MANEUVERS

MANEUVERS

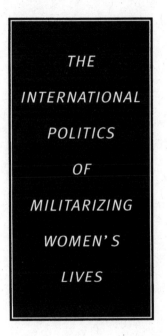

THE
INTERNATIONAL
POLITICS
OF
MILITARIZING
WOMEN'S
LIVES

CYNTHIA ENLOE

UNIVERSITY OF CALIFORNIA PRESS
Berkeley   Los Angeles   London

University of California Press
Berkeley and Los Angeles, California

University of California Press, Ltd.
London, England

© 2000 by The Regents of the University of California

Enloe, Cynthia H., 1938–
    Maneuvers : the international politics of militarizing women's
lives / Cynthia Enloe.
        p.   cm.
    Includes bibliographical references.

    ISBN 978-0-520-22071-3 (alk. paper)

    1. Women and the military.   2. Women and war.   I. Title.
U21.75.E5524   2000
355'.0082—dc21   99-28136
                                                         CIP

Printed in the United States of America

12   11   10   09
10   9   8   7   6   5   4   3

The paper used in this publication meets the minimum
requirements of ANSI/NISO Z39.48-1992 (R 1997)
(*Permanence of Paper*).

To the memory of my mother
Harriett Goodridge Enloe
1907–1983

CONTENTS

PREFACE

A fax machine never sleeps. If it rings around 11:00 at night—perhaps it is Australia, a friend from the other side of the dateline sending the latest about a prolonged sexual harassment case aboard the Australian navy ship *Swan*. If the fax rings at four or five in the morning, it's more likely that the message is coming from London; a friend already having read the morning papers is passing along news of the Labor government's waffling on its earlier election campaign pledge to lift the ban on gays in the British military. If the fax paper scrolls out of the machine when the sun has risen over the neighborhood's rooftops, it could be from Santiago, Ximena regaling me with the tale of an infamous army former torturer hiding out in the military's gynecology hospital. Coming home in the evening, I may find that Jeff, Nike's global nemesis, has faxed an update on the Indonesian government's use of its security forces to put down demonstrations by women workers employed in that country's sneaker factories. A lot of people these days are keeping track of their own countries' militarized gendered maneuvers.

Fax and e-mail are only the latest in a long line of successors to the carrier pigeon. I confess that I still relish the postcard arriving by ordinary mail that commemorates an anonymous wartime suffragist, or the manila envelope holding a precious feminist newsletter from Belgrade with its analysis of resurging nationalist militarism.

Over the past decade I have found that it is only by lots of us piecing together all sorts of information that we can make full sense of how militaries rely both on women and on presumptions about femininity. And still I keep learning things that surprise me.

Initially, I was nudged to think about women's experiences of militaries from two seemingly quite different directions. First, women students in the early eighties wanted to know more about women in uniform. Second, my own mother's life kept beckoning me to ask fresh questions. These early thoughts were bubbling up during the post–Vietnam War era in American popular culture. Sylvester Stallone wasn't the only one reconstructing war on the silver screen. Goldie Hawn was starring as Private Benjamin, a young widow making a new life for herself by joining the army. I can recall the skepticism with which European feminist friends greeted *Private Benjamin* when the film opened in Amsterdam. Were American women really this lacking in consciousness? Did they really imagine that the military offered just one more job opportunity, no different from the chance to work on a construction site or in a law firm? Yet it was a time, too, when American women peace activists were encircling the Pentagon with ribbon, while draftee-deprived officials on the inside were designing advertisements to enlist women volunteers to make up for their lost male conscripts.

Women *in* the military has never been an easy topic. It shouldn't be. Sexism, patriotism, violence, and the state—it is a heady brew. Indeed, it was a subject so enticingly hard to think through that, at first, I made it my chief preoccupation. I had just spent ten years studying male soldiers' experiences of racism in societies as different as Iraq and Canada, so it seemed logical then to focus my attention on women soldiers' dreams of service and experiences of sexism. But gradually I began to realize that paying attention only to women as soldiers was simply too confining. Militaries—and militarized civilian elites—have relied not just on sporadic infusions of a "few good women." Military policy makers have depended on—and thus maneuvered to control—varieties of women, and on the very notion of femininity in all its myriad guises.

At about this time in the early eighties I had begun reading my mother's diaries. She was still alive then. Now I wish I had asked her many more questions, especially those awkward ones that swim in a daughter's head but too rarely make it into speech. Before my father died two years ago, a decade after my mother, I could have asked him. After all, it was his intimacy with the military that had so shaped their lives together. But I didn't want to invite my father to interpret my mother's life. So I kept my questions to myself. My mother never had been in the military. No woman in my family has ever been in any country's military. But my mother's diaries hinted at life on the "home front" during World War II and at a militarized marriage during the subsequent Cold War version of American peacetime. Her cryptically penned entries set me to thinking.

In those years I was just becoming a feminist, just beginning to see the social landscape with new eyes, to broaden my curiosity, to ask new questions. Friends were glad to help. They directed me to New Words, Boston's wonderful women's bookstore; they lent me books, sent me drafts of papers—about the history of rape, of lesbian friendships, of women textile workers. It seemed that everything had a history, everything had a politics. My mother's diaries began to take on a new meaning. I began to get an inkling of the connection between militarized wives and women in the military. I was building a bridge from my mother to Goldie Hawn. The result was a book called *Does Khaki Become You?*

By the time, fifteen years later, that I began to think about revisiting the puzzles raised in *Khaki,* Hollywood was replacing Goldie Hawn's curly locks with Demi Moore's buzz cut. But I had become more sure than ever that women serving as soldiers—and their cinematic representatives—was not the sole story, not even the main story. Women *in* the military provides the focus for only one chapter in the larger saga of women *and* the military. Furthermore, I now believe more firmly than ever that the military is only one part of the story of militarization. How governments think about women as soldiers, how male soldiers and male civilians and women as voters and activists and wives and schoolgirls think about women as soldiers *does* matter. When the subject is treated as inconsequential or merely as a "human interest" photo opportunity, we do miss a chance to delve into the gendered dynamics of a society's political life. We witnessed this inattention when women came to comprise a surprising 11 percent of the then apartheid-bolstering South African military in the 1980s. We're seeing this inattention again today, as women rise from less than 1 percent of the 1980s Soviet army to 12 percent of the post-Communist Russian armed forces. Such failures of curiosity can stymie our efforts to understand how and when even a thoroughly patriarchal regime may subvert the orthodox sexual division of military labor in order to maintain itself in power.

However, readers will notice that I have placed the chapter on women-as-soldiers (Chapter 7) not at the beginning, but deep into this book. That placement is deliberate. One needs, I think, to take seriously the complicated militarized experiences of women as prostitutes, rape victims, mothers, wives, nurses, and feminist activists in order to make full sense of what happens when women are permitted in limited numbers to soldier in still-masculinized militaries. To invest one's curiosity solely in women as soldiers is to treat the militarization of so many other women as normal. If I slipped into that naive presumption, I probably would be allowing my own curiosity to become militarized.

I am even more convinced now than I was a decade ago that militaries need women to do a lot more than simply fill gaps in the ranks when their supply of "reliable" men runs short. Yet I also have been persuaded by the evidence that militaries and militarized civilian elites do not always get the results they so energetically pursue.

If we adopt the mainstream media's fascination with women-as-soldiers and thus devote only meager attention and thought to all the other militarized women, we will, by our own very inattention, I think, perpetuate militarized officials' capacity to manipulate many women's hopes and fears and skills. Any militarized government's manipulative capacity has relied on most people not being interested in military wives, on most people labeling as "trivial" the mixed feelings of military girlfriends, on most people turning military mothers, wartime rape victims, and military prostitutes into either abstract nationalist icons or objects of shame and exclusion. *In*attention is a political act.

Militaries rely on women, but not all women experience militarization identically. Militaries have needed, and continue to need, some women to provide commercialized sexual services to male soldiers, other women to commit themselves to marital fidelity in military families; simultaneously, they need still other women to find economic security and maybe even pride in working for defense contractors. At times governments even need some civilian women to act as feminist lobbyists promoting women's right to serve in the state's military.

Women who serve militaries' needs differently usually do not see themselves as bound together by their shared womanhood or even by their shared militarization. In fact, some militarized women will see their own respectability, income, or career chances thrown into jeopardy by the actions of other militarized women. Mothers of soldier-sons, for instance, do not have any automatic political affinity with women soldiers. A woman who is a military wife may go to considerable lengths *not* to ask her soldier-husband about the women who work in the discos around his base. Feminists working to help women soldiers overcome the institutional barriers of sexual harassment and homophobia inside the military may not give much thought at all to women as militarized mothers, wives, and prostitutes. Women devoting their energies to peace activism may think that the only militarized women worthy of serious intellectual attention are those women who have been uprooted or raped in wartime. In the 1980s I almost took for granted this separateness among the varieties of militarized women and their advocates. Today I am more interested to discover just how those divisions between groups of militarized women are maintained and what happens if tentative efforts are made to dismantle those divisions. The very disparateness of women's experiences of militarization has posed acute problems for feminist theorizing and feminist strategizing.

The "maneuvers" of the book's title refer to the efforts that military officials and their civilian supporters have made in order to ensure that each of these groups of women feel special and separate. Militarized officials need women themselves to nurture the boundaries that separate them from one another. Militaries have counted on military officers' wives to look down on the wives of enlisted men, and on all military wives to look down on women working in the discos around a military base. Militarized civilian officials have needed women raped by other regimes' soldiers to remain suspicious of antiwar women and, instead, to be willing to serve as nationalist symbols. Militaries have depended on women soldiers who imagine their service to be superior to that of both wives and prostitutes, and even of military nurses. The more distanced each group of women has felt from the other, the less likely any of them would be to notice how the political manipulations of gender affected them all. Thus the less likely any of them are to think about militarism.

Government officials have been remarkably successful in these divisive efforts. There are very few instances in any country of military wives joining in an alliance with military prostitutes and together devising a joint action along with women soldiers, all for the sake of dismantling the usually elaborate ideology of femininity constructed by military authorities to serve their own institutional interests.

For militaries and their supporters in both government and the general public have needed not only women, flesh and blood creatures. They also have needed ideas, especially ideas about femininity. Just as important to the maintenance of military life as has been the ideology of manliness, just as important as parades, alliances, and weaponry have been certain feminized ideas: "the fallen woman," "patriotic motherhood," "marital fidelity," "racial purity," "national sacrifice," and sexualized "respectability." Sometimes militaries even have needed a very particular version of the idea "liberated woman."

Paradoxically, these ideas turn out to be as potent as a B-52 bomber, while simultaneously they are as fragile as domestic harmony. The dynamics of this paradox create a peculiar narrative of our time: the military sex scandal. Military scandals occur—not just the globally head-lined American military scandals, but those less internationally featured that have occurred recently in Canada, Italy, Chile, and Australia—when those delicate maneuvers that have been designed to make ideas about gender work for military ends become confused, and when that confusion becomes visible to the public. The whole story of the political efforts to get women to act and think in ways that sustain the military turns out to be riddled with this paradox: the gendering of any country's military involves some of society's most powerful actors, senior officials of the state; but they often act as though they were on the verge of losing control, losing control of women. Sometimes they are.

Feminists have devoted increasing intellectual energy and scarce organizational resources to making sense of the militarization of women's lives. Indian feminists have sought to explain why so many Indian Hindu women have supported their new regime's nationalist policy of nuclear weapons testing. Serbian feminists have courted the Milosevic regime's repression when they have developed nonviolent forms of political protest. American feminists have struggled to craft strategies that support sexually harassed women soldiers without leaving deeper issues of American militarism unexamined. Okinawan feminists have tried to build alliances with male peace activists so as to effectively challenge the U.S. bases on their island without allowing those male peace activists to turn the rape of local women into merely a symbolic nationalist issue. Creating feminist theories and strategies to respond effectively to militarization's surprisingly multiple forms is not easy. Much of the discussion that follows here is meant to shed light on why that is so.

The book that launched me on this investigation of the militarization of women's lives was called *Does Khaki Become You?*—with the double entendre intended. The present volume revisits some of the questions raised there, examining them in light of developments in the 1990s. Other questions are broached here that I had not yet formulated back then: When do soldiers rape? How are high schools being

militarized? Are militaries getting more adept at handling military
wives? What are the risks that feminists face when they try to raise the
issue of wartime sexual abuse? I don't think I could have tackled these
questions had I not written and then rewritten *Khaki* a decade ago.
Thus this latest investigation self-consciously builds on what I learned
there.

Because *Maneuvers* and *Khaki* are separate branches on a common
tree of feminist exploration, I think it may be helpful for readers to
have access to some of their shared genealogy. *Does Khaki Become
You?* was published first in London, by Pluto Press and then by Pandora, the British feminist press. American publishers thereafter bought
the overseas rights. For an American writer, this sequence was a boon.
It meant that British readers, not American, would be that book's first
readers. The American military has been so powerful in its Hollywood,
CNN, and NATO versions that sometimes it seems as if it were the
only military worth talking about. This dominance poses a risk. It
tempts one (me) to think too simply. Treating the American military's
attempts—often slick, occasionally bungling—to secure women's cooperation in its mission as *the* feature story once again places this institution at the center of the analytical universe, either as the archetypal
villain or, more suspiciously, as the model of modernity and enlighten-
ment. Such a centering of the American story is, I think, analytically
dangerous.

As we enter the new century, the American military, admittedly, is
preeminent in the creation of roles for, and ideas about, militarized
women. On a recent trans-Atlantic flight I was seated next to a pleasant man in his late thirties. We exchanged a few words before each of
us became absorbed in the contents of our respective knapsacks. He
seemed totally familiar with the rituals of a seven-hour flight. A regular. It was only later, as the captain announced our approach to
Heathrow, that we struck up a conversation, now assured we wouldn't
be intruding on the other's in-flight reverie. He was returning to his
home in England, to one of the big American military bases that have
survived the post–Cold War overseas base closures. An African American, he had made a career of soldiering, rising to the rank of senior sergeant. He thought it had been a good life for a family man. His wife
liked it too. He confessed, though, that she didn't care for these frequent month-long trips he now had to make. He was a trainer. Ever
since the collapse of the Soviet Union and the breakup of Yugoslavia,
his skills had been in special demand. He already had helped train the

new army of Lithuania. He was just completing a tour in Slovenia. The
American military was offering itself up as a model to be emulated,
and officials in charge of many new governments were accepting the
offer.

Precisely because the U.S. military has become so physically and ideologically influential in today's post–Cold War world, we do need, I
think, to pay special heed to American manipulations of ideas about
women and to the appeal that those militarized ideas have for so many
women. In the late 1990s, the American armed forces provide not only
traveling trainers, but their own formulas for AIDS prevention and
peacekeeping. The U.S. also has become the world's leading exporter
of weaponry. Each one of these international military programs is providing a site for the export of American ideas about what should be expected of a man, what should be expected of a woman—not just of a
woman in uniform, but a woman in a soldier's home and a woman in a
militarized off-base disco.

Yet, for all its influence, the American military is distinct, just as
American feminisms are distinct. It is to underscore this distinctness
that in the following chapters I have compared American women's militarized experiences as wives, prostitutes, soldiers, nurses, mothers,
and feminists with the experiences of women from Britain, Russia,
Germany, the former Yugoslavia, Chile, Canada, the Philippines,
Rwanda, Indonesia, South Africa, Israel, South Korea, Vietnam, and
Japan. The American military's current preeminence has not made a
comparative curiosity obsolete. At this start of a new century, it has
made nonparochial investigation an even more urgent enterprise. The
processes of gendered militarization today operate internationally. We
need, therefore, to develop our curiosities internationally.

There are routes toward a distinctly feminist form of action on militarization that can look quite unlike the much talked-about American
liberal feminist route. For instance, British women's advocates have
not spent much time and political energy trying to widen the roles of
British women in the military. Among British women legislators—even
after the celebrated 1997 influx of 160 women into the masculinized
domain of the British House of Commons—there is no equivalent of
recently retired Congresswoman Patricia Schroeder. No British woman
parliamentarian, that is, has invested so much of her political currency
in promoting women as equal members of her country's military: in the
late 1990s House of Commons it just has not been a political priority.
Likewise, it has been German, South Korean, and Okinawan women

as well as British women, not their American counterparts, who have
had to cope with the men from two militaries—their own and a foreign military—living in and around their hometowns. As a result, it
has been feminists from these countries who have been tutoring their
American counterparts about militarized gendered nationalism, about
the pitfalls of organizing against foreign soldiers' abuses of local
women in ways that rekindle a local brand of masculinized nationalist
militarism. American women have a lot to learn.

Today American feminists are starting to absorb the hard lesson for
women of any international superpower: they will be weaker analytically and strategically if they don't take seriously the gendered experiences and feminist theories developed by women in other countries.
For example, America's well-developed anti-domestic violence movement only belatedly struggled to introduce the issue of violence onto
their country's military bases. In Chile, the sequence was reversed: it
was Chilean feminists' daring participation in their country's movement to oust an oppressive military regime in the 1980s that led them
thereafter to raise the issue of domestic violence in the civilian society.
The result has been that American feminists have invested enormous
energy in stopping domestic violence, yet many of them do not see
their country's military policies as "their issue"; by contrast, Chilean
feminists today constantly think analytically about militarism *because*
they are concerned about misogynist violence against women. Questions are whetted, too, by a newly internationalized curiosity. For instance, why have no American mothers been documented doing what
scores of Russian mothers did in 1995 and 1996—traveling to a war
zone, Chechnya in this instance, to retrieve their soldier-sons from
what they deemed to be an unjust military operation? The morning of
a new century is no time for parochialism.

Publishing *Khaki* first in Britain served as my inoculation. It was invaluable to have non-American readers in my mind's eye as I wrote. It
still is. Readers in South Korea, Australia, Canada, Serbia, Chile,
Japan, and Israel keep me from being too parochial, keep me from
slipping into that all too common presumption that American women's
experiences are those of the world's Everywoman, if such a mythical
creature even exists.

Many of the women and men who initially kept me informed about
the militarization's gendered course and kept me from treading too far
down the path to parochialism have continued to do so. To them I owe
a large debt of gratitude. Since the early 1980s, dozens of people, some

of whom I know only by correspondence, have continued to share with me their hunches, their data, their alarm. One of the best ways to read the Notes at the end of the book is as an extended thank-you. Everyone who has sent me a thesis, a clipping, or a video has helped teach me about what it means for a woman to live a life that has been militarized.

There are some people to whom I extend special thanks here for their generous help in writing the present book: in Chile, Ximena Bunster; in Canada, Sandra Whitworth, Maja Korac, Wenona Giles, Lucy Laliberte, and Deborah Harrison; in Australia, Jan Pettman, Anne Marie Hilsdon, and Ann Smith; in Britain, Debbie Licorish, Philippa Brewster, Candida Lacey, Marysia Zalewski, Julie Wheelwright, Nira Yuval-Davis, Ken Booth, Debbi King, Terrell Carver, Joanna Labon, and the late Anne Bennewick; in Ireland, Ailbhe Smyth; in South Korea, Insook Kwon; in Austria, Katrin Kriz; in the United States, special thanks to Joni Seager for her wit, her ever-sharp analytical questioning and our ongoing conversation, to David Enloe for his brotherly graphics sleuthing, to Margaret Enloe for helping me to decipher our father's years of war stories, to Lois Brynes for her editorial savvy, to Gilda Bruckman and Judy Wachs for their literate worldliness. Also in the United States, warm thank-yous to Serena Hilsinger, Amy Lang, Julie Abraham, Karen Turner, Saralee Hamilton, Caroline Becraft, Katharine Moon, Linda Green, Mary Wertsch, Mary Katzenstein, Angela Raven Roberts, Jeff Ballinger, Stephanie Kane, Doreen Lehr, Madeline Drexler, E.J. Graff, Pat Miles, Seungsook Moon, Georgia Sadler, Lory Manning, Betty Dooley, Frank Barrett, Lois Wasserspring, Alison Bernstein, Kristin Waters, Pat Cazier, Annie Mancini, Valerie Sperling, Constance Sutton, Mark Miller, Justin Brady, David Michaels, Suzanne Keating, Parminder Bhachu, Beverly Grier, Francine D'Amico, Bob Vitalis, Michelle Benecke, Dixon Osborn, Kate Rounds, Jayne Hornstein, Patty Dutile, Karen Dorman, Catherine Lutz, Harold Jordon, Karen Kampwirth, Simona Sharoni, Gary Lehring, Caroline Prevatte, Yoko Harumi, Keith Severin, Philippa Levine, Keith Gaby, and Brenda Moore. In Japan, warms thanks to Suzuyo Takazato, Carolyn Francis, Norio Okada, and Amane Funabashi. In the Philippines, Angela Yang. In the Netherlands, Shelly Anderson. In Cambodia and Mozambique, Liz Bernstein. In Israel, Isis Nusair, Rela Mezali, Dafna Izraeli, and Hanna Herzog. In Thailand and the United States, Gai Liewkeat. In Croatia, Maria Olujic. In South Africa, Jacklyn Cock.

Books don't just "happen." They are produced and sold by people who make choices. Books that take seriously women's experiences and ideas about political life come into print and are available for the rest of us to read because of those feminists who make choices at all levels of the publishing industry, from editors to booksellers. Each of them depends on the other. And we, the readers, need them all. This newest exploration has been the beneficiary of the sophisticated editorial vision of Naomi Schneider. All of my thinking-in-print has benefited from the collective wit, wisdom, and entrepreneurial skills of feminists in publishing.

A book has a deceptively finished feeling. The ink giving shape to ideas has dried. The glue holding the pages together in a certain order has hardened. But I am more convinced now than ever that the questions that provoked me to write this book are only partially answered. We scarcely know enough about how militaries rely on, and thus try to control, women's talents, women's aspirations, women's nightmares— and how women weigh and respond to those maneuvers.

Thus we just have begun to understand how particular women's lives become militarized—and what would happen if those subtle daily processes of gendered militarization were to be reversed.

Somerville, Massachusetts, 1999

How Do They Militarize a Can of Soup?

For several years I kept a can of Heinz tomato and noodle soup on the kitchen counter. I had bought it in a London supermarket. I don't know whether Heinz marketed this particular canned recipe around the world or decided it would sell best only in Margaret Thatcher's Britain. At the time it seemed more Reaganesque than Thatcherist. I was never tempted to eat the contents. I brought it back to Boston in my luggage just so I could keep looking at it, puzzling over its deeper militarized meanings.

The formula was a familiar one. The Heinz chefs had added little pasta bits to the condensed tomato soup. But instead of the usual alphabet letters, the soup designers had cut their pastas into the shape of Star Wars satellites.

One can only conjecture about the conversation at the Heinz headquarters when this innovative soup design was first proposed. Since marketing specialists know that women do most of the food shopping, they must have imagined that Star Wars noodles floating in a tomato liquid would be appealing to women. Why? What would catch a double-burdened woman's attention, what would "speak to her," as she moved purposefully along her local grocery store aisles on the way to or from her paid job? The designers and dietitians sitting around the corporate table probably tried to imagine a typical mealtime in the household of a busy woman. Tomato soup is healthy. But a mother has to get a child to eat the healthy meal she has prepared. Sometimes that can be a challenge. Little a, b, and c's might not be sufficiently enticing to a frenchfriesandacoke-lusting child. But add little space weapons. Maybe that would get the young diner to dig the spoon down deep into the mealtime soup bowl. Everyone would be happy—the vitamins-phobic child, the harried mother, and the soup company.

Militarization, therefore, affects not just the executives and factory floor workers who make fighter planes, land mines, and intercontinental missiles but also the employees of food companies, toy companies, clothing companies, film studios, stock brokerages, and advertising agencies. Any company's employees are militarized insofar as they take their customers' fascination with militarized products as natural, as unproblematic. Employees are militarized also insofar as they imagine that promoting military ends serves the general welfare. Such employees may go further than just taking these militarized values as a given; they may start to define these values as a corporate resource, something to be reinforced and exploited. Latex condoms designed to look like army camouflage, films that equate action with war, fashions that celebrate brass buttons and epaulettes—each has been consciously designed by someone.[1]

In the Star Wars soup scenario a lot of people have become militarized—corporate marketers, dietitians, mothers, and children. They may not run out to enlist in the army as soon as they have finished their lunch, but militarization is progressing nonetheless. Militarization never is simply about joining a military. It is a far more subtle process. And it sprawls over far more of the gendered social landscape than merely those peaks clearly painted a telltale khaki.

THE MILITARIZATION OF CARMEN MIRANDA

The pervasiveness of militarized values is a principal reason for the student of militarization not to become fixated on men or women as soldiers. True, militarization does make us pay more attention to people inside the military. Still, many people can become militarized in their thinking, in how they live their daily lives, in what they aspire to for their children or their society, without ever wielding a rifle or donning a helmet.

Militarization does not always take on the guise of war. Much discussion of women and militarism occurs in times of open warfare—women in the Kosovo or Chechnyan wars, women during World War II, women in the American Civil War. As a result, even though the best of this research does indeed shed light on the home front's transformation—and resistance to that transformation—it is easy to slip into imagining that militarization is always accompanied by government-directed overt violence, by war. Yet what the exploration of the lives of military wives and of women working as military prostitutes reveals for us is that militarization creeps into ordinary daily routines; it threads its way amid memos, laundry, lovemaking, and the clinking of frosted beer glasses. Militarization is such a pervasive process, and thus so hard to uproot, precisely because in its everyday forms it scarcely looks life threatening.

It is by taking women's experiences of militarization seriously, I think, that we are most likely to understand it fully. The militarization of women has been crucial for the militarization of governments and of international relations. The militarization of women has been necessary for the militarization of men. And because the militarization of women takes such humdrum forms, because it tends to insinuate itself into ordinary daily routines where it is rarely heralded or even deemed noteworthy, investigating the militarization of women can sharpen our sometimes dulled analytical skills.

Militarization is a step-by-step process by which a person or a thing gradually comes to be controlled by the military *or* comes to depend for its well-being on militaristic ideas. The more militarization transforms an individual or a society, the more that individual or society comes to imagine military needs and militaristic presumptions to be not only valuable but also normal. Militarization, that is, involves cultural as well as institutional, ideological, and economic transformations.[2] To chart the spread of militarization, then, requires a host of skills: the ability to read budgets and interpret bureaucratic euphemisms, of course, but also the ability to understand the dynamics of memory, marriage, hero-worship, cinematic imagery, and the economies of commercialized sex.

Militarization, on the other hand, doesn't shape everything all the time. If it did, it would be impossible to distinguish. For instance, even a gun can be militarized or *un*militarized. If the gun, an instrument designed to inflict pain and harm, is used to hunt rabbits by a person for whom eating rabbits is necessary for his or her diet, that gun and its user are not very usefully thought of as militarized. The gun's use may still be controversial, of course, igniting useful debates about cruelty to animals, about public safety. But if this gun begins to be seen by its owner not only as a tool for obtaining an essential food but also as an instrument to ensure the security of the society against diffusely imagined enemies, or as a symbol of manly self-expression or masculinized citizenship dependent on the superior control of violence, *then* that gun and its owner—and anyone who admires or abets the owner—are cruising down the ramp onto the militarization highway.

It is precisely because guns are so easily converted from unmilitarized to militarized instruments that they and their suppliers and wielders are worthy of close attention. For instance, the South African sociologist Jacklyn Cock urges her fellow citizens to pay close attention to the spread of guns in post-apartheid South Africa. She argues that the proponents of demilitarization must look beyond the country's reorganized defense force. Cock understands that the diffusion of guns—many distributed by newly decommissioned soldiers—to private armies, bandits, and tourist-luring hunting companies needs to be monitored today if South Africans' hopes for thoroughgoing demilitarization are not to be dashed.[3]

Today in the United States there is considerable concern about the seeming assimilation of military gear, tactics, and cultures into such supposedly nonmilitary departments as the Federal Bureau of Investigation (FBI) and the Federal Bureau of Alcohol, Tobacco, and Firearms (BATF).[4] Paradoxically, some of those Americans who have sounded the loudest alarms about the FBI and BATF's militarization have themselves adopted hypermilitarizing modes of protest, organizing themselves into what they call "patriotic militias."[5] Without a self-conscious avoidance of militarized forms of public action, the militarization of one sector of public life can generate an equally militarized response, apparently based on the assumption that the only effective response to official militarism is the militarization of dissent. This assumption may prove to be a tragic failure of political imagination. There is an alternative response: the demilitarization—in equipment and mind-set—of both the civilian agency's personnel and the forms of dissent developed by its critics. As feminists in Okinawa, Northern Ireland, and Serbia have noted, opposing militarization must be done in ways that avoid privileging masculinity. Militarization, as we will see, whether it occurs in the corridors of a government or on the streets during a protest, requires *both* women's and men's acquiescence, but it *privileges* masculinity.

Militarization is a specific sort of transforming process, but the list of what can be militarized is virtually endless: toys, jobs, the profession of psychology, fashion, faith, voting, local economies, condoms, and

Figure 1 Carmen Miranda, here performing for American soldiers and sailors, was among those 1940s Hollywood stars whose talents were mobilized to sustain troop morale during World War II. In Washington officials' eyes, Miranda was especially important as a symbol of U.S.–Latin American friendly relations. (The Academy of Motion Arts and Sciences, Los Angeles, CA.)

movie stars.[6] Thus, for example, the Brazilian singer and comedian Carmen Miranda was militarized by her Hollywood studio employers during World War II. Eager to cooperate with the Roosevelt administration's wartime effort to keep Latin American governments friendly to Washington, her Hollywood employers launched Carmen Miranda into film roles as the all-purpose Latina, building bridges between north and south while simultaneously entertaining U.S. troops.[7] The militarization of Carmen Miranda also played a part in enhancing the masculinization of public life insofar as Miranda was turned into a tool for building an alliance between the men running Hollywood studios, the men making policy in Washington, and the men determining foreign policy in the capital cities of Latin America. That is, Miranda's feminized place in the center of the militarized movie screen served to camouflage men's place in the center of the political stage.[8]

Cabaret singers, stand-up comics, dancers—any entertainer can be militarized, often quite willingly, if she or he converts performance talent into the means for sustaining the morale of soldiers.[9] Morale. Masculinized, militarized morale. A great deal of official energy is invested in mobilizing women in particular to sustain the morale of male soldiers. Women who are the targets of these official efforts have to make decisions about whose morale and for what ends they are willing to sing.

Civilian voters can be militarized. Britons talk, for instance, of certain elections as being "khaki elections." That is, each rival party's success in garnering votes in this sort of militarized election depends on their presenting themselves as war victors. A khaki election always favors the party or candidate most enthusiastic about war waging or most intimately associated in voters' minds with the arts of war. It is assumed in such an election that voters will lean toward the party whose candidates can demonstrate military skills, success in a military organization, or militaristic public attitudes toward outsiders. Not only is it assumed that voters will be convinced that these attributes translate into potential for solving problems facing civilian society, but also it is widely imagined that voters will conclude that those skills and organizational experiences are the *most* suited for civilian problem solving. Typically, a khaki election—in Britain, the United States, Liberia, Russia, or Serbia—privileges male candidates and masculinized party platforms because in so many societies only masculinized leaders are imagined to be credible wielders of militaristic formulas.[10] On voting day, such an effort to turn an election into a khaki election may provoke a gender gap, women being less inclined than men to vote for the war-enthusiastic party.

But not always, and not always dramatically. The militarized woman voter is not an oxymoron.[11] Some feminists and anti-war activists take heart, however, in the gender gaps when they appear. For instance, in early 1998, when the Clinton administration and the government of Tony Blair joined political hands to build up a military threat in the Persian Gulf in order to compel Iraq's Saddam Hussein to accept UN weapons inspectors, pollsters revealed that British women were notably less enthusiastic about the Blair policy than were their male counterparts. In early February 1998, 68 percent of the British men surveyed told pollsters that they "supported British involvement in military action, including bombing raids, against Saddam Hussein's Iraq"; only 45 percent of British women voiced such support.[12] A 23 percent difference is deemed significant by polling experts. But the real test may come only when a government actually launches a war. As demonstrated in the United States during the 1990–91 Gulf War, many women opposed to a war-waging strategy before the fighting begins may move to a more supportive or at least more ambiguous position once "their boys" or "their sons and daughters in uniform" are thrust into immediate danger.[13]

In April 1999, six weeks into the Belgrade regime's campaign to displace ethnic Albanians in the Yugoslav province of Kosovo and one month into the U.S./NATO bombing attacks to stop such ethnic cleansing, the gender gap between American women and men was narrower than it had been on the eve of the Gulf War. When an NBC/*Wall Street Journal* poll asked whether the United States and NATO should continue bombing or stop to permit negotiations, 59 percent of men supported continued bombings and 46 percent of women did: a thirteen-point gap. Reflecting on this seemingly narrowed U.S. gender gap, one woman analyst suggested that many women had had their earlier opposition to the use of U.S. military force softened by their exposure to media images of Kosovar women turned into desperate refugees and victims of wartime rape.[14]

In recent years my curiosity about suffragists—those women who campaigned for women's right to vote—has been rekindled. As I have delved into the often surprising histories of these campaigners, I have begun to appreciate more fully just how difficult it was for many of them to navigate between the rocks of misogyny and the whirlpools of militarism. Should suffragists see their country's entrance into a war as a strategic opportunity to prove women's value to the governmental male elite? Is it wise for feminists in the postwar years to hold up women's wartime contributions as proof of women's competency to act as full citizens?

Both British and American suffragists argued fiercely among themselves over these knotty questions during World War I. Although previously they had disagreed sharply over campaign tactics, leading British suffragists Millicent Fawcett and Christabel Pankhurst agreed in 1915 that suffragist women's energies should be devoted to aiding the British government win the war against the Germans. Many suffragists were propelled into this political position by the anger they felt upon hearing media stories of German soldiers raping Belgian women. Nonetheless, in calling on suffragists to contribute to the war effort, these suffrage activists were willing to alienate scores of women within their

Figure 2 Because their government was draining the civilian economy of young men to fight in the trenches, many British women gained access to jobs during World War I that, until 1914, had been defined as suitable only for men. Pictured here are women newly hired to drive the Post Office's horse-drawn mail vans. (The National Postal Museum, London EC1A 1LP, England, UK - file #: NPM 92/7.)

respective organizations who were convinced that securing women's rights and opposing war were inseparable. In April 1915, Pankhurst was among the organizers of a large demonstration in London calling for "women's right to serve." Their target audience: the men who owned munitions factories and the men who worked in them, many of whom were reluctant to permit women to take men's places on the wartime assembly lines.[15] At the same time, however, those advocates of women's voting rights who believed that the only way to ensure the demise of patriarchy was to create cross-national alliances to oppose jingoist patriotism were taking their own organizing steps. In 1915 these women—among them Jane Addams from the United States and Helena Swanwick from Britain—created the Women's International League for Peace and Freedom (WILPF).[16]

The internationalist WILPF campaigner and the suffragist munitions worker were early-twentieth-century women connected to each other by a debate that still goes on today: is women's liberation advanced or derailed by women's active contribution to their own country's war waging?

As a young American woman, Rose Monroe was discovered by Hollywood in the 1940s while she was working in an aircraft parts factory in Ypsilanti, Michigan, and was turned into the feminized model for the newest world war. Rose Monroe became "Rosie the Riveter," America's wartime icon.[17] Fifty years later the question that her iconographic symbol prompts is still with us: was Rose/Rosie maneuvered or empowered—or both?

This question is not just about historical interpretation. This question is still a pressing one today when the manufacture of military hardware and software is big business. Despite defense industry layoffs in post–Cold War United States, Canada, Russia, and Britain and despite downturns in sales from the 1997–1999 Asian economic crisis, military weapons contracts remain the objects of intense corporate competition and fierce international trade rivalries: "Over lamb chops and red wine, the Senators heard Secretary of State Madeleine K. Albright explain NATO expansion. The guest list included Bernard L. Schwartz, chairman of Loral Space and Communications, a company partly owned by Lockheed Martin. Mr. Schwartz personally donated $601,000 to Democratic politicians for the 1996 election. Lockheed Martin itself gave $2.3 million to Congressional and presidential candidates in the 1996 election."[18]

Madeleine Albright, the first woman to hold the post of U.S. Secretary of State, was convinced that bringing countries such as the Czech Republic (her birthplace), Poland, and Hungary into the North Atlantic Treaty Organization (NATO) would ensure a long-term peace in post–Cold War Europe. But this dinner was not organized by the secretary of state. The lamb-chops-and-wine affair was hosted—in the private, prestigious, and formerly male-only Metropolitan Club—by the U.S. Committee to Expand NATO,[19] a group to which many defense manufacturing executives belong. The expansion of NATO, with the accompanying pressures on the new member governments to upgrade their militaries to meet NATO's high-tech standards, is just one maneuver that is raising defense industry hopes for a profitable future. But how does an expanded NATO affect the future for Rosie's granddaughters? Will they see a skilled job in the defense industry as a ticket to a better life? Will NATO's 1999 bombing operations in Serbia and Kosovo make that ticket seem all the more golden in the eyes of North American and European women?

As suggested by new investigations into the complex lives and ideas of both suffrage campaigners and women industrial workers, some maneuvers designed to militarize women succeed because of women's own cooperation. A militarizing maneuver can look like a dance, not a struggle, even though the dance may be among unequal partners.[20]

Over the centuries, women who are mothers also have found it hard not to succumb to militarizing maneuvers. Yet, when motherhood's militarization is resisted, when mothers refuse to believe that mothering is made easier by their child's fascination with real or make-believe weapons, then militarization within a society becomes very difficult to achieve. For this reason serious students of militarization keep a close watch on toy sales. Researchers seek answers to such questions as: What toys are aggressively marketed by multinational companies such as Mattel and Hasbro? How do giant merchandisers, such as Toys R Us, appeal to girls and to boys by the way they lay out their store displays? How do mothers juggle their own ideas about femininity and masculinity? Do the choices that mothers make about their daughters' and their sons' play determine their children's popularity? The answers at any given moment in any country will affect corporate profits. They also will shape relationships within families. But these answers may also influence an entire society's collective attitudes toward violence, soldiering, and gender. Even the mother who hopes her son will eat tomato soup if it is enhanced with Star Wars pastas may hesitate before fulfilling the boy's wish for a make-believe laser gun.

In 1997, Hasbro, one of the world's toy manufacturing giants and the creator of G.I. Joe, introduced a new toy soldier, G.I. Jane. Hasbro marketing executives preferred to call their newest creation, not a soldier, but a "female action figure."[21] On the other hand, these company executives proudly described G.I. Jane as a doll "portrayed in authentic military gear," that is, helmet, boots, pistol, and other equipment of an army helicopter pilot. Hasbro actually created four G.I. Janes—one blonde, one brunette, a third redheaded, and a fourth doll whose skin was darker than that of the other Janes and whose hair was black. The 1990s G.I. Jane was not Hasbro's first female military doll. Back in 1967, on the eve of the U.S. war-making escalation in Vietnam, when women were only 2 percent of the total American military's personnel and most served in the nursing corps, Hasbro had introduced G.I. Joe Nurse. But the doll was soon withdrawn from the market because, as a corporate spokeswoman explained, "boys didn't want to play with a nurse." On the brink of a new century, the market may prove friendlier. Thousands of American women are serving or have served in the

military, many of them African American and Latina women. Moreover, some toy-buying mothers and aunts may see G.I. Jane as a step
forward in the cultural history of child's gendered play. G.I. Jane, Hasbro strategists hope, will represent girls-in-action.

The potency of motherhood in the processes of militarization is one
reason that women in militarizing countries—from Britain during the
Boer War, to Chile under the Pinochet junta, to Croatia in the midst of
its 1990s civil war—have had to think so hard about the rewards and
risks of engaging in "patriotic mothering."[22] Mothering is an unpaid
job. It may provide great satisfaction, but it also is work. Mothers are
often confined to housework; they are presumed too parochial or too
emotional to have anything to say about their country's public decisions. Thus, many women have greeted with enthusiasm any politician
who has proposed that mothering is a *national* activity. Some women
feel deeply validated when that same politician goes on to call for
mothering to be defined as a vital contribution to the nation's war effort, because warfare has been imagined by many to be the quintessen-
tially public and national activity.

Leaders on all sides in the 1990s Yugoslav civil war calculatingly
dipped their ladles into this maternalist ideological brew. But the formula can be traced back far beyond the 1991 outbreak of strife in the
Balkans. The militarizing appeal to women in many countries has derived from the common patriarchal practice of relegating women's
child care to the private sphere. Insofar as women are presumed to be
the chief caretakers of sons and insofar as political leaders wanting to
raise armies need to persuade mothers to offer up their sons to military
service, women will be encouraged to see their maternal duty as a public duty and to release their sons (and sometimes daughters) for some
higher good. The pressure to see good mothering as patriotic mothering is difficult—and even risky—to resist, especially if one's son and
one's husband support the political leaders in the militarized campaign.[23] As we will see in Chapter 7, however, when women define
good mothering in a way that subverts sons' compliance to calls for
soldiers, governments quake. Militarizing gendered maneuvers do not
always succeed.

WHEN HIGH SCHOOL GIRLS MARCH

Militarization is a complex process, frequently a contested one.

The reduction of militarism in some arenas can occur at the same
time as its expansion in other arenas. Within the European Union

(EU) today, for instance, militarization seems to be retreating and expanding simultaneously. On the one hand, European leaders on both the left and the center-right are hailing the closer integration of Europe's once-rival states into an enlarged European Union as a movement that can guarantee regional peace. On the other hand, some of these same leaders are taking steps to create a military arm of the European Union, a new "Eurocorps" capable of acting separately from the United States, and are putting into place anti-immigration policies that some critics say are building a new "Fortress Europe." The most starkly visible evidence of this version of an integrated Europe is the militarization of the EU's borders: "The eastern borders of Germany, for instance, are patrolled by a double line of border guards using dogs, patrol boats, helicopters, radar, heat detectors and night vision.... While marine guards patrol the Spanish coastline, barbed wire, closed circuit TV and electronic monitoring are used to fortify the frontiers of the north African enclaves of Ceuta and Melilla."[24] This militarizing strategy is not without its gendered consequences. It appears to make the organized smuggling of women (thousands destined for EU brothels) across these fortified borders all the more profitable: pointing to the EU helicopters and patrol boats, smuggling syndicates raise their prices.[25]

In the United States as well, evidence shows that militarization has not been rolled back uniformly in the 1990s. The American media headlined the loss of defense manufacturing jobs and the closure of scores of military bases, but on other fronts, militarization moved forward apace. One of these fronts—most discussed among Latino community activists and among the advocates of immigrants' rights—has been the increasing militarization of life along the U.S.-Mexican border. The Defense Department has become increasingly involved in the operations of not only the Justice Department's Border Patrol but local police forces as well.[26]

Another front, not as likely to be a topic of American national political discourse, has been the post–Cold War militarizing trends that are occurring in public education. Local school board members, administrators, and teachers in towns across America today are weighing the advantages of militarizing local public education. In many towns, the proponents of militarized education have won those debates, though often over considerable opposition. In the United States in the mid-1990s, the fastest-growing program in the Department of Defense was the Junior Reserve Officer Training Program, or JROTC.

JROTC is a Pentagon-designed program of military training intended to be adopted by American high schools. By late 1995, Defense Department officials were allocating (with Congressional approval) $173 million to promoting high schools' adoption of JROTC programs.[27] Thousands of parents and high school administrators agreed that JROTC would enrich a school's curriculum. By 1998, 330,000 American high school students, some as young as fourteen, were enrolled in JROTC.[28] Twenty-six hundred high schools across the country were officially participating.[29] School board members in southern states had become especially enthusiastic: by 1995, 65 percent of all the JROTC units were located in the south.

Sex discrimination in American school curricula and sports programs was being successfully challenged; the architects of JROTC adapted as well. By 1995, high school girls from all racial groups comprised 40 percent of the JROTC cadets, although the great majority of instructors, mostly retired military officers, continued to be men. Those schools with large proportions of Latino and African American students were among the most likely to sign up for the JROTC program. Black students represented 34 percent of all the students in schools that accepted the Army's JROTC, but they made up a greater proportion, 42 percent, of all the JROTC student participants. Nationally, by 1995, students from all racial minority communities comprised more than half the JROTC students.

The obstacles faced by those parents who wished to keep soldiering out of their children's school curriculum are revealed by the experiences of Anne Boylan. She lives in Delaware, where her children attend public schools in a district that extends from urban Wilmington to the university town of Newark and its surrounding rural townships.[30] Her children's school board agreed to adopt the JROTC program in 1996. Although the program was billed as a high school activity, recruiting for JROTC was begun among students in their last term of junior high school. Boylan, a mother, a feminist, and a women's studies professor, was dismayed that so few teachers had raised their voices in skepticism over the alleged benefits of JROTC. Especially notable, she believed, was the silence of social studies teachers; they seemed unconcerned about the content of JROTC's American history curriculum, which featured the role of the military in this country's development. She and other parents critical of JROTC tried in vain to point out that, despite Defense Department promises of budget relief to financially hard-pressed school districts, the department's payments in practice covered only one-third of the school's financial expenditure for the program. Boylan and her small band of anti-JROTC parents could cite only one victory: they did succeed in persuading the principal to ban JROTC from bringing guns—real or make-believe—into the school. They failed in their parallel efforts to prevent the JROTC-uniformed cadets from being given the sole responsibility for raising the American flag on the school grounds each morning. Although this activity was a seemingly minor one, Boylan believed it was symbolically significant: "Will school children now imagine that a member of the math club or the French club is somehow less of a full American citizen than a member of the JROTC is?"[31]

School board members, along with many parents, have accepted the military's argument that, in post–Cold War America, militarized training in high school will instill discipline in "marginal" students, will teach patriotism, and will provide a post-school career track. Although Defense officials assure local parents that the JROTC is not intended to encourage teenagers to enlist in the military, approximately 45 percent of JROTC graduates do enter military programs.[32]

The introduction of this energetically promoted program for early teenage Americans has not occurred without debate, but the number of communities in which it has been voluntarily adopted suggests that militarization is not a process that became passé in the United States when the Berlin Wall came down. Militarism is far too adaptable, far too appealing to be dismantled as quickly as a wall.

LESBIANS AND GAY MEN IN THE MILITARY

In some countries gay and lesbian activists have been among the most careful civilian monitors of their respective militaries. During the 1990s, these activists, perhaps more than the activists of any other movement, taught their fellow citizens much about the prevailing masculinized cultures in their governments' militaries. There has been, nonetheless, an attendant risk in challenging the military at such close quarters. The militarization of the American gay and lesbian rights movement, one might argue, has become more intense, not less, in recent years. There is evidence that, to a lesser extent, so too has the militarization of its political counterpart in Britain.

The topic of gays in the military moved from being a little known fact of military life to being a touchstone of fin de siècle American politics. During World War II and the Vietnam War, those men and women who joined the military already conscious of their homosexuality or who, as so often happened, came to that consciousness only while serving in the military, coped privately or in small groups with those rules that made their sexuality a punishable offense. But by the late 1980s several widely reported court cases, plus increasingly public gay and lesbian organizing, had turned a once-private problem into a political issue.[33]

The 1992 campaign pledge of then–presidential candidate Bill Clinton to lift the existing ban on gay men and lesbians serving in the U.S. military was not the start of this politicizing process, but it did attract the attention of newspaper editors, television talk show hosts, members of Congress, lobbying groups, and ordinary voters who heretofore had paid little attention to military investigatory practices or the career paths of gay and lesbian soldiers.[34]

It is the very centrality of the military in American popular culture that has made it so hard for gay rights activists to avoid having their own campaign militarized. Here is the resultant dilemma: how do you campaign to allow gay men and lesbians to participate in soldiering *without* fostering the notion that soldiering is an exceptionally valued activity?

This dilemma is hardly new. Any group excluded from its country's military, a military that possesses symbolic or actual policy-making power, has had to unravel this conundrum. Or, if the group chooses not to think about the puzzle, not to see itself as acting out a dilemma, then it is likely to become militarized through the very act of pressuring the military to open the doors a bit wider. When World War I began, the British and American women who were campaigning for the right to vote divided among themselves when they tried to figure out if "the right to serve" should be militarized so that women's indispensability to their war-waging governments would have to be admitted. African American women and men from the American Revolution to the Gulf War have debated different approaches to resolving this dilemma. As recently as September 1995, the Congressional Black Caucus sponsored a celebration in Washington to honor African American veterans of the Korean War. Sanford Bishop, a black congressman from Georgia who was a member of both the Black Caucus and the House Veterans' Affairs Committee, sent out a letter urging people to attend. He told his letter's recipients, "We think it would be an excellent opportunity to call attention to the achievements of the U.S. military as a model of equal opportunity."[35] Similarly, South

Africa's newly empowered black women and men—including South Africa's well-organized gay men and lesbians—have tried to reap the most valuable benefits of post-apartheid political inclusion without being insinuated into what some thought to be its most oppressive institutions.[36] Is soldiering in the country's reorganized military a distributor of valuable benefits or an instrument of oppression—or both?

Despite all this thoughtful discussion over several generations, the way out of the dilemma remains far from clear. The most optimistic calculation is to figure that when a country's military admits a once excluded or despised group, that institution is transformed and made more compatible with democratic culture. In this perhaps too-sanguine scenario, the outsider group campaigning to enter the military doesn't become militarized; rather, the newly diversified military becomes democratized.

The gays-in-the-military debate, as it has occurred in the 1990s United States, has highlighted the military's reliance on ideas such as masculinity and heterosexism. Greater exposure has proved positive. Any debate that reveals the ideological foundation of a powerful institution is a valuable debate. But militarism itself has been scarcely disrupted. Perhaps its roots have been sent down even more deeply into the soil of American political culture. The reason lies in the way that soldiering was portrayed during the campaign. Soldiering for the state was—and still is—represented by many gay rights advocates as well as by heterosexism's proponents as an activity that many of the country's most talented, most selfless citizens want to do and should have the right to do. Soldiering as an activity and the soldier as a public figure may have gained, not lost, stature in U.S. political culture as a result of the 1990s gays-in-the-military debate.

The dynamics of the debate, however, have not had identical resonances for women and men. For lesbians and for women of all sexual orientations, this contention that soldiering and soldiers symbolize the best in citizenry has a special salience. First, in order to be taken seriously as full-fledged citizens, women of all races in the United States have had to form movements, lobby all levels of government, argue with fathers, brothers, and husbands. Any debate that has the effect of defining a "real" citizen is a debate that affects all women, whether they join in the arguments or not. Also, hundreds of women have been forced out of the U.S. military on grounds of homosexuality during witch-hunts—those systematic investigations designed to disclose the sexual preferences of scores of uniformed women simultaneously, usually by intimidating each woman to the point that she will reveal information about other women. These campaigns have had all the signs of being aimed at marginalizing women per se, not simply lesbian women.[37] Thus even feminists whose political inclinations were anti-militarist found themselves outraged in the 1990s when stories of particular women discharged from their chosen profession gained public notoriety.

For instance, many feminists watched Barbra Streisand's 1995 prime-time television docudrama of lesbian army colonel Margarethe Cammermeyer.[38] The film "worked" for many viewers, even for many skeptical peace activist feminist viewers, not only because the relationship between Cammermeyer, a career army nurse in the Washington State National Guard, and her lover was portrayed with relative complexity and humanity, but also because the director and actors created a narrative that portrayed Cammermeyer as an asset to the military: she was dedicated, mature, disciplined, patriotic, skilled, and experienced. She was everything a modern military commander could wish for. It was patently unfair and irrational, the film's plot implied, for this woman to be excluded from an institution to which she had devoted most of her adult life.

Off the film set and behind the scenes in the U.S. Justice Department, Attorney General Janet Reno seemed to agree. In the Justice Department offices, debates developed between Reno and her legal staff over whether to pursue Cammermeyer after a lower court had reinstated her in the military. Reno voiced the opinion that the federal government would look foolish if it entered an appeal; the lower court's decision in favor of Cammermeyer should be allowed to stand. According to one of the Justice Department's policy participants, Reno told her aides that "this woman is no threat to anyone."[39] In the end, however, the attorney general and her senior advisors concluded that they had to go ahead with the court appeal because to do otherwise would be to undercut the Clinton White House, which had spent so much of its political currency in 1993 crafting the revised anti-gay ban.[40] The decision-making process that went on inside one federal department sheds some light on the myriad dynamics that can promote the militarization of civilian officials.

In the wake of the news stories, the published autobiography, the Streisand film, and the court cases, Colonel Cammermeyer continued to receive invitations to speak at colleges and high schools. She described her message as less about the value of military service,

however, than about providing support for young gay men and lesbians. While her court appeals were pending, she continued to serve in
the military, but she described the institution by saying, "The military
isn't good about dealing with the realities of sexuality, either heterosexual or homosexual."[41]

Issue definitions in American political life are not easy to control in
this day of fiercely competitive media. One of the principal dynamics
that has militarized the gays-in-the-military issue in the United States
has been the pressuring of advocates to offer up to the media those gay
and lesbian soldiers in whom mainstream media producers and editors
can find no fault on any grounds *other* than their violation of the government's homosexual ban. Presenting gay and lesbian soldiers as
paragons of soldierly virtue consequently became the strategy chosen
by activists for exposing the utter irrationality of the Defense Department's ban. It was an effective strategy: it narrowed the terms of political debate, and it convinced many American citizens who had no personal stake in gay rights.

This strategy, however, also had other consequences. The very
confines and contours of the resultant public debate made it seem as if
the highest caliber of American citizens were those who chose the military as their career. These lesbian and gay model soldiers took on the
status of paragons of citizenship. They could have been architects or
social workers, carpenters or journalists, yet instead they chose to be
professional soldiers. In so doing, the anti-ban debaters implied, these
soldiers had a better chance than any of their civilian compatriots did
of performing a valued service to their nation. During 1993, as these
lesbian women and gay men gained national recognition through their
exemplary soldiering, as their merits and patriotism became the focus
of congressional hearings and nighttime television shows, perhaps homophobia did recede in American culture. But militarization advanced.

Some American lesbian feminists voiced reservations about the
strategy of presenting gay soldiers as model citizens. Informal debates,
for instance, took place inside large women's advocacy groups such as
the National Organization for Women (NOW). Members of NOW
had long been divided on the question of whether women's entry into
the military was a step toward "first class citizenship." During the
Carter years NOW's national leadership submitted a powerful amicus
curiae brief to the Supreme Court urging that compulsory military registration cover young women as well as young men.[42] Yet NOW had a
history of homophobia to overcome. During the late 1980s and early

1990s, therefore, NOW's new leadership, together with its local chapters, took deliberate steps to support gay and lesbian rights. When the Clinton proposal to lift the gay ban propelled the issue onto center stage, many NOW members believed that the organization should be allied with those women's groups who were forcefully expressing their solidarity with gay men and lesbians. Other NOW activists were not so sure. They saw not just an opportunity but a dilemma.

This early 1990s debate among activist American women about militarism did not attract much attention in the mainstream media. Press editors and television producers were not interested in a public debate over the role of militarism in American culture. Media managers seemed to think that this debate wouldn't attract consumers or hold advertisers. Instead, editors and producers seemed interested in sexuality and in the military as an embodiment of patriotism. Most of their readers and viewers seemed to share their preference. Consequently, the presumed legitimacy of the military as an institution and soldiering as an activity became even more firmly entrenched in American political culture.

Still, these marginalized lesbian feminists voicing concern about the valorizing of lesbian soldiers did set off discussions among women active in both lesbian political circles and the peace movement. In the aftermath of the Gulf War, for instance, Sherri Paris, writing for the California gay paper *Lavender Reader,* explained why she "didn't support the troops," even if some of those troops were lesbians: "Now I could tell you in that moment I felt compassion for Donna Jackson [an American woman soldier who had been discharged after she had publicly revealed that she was a lesbian], that I saw her as a fellow human being rather than a symbol of the war I hate, and that I respected her for having the courage of her convictions. If I told you that, I'd be lying. My sympathies were reserved for those that Donna was willing to kill if she could do it as a lesbian."[43]

The first national political debate among Americans about the policies toward heterosexuality and homosexuality in their government's military ended in 1993, not with a bang, but a whimper: the new ambiguous, largely unenforced policy of "don't ask, don't tell, don't pursue." It was a solution hammered out in the end by a group of men: the president, the armed services chiefs of staff, and the most powerful members of the House and Senate Armed Services Committees.

The long-standing and persistent practices of militarized homophobia have mobilized many proponents of lesbian and gay rights. The

result has been another paradox: the very stubbornness of their country's official militarization apparently has made it almost impossible
for the American lesbian and gay campaigners to avoid becoming militarized themselves.

Since 1988, when the Gay and Lesbian Military Freedom Project
was created, there had been small but determined efforts to change the
military's homophobic policy. The project's members had concentrated
on court challenges and on cultivating contacts within the Defense Department and the staffs of the most influential congressional committees. This strategizing, removed from most lesbians' and gay men's
daily lives, created a chasm between the movement's leaders and supporters. Responsibility for this chasm, says prominent lesbian activist
Urvashi Vaid, lay with gay and lesbian rights leaders' excessive preoccupation with backroom political dealings, with their concern more for
what senators and White House officials found palatable than for what
lesbians and gays in Wisconsin or New Jersey thought.[44] The resultant
gap left most gay and lesbian leaders unprepared for the nationwide
torrent of attention when the issue leaped onto the political stage in
1992: "Suddenly, we broke through. And like characters in a slapstick
comedy, we came tumbling through the door, falling on top of each
other and stumbling for footing as we adjusted to the sudden lack of
resistance. We failed to realize that the resistance had not disappeared;
it had changed. The door was still shut, but it was masked by a welcoming facade."[45]

What Vaid has described is a subtle form of militarization. Military
policy is among the most centralized policy areas in any country; furthermore, military policy usually is shrouded in a secrecy that is legiti-
mated by notions of "national security." Consequently, the leaders of
any movement that seeks to alter military policy will be tempted to
adopt a style of political bargaining that shuts out its local supporters.
In other words, any popular movement is prone to militarization if its
activists believe that altering military policy can be achieved only if the
movement's leaders are willing to engage in elitist state politics. Every
transformative movement, including those informed by feminism, takes
a risk if it engages with the central state's elite.[46] It might be a risk well
worth taking. But engagement with those state policy makers whose
specialty is military affairs doubles that risk precisely because centralization, secrecy, masculinized pride, and masculinized expertise are so
tightly woven into the very processes of state military policy making.

One popular effort to tackle military policy that thus far largely has avoided the tendency toward movement centralization is the organizing by local communities to expose and then force the military to clean up toxic pollution on and around military bases. The leaders of this movement in the United States have been women, many of whom refer to themselves as "just ordinary housewives." They have been held in patriarchal contempt by local military base commanders for their alleged feminine naïveté and "hysteria." But, according to feminist geographer Joni Seager, who has charted their organizing, these women-led environmental groups have persisted and have managed to sustain authentically grassroots connections.[47] Their success shows that although dealing with any military does pose militarizing temptations for a popular movement, giving in to those temptations is not inevitable. Resisting a militarizing temptation, however, does require activists to self-consciously analyze it, something the American opponents of the military's ban on gays and lesbians may not have done sufficiently in the early 1990s.

The congressional political debate on gays and lesbians in the military riveted Americans during the early months of 1993. The House, the Senate, and the presidency were then all under Democratic control. The Senate Armed Services Committee, led by Georgia Democrat Sam Nunn, managed to dominate the proceedings. This committee's domination was surprising to many long-time observers of military politics because on matters of personnel—rather than procurement or doctrine—the House Armed Services Committee traditionally had taken the initiative. It had been the House committee's usual influence on military personnel issues that had provided women congressional representatives, especially Colorado Democrat Patricia Schroeder, with leverage in the late 1980s and early 1990s during discussions of women as military wives and women as military personnel. How the House committee, chaired in 1993 by the usually outspoken liberal African American California representative Ronald Dellums, was so thoroughly marginalized in the gays-in-the-military debate has yet to be fully explained. The silencing of the House Committee served to further masculinize this state policy-making process. The Senate committee in 1993 was dominated by Sam Nunn, who in turn was in agreement with Chief of Staff General Colin Powell: both Nunn and Powell were adamant in their opposition to relaxing the ban on gays in uniform.

When the final legislative formula, which made only minor changes in the official homophobic policy, came to a vote in the House of Representatives in 1993, the gendering of that institution's own operations was clear. Voting *against* "don't ask, don't tell, don't pursue" legislation were:

Republican men	6%
Republican women	17%
Democratic men	41%
Democratic women	78%[48]

The implementation history of the new policy between mid-1993 and early 1998 suggests either that the constitutional precept of uniformed military officers' subordination to civilian authority is routinely breached *or* that the U.S. military's disciplinary chain of command is far looser than is often presumed. The independent watchdog organization Servicemembers Legal Defense Network (SLDN), for instance, found, first, that while the new policy forbade the practice of asking a potential recruit about her or his sexual preference, this provision took three years, until 1997, to be implemented.[49] Second, lawyers for the SLDN found routine violations of the new policy's requirement that Pentagon investigators not ask women and men in the services about the sexual practices of their colleagues and friends; third, they found open defiance of the policy's requirement that military investigators not take a soldier's presence at a gay club or at a gay rights rally (out of uniform) as indicator of homosexuality. Furthermore, according to the findings of SLDN's civilian monitors, the number of military violations of the policy in 1994 through 1998 rose steadily.[50] Lesbian women and gay men in uniform who were trying to remain in the military while escaping notice during this period told of going to extraordinary lengths in order to not arouse suspicion. All lived double lives. Many got married. One man told of taking part in group sex with a Filipino prostitute simply so that his military friends would not suspect him of homosexuality.[51]

That the elected civilian officials in Congress and the White House never took steps to compel the military to adhere to the 1993 policy of don't ask, don't tell, don't pursue might reflect their own deferential attitudes toward the military. Alternatively, the failure of these civilians to bring the military into compliance could be explained by their earlier support of the notion that U.S. national security is best achieved through the continuing harassment of any military personnel suspected of being gay. Either of these two explanations suggests the militarization of American elected officials at the end of the twentieth century.

Given this pattern, it is not surprising that numerous gay and lesbian activists have devoted resources to challenging the Defense Department. Much of their activity has moved outside of Congress and the media and back into the courts, the political arena in which their activism began a decade earlier. In mid-1995, a Navy board of inquiry for the first time sided with a homosexual who had come out but who argued before the military's court that simply being a homosexual should not be the basis for discharge. Lieutenant Zoe Dunning had carried on her fight inside the Navy for two years. On June 16, 1995, she made history. Her claim that being a lesbian should, on its own, not prevent her from continuing to serve in the military was endorsed by the Navy's tribunal and thereafter by the civilian Secretary of the Navy.[52] It was unclear whether Zoe Dunning's victory would act as a precedent. It was likewise uncertain whether those civilian judges who will be hearing a string of suits in coming years will continue to see homosexuality alone as fair and reasonable grounds for discharge.[53]

It has been a common practice of men and women appointed to federal judgeships in the United States to defer to Congress and the president in matters that they consider to fall within the bounds of national security. In this sense, the judicial culture of America is a militarized culture. Thus, for example, the judges presiding over the federal judiciary's Ninth Circuit reiterated their belief in the courts' "traditional deference to military judgment" as the foundation for their opinion approving the Navy's dismissal of Petty Officer Mark Philips in 1997.[54]

The dynamics of gays in the military as a public issue are not globally Americanized. The analytical danger is that—due in no small part to the current structure of the international media ownership—the American debate has become the best known on several continents, which makes it more difficult for lesbian and gay activists and campaigners against state-sponsored homophobia in other countries to craft a movement strategy and a public discourse that avoid some of the pitfalls encountered by their American counterparts. Americanization takes a host of forms. But one of those forms is militarization.

Israel, Australia, Canada, Zimbabwe, the Philippines, South Africa, and Britain have all had post–Cold War public discussions of the doctrine that heterosexism is necessary for genuine national security.[55] In each of these countries, some lesbians and gay men have experienced soldiering as an opportunity to build community, to create emotional relationships, and to explore their own sexuality, even while they have feared investigation, exposure, and punishment.

In each of these countries, the very campaign to permit gay men and lesbians to soldier may result in a deepening of militarization. Just how militarizing any of the campaigns' unintended consequences actually are will be determined by how many gay and lesbian citizens join together with their heterosexual compatriots in believing that soldiering is good citizenship writ large, or epitomizes public service, or amounts to laying down one's life for one's country. To the extent that any one of these equations is taken as culturally *un*problematic, it is likely that the campaign to overturn a gay ban will further entrench militarism, even if campaigners succeed in overturning their own military's ban.

In 1990s Britain, one could watch activists trying to cope with this risk of unintended militarization.

It was a warm day in June, a lovely day for a parade. An estimated 160,000 lesbians and gay men and their supporters turned out for Britain's 1995 Gay Pride march. Among the joyful participants was Liz Campion. With her daughter riding happily on her shoulders, Liz Campion paraded in her navy uniform. Although she recently had been dismissed from the military on grounds of her homosexuality, she wanted to be certain that people along the London parade route realized that lesbians were currently serving in the British military. Lieutenant Liz Campion was one of a group of increasingly activist British gay men and lesbians challenging dismissals from that military on the grounds of homosexuality.[56]

The British campaign to end the ban on gays and lesbians in the military has not had precisely the same consequences as the American campaign. This difference is because soldiering in 1990s British political culture is held in somewhat less awe and because senior uniformed officers are less likely to take high-profile policy-making positions. Some of the relative lack of national emotion emanating from the British debate also may be due to the demise of the empire: the military as an institution seems somewhat less a symbol of the country's world stature than it still does for many Americans. Perhaps the difference is due as well to the unappealing character of soldiering most visible to an ordinary British citizen watching the evening television news during the last decade: soldiers patrolling the streets of Belfast. Unlike their Russian and American counterparts, Britain's retired generals are not touted as potential political leaders.[57] None of the British prime ministers in the last century—and none of their principal rivals—has been a member of the professional military. None of the three men who vied for the prime minister's post in the watershed election of May 1997 portrayed himself in his campaign ads as a younger man in the uniform of British military. And few citizen-voters seemed to take any notice of this absence.

This is not to say that militarism plays no significant role in British political life. The Queen's annual June birthday appearance finds her dressed in the red tunic of a royal regiment as she inspects her soldiers. Prince Charles and other members of the royal family regularly appear in military attire. Several members of Parliament—especially men on the Conservative Party's benches—are military veterans. Margaret Thatcher won her 1983 national election in part by taking credit for the British military success in the Falklands war against the Argentinean military. The British military's academy, Sandhurst, has the power to confer on its graduates a privileged status within the country's hierarchical class system. The thirty-year government policy of militarizing the ethnic conflict in Northern Ireland lost neither the Labour nor the Conservative party many votes among ordinary Britons. During periods of economic recession, thousands of young British working-class men have looked to soldiering to save them from poverty. Thousands of Britons continue to work in military industries. Britain's arms exports were sufficient to make it the second-largest international arms seller in 1996.[58] The new Labour Party leadership of the mid-1990s sought—successfully—to win British voters' support by sanding down the once-sharp edges of the party's antimilitarist electoral platform.[59] The 1998 political alliance between Prime Minister Tony Blair and President Bill Clinton in support of threatening military action in Iraq was approved by 57 percent of Britons polled.[60] In 1999, Blair was among the nineteen NATO leaders pushing hardest for an expanded bombing campaign to stop ethnic cleansings in Kosovo.[61] Around Britain, museums, monuments, and textbooks continue to feature military heroism as proof of British civilization's past greatness.

Nonetheless, the contemporary American eye sees in British political culture today a notably lowered profile of citizen-as-soldier. Significant credit for this lowering might be due to the British women's movement, which since the 1970s has been particularly focused on gendered economic class issues and rather less so on individual women's professional achievements. Particularly successful in arousing a cross-class British antimilitarism alliance was the 1980s Greenham Women's

Peace Camp. The movement's chief political target was the U.S. cruise missile housed in a rural region an hour's bus ride west of London, a missile that symbolized in the 1980s the militarized partnership of British government with Washington. But this feminist campaign soon raised broader issues, especially the prominence of masculinized militarism in Britain's national culture. As a result, without ever focusing on women as soldiers, the Greenham activists' efforts may have discouraged British feminists from believing that women had to become soldiers in order to become first-class citizens.[62]

To shed light on the character and extent of British militarization in general, one must study how the debate over gays in the military has been fashioned in such a mixed political setting, with cultural and economic forces pulling Britons and their institutions simultaneously away from and into the embrace of militarism. Many British gay men and lesbian activists in the campaign to overturn the Ministry of Defence ban do claim the "right to serve." They, like their American counterparts, have hesitated to analyze militarism, choosing instead to focus public attention on the unfairness and unreasonableness of heterosexist military rules.[63]

During 1995, the British Parliament held hearings. The Ministry of Defence quoted the retired American general Colin Powell in support of its own exclusionary policy.[64] British courts handed down a series of judgments supporting the government's ban, though on ever narrower grounds. News of the Conservative Defence Ministry officials' decision to "review" their current exclusionary policy was reported by some of the national daily papers. Ministry reform alternatives included allowing gay men and lesbians to soldier, but not in combat positions or in any post that required soldiers to work together in "close quarters."[65] Labour Party leaders—then in the opposition—pledged to overturn the ban if they won the 1997 parliamentary election.[66] Stonewall, a principal British gay rights organization, devoted its resources to challenging the existing policy and holding the Labour Party to its promise.

Still, all these aspects of the British campaign add up to something less than the American version of issue-saturation. The gays-in-the-military debate in Britain did not monopolize public discussion. In 1995–96, the government of Conservative Prime Minister John Major was fragile, but no commentator put the topic of gays in the military on a list of the top five issues threatening his party's parliamentary majority. Instead, among the politically salient issues that ordinary British voters were using to evaluate party rivals, the economy, the National

Health Service, mad cow disease, and the European Union all far out-ranked the government's continuing ban on gay men and lesbians in the military. Nor did Britain's feminist groups feature the issue; they spent much more energy promoting women as parliamentary candidates and sounding warnings over the feminization of Britain's low-paid part-time jobs. Most significantly, the individual women and men who were forced out of the military on charges of homosexuality were not trans-formed by campaigners or the media into Model British Citizens.[67]

During the mid-1990s openly gay Dutch soldiers served in UN peacekeeping forces alongside British soldiers in Bosnia, but the British government continued to justify its NATO exceptionalism as a matter of national sovereignty. Sovereignty had become a matter of special po-litical sensitivity in contemporary British culture. It continues to be de-bated in many arenas, as Britons try to come to terms with their shrunken role in world affairs, with the multiracial character of pres-ent-day British communities, with Scottish and Welsh Britons' gains in regional autonomy, and with Britain's membership in an increasingly integrated European Union. Defenders of Britain's gay ban have re-vealed that the confusion over British identity in the post–Cold War world could be not only militarized but also sexualized. John Wilkin-son, an influential Conservative member of Parliament, demonstrated in 1995 how the issues of homosexuality, defense, and sovereignty could be fused: "How we run our armed forces is a matter for the British Par-liament and people alone. It is the view of the forces, and has been the view of successive Governments that it would be inappropriate to insist that the forces accept these people [homosexuals]. People's sexuality runs very deep and it affects the way in which people get on with their colleagues. It can prejudice their behaviour in an invidious way."[68]

Wilkinson and civil servants in the Ministry of Defence were nerv-ously looking over their shoulders at the European Court. While American gay rights advocates were parochially limited to U.S. institu-tions in their campaign to reverse the ban, British campaigners could draw on a set of institutions created to realize European integration. In Europe gay rights in and out of the military was acquiring the status of an internationally recognized human right.[69] Could this European de-velopment inadvertently militarize the concept of international human rights?

In the late 1990s, the British military looked rather silly, said its critics. Spokespeople for Stonewall reminded journalists and members of Parliament that the British military was the only European NATO partner, besides Greece, that totally excluded men and women from its armed forces on the grounds of homosexuality.[70] In 1994, the Ministry of Defence did bow to pressure and accept Parliament's legislative amendment that disallowed treating a soldier's homosexuality as a criminal act. But homosexuality remained a basis for exclusion or forced discharge. Military recruiters continued to ask potential recruits if they were gay or lesbian, and each of the services maintained its own police force to investigate service members for suspected homosexuality.[71]

The Defence Ministry investigations of individual women turned into witch-hunts when the military's interrogators used one woman's vulnerability to learn about other women suspected of lesbianism and when those allegations and suspicions were fed into the ministry's global computer system. Caroline Meaghr, a staff sergeant in the Royal Military Police, recalled witch-hunts that she officially took part in before she herself came under investigation:

> There would be a very detailed search of [the suspected women's] possessions. We would read every letter. We would look everywhere for evidence. This would be followed by very long interviews two to three hours at a time.... I sat there a few times and I wanted to say, "Don't answer these questions." But it is a rank thing and the interviewers are male sergeants and staff sergeants and the women felt obliged to answer....
>
> Everyone who had ever been mentioned in an investigation, even if they were just friends on the fringes, would be named. If their name was on the index [a file of suspected lesbians kept by the British military police] the investigator would use it to bully the woman—it might intimidate somebody into confessing.[72]

Between 1990 and mid-1994, the Ministry of Defence dismissed 260 army personnel on the grounds of their sexuality: captains, squadron leaders, chaplains, and ordinary soldiers. Rank alone did not seem to make a soldier vulnerable or immune. But gender did. Like military investigators in the United States, Britain's military investigators appeared to focus their attentions more on women than on men. Of the sixty-four personnel dismissed by the Ministry of Defence in the period between 1992 and mid-1994, thirty-three were women. That is, although women comprised only 6 percent of all British military personnel, they made up over *half* of those discharged on grounds of alleged homosexuality.[73]

Liz Campion, the dismissed naval intelligence officer, charged that the Royal Navy knew for years that she was a lesbian, that naval investigators chose their targets on whim: "There are many, many gays and lesbians serving but they [the Royal Navy] turn a blind eye to it.... They only sack a few to keep the rest in hiding. It is a lottery system and you don't know if or when your number is up."[74]

In March 1996, the Ministry of Defence released their long-awaited 400-page report. Prepared by the ministry's Homosexual Policy Assessment Team, the report rejected all alternatives and recommended no change in the current ban on homosexuals in the military. The Conservative armed forces minister, Nicholas Soames, grandson of Winston Churchill, told his fellow members of Parliament that "any relaxation of the prohibition would damage operational effectiveness, leading to breaches of trust at critical moments and loss of morale."[75] The issue subsequently returned to the House of Commons select committee on the armed forces. Labour's parliamentary leadership, sitting across the aisle on the opposition benches, voiced caution, preferring to let the Commons select committee take the lead on proposing any changes. Labour leaders, despite their earlier campaign pledge to lift the ban, had been in close contact with members of the Clinton administration over a wide range of political strategy issues. Commentators speculated that Tony Blair and his Labour front bench, working hard to win the upcoming 1997 election, were trying to avoid what they saw to be Bill Clinton's political error in making a prominent issue out of lifting the gay ban.[76] In the 1990s, electoral strategic lessons were becoming an item of trans-Atlantic trade.

It may be the sheer meanness of the ban, especially when coupled with policy makers' rejection of all the evidence demonstrating the irrelevance of a soldier's sexual orientation to her or his successful performance of military tasks, that has driven gay and lesbian activists in Britain as well as in the United States to skip over what militaries actually *do*. The glaring unfairness has prompted an activist response that has paid little attention to the special character of the military in world affairs and instead has treated the military as if it were a public institution no different from a hospital, a fast food franchise, or a legislature.

Challenging Stonewall's campaigners and Edmund Hall, author of *We Can't Even March Straight,* was Peter Tatchell, another British gay activist, who combined his antihomophobia with antimilitarism. Tatchell responded with a pamphlet entitled *We Don't Want to March Straight,*[77] in which he asked rhetorically, "Why should we drop a single drop of queer blood to defend a homophobic state which treats us as second-class citizens?"[78] Then he cast his critical net over a wider political field. Tatchell questioned whether lesbians and gay men should seek to serve in an institution with a hierarchical, antidemocratic culture. He went further. Like American Sherri Paris, Tatchell refused to lend his support to members of his gay community when they joined an institution with a record of oppressing other peoples at home and overseas.[79]

In May 1996, the House of Commons select committee issued its report: it supported the continuation of the Ministry of Defence ban on homosexuals in the military, concluding that allowing gay men and lesbians to serve would, as the ministry had claimed, undermine morale and operational effectiveness.[80] The members of Parliament (MPs) on the cross-party select committee did include in their report some criticisms of the Defence Ministry's practices. In particular, they warned ministry officials not to pressure military chaplains to reveal information about sexual preference garnered from their allegedly confidential sessions with soldiers. They also warned the military not to relax its antiracism efforts simply because it was being supported in its heterosexist principles. The MPs' report criticized the ministry for "dragging its feet" on tackling racism in the armed forces and for taking meaningful actions against racist behavior only when pressed to do so by the Commission for Racial Equality.[81]

Two days later, the government of Prime Minister John Major called for a vote in the full House of Commons on its armed forces bill, which included a clause continuing the military's gay ban. Just before the vote, Conservative backbench MP Edwina Currie proposed an amendment to permit sexual activity, homosexual and heterosexual, so long as neither was prejudicial to good order or command relations. The Currie amendment sparked what one reporter described as "impassioned debate" among the MPs.[82]

The leaderships of the two dominant parties adopted rather different strategies in this debate. The Conservative leadership, under Major, imposed on its MPs a "three-line whip," that is, strict party discipline. By contrast, the Labour leadership, under Tony Blair, decided to impose on its MPs no whips at all; that is, it allowed Labour MPs a free vote. Blair himself abstained in the ultimate vote. Labour's front bench chief spokesman on defense issues, John Reid, did vote—in favor of sustaining the ministry ban. Many of Labour's MPs avoided even that level of visible choice; they stayed away from the House that day.[83]

In the 1996 vote, the Conservative leadership's bill sustaining the ban passed in the House of Commons 188 to 120. Eight Conservative

MPs defied their party's whips and voted for lifting the ban. Among the eight were renegade backbencher Edwina Currie and the only openly gay Conservative member of Parliament, Michael Brown.[84] One gay critic observed that "it is somewhat ironic that gays can serve in Her Majesty's government but not in Her Majesty's armed forces."[85]

In the wake of the select committee report and the Commons vote, a newly formed women's group, Lesbian Voices, was organized specifically to lobby Parliament. Among its founding members was Liz Campion, the lesbian dismissed from the Royal Navy the year before on charges of homosexuality. Campion responded to the 1996 House of Commons vote: "The idea that lesbians should be sacked for presenting some hypothetical sexual threat to other women while heterosexual men continue to present an actual sexual threat to all women, including lesbians, is utterly ridiculous."[86]

Following the 1996 parliamentary setback, British anti-ban campaigners announced that they would move their campaign focus from London to Strasbourg, the site of the European Court of Human Rights. The legal process would be a slow one, but it was expected to produce a judgment against the British government. In the two years following its 1997 electoral victory, Tony Blair's Labour government studiously avoided any dramatic change in the military's anti-gay policy, all the while keeping one eye on the judges in Strasbourg. Finally, in April 1999, when it became clear that the European Court was likely to find the British government in violation of human rights, the Blair government announced that it would submit to Parliament a bill that lifted Britain's ban on gays and lesbians in the military. Given Labour's overwhelming majority in the House of Commons, the bill was certain to pass.[87]

Perhaps the Blair government was emboldened to take on its still-resistant military senior command by the decline in British voters' homophobia. Already in 1995, opinion polls had revealed that a majority of all Britons (69 percent of women, 55 percent of men) approved of military service for a "declared homosexual living in a stable relationship with a partner."[88] Tony Blair's appointment to a post in his Cabinet of an openly gay MP, Chris Smith, and the announcement by a second Cabinet minister and Labour MP, Angela Eagle, that she was a lesbian seemed to make no dent in Blair's popularity ratings. It may be that the British government's ending its gay ban while its American ally held on to its ban is explained not by Britons' lessening militarism but by their lessening homophobia. Rises and falls in any society's homophobia and militarism need to be monitored simultaneously but distinctly. While one shapes the career of the other, they are not synonymous.

The militarizing processes running underneath both the American and the British political struggles over the military exclusion of gay men and lesbians are difficult to detect and painful to map. Yet this very difficulty makes efforts to detect and map the processes all the more important. Militarization can come in many guises. It can ride on the back of a worthy cause. Thus, a public discourse can be militarized if, in the name of celebrating the contributions that lesbians and gay men have made to society, homosexual soldiers are held up as the models of "good citizens." A public discourse, however, also can be militarized if the military and soldiering are discussed in a way that normalizes, or "civilianizes," each. Treating the military as if it were just another job site and treating soldiering as if it were just another job—as if its members were no less likely to wield organized violence than, say, hospital orderlies or Webmasters—may strip a military of its immunity from the country's antidiscrimination laws, but that same rhetorical strategy may serve, unwittingly, to militarize public conversation by camouflaging the military's distinctiveness.

MILITARIZATION, MASCULINITY, AND MEMOS

Thinking about militarization allows us to chart the silences. It enables us to see what is not challenged or, at the very least, what is not made problematic: elevating a good soldier to the status of a good citizen; expanding NATO in the name of democratization; seeing JROTC as simply a program to enhance school discipline; imagining Carmen Miranda's wartime movie roles as nothing more than harmless comedies. The silence surrounding militarization is broken when military assumptions about, and military dependence on, gender are pushed up to the surface of public discussion.

Here comparisons can help. The British campaign to end the ban on gay men and lesbians in the military, like its American counterpart, has been notably narrower in its assessment of the military as an institution and militarism as a package of assumptions than was, for example, the 1980s antimissile campaign inspired by the Greenham Women's Peace Camp. Whereas Greenham's feminist activists eventually moved from a focus on a single weapon, the cruise missile, to a far-reaching critique of both patriarchy and militarism, gay and lesbian rights advocates are tempted to question heterosexism in British culture while accepting militarism as a given.[89]

It has been feminists' self-conscious investigation of what serves to privilege masculinity that has prompted so many—though not all—feminists in so many countries to go beyond questioning equality inside the military, to question militarism itself. Feminists from India, Zimbabwe, and Japan to Britain, the United States, Serbia, Chile, South Korea, Palestine, Israel, and Algeria all have found that when they have followed the bread crumbs of privileged masculinity, they have been led time and again not just to the doorstep of the military, but to the threshold of all those social institutions that promote militarization.[90]

Thus it is that in the middle of conversations about ethnic conflicts, upcoming elections, gay liberation, human rights violations, sweatshops, military base closures, and UN peacekeeping, it is often feminists who are most vocally skeptical about leaving militarism unexamined. So many feminists have discovered in their own work that if any one of these issues is seemingly resolved without militarism being dragged out of the shadows into the bright light, that issue's resolution is likely to leave masculinity's privileged status still untouched. Women who have learned to look for militarism under the rock of patriarchy have concluded that, for masculinity's privilege to be challenged effectively, militarism must be measured and weighed explicitly. Only then can a society make truly meaningful decisions about how women should relate to men, to each other, and to the state.

Militarization and the privileging of masculinity are both products not only of amorphous cultural beliefs but also of deliberate decisions. The tomato soup acquired Star Wars pasta shapes because someone decided it would promote sales among harried women shoppers. High school students drill and learn military history because government officials, local parents, and principals made decisions. Camouflage patterns or epaulettes appear on fashionable clothes because some designers made a profit-making fashion choice. Army units are called in to put down women factory workers' protests because a government official made a political calculation. A candidate's military record is featured in his (rarely her) election campaign ads because someone decided that this image will appeal to certain voters. During a gays-in-the-military campaign, certain issues are raised while others are left lying dormant because someone in the movement made a strategic assessment.

Many more decisions are made in any country's political system than most of us realize. Conventional wisdom *under*counts the decisions that are necessary to keep patriarchy alive and to sustain a society's militarization. The common conception is that decisions are driven by tradition or culture rather than by deliberate, conscious thought. Nowhere is this easy assumption more pervasive than when patriarchy and militarization converge—in the gendering of militarization. Commentators on both domestic and international politics have spent many years *not* investigating how militarization occurs and how its progress relies on particular constructions of femininity and masculinity because many of these observers have lazily assumed that either tradition or culture was at work—*and* that neither tradition nor culture required explicit decisions for their maintenance.

The reality is less ephemeral. Women's myriad relationships to militarist practices and to the military are far less the result of amorphous tradition or culture than they are the product of particular—traceable—decisions. But the persistence of the presumption that women's militarization is simply the outcome of nature or custom is one of the things that grants gendered militarization its stubborn longevity. Thus, once it is made clear that the peculiarities of women's lives as military wives or as military prostitutes or as wartime rape victims is the result of memos, not tradition, it will be harder to treat the consequences as apolitical.

Just the assertion that there are more decisions—and decision makers—than are usually assumed may carry the ring of a conspiracy theory. Yet one does not have to wallow in paranoia (itself often a fertile ground for militarizing fantasies) in order to ask "who decides what?" Finding the memo that sets out criteria for the "good" military wife, uncovering the ruling that sets a woman soldier's hemline, discovering the official agreement that requires disco women to undergo vaginal exams—uncovering any of these actions, but especially all of them together, may reveal a gendered military system that is more political than it is cultural. Or finding those memos may show just how politically constructed any national or international culture is.

Still, these findings may not add up to a monolithic militarized political elite that always knows exactly what it wants from women. Setting out to pinpoint the decisions—and the decision makers—can uncover not a neatly packaged conspiracy, but instead tension, contradiction, and confusion. Surprisingly, the search for those decisions that have promoted gendered militarization often reveals ambivalence, that is, both men and women with mixed feelings. Masculinity-privileging militarization, however, can survive, even thrive, on mixed feelings.

The Laundress, the Soldier, and the State

Measuring the crumbling remains of Roman sandals is a tedious business. One has to be inspired by a strong hunch that one is on the trail of something significant. Carol van Driel-Murray, the Dutch archeologist, thought she was.

> Flavius Cerialis, the commander, [was equipped] with exceptionally elaborate openwork shoes (which for full effect must have been worn with coloured socks); his wife, Sulpicia Lepidina, with a narrow, extremely elegant foot.... She had sensible closed shoes as well as fashionable sandals stamped with the maker's name: Lucius Aebutius Thales, surely the first designer label in history.[1]

All of Carol van Driel-Murray's colleagues in the 1990s seemed sure, and had been sure for decades, that the Roman troops sent by the emperor to conquer Britain had been unmarried. She had a sense that most of her male archeologist colleagues were a bit too fond of this bachelor-soldier image.[2] As she measured the sandals found on the sites of various British Roman garrisons, meticulously charting her findings on statistical graphs, she began to create a picture far more complicated than that of a garrison full of male bachelors. She found sandals too small for men. A lot of them. Some were designed for the commander's wife, many were in the style common among ordinary women and children. Her conclusion: there were women living inside the Roman garrisons.[3] Thanks to Carol van Driel-Murray's intellectual tenacity, the Roman conquest of Britain was about to undergo a serious reimagining.

So was soldiering. So was military strategy.

Most military history—and a great deal of contemporary military reporting—is written as though women were invisible at worst, a mere "human interest story" at best. This approach underestimates the impacts of militaries on women's lives. The conventional approach to military affairs makes another, even more serious, mistake: it underestimates the extent to which states' militaries have relied on women in order to conduct their military operations and in order to sustain the military's political legitimacy. The militarization of women—from women who left behind their sandals inside the British Roman garrisons to women whose lives today are tied to militaries in Serbia, Rwanda, the United States, Israel, South Korea, and Britain—has been so pervasive because so many military officials have presumed that they have needed to control not only women, but the very idea of "femininity."

Out of their sense of need, those military officials and civilian state authorities responsible for preparing for and waging war have tried to maneuver different groups of women and the ideas about what constitutes "femininity" so that each can serve military objectives. Sometimes these maneuvers have thoroughly succeeded. Women have so internalized the militarized sense of their duties, sources of pride, bases of anxiety that they have virtually no awareness that they have been maneuvered. They talk instead about "opportunities" or "adventure" or "love" or "shame" or "belonging" or even "liberation."

Yet at other times, the militarizing maneuvers have been so blatant, so brutal or threaded through with hypocrisy, that many women have felt pushed around, even oppressed. Under these circumstances, many women may resist the militarizing maneuvers. They might even be prompted to openly discuss militarism. Imagine, for instance, an American "Rosie the Riveter" talking today to a Korean "comfort woman." These two women would have experienced the same war and experienced it self-consciously as women. They both would possess detailed memories of how the waging of that war profoundly shaped their lives. Still, between these two women yawns a chasm, a gaping divide in levels of consciousness. The first woman would likely be insulted if she were told she had been maneuvered; the second would perhaps feel validated.

Male military policy makers—uniformed and civilian—have believed that they need to control women in order to achieve military goals. In scores of different societies, they have acted as though most men are not natural soldiers, as though most men need to be continuously reminded that their tenuous grasp on the status of "manly man" depends on women thinking of them as such. Moreover, military policy makers have acted as if the military's own legitimacy as a state institution requires perpetual shoring up through affirmation not only by the country's men, but by its women as well. Yet men commanding military forces have been uncertain about which sort of maneuver proves most effective—direct or indirect exertion of control over women. Should women (as morale-boosting wives, mothers, prostitutes, nurses) be made integral cogs of the military machine? Or will the military's masculine image, mobility, and customary ways of operating be better protected if less direct structures of control were devised, keeping women available but at arm's length? One of the reasons that many women who have been maneuvered to play a militarily supportive role have developed so little consciousness of the militarization of their lives is that that process has occurred quite indirectly or because military officials designing that process have waffled. Women haven't been able to see the gendered militarization process clearly because it frequently has been implemented in a spirit of ambivalence.

Long before militaries had women's corps, married quarters, AIDS-prevention classes, and legions of civilian clerical workers, they had women in tow. There are those telltale women's sandals found in Roman garrisons on the British frontier. In the mid-seventeenth century, one European army was reported to have had 40,000 male soldiers and "100,000 soldiers' wives, whores, man servants, maids, and other camp followers."[4]

"Camp followers"—this label was attached to those civilian women who followed male soldiers. To "follow" is not to be a part of, but to be dependent on, to tag along. The implication is parasitic. Poor women who followed on foot and in wagons behind medieval European armies were deemed mere (unclean, untrustworthy, unrespectable) camp followers. Centuries later, so were those impoverished German women who during World War I tried to sustain the economies of their households after the Kaiser had conscripted their husbands. Many were driven to take up prostitution—servicing other German male soldiers. The German authorities began to see these women as subversive camp followers, undermining the health and morale of the army. The authorities labeled these women "secret prostitutes" and sent out special police units to control their sexual activities. At the same time, however, many resentful German wives noted that these commanders pursued a policy of distributing prophylactics to their troops, thus institutionalizing the presumption that soldiering men will seek sexual relations with women whether they are married or not.[5] Once again, military policy makers, in an attempt to determine which maneuver proved most effective, devised policies on women in wartime that inclined toward confusion and contradiction.

Three decades later, German women sought out relationships with American troops of the occupying army as a means to survive the devastating conditions in the immediate aftermath of World War II. In the eyes of the victorious U.S. authorities who were trying to restore a postwar order and simultaneously maintain discipline in their own military ranks, these German women too were disreputable, immoral, sexually promiscuous parakeets—that is, camp followers. Explicit steps would have to be taken, in coordination with the fledgling post-Nazi German authorities, to control such female behavior.[6] On the other side of the globe at the same time, American commanders were nervously assessing the postwar relationships between American male troops and local Chinese women. In the wake of a much-publicized December 1946 rape by two American soldiers of a nineteen-year-old Beijing National University student, Shen Chung, student nationalists took to the streets to claim that, even though the United States and the Chinese had just spent four years fighting together against Japan, the stationing of American military units on Chinese soil was a violation of that country's sovereignty. At first, the American command adopted the camp follower explanation, wondering aloud whether the Chinese young women might not have been inviting such behavior. Only when the State Department warned of the seriousness of the Chinese protests as threats to larger U.S. political postwar objectives did official attention shift away from the sexuality of Chinese women.[7]

As these recent revelations about the militarized sexual politics of early post–World War II Germany and China suggest, the idea of the woman-as-camp-follower can become publicly salient whenever authorities imagine women impoverished by war to be strategizing to survive by creating some sort of relationship with men as soldiers. Under these militarized conditions, the feminized categories of refugee, war victim, prostitute, girlfriend, and war bride can become conflated in policy makers' anxious minds. Viewed through this mist of anxiety, a camp follower is a woman who is performing her own maneuver. She consequently is not securely under patriarchal control. She is devising her own individualistic strategy for gaining whatever benefits she can from a masculinized military.

Many woman who have followed militaries and who have lived off the table scraps of military operations have indeed been resourceful and energetic survivalists. On the other hand, it is a mistake to picture these women as autonomous entrepreneurs. Listen to political scientist Katharine Moon's description of the Korean women who later became prostitutes servicing American male soldiers stationed in their country:

> Most, especially among the earlier generations of prostitutes (1950s–70s), came from poor families in Korea's countryside, with one parent or both parents missing or unable to provide for numerous family members. [They] were camp followers of troops during the Korean War; they did laundry, cooked, and tended to the soldiers' sexual demands. Some had been widowed by the war, others orphaned or lost during a family's flight from bombs and grenades. Many of [them] considered themselves "fallen women" even before entering prostitution because they had lost social status and self-respect from divorce, rape, sex, and/or pregnancy out of wedlock.[8]

Focusing exclusively on the much-touted craftiness of camp followers is analytically—and politically—risky. Such a focus risks underestimating the explicit need that military commanders had for these working women. As always, recognizing any woman's agency—her capacity to think and act autonomously—should not lead us to be uncurious about a larger institution's efforts to put that woman's labor and emotions to work for its own patriarchal ends. To reveal a camp follower's and a military commander's simultaneous strategizing is not to argue that they are equals on the field of maneuvers.

Historically, women camp followers were barely tolerated by military commanders. So long as they provided supplies and services that the military did not want to bother with itself, so long as they kept rank and file men satisfied enough not to mutiny or desert, they were allowed to follow the armies from battle to battle. But as soon as a commander decided that the women were slowing down the march or tainting his troops' reputation as an efficient fighting force, camp followers were summarily purged.

The commander's periodic purge required the discrediting of women who followed and serviced the troops, for it was far easier for

commanders to send the women out of camp if they could be portrayed as rootless, promiscuous, parasitic, and generally a drag on the
military's discipline and battle readiness. Thus *camp follower* was
commonly equated with *prostitute*. The very fact that the camp follower was a woman who allegedly *chose* to make her life among rough
men was presumed proof enough of her loose character. Despite useful
functions that camp followers might temporarily provide the military,
a commander who wanted to rid himself of the women in his trains
could claim that camp followers were fundamentally nothing more
than whores. Furthermore, they could be replaced by other women
when the need again arose. In the late twentieth century, women who
have been mobilized to serve the military's needs are still vulnerable to
the stereotype of camp follower—dispensable, disreputable—no matter how professional their formal position is in the military.

MILITARIES NEED CAMP FOLLOWERS

Before the twentieth century, a woman traveling with an army (unless
she traveled disguised as a man) ran the risk of being disciplined or dis-
paraged as a common prostitute. In reality, these thousands of women
were soldiers' wives, cooks, provisioners, laundresses, and nurses.
Sometimes they served in all these roles simultaneously. It was as if
what we now think of as military base towns—in North Carolina or
South Korea or Chiapas—moved en masse across the land on horse-
back, in wagons, and on foot.

When they weren't being reduced verbally or physically to the status
of prostitutes, camp followers were performing tasks that any large
military force needs but wants to keep ideologically peripheral to its
combat function and often tries to avoid paying for directly. Sir James
Turner, in cautioning his fellow officers in seventeenth-century Britain
not to be too quick to rid themselves of women, reminded them that
"[camp followers] provide, buy and dress their husbands' meats, when
their husbands are on duty or newly come from it; they bring in fuel
for fire; a soldier's wife may be helpful to others, and gain money to
her husband and herself, especially they are useful in camp and lea-
guers, being permitted (which could not be refused them) to go some
miles from the camp to buy victuals and other necessaries."[9]

Individual male soldiers also recognized that women could ease
their hardships. A seventeenth-century soldier with a wife in camp who
proved a skilled sutler, cook, and nurse was envied by the other sol-

Figure 3 British male soldiers have gathered for a meal on the Turkish battlefield in 1855. The woman camp follower, barely visible here, is integral to the cook crew, yet scarcely of interest to the photographer. What would we learn about the Crimean War if we knew her full story? (Photographer: R. Fenton, "Cookhouse of the 8th Hussars, Crimean War, 1855," The Arts Council of Great Britain, London, UK.)

diers. If the husband was killed, his comrades vied to gain her services for themselves.

> I should have mentioned that one of my comrades was married to a pretty Scotchwoman, who lived in camp with him, and got a good deal of money by keeping a scuttling tent for the officers. The man was killed. In such a situation, the woman must not remain a widow and with such qualifications, she was a prize to any man. Another comrade said to me, "I advise you to marry Kate Keith. If you won't, I will. But there's no time to be lost, for she'll have plenty of offers."
> I took a few hours to consider of it, and determined upon soliciting the hands of Kate Keith.... The little black-eyed Scotchwoman accompanied me to the chaplain of the regiment the second day after her husband had fallen.[10]

To wage war against the American colonial upstarts, the British army regularly included women in its regiments. Historians estimate that 20,000 British women made the trans-Atlantic voyage so that they could march with the redcoats.[11] On Long Island in 1779, for instance,

British women could be found selling liquor to British soldiers, doing soldiers' laundry, sewing linens under the supervision of male soldier-tailors, and nursing sick men in army hospitals. The 23rd regiment stationed there, preparing for the New York campaigns, recorded feeding 469 men, 61 women, and 60 children on November 21, 1779. Nearby on that same day in the middle of the revolutionary war, the 37th regiment recorded feeding 57 women and 38 children along with their 499 male soldiers. Almost all these women were married to British soldiers. Other women "following" the British troops were mentioned, but not so meticulously accounted for.[12]

A woman officially recorded as a soldier's wife had had her oceanic passages to America paid for by the British military. In return, she was subjected to military policies designed to make her serve military objectives. Local British commanders devoted considerable thought to regulating the women inside their encampments. Women were told where to walk in the long lines-of-march that could stretch over miles of the American landscape. Women were instructed on where they could and could not sell their liquors. They could be court-martialed if discovered plundering an American's property. They were threatened with dismissal from the regiment (and thus lost their food and lodging) if they didn't answer the commander's call for nurses. A widow deemed by a soldier's superior to be insufficiently moral could be prevented from remarrying.

Evidence suggests that at least some women in the British regiments defied these attempts to control them. They cursed loudly, they acquired debts, they plundered when they could, they set up canteens outside the camps, they had sexual liaisons with other women's soldier-husbands. But if a woman did sustain her reputation in the commander's eyes for being the model regimental woman, "sober and industrious," she could count on the military paying her passage home to Britain when her husband was killed in battle.[13]

One American spectator watching the Britons' sad parade through Cambridge, Massachusetts, whets our curiosity: "I never had the least idea that the Creation produced such a sordid set of creatures in human figure—poor, dirty, emaciated men, great numbers of women who seemed to be the beasts of burden, having a bushel basket on their backs, by which they were bent double, the content seemed to be pots and kettles.... various sorts of furniture and utensils, some very young infants who were born on the road, the women, clothed in dirty rags."[14]

On the other side of the American Revolution, George Washington was of two minds about the scores of women who "followed" the male troops of his Continental Army. On the one hand, these women were known to care for the sick, to brave British fire in order to refill and carry water canteens to their husbands and friends, and to do laundry. In one New York regiment, record keepers in 1779 reported two washerwomen doing the laundry for every twenty-four male soldiers.[15] This resource was not one that the commander of the under-equipped colonial army could sneeze at. On the other hand, in August 1777 Washington wrote: "The multitude of women in particular, especially those who are pregnant, or have children, are a clog upon every movement."[16] He thus urged his commanders to "get rid of all such as are not necessary."[17]

Necessary. That was Washington's proviso. Yet soon after, during the early months of the Continental Army's wintering at Valley Forge, there remained in that encampment alone an estimated 400 women among 16,000 men.[18] Imagine the story of the American Revolution if it could be told by the scores of women who followed—and served—the British and American troops.

Some women who have followed soldiers have become totally dependent on the military. At the end of the Thirty Years War, one camp follower asked plaintively: "I was born in war; I have no home, no country, no friends; war is all my wealth and now whither will I go?"[19]

Her plaintive question sounds not unlike that posed by many American civilian women in the 1990s. When the military bases on which they and their towns depended were slated for closure, many responded with anxious queries. Likewise, women married to soldiers complained when their husbands were forced into early retirement. It was as if the women were being afflicted with a personal injury. The military on which they had come to rely—for income, for housing, low-cost medical care, for public status—was going to betray them. The sounds of the guns may have been far off in the distance, their skirts might not have been dragging in the mud of the march, but these modern women, like their camp-following foresisters, had developed a dependency on war preparing and war waging for their economic and emotional security.

Kristin Waters is a feminist philosopher. She is also the product of an American military base town. In her hometown of Rome, New York, the Air Force had not been a coercive instrument of state power. That may be the way political scientists would describe it, but to Kris and her family, Griffiss Air Force Base was a neighbor, a good neighbor; it provided jobs, retail customers, special school programs, and a sense of local pride. The Waters family owned the local newspaper, *The Daily Sentinel.* "My grandfather and father had very, very close relations with the base commander."[20] Her mother's relations with the base were just as intimate. She was treated by the local military officers as an "honorary military wife." This recognition served the military's purposes of gaining the cooperation of the local civilian elite, a cooperation essential for any base commander's success in handling the delicate relations between the town and the base. Yet Mrs. Waters did not feel used. She took the label "honorary military wife" as a compliment. It gave her satisfaction, a role to play, a respected status. It also gave Kris Waters's mother a personal investment in the base. When word came that Griffiss would be closed as part of the post–Cold War base closures occurring all over the country, *The Daily Sentinel* carried a half-page lead headline in full color: "Farewell to Arms."[21] It was not just the men in the Waters family who felt the base closure as a blow. "My whole family went into mourning."[22]

Today's military forces are such complex organizations administratively and technologically that they demand ever greater support services. Napoleon is routinely quoted as observing that armies travel on their stomachs. But this observation scarcely captures the range of support services that commanders and their government superiors require to keep their forces prepared for battle.

Women are being used by militaries to solve their nagging problems of "manpower" availability, quality, health, morale, and readiness. Exposing the character and operations of the military as an institution can be done not by concentrating on the usual topic—male soldiers—but by focusing on those women most subject to military exploitation: military prostitutes, military wives, military nurses, women soldiers, women defense industry workers, and "civilianized" defense workers. By paying close attention to these women, women who straddle military and civilian positions, we can learn how and at what price women become militarized.

Military policy makers have needed women to play a host of militarized roles: to boost morale, to provide comfort during and after wars, to reproduce the next generation of soldiers, to serve as symbols of a homeland worth risking one's life for, to replace men when the pool of suitable male recruits is low. But the military usually does not need—or want—all women to provide all these militarized services. Rather, government officials have needed women of some classes and some races and some ages to serve some of these functions while they have required women of other classes, races, and ages to perform other militarized functions. The gendered divisions of labor have worked best— "best" as measured by military criteria—when women acting in each role have felt unconnected to, even wary of, women in the other roles. The officer's wife thus serves her soldier-husband's military best if she holds the poor camp follower in contempt. In some instances, one group of militarized women might even be exploited for the sake, allegedly, of protecting women of another, more valued, group.

Thus Sancho de Londono, a Spanish officer, explained in 1589 how prostitutes were integrally necessary to well-run militaries: "For, accepting the fact that well organized states allow such persons (prostitutes/camp followers) in order to avoid worse disorders, in no state is it as necessary to allow them as in this one of free, strong and vigorous men, who might otherwise commit crimes against the local people, molesting their daughters, sisters, and wives."[23]

All the military's needed support services can be provided to the military by women only if the military can be ensured of sufficient control over women. The key to that control is to define women as creatures marginal to the military's core identity, no matter how crucial in reality are the services they perform (and the symbolism they provide) to the smooth operations of the military. By contrast, when women begin to act in their own interests, military commanders suspect that their control is slipping. Then begins a search for alternatives. Military policy makers have tried to continue using women, even at a time when many women are self-consciously striving for autonomy. In the long history of the militarization of women, the newest maneuver has been to camouflage women's service to the military as women's liberation.

MORE THAN JUST ONE MORE PATRIARCHAL INSTITUTION

Women who have joined their country's army to acquire training as mechanics only to find themselves sexually harassed by their supervising officers can identify with civilian women secretaries who feel pressured to go out to lunch or be "friendly" with their male bosses in order to gain a pay rise. In a multitude of ways, all of which affect women, the military resembles other patriarchal institutions.

On the other hand, the military is distinctive, and the experiences that women have had in coping with military efforts to use them de-

mand special attention. Perhaps most important is the military's intimate relationship with the state—with the central government and the
laws and ideologies that sustain its authority. No other public or private institution comes so close to being the sine qua non of a state.
Some states (Costa Rica, Iceland, Japan, Haiti) have made attempts at
disestablishing their armed forces; but in most instances, under different guises, military institutions have reemerged (a very powerful one in
the case of Japan).[24] The claim that a state is not a genuine state in the
eyes of the "international community" unless it has its own instrument
of organized coercion—an army—carries a lot of weight, even in a society not usually considered highly militaristic.

The close identification of the military to the state thus gives the
military a kind of influence and privilege rarely enjoyed by a large corporation or a public health agency. This special status permits the military to exercise powers denied to other institutions. It can keep secrets;
it can create its own court system; it can conscript the labor it needs; it
can own or control vast complexes of research and manufacture; it can
be exempted from laws requiring nondiscrimination; it can run its own
universities; it can back up its policy directives with tanks; it can form
its own alumni associations; it can operate its own hospitals; it can
have its own representatives placed in the government's overseas em-
bassies. The military branch of government is not interchangeable with
that government's labor ministry or its environmental protection
agency, even if they too wield the state's authority and spend the public's money.

The military can use this extraordinary status in relation to the state
to define national security. The concept of national security has, in
turn, been used to define the social order supposedly necessary to ensure that national security. In this circular process, national security
can come to mean not only the protection of the state and its citizens
from external foes but, perhaps even primarily, the maintenance of the
social order. The social order includes in its turn those gender definitions that bolster ideological militarism.

Out of this same expansive concern for the social requisites of national security, military professionals and defense bureaucrats keep
track of demographic trends, worrying not only about overall birth
rate declines, but about high birth rates among those ethnic groups
that the current government does not trust. Racism and militarism become mutually supportive in such a national security state. In the

process, the lives of all women—the trusted and the distrusted—are militarized.

Consequently, the behavior of the military as an institution—in particular, how it treats women and women's own capacity to respond to military control—cannot be deduced simply from our studies of and experiences with other patriarchal institutions such as the courts, legislature, family, church, or business firms. Those analyses do give women an invaluable vantage point from which to pose questions, make connections, see hidden implications. But the military's use of its usually privileged status within the state has to be taken into explicit account if we are to fully understand how it can penetrate women's lives.

Few other institutions can command such vast financial, labor, and material resources as the military. With its budgetary appetite, the military can distort a country's whole public spending structure—as well as its trade relations with foreign countries. Public services intended to reduce society's economic inequalities are cut when military funding proposals outstrip the government's current revenues. Women are especially vulnerable to economic recessions; they are usually the first to be laid off or cut to part-time and the first affected by service and welfare cuts. Some economically vulnerable women may even enlist in the military in order to compensate for the loss of civilian jobs. Thousands of job-hungry Russian women, for instance, began volunteering for the Russian military in the 1990s, while their brothers were avoiding conscription notices in droves. In the same decade some South Korean women, likewise, have looked to soldiering to offset the collapse in their country of such feminized industries as electronics and sneaker manufacturing. The sexism that distorts the employment and unemployment patterns in the civilian economy can intensify the militarization of at least some women's labor: under these sexist economic conditions, some jobless women may take jobs in the prostitution industry; others may enlist in their country's military.

WEBS OF MILITARIZED WOMEN

In the early 1970s British and American military recruiters, faced with the ongoing Cold War and many women's decision to have fewer children, began to worry that they were running short of their preferred white male recruits. Recruiters responded in part by urging young women to seek enlistment into selected military posts as their path to

"first-class citizenship," to financial independence and upward mobility. This recruitment took place during the early years of the "Second
Wave" of the American feminist movement. The call was appealing.
The military—so central to the workings of political power in American public culture—looked as though its previously masculinized walls
might be scalable after all. In other countries, too, significant numbers
of women pressed to join their militaries. Two decades later women
comprised 10 percent or more of uniformed military personnel in
Canada, the United States, and South Africa. By 1998, eight years after
the end of the Cold War, women accounted for 10 to 14 percent of soldiers in the militaries of Australia, Canada, Israel, New Zealand, Russia, South Africa, and the United States.[25]

The recruitment of women may amount to a cruel hoax: militarism
and the military, those instruments of male ideological and physical
domination, riding on the backs of individual women's genuine desire
to find ways to leave oppressive family environments, delay or avoid
marriage, serve their countries, and acquire "unfeminine" skills. What
we need are carefully calibrated analytical tools with which we can
measure the extent to which a woman's joining her government's military enhances her own autonomy and, by so doing, reduces the potency of those masculinity-privileging beliefs and processes that push
most women to the margins of political life.

To pursue this exploration, we need to chart the web of gendered relationships among those women who join the ranks and those who
work in the discos outside the base and those who sustain the families
of those women soldiers' male colleagues. At the same time we need to
make sense of feminists' efforts to support some militarized women
while keeping their distance from others. It is not easy for feminists to
mobilize support for their own military's camp followers. To do so effectively, local feminists become international, while internationally
adept feminists relearn the intricacies of local webs of militarizing pressures.

3

THE PROSTITUTE, THE COLONEL, AND THE NATIONALIST

The United Nations Fourth Conference on Women seemed to offer a good chance for the Clinton administration to demonstrate its commitment to women's rights. Prominent women's advocates such as Madeleine Albright, then the U.S. ambassador to the United Nations, were appointed by the White House to the official U.S. delegation. Hillary Clinton was set to deliver at the conference a rousing indictment of misogynist violence and economic discrimination. But what exactly would the American government's delegation to the UN conference propose when it arrived in Beijing in September 1995?

The State Department was a hub of activity in the weeks leading up to the conference. Timothy Wirth, President Clinton's appointee in the State Department's human rights post, coordinated the activity. Those women's groups with access to State Department officials were invited to make suggestions. The Feminist Majority, a Washington-based advocacy group, suggested that the U.S. government propose that all the world's governments critically assess their own participation in military prostitution. These Potomac-wise women "knew the ropes." They worded their proposal carefully:

> Problem: Trafficking in women and girls is on the increase worldwide. It has been documented that U.S. military personnel stationed at overseas bases make use of local prostitutes. In addition, there are cases where retired U.S. military personnel return to cities adjacent to previous base assignments to profit from prostitution operations.

Recommendation: Hold congressional hearings on the relationship between the U.S. military and the local prostitution trade at overseas U.S. bases. Through congressional action, reform the Uniformed Code of Military Justice to make the exploitation of prostitutes at or around military bases a punishable offense.[1]

The State Department officials' initial response was positive. In this era of AIDS, as well as of U.S. overseas military base closures, taking a stand against military prostitution seemed a position that could be politically painless and attract widespread support. It would also make the Clinton administration look like a leader in making the post–Cold War world more friendly to women.[2]

But something happened. No mention of military prostitution appeared in the American government delegation's final list of proposals to the UN conference in Beijing. It is not yet clear why. Whether or not prostitution should be seen as a violation of women's human rights, in the same way that domestic violence has been increasingly understood to be, remains a question of some controversy among women advocates, including those who attended the Beijing conference in 1995.[3] But this intrafeminist debate does not seem to be what caused the disappearance of the antimilitary prostitution plank from the U.S. proposal. Maybe the topic was deemed an insignificant issue by the State Department civilians, and so it was pushed off an already crowded agenda by issues to which they assigned more weight. Or perhaps people across the river in the Pentagon vetoed its inclusion. Maybe Defense Department officials had to inform their State Department counterparts, whom they had long imagined naive about military affairs, that women's relationships to militaries were far more "complicated" than their diplomatic colleagues presumed. Thus, in the end, condemning the military's involvement in prostitution at an international women's conference might have been deemed too risky for this American administration. Military prostitution, after all, has had a long, entangled international political history.

SEXUALITY AND MILITARY POLICY MAKING

Stand in the middle of Key West, Florida; Fayetteville, North Carolina; Halifax, Nova Scotia; Mombassa, Kenya; or Portsmouth, England— any town long used as a military base. From here you can trace the history of the relationship between militarism, sexuality, and military policy. Ask where the red light district is today and where it has been.

Track down the retired men who, when they were colonels, commanded this base: how did they handle their troops' sexual expectations in a way that maintained town-base harmony? Interview police commissioners about their cooperative understandings with the military police. Ask local "respectable" women what neighborhoods they still tell their daughters to avoid. Look through the town's public health records under "venereal disease." Talk to bar owners and to the local clergy. Have conversations with the women who make their living working in bars and hotels; ask them what services off-duty male soldiers—or sailors or airmen—have expected. It will take a multipronged investigation to piece together the town's history of militarized prostitution—and the decisions the town has taken to create and maintain it.

Through wartime mobilization, postwar demobilization, and peacetime preparedness maneuvers, sexuality and militarism have been intertwined. They have been constructed and reconstructed together, usually with the help of deliberate policy decisions. *Together,* ideologies of militarism and sexuality have shaped the social order of military base towns and the lives of women in those towns.

Exploring militarized prostitution is important first because the lives of so many women in so many countries have been directly and indirectly affected by this institution. Second, the subject should attract our attention because so many men have had their expectations of, and fantasies about, women shaped by their own participation in militarized prostitution. Third, military policy makers' attempts to construct a type (or a particular array of types) of masculinity that best suits their military's mission are exposed by taking seriously their military prostitution policies. Fourth, we need to think carefully about militarized prostitution because calculations about it have shaped foreign policies and international alliances. Fifth, understanding any military's policies on prostitution will throw light on the thinking that lies behind its policies on rape, recruitment, sexual harassment, morale, homosexuality, pornography, and marriage. Finally, devoting analytical energy to unraveling the politics of military prostitution may help us explain why prostitution policies of a foreign military can often capture the attention of local male nationalists while those same protest leaders not only continue to ignore the prostitution policies of their own country's military but also stubbornly resist local feminists' efforts to make sexuality an explicit issue in the wider nationalist movement.

Those women controlled by the military as wives, nurses, and soldiers and those women trying as feminists to alter the patriarchal practices of their society's nationalist or peace movements each may have much more in common with women controlled by a local or foreign military as prostitutes than the former usually want to admit. In fact, the very distance these women seek to put between themselves—for the sake of sustaining their status as "respectable," as "serious," as "patriotic," as "professional"—and those women who work in the discos, brothels, and massage parlors around a military base may contribute to the maintenance of the complex system of military prostitution.

From the Crimean War to World War II, from the American Revolution to the wars in the former Yugoslavia, military officials have acted as though prostitution were simultaneously a resource and a threat. In 1870s Italy, for example, a military commander ordered "strict military surveillance" over brothels among whose clients were soldiers. His intent was to add military regulation to the already existing police regulation in order to prevent his men from being infected with venereal disease.[4] Likewise, when the U.S. Marine Corps set up their occupation command in the Dominican Republic in 1916, they took steps to open up opportunities for local middle-class women to practice law and medicine. But along with modernity, the American military occupying officials saw themselves as bringing social order to this allegedly benighted Caribbean nation. Thus these same American military commanders established a red-light district in the capital. In their eyes, making prostitution safe for foreign and local men—and, indirectly, protecting local middle-class women from their disreputable sisters—was part and parcel of their militarized packaged progress.[5]

The history of the various attempts to control the sexual behavior of soldiers and the women whose bodies they buy is especially hard to chart because so many women who have been subjected to such control have lacked the resources—money, literacy, fluency in the language of military officialdom, access to other women's support—that have allowed some women a voice and a place in written histories. We consequently are only now beginning to piece together an international history of that prostitution that has existed outside of direct military control.[6]

Tracing military prostitution policies is made doubly difficult by senior officials' denying that their country even has a formal policy on prostitution for soldiers. Military elites—generals, admirals—and their civilian colleagues frequently pass the messiest, the most unmilitary responsibilities further down the chain of command to the level of field officers, to the colonels. Still, because most men who achieve the

lofty ranks of general and admiral have themselves climbed the ranking ladder, they each have had the experience of being the colonel (or
commander) handling the messy, unmilitary matters such as prostitution. It is because they managed to handle those matters well—kept
operations running smoothly, did not allow scandal, took steps to ensure that no civilian issue arose—that these men were positively evalu-
ated by their superiors and promoted up the ladder, away from daily
worries about bar brawls and venereal disease.

Thus, military prostitution policies often are made at precisely those
levels in the political system at which politicians and citizen groups
have great trouble monitoring and holding the military as a whole accountable. At the same time, central government civilian authorities
often find it politically safer to let local municipal officials do the negotiating with military commanders on questions involving prostitution—questions of business zoning, public health, licensing, policing.
This civilian political strategy only serves to further fragment and
camouflage the political decision making that regulates the daily
processes that add up to military prostitution. The strategy makes it
harder for citizens outside these closed policy circles to see prostitution
as an industry and as an integral part of a distinctive national security
doctrine.[7]

Yet the absence of a written, centralized prostitution policy does not
mean that a military elite has no policy. It may only suggest that the
military is aware that its attitudes and practices surrounding sexuality
are fraught with contradictions and political risks. Those risks can be
strategically minimized by a combination of decentralized responsibility, informal decision making, and official acknowledgment only of
prostitution as a "health issue." Under certain circumstances and at
rare times, however, militarized prostitution does become visible and
does acquire the status of a public issue.

THE CONTAGIOUS DISEASES ACT: USING WOMEN TO CONTROL SOLDIERING MEN

In 1857, William Acton described the daily life of a woman working
(often to escape rural poverty) as a prostitute in an English military ·
town such as Portsmouth: "(Her) daily gains are not large. The generous and prodigal Son of Mars who had lately received his pay or his
loot money will, perhaps, bestow half a crown in return for the
favours granted to him, but the usual honorium is one shilling. [To obtain a] subsistence a woman must take home with her about eight or

ten lovers every evening, returning to her haunts after each labour of love ... to dance or drink beer until a fresh invitation to retire is received by her."[8]

Despite their poverty and dependence on tavern keepers and soldiers, however, the prostitutes were not totally without resources of their own: "For help when her own resources fail her, she depends on the contributions of those of her companions, whom chance has for the time being more befriended; and in justice to these women, it must be said that they are always ready to afford each other this mutual assistance.[9]

After 1864, women compelled to earn shillings from sex with soldiers would need each other's support all the more. For in that year the British all-male Parliament passed the first Contagious Diseases (CD) Act. This law was followed by the Acts of 1866 and 1869; eventually eighteen British towns were brought under the acts. The government's formula was this: the military could control male soldiers' sexuality by controlling the poor women with whom they were most likely to have sexual relations. The acts applied only to women in specific navy ports and garrison towns such as Colchester and Portsmouth. Local police and judges in those towns were given sweeping powers to compel any woman vaguely suspected of prostitution to undergo a humiliating, painful genital examination. Any such woman could be officially categorized as "prostitute" by the health and police authorities. Thereafter she would be subjected to surveillance, treatment, and repeated medical examination. By contrast, the civilian men who engaged in procurement and who ran the pubs that the women used were left outside the acts' control.

The CD acts militarized not only poor women, but also local police, health, and court officials: all were made to serve the needs of the Victorian-era British military. All thereby were made to serve the empire-building project. The Portsmouth woman arrested on suspicion of prostitution, her arresting officer, the doctor who conducted the forced genital exam on the woman—all were playing their parts in ensuring that the British soldiery could expand the crown's authority in Asia and the West Indies and Africa. It took—and takes—more than gunpowder to colonize another people. It takes the militarization of women's relationships to men.

The CD acts were imagined by their drafters to be a postwar reform. In both the United States and Britain, the 1860s and 1870s were decades during which the social lessons of costly wars were fashioned.

In America, the emergence during the Civil War of General Joe
Hooker's girls—later to be known simply as hookers—led to a postwar flood of anti-vice literature, condemning "loose women" who
preyed on men.[10] Both capitals during the American war—Washington on the Union side and Richmond on the Confederate—became
known for their brothels. In Washington alone, "not including Georgetown," the number of prostitutes grew from a prewar 500 to a
wartime 5,000. Georgetown's count was harder for authorities to carry
out because so many brothels designed to sexually service Union
officers were provided with a respectable front; their prostitutes were
passed off as officers' wives or as proper salon hostesses.[11] American
authorities' attempts to control prostitution were less than successful.
Two women archeologists digging under the Washington Mall in 1999
discovered evidence of a brothel that continued to thrive in the
post–Civil War capital, providing sexual services to the all-male Congress and to male special interest lobbyists. Its owner was Mary Ann
Hall.[12]

In Britain, however, postwar assessments of the Crimean War
prompted many social commentators to conclude that the disappoint-
ing British military performance was due to the moral and physical de-
generation of its male soldiery and to demand central authorities' action. Military reformers were especially worried about reconciling
soldiers' presumed male sex drive with military efficiency. Left uncontrolled, soldiers' "natural sex drive" led them into a vicious downward
spiral of indebtedness, drunkenness, illness, and poverty. If men married, their wives might both drive them into debt and reduce their devotion to soldiering in the distant colonies. But if men serving the military were allowed to satisfy their sexual needs in the company of
greedy, unclean women, the postwar reformers reasoned, those women
would continue to undermine the country's military capabilities,
thereby jeopardizing the entire imperial enterprise. "Clearly the [Victo-
rian] army was fostering a certain kind of man and this had crucial implications for the treatment of the women with whom the men were
permitted to consort. It would appear that the attitude was that military life called for a special kind of man reared away from the distrac-
tions of women.... Women threatened a man's loyalty and vigour and
were a financial drain."[13]

Military reformers in 1860s and 1870s Britain presumed that soldiers, to be real men, had to satisfy their sexual "appetites." That was
a given. But military commanders saw each of the various outlets for

sexual activity as potentially threatening to military effectiveness as they imagined it. For instance, commanders, especially those responsible for sending sailors on long sea voyages, feared homosexual relations between men confined to each other's company, frequently in close quarters. Commanders imagined then, as now, that homosexuality somehow made men less able and willing to serve as effective fighting men. On the other hand, commanders were nervous when their male soldiers sought sexual relations with women, fearing that those women would dilute the men's loyalty to the military as well as ruin their health. So military officials faced a dilemma: how could they reconcile their ideas about soldiers' manly sexual appetites with their ideas about the impact of sexual relations on military operations?

Prior to the 1864 CD act, British commanders had tried to prevent venereal disease in the ranks by compelling soldiers themselves to undergo genital examinations performed by a military medical officer. Under this system militarization was relatively contained; military criteria and military objectives were imposed mostly on formal members of the military itself: officers, rank-and-file men, and the military's own doctors. Married soldiers were exempted from the compulsory genital examinations. Commanders and military doctors reasoned that married rank-and-file soldiers—a very small proportion of all soldiers at the time, since marriage was presumed to divide a soldier's loyalties— were not as tempted by prostitution as were their bachelor comrades. Furthermore, in Victorian Britain married men generally were considered more respectable and thus deserved to be spared the humiliation that the genital examinations entailed.[14]

This relatively confined control system proved ineffective. British officers, as men, seemed loath to inflict what they saw as a humiliating and degrading ordeal on other men.[15] Officers exercised clear authority over rank-and-file men, but the British military worked best when that authority could be cushioned by a mix of paternalism and male bonding.

The armed forces, especially as portrayed by heavy-handed enthusiasts of militarist ideals, may seem simplistically hierarchical. But in reality most military institutions resemble those of Victorian Britain insofar as male bonding cuts across and often contradicts the more formal hierarchical concepts of the chain of command and centralized control. Most armies and navies are built on a patriarchal bonding between men as men. On the other hand, most men also are stratified by rank in a way that commonly accentuates those inequities of class and ethnicity already existing in civilian society at large. Relations between men are never simple. At the heart of relations between militarized men is this persistent tension between hierarchy and male bonding. A military's prostitution policy usually is crafted by officials with an eye toward sustaining this ambivalence, not resolving it.

In Britain the Contagious Diseases Acts of 1864, 1866, and 1869 established a state policing system for compulsory periodical genital examinations of any woman that local police and judges suspected of being a prostitute. Josephine Butler was among the feminist leaders of the campaigns in the 1870s and 1880s to repeal the CD acts. In the midst of what became one of nineteenth-century Britain's most explosive political controversies, Butler described how these military acts subjected women to men's control:

> I recall the bitter complaint of one of those poor women [picked up under the Acts]: "It is men, men, only men, from the first to the last, that we have to do with! To please a man, I did wrong at first, then I was flung about from man to man. Men police lay hands on us. By men we are examined, handled, doctored.... In the hospital, it is a man again who makes prayers and reads the Bible for us. We are had up before magistrates who are men, and we never get out of the hands of men till we die!" And, as she spoke I thought, "And it was a parliament of men only who made this law which treats you as an outlaw. Men alone met in committee over it. Men alone are the executives. When men, of all ranks, thus band themselves together for an end deeply concerning women, and place themselves like a thick impenetrable wall between women and women ... it is time that women should arise and demand their most sacred rights in regard to their sisters."[16]

Led by Butler and other women who were to become key figures in the subsequent British suffragist movement, the campaign to repeal the CD acts can be understood as a successful feminist movement against militarization, against a collusion between the military and the state to control women. Judith Walkowitz has shown that the feminist campaigners argued that what began as a regulation of poor women to serve supposedly narrow military needs—in other words, to prevent venereal disease among rank-and-file soldiers—quickly became a springboard for the expanding state control of all women's sexuality.[17] More recently, historian Susan Kingsley Kent has warned those of us still trying to understand the British suffragists not to dismiss these women's analysis of sexual politics as merely an incidental side pursuit.[18] The suffragists took sex seriously indeed. From the years after the Crimean War to the weeks leading up to Britain's entry into World

War I, suffragists of all stripes would be deeply influenced by Butler and her insistence that prostitution was at least as much a barrier to British women's full exercise of rights as were patriarchal universities, churches, and houses of parliament. Failure of middle-class women to make common cause with poor women working as prostitutes, Butler warned her fellow activists, would only preserve the debilitating influence of the ideology of "feminine respectability."[19] Her listeners did not always heed her admonition.

Although no women representatives sat in Parliament, the anti-CD-acts activists waged their campaign so persistently—for twenty years—and with such strategic acumen that ultimately they compelled a majority of male MPs to vote for the repeal of the acts in 1886. Victory for the CD-acts repealers was a significant step toward building a national political women's movement in Britain, but repeal did not end Britain's militarized prostitution. Nor did Parliament's repeal lift the CD acts in the rest of the British colonies. In India, Hong Kong, Singapore, Ceylon, Australia, Jamaica, Gibraltar, and Egypt, British colonial officials waged their own campaign—to keep the CD acts in place. Historian Philippa Levine has uncovered this 1888 elite justification for maintaining the control of those women in prostitution who provided commercialized sex to Britain's soldiers stationed in India: "It is impossible to exaggerate the importance of preserving the health, and with it the efficiency, of the British Army in India. The intents, moral as well as material, which depend upon the efficiency of that Army, are interests of the First magnitude.... There are very strong grounds for maintaining and enforcing the operation of these Acts in India."[20]

Philippa Levine, whose investigation of British prostitution policies has taken her on a global tour of dusty but revealing colonial archives, has been on the trail of Britain's imperial military prostitution policy making. She has found that late-nineteenth-century British colonial authorities in India were anxious about all sorts of interracial sexual contacts. If white British soldiers purchased sex from Indian prostitutes, commanders worried. But if white prostitutes sold their sexual services to Indians, they also worried. When thinking about colonized, militarized sex, these elite imperial men exhibited what Levine aptly calls a "taxonomic urge."[21] It is an urge to categorize-for-the-sake-of-refining-control that future male officials would come to share. It stems from a determination to make sure that certain kinds of men have certain kinds of sexual relationships with only certain kinds of women.

Butler, through her antiprostitution journal, *Dawn,* continued to try to rally international opposition to government-supported prostitution not only in the British empire, but in the Dutch and French empires as well. Nonetheless, most of her supporters in Britain turned their attention homeward. Few British suffrage activists made their government's ongoing attempts to control prostitution overseas for the sake of securing British soldiers' well-being a matter of suffragist concern.[22]

On the other hand, activist local women in several British colonies did take up the cause of repealing the CD acts. In Egypt in the 1930s, the first wave of Egyptian middle-class and upper-class feminist nationalists found that the weekly medical exams forced on those Egyptian women who served as prostitutes for British troops were a perfect example of why Egyptian nationalism required an explicit discussion of the lives of women of all classes. These feminists, having been stunned by the emergence in the early 1920s of patriarchal attitudes among their male nationalist compatriots, had since then been pursuing an international strategy. They had joined with British and Continental European feminists in the International Alliance of Women (IAW) to combat the growing practice of trafficking in women. But Egyptian feminists, such as Huda Sha'rawi, could not persuade other IAW colleagues, many of them from countries possessing their own colonies, to formally denounce British officials' continued exertion of control over women in prostitution. The Egyptian feminists in the 1930s were caught between, on the one hand, their own male nationalists, who saw women prostitutes serving British soldiers solely as symbols of a "prostituted nation," and, on the other hand, European feminists, many of whom were reluctant to cast blame on their own countries' soldiers.[23] Egyptian feminists' resultant frustrations would be shared by other feminists seven decades later.

SEXUALIZING WAR, MILITARIZING WOMEN, RACIALIZING ARMIES: THE WORLD WARS

British women foresaw the likelihood of their government using the outbreak of World War I to justify the revival of the hated CD acts. They held a rally in 1914 to protest any attempt to reestablish such controls.

Prostitution became a formal political issue at the highest levels of wartime policy making, however, not only because of women's activism but also because of conflicting interests among elite men. When the prime ministers of Canada and New Zealand came to London at the outset of the war against Germany for a meeting of the Imperial Defence Committee, they had sex on their agendas. Both men were outraged at what they claimed was the seduction of their innocent boys from the colonies by the aggressive whores of London's Soho. If the British government did not control their allegedly voracious women, the Canadian and New Zealand prime ministers threatened, they would pull their soldiers out of the British war effort. At the same time, Britain's own military field officers were complaining about the loss of soldiers due to the rampant spread of venereal disease. Although these problems ignited a running debate inside the government over how to control women, not until the latter days of the war did the British government issue a formal directive. Instead, officials simply directed local authorities to impose greater control over women in their areas. In Cardiff, Wales, local officials imposed a curfew on women "of a certain class"—suspected prostitutes—between 7:00 P.M. and 6:00 A.M. In another town, Grantham, the local senior military officer instructed military and police authorities to enter any residence they believed might be breaking his imposed curfew. Thus, while feminists managed to prevent the reimposition of the CD acts, they were not able to stop the government from policing women in the name of the war effort.[24]

Some British women were energized by the suffrage movement, which had become progressively militant in the years just prior to 1914, and were eager to take a more direct role in this wartime policing. Those women activists who took their sexual politics down the path of social purity argued to the still all-male government policy-making elite that women were better equipped than were men to control women for the sake of war-waging efficiency. For instance, the newly formed Women Police Service took as their mission to warn young girls and soldiers' wives of "the moral dangers their casual or wild behaviors might engender."[25] This priority fit neatly with male officials' belief that "real" prostitutes posed less of a threat to Britain's soldiers than did ordinary white British women, "amateurs" or "free lancers" who hung around military camps seeking to distract, ensnare, and probably infect those naive white British boys unused to such sexual propositions.[26]

All male soldiers fighting for Britain against Germany in World War I were not treated alike by British military officials. The "taxonomic urge" among those officials remained powerful. As they designed their war-waging policies, many authorities continued to overlay gender categories with racial categories. When military officials imagined encounters between civilian women and male soldiers, they saw not only anatomies but skin colors.

An estimated 2.5 million men from Britain's colonies fought for Britain during World War I. In France alone, some 135,000 Indian men fought as soldiers for the British. Black South African men and men from the Gold Coast (later Ghana), Rhodesia (later Zimbabwe), Nigeria, Fiji, and the Caribbean were mobilized to serve the British war effort either as regular soldiers or as civilian laborers.[27] Men came from as far away as the Cook Islands to fight for the British Crown. In the modest, quiet town square of Avarua, the capital of the Cook Islands, stands today a simple black marble monument. Few people in this tiny south Pacific island country today stop to look at it as they go about their daily errands. Carved in the surface of the polished black stone are these words:

> To The Glory of God
> And in recognition of the loyalty of the Natives
> Of Rarotonga, Aitutaki, Mangaia, Atiu,
> Hauke, Mitiano, Manihiki, Rakananga, and
> Pukapuka Islands, of the Cook Group,
> Who sent their sons to the number of five
> Hundred to help the Empire in the Great War.
> 1914–1918[28]

White British male officials worried about the sexuality of these Cook Island men and about the sexuality of their Indian, African, and Caribbean soldiering counterparts. Once again, Philippa Levine has charted their official anxieties. Authorities needed these colonial men, needed their "warrior" skills, but feared the sexual disorder that might ensue if local white women found these warriors too attractive. Their solution: government controls imposed on nonwhite male soldiers serving in Europe would be more rigorous than those imposed on the white British soldiers or the white soldiers from Canada, New Zealand, and Australia. But officials' racialized sexual categorizing went further. African troops were more severely limited in their contacts with white women than were Indian troops.[29]

Some white British women had their own ideas about race, masculinity, imperialism, soldiering, and sexuality. They sought to create personal connections with nonwhite men from the colonies. This action worried white men in government. It outraged some white men outside of government. A race riot broke out in London's working-class East End in 1917 when young white men attacked black men's houses. Their incentive: they were angry at "the infatuation of the white girls for the black men."[30] In the northern manufacturing town of Sheffield, the press reported that Salvation Army workers were shocked by young white Englishwomen "consorting with and listening to the persuasions of coloured men."[31] A world war was a managerial challenge for sexually minded, racially preoccupied officials. Women would not always behave.

Three decades later, during the Second World War, the connections between race, men's "sex drive," soldiers' morale, venereal disease, health requisites for victory, prostitution, and women reemerged to occupy minds. German historian Claudia Schoppmann, for instance, has uncovered evidence that suggests that SS officers of the Nazi regime forced some women suspected of being lesbians to work as prostitutes in the brothels that the officers organized. These women were to sexually service not only German soldiers but also men imprisoned in labor camps. The official Nazi reasoning appeared to be that, although lesbianism was not officially designated as a crime (male homosexuality was), those German women who refused to fulfill their proscribed national roles as wives and mothers could be "reformed" by coerced heterosexuality. At the same time, this logic held, the morale both of men conscripted into the army and of men forced to produce munitions could be enhanced by access to prostitutes.[32]

On the Allied side, ambivalence and fragmentation were hallmarks of policy. Once again, officers directly in charge of rank-and-file troops were torn between their belief that any soldier who was a "real man" needed sexual access to women and their fear that uncontrolled sexual relations with local, or "native," women would undermine the physical and moral vigor of men, making them less valuable in battle.

This ambivalence may help explain why military prostitution policy differed from one war zone to another, reflecting the varying dispositions of different field commanders, differing race and class origins of local women, how those origins affected relations with the British soldiers, and the lesser or greater opportunities soldiers had for recreation between battles. In Tripoli, North Africa, in the Second World War, British army commanders permitted brothels to remain open but compelled women working as prostitutes to undergo military medical examinations. Some of Tripoli's brothels were even brought under the direct control of a Royal Army Service Corps noncommissioned officer.

Each of the army's different ranks and racial groups had its own brothel: one for nonwhite soldiers, others for white men in the ordinary ranks, still another for noncommissioned officers and warrant officers, and the most exclusive brothels reserved for British officers.[33]

One soldier described Britain's militarized prostitution system in Tripoli in the early 1940s:

> The army, with its detailed administrative ability, was able to organise brothels in a surprisingly short time and a pavement in Tripoli held a long queue of men, four deep, standing in orderly patience to pay their money and break the monotony of desert celibacy. The queue was four deep because there were only four women in the brothel. The soldiers stood like units in a conveyor belt waiting for servicing.... Brothels for officers were opened in another part of town, where a few strolling pickets of military police ensured that the honoured ladies were not importuned by those who did not have the King's Commission.[34]

Who were these four women? We are told nothing, only that they were Italians.[35] As in Tripoli, British India's military brothels in Delhi were differentiated so as to match the British army's own class and race stratifications: "The officers' brothel was in Thompson Road and cost 75 rupees. Most of the women there were white, some of them the wives of absent officers keen on a little money."[36]

Throughout both world wars ran a controversy that has yet to be resolved. In both military and civilian corridors of power, women figure in this debate as allegedly passive creatures whose sexuality is merely designed to service individual men and male-defined institutions. The perpetual question is this: How can women be controlled so that they can be made available to satisfy individual male soldiers' presumed sexual needs and yet not jeopardize military efficiency?

British and American officers disagreed in their approaches to prostitution during the Second World War. While the British adopted an attitude of relative resignation and fined a male soldier hospitalized for venereal disease at the rate of one shilling and sixpence per day lost, their American counterparts treated men suffering from venereal disease as criminals, often putting them behind barbed wire so they would feel humiliated.[37] Both militaries, however, officially filed all prostitution policy papers under the heading of male soldiers' health, as merely an offshoot of their anti-venereal disease programs. This categorization protected the military against criticism at home, while it made the military's dependence on the control of women invisible.

British and American military establishments also shared a self-image that they were not like—in other words, were of a higher moral caliber than—the French. That is, they did not want it assumed that all military institutions fighting a common enemy shared identical notions of masculinity, femininity, sexuality, and civilization. In reality, at the same time that these institutions were creating stereotypes of the enemy in order to boost their soldiers' morale, they were often constructing stereotypes of their allies, stereotypes that depended on those same four notions.

Thus, the British and American common approach was to deny direct involvement in regulating sexual services for their male soldiers and so distinguish themselves from their French allies' "continental system," which entailed the direct military control of brothels. The alleged distinction, however, is more real on paper than it is in practice. But the claim protected each military from civilian criticism back home.[38]

In the aftermath of the Japanese bombing of Pearl Harbor, Hawaii sat uneasily in American military strategists' minds. Was it best thought of as the World War II "home front" or as a foreign colonial base? Japanese Americans in California, Oregon, and Washington (as well as in Canada's British Columbia) were interned in prison camps on the desert, whereas Japanese Americans in Hawaii were treated as too valuable to Washington's war-waging efforts to be interned. Likewise, prostitution was openly organized by public officials for the pleasure of American soldiers and sailors in Honolulu by military and civilian officials, whereas back on the mainland such open collaboration between brothel owners and public officials would have set off an outcry.[39] In 1943, a French military official would have felt quite at home in the militarized sexualized environment of Honolulu. Today, some of the island state's feminists contend that Hawaii's contemporary militarized culture has its roots back in World War II.[40]

On the mainland, American civilian authorities shared their British counterparts' worries that wartime so disrupted the social order that home front women had to be placed under tighter control. "Victory girls" were American women so labeled because they supposedly "pursued sexual relations with servicemen out of misplaced patriotism or a desire for excitement."[41] Many of these victory girls were in fact Rosie the Riveters, women able to get well-paying jobs outside the home for the first time and translating that newfound economic autonomy into a sense of social freedom.

The American government's response to women's seeming liberation was a program that merged public health with military efficiency. From 1942 to 1945, local health and police officials were empowered to arrest any women they suspected of "sexual delinquency" and to subject them to mandatory venereal disease tests. The intent was not just to protect soldiers but to ensure that the exigencies of wartime did not radically alter gender roles in American society. The antivice campaigns became part of the larger anti-Axis campaign in various American cities, though not all local authorities docilely complied with the instructions of the government's Social Protection Division (SPD). (The SPD, perhaps not coincidentally, was headed by Eliot Ness, the legendary FBI gangbuster of the 1930s.) Baltimore officials, for instance, were reluctant to force anyone to take mandatory health tests and dragged their feet in creating a local social protection committee. Other cities did comply, often enthusiastically. FBI statistics indicated a 95 percent increase in American women officially charged with moral violations between 1940 and 1944.[42]

There was little protest by Americans against these violations of women's rights and the complementary militarization of local police forces, courts, health services, and social workers. Protection of servicemen became, for many citizens, a legitimizing umbrella for the expansive state control of those women portrayed as the twentieth-century urban American equivalent of camp followers.

The 1940s wartime era frequently is remembered nostalgically by Canadians and Australians as well as Americans as an era of new opportunities and liberation for women. It might usefully be thought of as a time of increased governmental efforts to control women's sexuality.[43]

VIETNAM: PROSTITUTION IN WARTIME AND MARKET-TIME

On the heels of World War II came the first Vietnam war. In the United States, Americans paid little attention. This first Vietnam war, sometimes called the Indo-China war (1945–1954), was fought by the French against the Communist-led but broadly nationalist Vietnamese independence movement. The Vietnamese had endured decades of French colonialism as well as the Second World War and yet had preserved enough social cohesion to resist coughing up dislocated, impoverished women to service the French military's sexual needs. French military officers resorted to imported non-Vietnamese women, who were turned into prostitutes for French soldiers. Arab North African women who could not speak French or any of the several languages common in Vietnam were preferred by the military: these women could have sex with the French troops without their commanders worrying that lonely soldiers would whisper military secrets in moments of indiscretion.[44]

By 1954, when the French had withdrawn in defeat and American soldiers had begun to fill the "vacuum," war had so disrupted South Vietnamese society that thousands of local Vietnamese women were desperate enough to be available for a prostitution industry that grew ever more expansive as the war dragged on.[45] American military officials militarized local prostitution by degrees. One American veteran described the evolution between 1965 and 1973: "First bar girls, then massage parlors for the Marines at Da Nang, then a shanty town of brothels, massage parlors and dope dealers known as Dogpatch soon ringed the bases."[46]

Prostitutes were made officially welcome to many U.S. bases in Vietnam as "local national guests." The American base at Long Bin was a militarized city of 25,000 people. It employed hundreds of Vietnamese women on base as service personnel. Another American recalled: "There were mama-sans and hooch-girls all over the place. Everything was clean."[47] Soldiers also could bring onto the base as local national guests any of the fifty to sixty girls who waited outside the wire fences.[48]

Official Washington again gave U.S. commanders in the field considerable discretion when it came to regulating prostitution on their own bases. An American historian who lived in a central Vietnam village whose daily routines were regularly interrupted by operations stemming from a nearby U.S. base later wrote that the army colonel in charge of Camp Eagle, headquarters of the 101st Division, issued his own policies on prostitution. Concerned that Vietnamese women working as prostitutes interfered with his soldiers' effectiveness, this colonel banned prostitutes from his base. Flowing from a seemingly related calculation, he also prohibited Vietnamese women being hired as personal maids to his troops, a common practice on other American bases.[49]

As the history of Britain's CD acts at home and in the colonies reveals, militarized prostitution is sustained by policies that are racialized as well as sexualized. During the U.S. war in Vietnam, relations between American white and black male soldiers grew so intense that there developed separate brothels for black and white soldiers. "Blacks were often casually addressed as spook, nigger, boy, and spearchucker by both white enlisted personnel and officers," one historian tells us. "And some thought it humorous to tell the Saigon bargirls that blacks were 'animals' and 'had tails.'"[50] A Vietnamese woman who was a prostitute servicing white soldiers was likely to be murdered by white soldiers if she was discovered providing services also to black soldiers.[51] Between 1968 and 1972, the Saigon entertainment districts that were frequented by white soldiers became increasingly uncomfortable for black soldiers. Khanh Hoi, the neighborhood whose bars and nightclubs attracted African American patrons, was the same district that France's black male troops from Senegal had found welcoming during the first Vietnam War fifteen years earlier.[52]

By 1972, on the eve of the American military's withdrawal, prostitution had become an industry, the result of what Kathleen Barry calls "the industrialization of sex."[53] That is, prostitution was not simply a matter of personal choices or of private sexual desires. There were institutional decisions, there were elaborate calculations, there were organizational strategies, there were profits. The U.S. allies—the governments of Australia, South Korea, and the Philippines—also had sent thousands of men to fight in Vietnam; they too made calculations and decisions about their male soldiers' sexual needs and about how Vietnamese women could best meet those needs. The war stories from the soldiers in these countries have barely begun to be told in public.[54] At the war's end, between 300,000 and 500,000 Vietnamese women were working as prostitutes in South Vietnam. An estimated four-fifths of them were afflicted with venereal disease.[55]

After the departure of the American military in 1975 and the fall of the U.S.-backed Saigon regime in April 1975, the Hanoi government, now ruling a unified Vietnam state, introduced a program to rehabilitate the thousands of women in the south who had been prostitutes. In the early 1980s, however, visitors to Ho Chi Minh City (formerly Saigon) reported that prostitutes had been removed from bars but that young Vietnamese women called Cinderellas were paid by the government to dance with foreigners at a weekly ball held in the former American Officers Club. During the day these women were office workers or shop assistants, but on the night of the officially organized party, they wore Western jeans and blouses: "They dance with French, Scandinavian and Russian partners, mostly technicians on projects, and they go home alone at night."[56]

By the early 1990s, Vietnamese women researchers were sounding an alarm. Despite the government's 1970s prostitute reeducation program and its more recent AIDS prevention campaign, women researchers in Hanoi and Ho Chi Minh City were documenting a new upsurge in organized prostitution. According to Vietnamese women's studies researcher Le Thi Quy,

> In recent years when prostitution has been on an alarming increase, there is a strong tendency of women coming from rural to urban areas [to practice] sexual intercourse for money....
>
> [Yet] now prostitution is not only confined in cities but has also expanded to the rural mountainous and coastal areas (usually at mountain and sea side resorts). It is noted that many villages and townships have already their brothels.[57]

The male clients in 1990s Vietnam were both local and foreign. Most had traded in their khakis for pinstripes, their rifles for cellular phones. Prostitution in today's Vietnam continues to be fueled by the convergence of four conditions: Hanoi's policies designed to accelerate foreign investment, to promote consumerism, and to privatize state companies and social services; the arrival in Vietnam of thousands of overseas businessmen and male tourists; the absence of a strong women's movement independent of the ruling party; and the rising unemployment of Vietnamese women.[58]

Vietnamese women's experiences of prostitution over the last five decades suggest that militarization causes the expansion of prostitution, but that prostitution's relationship to *de*militarization is mixed. Certain kinds of demilitarization—for example, that attempted by the Hanoi government immediately following 1975—can drastically reduce prostitution. Other kinds of demilitarization, however—such as that pursued by Hanoi officials (with the encouragement of international economists and investors) since 1986 in the name of a "free market economy"—can spark a resurgence of prostitution.[59]

MILITARY BASES, TOURISM, AIDS, AND PROSTITUTION

Tourism, at first glance, seems far removed from militarism. Tourism's promoters glorify leisure, they urge the tourist to shed stress, discard discipline. Tourism usually is portrayed as a search for peace, not violence. And yet, in reality, tourism can push women into prostitution just as surely as does militarism. In many parts of the world, in fact, the presence of brothels for male soldiers has laid the groundwork for the development of brothels for male tourists.[60] That is, militarism and tourism may not be polar opposites after all. They may be kin, bound together as cause and effect.

Although the Thai monarchical state has been complicit in fostering the prostitution of Thai women and girls since the seventeenth century, in the 1980s prostitution took on a major role in that country's economy.[61] In the 1980s the tourist industry became a major foreign currency earner for Thailand's conservative government. Twenty years earlier the biggest flow of foreign "tourists" into Thailand wore khaki and olive drab. Some were the men of the American army and air force who were stationed on the large U.S. air force bases in Thailand, built as launching pads for bombing missions into Cambodia and Vietnam. Others were American soldiers who came from Vietnam combat zones to Bangkok and to Thai beach villages to the south of Bangkok for rest and recreation.

On the U.S. bases themselves, most of them located in Thailand's impoverished northeast, military commanders maintained an arm's length approach to control of women by counting them officially as "special job workers" (dancers, masseuses, entertainers). At Udon Air Force Base, the number of special job workers grew from 1,246 in 1966 to 6,234 in 1972.[62]

One American man, now in his forties, tries to recapture what it felt like to be nineteen in 1970 on a U.S. fighter base in northern Thailand: "In the relative cool of the evening, we'd bring our drugs—marijuana, speed, heroin (for some)—a cooler full of beer, and a tape player. We'd sit out there waiting for the fighters to return from their missions, from their forays over Vietnam and undoubtedly Laos and Cambodia, as well. When the planes landed, afterburners shot out huge flames from the rear of the aircraft, lighting up the night sky."[63]

Gregory DeLaurier had signed up for the air force in order to avoid the army's draft. He thought that the air force offered less likelihood of being killed in Vietnam. He was right. But there were other political conditions that he would share with those less fortunate American men who served in the ground forces across the border: the politics of wartime commercialized sexuality.

> "Watch out for those LBFMs, son," said the sergeant. LBFMs? We'd only been in Thailand a couple of days and were about to hit the town for the first time. "Little Brown Fucking Machines, buddy. You don't want your dick to fall off do you?" He threw me a pack of condoms. "These Thai honeys'll fuck your brains out but goddamn won't they give you the clap." Forewarned, we went to town.[64]

Clearly, American sergeants (in the 1970s, unlike today, they were overwhelmingly male and white) had a role to play in creating militarized prostitution in northern Thailand. In the process, they helped to chart young male soldiers' mental map of femininities: "There were two kinds of women in our world in Thailand: those who did our laundry, and prostitutes, and the latter far outnumbered the former. They were by and large our age, some younger—some much younger, some older.... Many of them were forced into doing what they did, but all I knew then was that for a few dollars, a radio, a couple of cases of food taken from the base, I could buy a woman."[65]

By the end of the 1970s, an estimated 100,000 women in Bangkok were working as prostitutes; 70 percent of them suffered from venereal disease. "This means that 30 percent of the female labor force in Bangkok suffer[ed] from venereal disease as a result of earning a living."[66]

A decade later, the child prostitution barely alluded to by Gregory DeLaurier had expanded in Thailand, driven by foreign and local men's new fear of AIDS and their belief that having sex with a young girl would provide them protection. Though denied by the Thai Ministry of Labor, local and foreign investigators documented the system by which young children from poor farm families are kidnapped and put to work to increase Thailand's gross national product. Some boys and girls end up working for little or no wages in small factories. Many of the girls are taken to work in brothels serving Thailand's booming tourist industry.[67]

The Thai military, long the recipient of American support, became a principal player in the prostitution industry during the Cold War. Individual officers used their connections with businessmen, together with their control over border regions, to profit (along with police officers) from the recruitment and sale of women's sexuality.[68] Ordinary soldiers (along with male civil servants) were such regular users of prostitutes that in the 1990s AIDS prevention officials made Thai military personnel the object of HIV studies and of a campaign to increase condom use.[69]

Conditions that promote organized prostitution:

1. When large numbers of local women are treated by the government and private entrepreneurs as second-class citizens, a source of cheapened labor, even while other women are joining the newly expanded middle class[70]

2. When the foreign government basing its troops on local soil sees prostitution as a "necessary evil" to keep up their male soldiers' fighting morale

3. When tourism is imagined by local and foreign economic planners to be a fast road to development

4. When the local government hosting those foreign troops is un-
    der the influence of its own military men, local military men
    who define human rights violations as necessary for "national
    security"

All four of these prostitution-cultivating conditions existed in Thailand
in the 1970s.

In the mid-1990s, Thai feminists have been part of the pro-
democracy movement that has elected civilian politicians to power in
Thailand. The Thai military remains a potent political force, but there
has developed an opening for women's advocates to press Thai government agencies to crack down on corrupt police officers, brothel owners, and on those who procure women and, increasingly, girls—girls
are deemed "safer" by many local and overseas male clients who want
to buy sex in the age of AIDS.[71] Only in 1997 did the still-masculinized
civilian political elite, under increasing pressure from an organized
women's rights movement, pass a law making it a crime to be either a
procurer or a customer of a child in prostitution.[72]

As the fear of AIDS has become global, the connections between sex
tourism, the military, and now, medical researchers have become more
dense. The U.S. military has offered itself as a model of AIDS prevention for other forces to copy. The assumption behind much of the international militarized AIDS prevention work being conducted in
countries as disparate as Uganda, the United States, and Thailand is
that women working as prostitutes are the chief carriers of the HIV
virus. It is prostitutes, many assume, who spread AIDS among a country's soldiers. Male soldiers travel around their own countries and
abroad. That these soldiers will go to prostitutes is thought to be
natural, inevitable. The challenge, then, it is implied, is to keep those
soldier-clients from contracting AIDS and spreading it to their respectable wives or girlfriends. This 1990s internationalized model is
a direct descendent of the model informing British legislators'
1860s–1900s CD acts enforced at home and throughout the empire.
The CD acts, too, put the onus on the women in prostitution. The CD
acts, too, were grounded in assumptions about the naturalness of
men's—especially soldiering men's—"sex drive." The CD acts, too,
were the launchpad for an international effort to control women's sexuality. The patriarchal militarized politics of sexually transmitted diseases (STDs) did not start de novo in the 1980s.

The U.S. Navy officers in command of the aircraft carrier *Midway*
and its battle group seemed to share this long-cherished institutional

presumption when they decided to make a stop at the Thai beach re-
sort town of Pattaya in March 1991.[73] The convoy was heading home
to its base in Japan after a successful operation in the Gulf War, a war
that was waged under an explicit U.S. policy of not permitting prostitution. This no-prostitution-allowed-in-Saudi-Arabia policy was intended to show Washington's sensitivity to the nervous Saudi regime.
But surprisingly, this policy had the unintended effect of making it
clear that any flourishing prostitution industry around American bases
was *also* the result of policy decisions.

Much technical coordination is required to stop a modern aircraft
carrier and its support ships. This March 1991 stop at Pattaya was not
made casually. During the 1970s, Pattaya had been transformed from a
quiet Thai fishing village into a favored destination of soldiers and international pleasure seekers during the Vietnam War. By the early
1990s, some of Pattaya's current bar owners were Americans who had
settled in Pattaya after that war. AIDS, however, had cut into Pattaya's
tourism business in the late 1980s, so the American military's decision
to stop there in 1991 was greeted with enthusiasm by local business
proprietors. "Welcome U.S. Navy to the Red Parrot Sexy Life Show,"
read one banner. "Thank you, Mr. Bush," read another.[74]

Seven thousand U.S. sailors went ashore at Pattaya that day. Aboard
their ships, American officers had given their men preparatory briefings
on safe sex. There was little question that the navy's post–Gulf War
stopover in Pattaya was to be sexualized. Lieutenant Sherman Baldwin
of the *Midway* explained: "We're beating men over the head to use
condoms. The Navy is doing all it can do in terms of information and
education to get the word across to every 18- and 19-year old sailor
about how to protect themselves."[75]

Throughout the 1970s, the Philippines joined Thailand as among the
world's most militarized societies. Feminists from these two countries
have been in the forefront of the international movement to uncover the
connections between homegrown militarism, foreign bases, tourism
politics, and the industry. Until the closure of the U.S. Philippine bases
in the early 1990s, thousands of young Filipinas migrated in search of
jobs from their usually rural homes to sexualized entertainment businesses near military bases. The two largest American military bases
were the Subic Bay Base, servicing the U.S. Navy's Seventh Fleet, and
the Clark Air Force Base. Washington began creating bases in the
Philippines during its colonial rule of the island nation. The leases on
the bases were renewed by a 1979 agreement between Washington and

the regime of the country's authoritarian president, Ferdinand Marcos, a close U.S. ally. Those bases had become linchpins in U.S. Asian policy. Insofar as those bases, in turn, depended for their operation on maneuvers to control women's sexuality, the U.S.-Philippine government-to-government alliance was a sexualized national security alliance.

The 1980s were a period of political excitement for many Filipinas. Some women became active in movements against President Ferdinand Marcos's oppressive militarized "croneyism," a brand of politics that prevailed from the late 1960s to 1986. Other Filipinas became politicized as they joined small autonomous grassroots groups that addressed the linked problems of landlessness, ill health, and domestic violence. Still other women invested their energies in the movement against the American bases in the name of Philippine sovereignty. Some women made the connection between all three levels of political distortion.

In response to mounting public criticism, American officials claimed that Clark Air Force Base injected $50 million into the Philippine economy in 1981, of which $13 million was spent on salaries for Philippine workers. Subic Bay reportedly spent $120 million in the Philippines that year, of which $47 million was in the form of salaries to local workers on the base.[76] The Marcos regime, in the years leading up to its 1986 overthrow by an alliance between a mobilized populace and a disaffected military, was desperate for revenues with which to pay off its mounting foreign debt and to support its expanding police and military force. Filipino officials thus welcomed such figures, pointing to them to justify its continuing collaboration with the U.S. military base officials.

Olongapo is the Philippine town that hosted the U.S. Navy's Subic Bay personnel. The town mushroomed from 40,000 Filipino residents in 1963, just prior to the escalation of the American involvement in Vietnam, to 160,000 in 1982.[77] Olongapo became as militarized as Portsmouth, England. In addition, like their counterparts in colonial India, many of Olongapo's women became dependent on a foreign army with a long history of racist relationships with Asian civilians.[78] But local businessmen in Olongapo made what was by then a familiar argument to wary town officials: "Instead of endangering our decent and respectable women to the possibility of rape and other forms of sexual abuse, better provide an outlet for the soldiers' sexual urge and at the same time make money out of it."[79] These businessmen were seen by American military commanders to be people with whom any diplomatically wise commander should cultivate close relationships.

By the end of the Vietnam War in 1976, Olongapo's town hall had 6,019 women officially registered as "hostesses." The town recorded no one in the category of "prostitute."[80] Prostitution allegedly was illegal in the Philippines. Thus the local government officials colluded with both the local businessmen and the U.S. Navy in making women's work in the prostitution industry invisible.

Filipino women working in the clubs and massage parlors catering to Subic Bay sailors knew what was expected of a hostess:

> The actual act of dropping one's panties, spreading one's legs and doing all possible motions during a sexual encounter with a customer in order to earn money is easy to do. What is difficult to do is to convince oneself to do it and to keep doing it.[81]

> Often times, I do not feel anything during sexual encounters. There are times when I am hurt. If I keep doing it, it is because I need money for myself and my children. I have learned to do the motions mechanically in order to satisfy my customers. If you do it very well, they will keep coming back—and that means money.[82]

The prostitution system was militarized, capitalized, and masculinized. Still, women working in the system attempted to pursue their own goals. Sandra Sturdevant and Brenda Stoltzfus conducted lengthy interviews with women working in the discos around the Subic base, revealing the complex assessments that women made daily in order to support their children and often their parents, comply with their club-owning employers' rules about things like "ladies' drinks" and "bar fines," and the sexual performance expectations of their American clients.[83] Their interviews showed Filipinas working as prostitutes to be anything but passive sex objects. Some former prostitutes helped to form Buklod Center in Olongapo to provide support and advice to women working in the bars. They went on strike in the late 1980s to stop bar owners from forcing them to fight boxing matches with each other for the entertainment of American sailors.[84]

Some Filipino women tried to transform the insecurity and degradation of prostitution into what looked to them to be the relative security of marriage to an American sailor or air force man. Lily was a hostess in Olongapo in the mid-1970s. Her story was not unusual:

> Jim and I were already going steady for six months. So for six months I had not been working in the club. It was some kind of relief.... Though I was not married to the serviceman, I had the feeling of being his wife. Besides, he promised he would marry me someday. I considered myself lucky, since most of us really look forward to a day when a serviceman

proposes marriage. Many of us think marriage to a sailor is the only way out of this job.... Little by little I was convinced that life was not that hopeless, even for a prostitute. Until my big disappointment came....

Jim was to transfer to another place of duty back in the United States. He then told me he was going to marry me.... I was ignorant about those papers so I just waited for what was going to happen.... But a day before departure, he told me that the marriage papers could not be processed on time.... He knew I was already six months pregnant.... He said he would plead with his commanding officer. However, he did not come home that night. Neither on the following day.... I found out he had already left for the United States. It was too late for me to realize I was fooled.... Emotionally, because he made me believe that he loved me and I learned to give a loving response, which was difficult for me who had been used to an exploitative sexual relationship. Economically, because Jim took with him all my savings which he asked me to withdraw the day before.... The more I am now convinced that men are all the same—manipulative and exploitative.[85]

The Filipino interviewer added: "Since then Lily never trusted any of her customers. Instead, she cunningly handles them in such a way that she gets the most out of every transaction. In her own words, 'It is very likely that after some time working in the trade, a woman will really succumb to mistrust, pretense, and deception which characterizes prostitution.'"[86]

In the world of militarized women, the calculations around marriage are reminiscent of those made by nineteenth-century American and British middle-class women. A militarized woman indulges in sentimentality at her peril.

The Filipino women employed in bars and discos were working against great odds. Many women were afraid of losing their jobs. The formal agreements between Manila and Washington elites, Manila and Olongapo elites, and the racially infused sexual politics of individual American servicemen each acutely limited the women's capacity for action. To calculate and to cope is not to be passive. But these actions also should not be mistaken for empowerment.

Many women in Olongapo's entertainment industry had children to support. The impoverishment of many women and the return to the United States of many of their navy fathers led to an increasing number of street children. The combination of military and civilian men who were now fearful of AIDS and who believed that sex with young girls offered their best protection against HIV and businesses willing to capitalize on such masculinized anxiety prompted a remarkable escalation in child prostitution in and around Olongapo City. By the mid-

1980s an estimated 200 children were recruited into prostitution in Olongapo. Male clients paid more for sexual access to a Caucasian-looking child than for a child who looked black-fathered.[87]

By the time the Marcos dictatorship fell in 1986, an estimated 300,000 to 500,000 Filipinos worked as prostitutes. Most were young women, but some were young men and a growing number were children. Around the U.S. Subic Bay navy base alone, there were approximately 15,000 to 17,000 prostitutes.[88]

The new, democratically elected regime of President Corazon Aquino was far more sensitive to the Filipino women's movement's critique of sex tourism, yet it was still eager to please the American government. Furthermore, in the late 1980s, the Aquino administration remained dependent on a U.S-backed Philippine armed forces, an institution with a reputation for masculinized posturing and abuse of civilians, including the sexual abuse of women activists thought by soldiers to be subversive.[89] Thus it took a citizens' anti-bases campaign, in which nationalist Filipinas played a major role—sometimes with an explicitly feminist interpretation of nationalism, sometimes treating women's status as if it would be enhanced automatically by the achievement of nationalist goals—with the support of the newly elected Philippine senate, as well as the devastating eruption of Mount Penatuba, to bring about the closing of Clark U.S. Air Force Base and Subic U.S. Naval Base, and with them, the 1993 demise of the militarized prostitution industry in Angeles City and Olongapo.[90]

Many women working in the discos and massage parlors around the U.S. bases felt understandably ambivalent about the loss of their livelihoods in the name of Filipino nationalism. Some were insistent that, if their degrading occupations were to be made a symbol of national humiliation by the anti-bases campaign, they should have a direct voice in creating the post-bases development plans for the two cities. They did not uncritically accept male activists' and male planners' assurances that the tourism and light industry profile being heralded as their salvation were devised with their best interests in mind—especially after the government had rejected a plan created by a women's group that built in explicit programs for retraining women in prostitution.[91] One community organizer for the Buklod Center, the Olongapo group created in 1987 and designed to empower current and former women bar workers, told feminists in Britain that the better-paying jobs that have come to Olongapo with the post-bases economic zone project did not go to former bar workers. Rather, because the bar workers received no skills training during Subic Bay's heyday, they could only watch as better-educated women from Manila were hired for jobs in the new factories.[92] Some women felt that the prostitution industry continued to offer them the most realistic opportunity to earn enough money to support themselves and their children and to send money each month back to their rural families who had come to count on the remittances of a working daughter.[93]

Other woman dislocated by the base closures in the early 1990s looked toward emigration to regain a modicum of economic security. Procurement agencies offered women new "opportunities" in Japan, Guam (both major sites of American military bases), Australia, and the United States. The regimes of both Aquino and her successor, Fidel Ramos, encouraged Filipinas to emigrate if they would send money home to their families and to their indebted government.[94] Mail-order-bride companies were heralded as an unemployed Filipina's salvation. Between 1989 and 1994, there were 94,926 Filipinos who became engaged to or married to foreigners. Most liaisons were between Filipinas and foreign men. Furthermore, the rate of such marriages was rising.[95] By 1996, 200 such companies operated in the United States alone.[96] Many Filipinas now married and living in Australia, however, have organized to challenge a racialized sexist presumption that is widespread among white Australians: that all Asian women married to white Australian men are either mail-order brides or former prostitutes—or both.[97]

This organizing has come at a time in Australia's own racialized and gendered history when more women activists have been trying to come to grips with racist dynamics among women in Australia and between Australian women and the women of the Asian and Pacific region, of which Australians are more and more self-consciously a part. This Australian Filipina organizing also comes at a time when Australia has become a significant player in the Pacific region's post–Cold War military system. The consequence is that Australian Asian women's political activism is making Australian white feminists consider the links between their stands on their society's gendered racism and its militarized regional diplomacy.[98] The ripples sent out by Filipino women's strategizing in the entertainment districts around Subic Bay have been felt as far away as Adelaide.[99]

Some women who had depended on Subic Bay's rest and recreation industry looked not south to Australia, but north to Japan. These women might be approached by recruiting companies offering them

jobs as "entertainers" or "dancers" in a Tokyo or Osaka club.[100] That
was the civilian option. The militarized option offered by the recruiters
was a chance to migrate to Guam, the militarized territory of the
United States, or to Okinawa, the Japanese island still dominated by
U.S. military bases. In the 1950s and 1960s, most of the women working as prostitutes around the American Okinawa bases were Japanese,
but the increased value of the yen in the 1970s and 1980s translated
into American military men being unable to afford the services of local
women. Prostitution procurers began to look outside Japan for
cheaper sexualized labor. By the 1990s, most of the prostitutes servicing American military men stationed in Okinawa were Filipinas.[101]

In the mid-1990s, Filipinos began raising the alarm about the remilitarization of Subic Bay. The U.S. government and the government of
President Fidel Ramos, himself a former general and West Point graduate, had signed the Continued Access Agreement. It required the approval of neither the American senate nor the Philippine senate. With
the agreement, U.S. naval ships once more could dock in Subic Bay for
repairs. By early 1996, Saundra Sturdevant could report, "Bars and
brothels at Barrio Baretto, a short jeepney ride from Subic, are booming and will boom more."[102] A year later, the mayor of Olongapo City
(the wife of the man who was mayor during the town's militarized,
sexualized era) tried to stymie local activists' efforts to direct legal and
political attention on the city's child prostitution industry, fearing such
attention would taint Olongapo's new reputation as a thriving modern
industrial zone.[103]

At the same time in the United States, Supreme Court justices were
hearing a case that had its roots in the mid-1970s Philippines but was
making judicial history only at the century's end. A Filipina, Lorelyn
Penero Miller, had been born to a Filipina and an American serviceman stationed in the Philippines. Lorelyn's father refused to legally acknowledge her as his daughter until just after she had turned twenty-
one. His delay meant that Lorelyn could not claim American
citizenship: under a law passed by the U.S. Congress, if the mother of a
child is an American citizen and the father is not, that child automatically gains U.S. citizenship; but if the mother is foreign and only the father is an American, then that child has no legal claim on U.S. citizenship. The intent of the Congressional lawmakers seemed to be that
children born out of sexual liaisons between American soldiers and
foreign women were excluded from American citizenship. When *Miller*
v. *Albright,* No. 96–1060, appeared before the Supreme Court, the

government's assertion prompted a clearly skeptical Justice Ruth Bader Ginsburg to query whether the government was "retreating" from its stand against sex discrimination.[104] The complex legacy of military prostitution perhaps was finally coming home.

In 1998, formal diplomatic and military negotiations were under way between the U.S. and Philippine governments to open up twenty-two other Philippine coastal towns to American operations, including troops' rest and recreation. First, the two governments were hammering out a Status of Forces Agreement (SOFA) whereby American military personnel would be granted partial diplomatic immunity if charged with crimes while in the Philippines. Second, the two governments were cooperating in the construction of new shipping facilities in the southern coastal port of General Santos, facilities that seemed to some observers to make that post ripe for increased use by the U.S. Navy.[105] There was no indication that the new Philippine president, Joseph Estrada, elected in May 1998 with support of many of the country's poorest voters, would oppose these developments. The Philippine Senate was divided over the policy of permitting the American forces expanded access.[106] Filipina groups warned that such an agreement would fuel sex tourism, the spread of AIDS, and child prostitution. They made connections that other anti-SOFA groups were not making: when the government announced that a beauty pageant would be made a part of the country's centennial celebration of its independence from Spain and its resistance to American colonization, Filipinas active in Gabriela protested. They and their Filipina American supporters saw the government's insertion of a beauty contest into a national celebration and the government's signing of a military rest and recreation agreement with the U.S. Defense Department as part and parcel of a common process: the objectification of women in the name of masculinized national objectives.[107]

Despite the 1990s base closures and the election of three civilian presidents, some Filipino women's lives remain fundamentally militarized at the opening of the new century. Moreover, the relative demilitarization that has occurred in other Filipino women's lives could be reversible.

LESSONS FOR TODAY FROM THE 1940s: THE "COMFORT WOMEN"

The early 1990s were years of World War II fiftieth anniversaries. Wreaths were laid, stamps were issued, reunions were held. Through-

out Europe, Australia, the United States, and Canada, a public eupho-
ria was generated by remembrances of "finest hours." In the midst of
the confusing and violent post–Cold War 1990s, here was the chance
to recall a "good war."

The cascade of World War II fiftieth anniversary celebrations provided the broad setting in which many Americans and Britons first
heard about the women from Korea, the Philippines, and China who
had been compelled to work as prostitutes on behalf of the Japanese
imperial army five decades ago. If the listener weren't careful, this
news could be heard as just one more bit of evidence that the Axis
was indeed the embodiment of evil that the forces of democracy did
well to defeat. If the listener paid closer attention, however, similari-
ties with British and American military prostitution policies might
come to mind.

In December 1991, Hak-Soon Kim took a daring step. The sixty-
seven-year-old Korean woman spoke out publicly about being enslaved
by the Japanese imperial army during the 1940s. As a young woman,
she had been forced to sexually service Japanese soldiers. Now, fifty
years after her ordeal, Hak-Soon Kim was speaking out. She was also
filing a suit against the Japanese government, holding it directly responsible for the damages she endured.[108]

> On arrival, the women, with feet bleeding from the long forced march,
> came under the supervision of the sergeant in charge of canteens, who
> chose the most attractive to serve the officers. As he instructed her: "This
> is the same as being in the front line. You never know when the Eighth
> Route Army [Communist] guerrillas will attack so you must always be
> prepared. You will now look after the officers and will have to work
> even harder than before for your country." He taught her how to bow in
> greeting to each officer and again in thanking him after the service was
> completed. The sergeant himself would earn points for the quality of
> service given by the women under his care.[109]

In the early 1990s, stories began to break about the Japanese imperial army's World War II forced mobilization of an estimated 200,000
Asian women to serve as prostitutes—what the imperial officials eu-
phemistically called "comfort women," but what Asian feminists think
are more accurately called "military sexual slaves." When reporting
these stories, a kind of smugness crept into some Western commentators' voices. The story, when repeated by the foreign media, was too
often treated as evidence of how peculiarly ghastly the Japanese were,
how "other" were the Japanese military's methods of waging war.

American nationalism has required repeated fertilizing. It has been bolstered by the telling of the story of World War II as if it were strictly a story of good guys (the Americans and their allies) versus the bad guys (the Germans, the Italians, and the Japanese). In reality, drawing that stark contrast between us and them hides more than it reveals. That common dichotomy underestimates how *similar*—not necessarily identical—each side's rationale was for its military prostitution policies as each elite tried to control different groups of women for the sake of waging a global war. The stories of the women enslaved to service Japanese soldiers are terrible, but evidence compiled by Yuki Tanaka and other historians suggests that Japan's policy makers, like their counterparts in so many militaries, designed a prostitution system in order to achieve the following: (1) to reduce the likelihood of their male soldiers raping local women, because rapes upset already-tense civilian-military relations; (2) to maintain their male soldiers' morale; and (3) to reduce venereal disease among male soldiers.[110]

The story hardest to dislodge from its archival hiding place has been that of the Japanese military's *official* complicity in the organizing and promotion of prostitution. In its reluctance to admit its institutional responsibility, the Japanese imperial military looks not at all exotically "other." It looks commonplace.

To compel the Japanese government fifty years later to admit past official complicity in militarized prostitution took a cross-generational, cross-national campaign organized by the approximately one thousand elderly women from all over Asia who had survived the wartime sexual slavery, in an alliance with younger Korean and Filipina feminists, Japanese feminists, and Japanese historians.

In their denials, contemporary Japanese male officials sounded strikingly akin to their British and American counterparts. Like them, these present-day Japanese civilian officials have felt far more politically comfortable with the presumption that women prostituting themselves with male soldiers was an inevitable, natural accompaniment of war; that, moreover, whatever organizing of and profit making from the wartime sex trade did occur was in the hands of private entrepreneurs over whom the military could not possibly exert any control.

Amanita Ballahadiu sat reservedly on the couch in a Wellesley College lounge. Around her clustered several dozen women students, women in their early twenties, young enough to be Amanita's granddaughters. She had been younger than they were now when the Japanese invaded the Philippines in 1941. Born in 1928 in central Luzon,

Figure 4 Remedios Felias, one of the Filipinas forced by the Japanese Imperial Army during World War II to serve as a "comfort woman," now in her seventies, took part in a protest in 1998 in Manila, pressing the Japanese government to provide direct compensation to the survivors of that military prostitution system. Felias is displaying the drawings she has made to tell the story of her own rape by soldiers five decades ago. (Agence France-Presse, "An Atrocity Illustrated" — "Remedios Felias, a 70-year-old Filipino..." Published in the *New York Times,* 11 October 1998, under the headline "An Atrocity Illustrated.")

Amanita had not been able to attend school, she explained, because her parents had needed her to take care of her younger siblings.[111] When the Japanese soldiers arrived in her province, they met with stiff resistance from Filipino forces. The Japanese accused Amanita's father of being a resistance sympathizer. When the troops burned the family's house, killed her brother and sister, and took her father away, she and her mother fled into the mountains and lived off roots. But soon thereafter, a group of Japanese soldiers found Amanita doing laundry by a stream and called out to her to join them; when she refused, they beat her and took her to their encampment.

"It was a life of hell for me.... What made it so painful was that I was only fourteen and had no knowledge of sex and no relations with men.... [Several days after being kidnapped and raped] I was assigned to one Japanese officer. He became very violent after coming back from raiding villages."

Just when she thought she was losing her sanity, Amanita managed to escape. She rejoined her mother, but still "became crazy." She would take off her clothes, crying "No, sir." Her mother nursed her daughter back to health, telling her that she could take up the fight against the invaders. With a rifle sent to her by a surviving brother, Amanita joined the resistance.

But speaking out after the war about her experiences of military prostitution required quite a different sort of bravery: "We tried to normalize our lives. I didn't want any more relations with men, but my father forced me to marry. This man I told [about her prostitution] and he accepted it. I had four children with him, but I didn't enjoy sex."

For fifty years, Amanita kept her secret from all but her husband. She recalls feeling "very low about myself." Then one day she saw on television a survivor of the "comfort women" system. This woman was talking publicly about her horrible experiences and calling on others to join her in speaking out: "I shouted with joy, 'Now is the time for the fight for justice.' I told my children. My children didn't want me to go. They felt *they* would be shamed. I told them, 'I've worked hard for you, given you an education, but now I must do something for myself.'"

Amanita went to the television station and made contact with the Filipina task force supporting the newly visible "comfort women." Her daughters eventually accepted her decision, though her son still refused to speak to her. Some people in her community ridicule her now. "Here comes the 'Japauki'," they say derisively, using the derogatory term for women who sexually serviced Japanese men. In the early 1990s, Amanita was earning her living as a cleaner in the homes of wealthy Filipinos. One of her employers fired her after she began to speak out, not wanting to be associated with a woman who had experienced what Amanita had experienced.[112]

Other women have come forward to tell their stories. No two are precisely alike, but together they expose a system. Kim Tokchin told her story to Korean women:

[It was] February 1937. I was 17 years old. I heard girls were being recruited to work in the Japanese factories.... [We took a train] to Pusan, where we boarded a boat.... we sailed to Nagasaki.... From that moment on we were watched by soldiers. I asked one of them: "Why are you keeping us here?".... He simply replied that he only followed orders. On the first night there I was dragged before a high-ranking soldier and raped.... On the fifth day, I asked one of the soldiers: "Why are you taking us from room to room to different men?" He replied: "You will go wherever orders take you."[113]

Kim Tokchin recalls being put on another ship, this one bound for Shanghai, the Chinese city then under Japanese military control. The fifty women were guided by a Korean man. From the port they traveled by truck to a large house located outside the city center. Several women, Koreans and Japanese, were already there. On the front of the house hung a sign, "Comfort Station."

The big house was divided by wooden panels into a lot of small rooms, each just big enough for one person to lie down in. There was a bed in each cubicle, and we spent most of our time incarcerated.... The Korean man who brought us seemed to be the owner, but Japanese soldiers came and inspected what we ate and checked whether the house was clean.... The comfort station we were in didn't belong directly to the army. So, when the troops moved to a new place the comfort station along with us women would move shortly thereafter....

In each room there was a box of condoms which the soldiers used. There were some who refused to use them, but more than half put them on without complaining. I told those who would not use them that I had a terrible disease, and it would be wise for them to use a condom if they didn't want to catch it. Quite a few would rush straight to penetration without condoms, saying they couldn't care less if they caught any diseases since they were likely to die on the battlefield at any moment.... About once every two months, an army surgeon gave us checkups.[114]

The five decades of silence cloaking the stories of the "comfort women" can be explained not just by the women's fear of being shamed and the Japanese postwar officials' desire to avoid any accountability. There was a third silencer: the U.S. government. After Japan's surrender in 1945, the American military occupation authorities prohibited the practice of selling Japanese women into overseas prostitution. However, American occupation authorities themselves took steps to bury the stories of the Japanese imperial military's forced prostitution program. They feared that such revelations might destabilize their new Cold War allies in Japan and Korea. Furthermore, American military occupation commanders seem to have been quite willing to accept initially the new prostitution system that the defeated

Japanese government quickly redesigned in 1945 specifically for the pleasure of the arriving "sex-starved" U.S. male soldiers:

> "We were told that our mission was to be a sexual dike to protect the chastity of Japanese women," remembers Tatsugoro Suzuki, who was [in 1945] the 25-year-old manager of a fine restaurant.... Mr. Suzuki had turned the restaurant into a brothel with 30 women supplied by the Government.
>
> "The charge to the soldier (only Americans were admitted) was the equivalent of eight cents, and that included a bottle of beer. Half the take went to the woman and half to the house."[115]

The American commanders imposed a ban on prostitution when they arrived, but it was imposed in theory, not in practice, according to a *New York Times* report: "A month after the troops landed, an American general came to me and said 'I need your help,' remembered Yasuhiro Komatsu, then a 25-year-old liaison officer between the American and Japanese forces in the city of Moji. Mr. Komatsu says that the American general demanded that Japan set up a brothel for his men."[116]

Where were the women for the brothels to come from? Japanese historians, today eager to uncover the full story of the Japanese experiences of the world war, have been unearthing new evidence. They have uncovered the archives of the Recreation and Amusement Association, the front organization that Tokyo officials created to recruit and manage Japanese women directed to sexually service the arriving conquerors. It has been harder to track down the women themselves. Some were recruited from factories; others were members of the imperial army's own women's corps. On September 9, 1945, the Interior Ministry ordered members of the women's corps to enlist in four Tokyo brothels that would service American soldiers. "You should bear the unbearable," the bureaucratic order urged, "and be a shield for all Japanese women."[117] Many of the women who provided commercialized sexual services for the American occupiers are thought to have died early because of the effects of venereal disease contracted from their soldier clients.[118]

The story of the Japanese government's organizing of, and the American military's complicity in, the 1945 prostitution system clearly had been known in Japan for some time. Yet only in 1995 was the story brought into the mainstream U.S. press. Thus the politics of military prostitution are multilayered. First, there are the politics of the actual recruitment and control of women to service male soldiers. Then there are the politics of suppressing information about that policy.

Third, there are the politics of trying to uncover that buried information. Finally, there are the politics of assigning present-day meaning to these newly uncovered stories. All four political processes have implications for women at the same time that all four processes depend on women.

Aside from confirming a contemporary diffuse sense among Americans that the Japanese imperial government deserved to be defeated in the "good war" of the 1940s, the "comfort women" revelations do not seem to have altered most Americans' political understandings of the gendered wagings of war. Yet in both South Korea and Japan, the elderly women's outspokenness has set off significant political debates. Feminists in each of these countries have become deeply involved in those debates, though they have not always been able to control the current meanings produced by these public discourses.

It was women who first insisted that the experiences of the "comfort women" be seen as a national political issue by the South Korean government. The Korean women activists wanted to make Korea's own Confucian ideology's inherently patriarchal assumption about feminine duty and feminine shame central to that issue formation. By contrast, the men at the top of the Seoul government, as well as many male nationalists in the opposition, preferred to craft the 1990s issue in such a fashion that local patriarchal complicity could be kept a nonissue. These nonfeminists were far more comfortable using the elderly women's stories to exert pressure on Japanese officials, men from whom they wanted apologies and compensation. Most important, the masculinized Korean political elite of the 1990s did not want the survivors' stories to fuel popular criticism of military prostitution still established around today's American bases in South Korea.[119]

Korean feminists found it difficult to maintain control over the issue-formation politics that swirled around the "comfort women" revelations in the 1990s. As feminist activist and theorist Insook Kwon has pointed out, nationalism is so tightly woven into South Koreans' political culture, including feminist politics, that campaigners found it almost impossible to compel Koreans to think about these wartime experiences of forced prostitution in a way that would make the public reassess Korea's own militarized and sexist beliefs and policies.[120]

For their part, Japanese feminists have been immersed for the last twenty years in discussions about their country's history of militarized prostitution. What does it mean for Japanese women's relationships with women in Korea and the Philippines today? What is Japanese women's particular stake in resisting the current reemergence of Japan's military as an instrument of their country's foreign policy?

Yamazaki Hiromi is one of the Japanese feminists active in pressing the current government to fully acknowledge the Japanese military's role in World War II sexual slavery. She helped found the Comfort Women Action Network through whose telephone hotline scores of Japanese male veterans, men who for fifty years had been keeping their own silences, now found their voices and telephoned to confirm the existence of army-run brothels during the war. But Yamazaki has urged her feminist colleagues to do more of their own soul searching. Why, she has asked, did Japanese feminists have to wait for Korean feminists to break the "comfort women" story? On the one hand, it should give Japanese feminists pause, make them dig more deeply into their own postwar consciousness. On the other hand, Yamazaki has contended, acknowledging their debt to Korean feminists provides a chance for Japanese feminists to weave a more authentic alliance between Japanese and Korean and other Asian women's movements, an alliance among genuine equals: "From my experience, this [uncovering of the 'comfort women' story] was made possible mainly through Korean women's double perspective on the issue, i.e., racism and sexism. It might sound abstract but they made us realize a consistent pattern of evasion by the Japanese women's postwar movement of the history of colonization and invasion, which in turn sustained the imposition of assimilation on Korean women in Japan as well as the discrimination against them."[121]

Even before the uncovering of the World War II sexual slavery, many Japanese women activists had organized to protest and halt the practice of Japanese male office workers taking trips to Thailand, South Korea, and the Philippines—the latter two countries each colonized by Japan in the early decades of the twentieth century—for the purpose of prostitution.[122] Thus in the 1990s Japanese feminists were politically prepared to make the connections between the practices of peacetime corporate sex tourism and wartime military prostitution. It has been a sometimes painful, if necessary, process to forge the analytical links between their society's past and present—as those British, French, Dutch, and American white women who also have been trying to face their own respective histories of racism, colonialism, and neocolonialism can testify.

Japanese feminist artist Shimada Yoshiko has created works that deliberately place Japanese pro-imperial women literally in the same frame as Korean women forced to serve as prostitutes to provoke discussion today about the complicity of ordinary Japanese women in their government's abuse of other Asian women.[123] She and other contemporary Japanese feminist historians and artists are questioning the common portrayal of Japanese women as solely victims during World War II.[124] Complicity is never easy to incorporate into one's memories. The construction of women as marginal to war waging, many present-day Japanese feminists are arguing, not only hides many women's suffering; it also camouflages many women's support for imperialist adventure and war. Even women who think of themselves as being advocates of women's empowerment may support their government's war waging. Pursuing a nationalist feminism can be a problematic maneuver.

Japanese feminists attending the Non-Governmental Forum at the Fourth UN Conference on Women in Beijing in 1995 joined with other Asian participants in a workshop designed to raise the contemporary issues surrounding the "comfort women" revelations. They circulated a petition protesting Tokyo officials' creation of an Asian Women's Fund, an attempt, the feminists charged, to avoid the government's direct responsibility for fully compensating the survivors of the sexual slavery program. In just three days, 2,250 people signed their petition.[125] One government's World War II prostitution policy was thereby being translated into a post–Cold War international feminist issue.

Succumbing to popular pressure, organized in large part by Japanese women's groups, the Japanese prime minister Ryutaro Hashimoto formally and publicly apologized in June 1996 for his country's sexual slavery policies six decades earlier. Yet he and his cabinet continued to refuse to pay reparations directly to the women who had been the targets of those policies. The prime minister, a member of the long-ruling Liberal Democrats, made his apology on an official visit to South Korea, a country that had once been a Japanese colony and since the end of the Cold War had become a major Japanese strategic and economic partner. "From the bottom of my heart I apologize and I'm regretful," he told a Korean audience.[126] Among those Koreans who had staged a protest to greet the prime minister's arrival were former "comfort women."[127]

The target for many of the Japanese, Korean, Taiwanese, and Filipino protests was the Japanese government's Asian Women's Fund, a private charity created with governmental support. The government claimed that because the Japanese state had already paid formal reparations for war damages, the survivors of the sexual slavery would seem to be best served by a nongovernmental charity. The government urged ordinary citizens to contribute so that the fund could distribute money to the elderly women. But feminists and other "comfort women" campaigners responded that the fund transferred the blame for the wartime prostitution scheme to the nation, whereas the responsibility rightly needed to be carried by the state. Feminists from all four countries thus traveled to Geneva in March 1996 to lobby the UN Commission on Human Rights, which had to vote on whether to accept Special Rapporteur Radhika Coomaraswamy's recommendation that the Japanese government, not the private Asian Women's Fund, pay compensation to the surviving "comfort women." The Japanese government felt vulnerable. Its officials did not want to jeopardize Japan's chances for being named to a permanent seat on the Security Council, something they had worked hard to obtain. But when the members of the Human Rights Commission did indeed vote to support the Rapporteur's recommendations, Prime Minister Hashimoto nonetheless made it clear that the Japanese government would not comply, that it would continue to make only indirect compensatory payments and thus would persist in refusing to admit direct responsibility for its state predecessors' World War II forced prostitution policies.[128] Japanese government officials' hope that the "comfort women" issue would finally go away were dashed again in 1998 when a Japanese court ruled that the government would have to go beyond vague apologies and directly compensate former "comfort women." Ruling in favor of three elderly South Korean women who brought suit against the Japanese government, Judge Hideaki Chikashita called the army's actions during World War II a form of sexual and ethnic discrimination and a "fundamental violation of human rights."[129] Judge Hideaki Chikashita was taking steps to lessen the militarization of judicial culture.

MILITARY ALLIANCES SEXUALIZED

Kim Yeon Ja is fifty-three years old now. She has made a new vocation for herself, teaching the children of Korean women and American male soldiers. For years she herself was a part of South Korea's extensive postwar prostitution industry. Telling her story, she chooses her starting point carefully.[130] Her father made a successful career in the South Korean police force, she explains, but then abandoned Kim and her mother because her mother was uneducated. Her mother tried to make

Figure 5 A South Korean woman working as a prostitute near a U.S. Army base must try to meet not only the sexual but also the material expectations of her American soldier customers. Thus she will go into debt in order to furnish her small room with a bed, a fan, a chest of drawers, a television, and a sound system. (Photographer: Saundra Sturdevant. "Women rent small rooms behind the club... (in South Korea)," in *Let the Good Times Roll* by Saundra Sturdevant and Brenda Stoltzfus, The New Press, New York, 1992, p. 191.)

a living as a salesperson. While a child in elementary school, Kim was raped by a distant male relative. Again, several years later, now in eleventh grade, Kim was raped, this time by another relative, a man who was in the South Korean army. Kim continued her education, graduated from high school in the early 1960s and obtained a job as a newspaper reporter in Seoul, but lost the job when the paper folded. Her economic situation became more precarious. She rented a small apartment and sold books and shined shoes. Unwittingly, she had rented a place in Seoul's red-light district. A woman who worked in one of the so-called GI towns that surround most of the American military bases scattered throughout South Korea advised Kim to move there because she could earn more money. Within a short time she was making her living as a prostitute; virtually all her customers were American soldiers. Through the 1960s and 1970s, she developed strategies for enduring the conditions of prostitution. It was not painful selling herself, she explained, "because I was in a drugged state most of the time."

Conservative Korean commentators typically have dismissed women working in prostitution as merely pursuing cash to feed their crass consumerist desires. A new generation of Korean and Korean American feminist researchers have challenged this conventional portrait. Katharine Moon is among this group; she points to studies that show that most women who enter the prostitution industry were then and are still poor women who believe prostitution is the only work that will earn them a livable income, an income that will support not only themselves but usually their children, their parents, and maybe their brothers who are still in school. Many of these women experienced sexual abuse as a prelude to entering prostitution.[131] This scenario is the less talked-about side of the 1960–1997 Korean economic "miracle."

At the entrance of each club in GI town (sometimes called "camptown" or "Americatown") was a board on which all the women employees' photos were posted. Each woman had to have a number beside her name. American military officials, Kim recalls, stopped by without notice to ensure that each woman's photo matched her bureaucratic number. In order to comply with U.S. military regulations designed to keep her male customers free from venereal disease, Kim and the other women in the bars had to submit to weekly vaginal examinations by approved physicians. A woman who failed the examination was denied the requisite health card that all bar owners insisted their women employees have so that their businesses could continue to win U.S. base commanders' approval. If a woman continued to practice prostitution without the health card, she was likely to be picked up by U.S. military police officers and sent to an anti-venereal disease hospital up in the mountains for a two-week treatment. Kim and the other women referred to this hospital as "the monkey house"; they dreaded being sent there.

The prostitution industry servicing American soldiers in South Korea has not been left to chance. It has been self-consciously shaped by two governments, each seeking to exert controls that would ensure that its own goals would be met. Thus, for instance, officials in Seoul since the 1960s have sponsored a Woman's Autonomous Association in each GI town. Each association in practice has been far from autonomous. Katharine Moon found that "local police and government authorities select the leaders of the associations and keep watch over

the women's activities."[132] A principal objective is to persuade the
women in prostitution to monitor each other, especially to guarantee
that every woman remains free of sexually transmitted diseases. This
practice has added an innovative twist on both the British government's nineteenth-century system and the U.S.-Philippine alliance's
more recent system.

There have been times, nonetheless, when women working in the
bars have taken genuinely independent organized action to challenge
the regulations devised by the U.S. military officials and their Korean
allies. The 1972 protest marked a first, Kim Yeon Ja believed. "We do
have human rights," Kim recalls the women newly realizing. "So one
thousand of us demonstrated in front of the base," calling for a reform
of the regulations that deprived them of a sense of autonomy and dignity. "They sprayed us with fire hoses." This was the military's sole response to the women's proposals.

By the mid-1970s women in the American base towns had developed organizationally. In 1976, an American soldier burned and stran-
gled a Korean woman in the entertainment district; no soldier was arrested, despite a witness. Shortly thereafter, a second woman was
murdered. Kim Yeon Ja recalls, "We were so angered by this injustice,
we ran barefoot to the base." At this point, the Korean police became
energized, promising the women that they would pursue the case.
Eventually an American soldier was arrested and convicted.[133] But under the terms of the U.S.–Republic of Korea Status of Forces Agreement (SOFA), the convicted soldier was not permitted to be jailed in
Korea. He was returned to the United States.

The SOFA is a major vehicle for cementing and sustaining a military alliance between the U.S. government and its international partners. A SOFA spells out in minute detail the conditions under which
American troops can be stationed on the host government's territory.
Health, surveillance, policing, finances—all are subjects of the intense
government-to-government negotiations that result in these formal
diplomatic agreements. The fine print of these alliance agreements is
not open to public scrutiny. In behind-closed-door negotiations over a
SOFA, governments' officials hammer out the sexual politics of militarization.

The actual implementation of any SOFA is left to American base
commanders. Anyone wanting a realistic sense of how a government-
to-government alliance works needs to keep an inquisitive eye on base
commanders. A base commander for a U.S. force overseas is not

Figure 6 The American military has taken deliberate steps to institutionalize its relationships with the clubs around its South Korean bases. Here a member of its Civilian Military Operations team mediates a conflict that has erupted between local Koreans and American male soldiers. Korean American soldiers are often assigned by their commanders to play this mediation role. (Photographer: Saundra Sturdevant. "The Civilian Military Operations (CMO) mediates, ... (South Korea)," in *Let the Good Times Roll* by Saundra Sturdevant and Brenda Stoltzfus, The New Press, New York, 1992, p. 201.)

merely an instrument of the policy makers in the White House or the State Department. He (rarely have U.S. women officers been promoted to base commander) is not even simply a cipher for Defense Department senior officials' designs. A base commander has his own concerns and his own career aspirations. Typically, he is a colonel. That is, he (and now occasionally, on some small bases, she) is at a very delicate point in his military career. In all militaries there are fewer slots for generals (or admirals) than there are for colonels. Not all colonels will be promoted. A colonel is a person who hopes to be a general. So much depends on how his superiors assess his performance as a base commander. A base commander has his own sources of information, his own social circles.

The base commander and his deputy commander (in the 1990s more American women officers are gaining assignments as deputy base

commanders) are likely to have a stake in creating smooth working relationships with local host-country officials and with local business
owners. It is standard procedure for American base commanders in
South Korea, for example, to develop mutual relationships with the local Korean Chamber of Commerce, many of whose members are the
proprietors of the bars and discos that are at the heart of the prostitution industry. Some American military officers, women and men, have
reported feeling quite uneasy with this part of their jobs as deputy base
commanders. On the other hand, their performance—and thus their
own chances for future promotion—will depend on how trouble-free
they can keep these base–local business relations.[134]

Researcher Katharine Moon has written perhaps the only feminist
analysis of the interstate negotiations leading to a revision of an SOFA.
Her investigation of the international politics of the early 1970s reveals
that male American government officials and male South Korean government officials each had their own particular reasons for wanting to
maintain male American soldiers' sexual access to Korean women, yet
each wanted to revise the ways in which that access was controlled.[135]

In the early 1970s, Moon finds, the American administration of
Richard Nixon was trying to disentangle the U.S. military from the unpopular Vietnam War. It proposed that in both Vietnam and elsewhere
in Asia local regimes assume more of the Cold War military burden. Simultaneously, Pentagon officials were becoming increasingly, and perhaps belatedly, alarmed at the ways in which hostilities between black
and white male military personnel in all branches were jeopardizing
American military effectiveness. Bars and brothels were among the
sites of the most frequent fights and of black charges of racial discrimination. For instance, "Near Camp Humphries, South Korea, a club
owner and his white G.I. patrons and backers paid a bounty to Republic of Korea (ROK) marines for every African-American they beat up
in the vicinity to discourage blacks from patronizing the bar."[136]
American base commanders were doing little to halt the discriminatory
behavior. The Black Congressional Caucus was taking up the issue.
The SOFA's renegotiation provided a chance for Defense Department
officials to try to lessen these intra-military racial tensions.

For their part, according to Moon's research, by the 1970s South
Korean senior officials were becoming less willing to play "younger
brother" to the United States in Cold War alliance politics and more
resentful of the original terms of the SOFA, which had made it clear
that this agreement was between unequals. For instance, it rankled that

the process by which health inspections and policing were conducted in the towns around the U.S. bases compromised Korean sovereignty for the sake of American soldiers' discipline and well-being. But the men who ran the South Korean government and its military—the 1970s was a period of widespread militarization in Korean political life—had their own opinions of women in general and of women working in prostitution in particular. The women were citizens of the ROK, not simply pawns in the American Cold War strategy; initially they could even have been characterized by Korean elite men simultaneously as "fallen women" and "patriots," because they were performing heroically for their country by making allied military men feel "at home." Descriptions of patriotic prostitutes notwithstanding, women in prostitution still were frowned upon, were deemed unrespectable not only for their lowly profession but for their intimacy with foreign men. It was out of this triple conservative version of nationalist patriarchal ambivalence—over sovereignty, femininity, and sexuality—that the South Korean male officials negotiated a revised SOFA with their American counterparts.

The two sets of officials together devised the "Camptown Clean-Up Campaign." The solution to these two governments' respective political anxieties—about racial conflict, global security, compromised sovereignty, regime stability—was to control more tightly those Korean prostitutes servicing American soldiers. As Katharine Moon's research demonstrates, it was not the entire elaborate web of relationships that constituted the military prostitution industry that was chosen as the target of new control. Rather, policy makers on both sides of the table felt more comfortable focusing on that part of the whole system over which they could exert the most control at the lowest ideological price: the prostitutes. Thus "purifying" the camptowns in the name of improving U.S.-ROK alliance relations was translated into purifying the women who worked as prostitutes. Their bodies would be more stringently controlled to ensure their purification and thus, by extension, the purification of American-Korean relations. In reality, this decision meant controlling access to these women's bodies so that they were equally distributed between U.S. white and black male soldiers. It meant, at the same time, enacting more interventionist measures to prevent women who had contracted venereal disease from infecting American male soldiers of any race.

Tightening the control over women's bodies, the diplomatic negotiators implied, would reduce soldiers' interracial hostilities, sustain soldiers' morale, bolster the self-esteem of ROK elites, and reconfirm U.S. commitment to protecting its ally from communist invasion. This was the Cold War; women's exercising their potential sexual autonomy could not be permitted to jeopardize states' formulas for security.[137]

South Korea's own military's involvement in prostitution—as individual soldier-clients and as institutional players in the country's sexualized entertainment industry—has attracted much less Korean political attention than has that of the American military. Two forms of Korean nationalism have blocked curiosity about Korean soldiers. First, the conservative strain of South Korean nationalism, as articulated by the country's political elites, military officers, senior civil servants, and corporate executives, has made the Korean military untouchable, even after its generals were pushed out of government by a popular pro-democracy movement in the 1980s. Meanwhile, South Korea's leftist nationalists have made American intrusiveness in their country's affairs a major object of their ire. While they led the campaigns to reduce authoritarianism in government and the workplace and, in particular, to reduce the generals' political power, they were reluctant to point an accusing finger at the sexual practices of ordinary male soldiers, most of whom are conscripts.

Korean feminists have sympathized with leftist nationalists. Many feminists themselves came out of the leftist nationalist movement—and continue to see themselves integral to that movement. In 1997, the centrist left, supported by a broad spectrum of Korean voters, managed for the first time to win a presidential election. Many feminists still see their alliance with the left-wing nationalist movement as their most reliable source of practical support and popular legitimacy. To give up their alliance with—or more daringly, to openly challenge—nationalists on the Korean left not only would require feminists to undergo an intellectual shift but would require them to muster considerable strategic courage in a society that still, despite its first expressions in the 1920s, looks at feminism as an alien import.[138]

Challenging U.S. militarized prostitution, by contrast, provides Korean feminists with an entrée into the prevailing populist nationalist discourse: foreign troops who abuse Korean women are, by extension, abusing the Korean nation; former military elites who allowed their American military peers to abuse Korean women likewise were violating the real Korean nation. To publicly criticize Koreans' militarized prostitution not only deprives a Korean feminist of this basis for allying with nonfeminist male nationalists, it exposes her to potential charges of national betrayal. At the dawn of the new century, when so

many Koreans are reeling from the economic crisis, to be seen as "unpatriotic" would carry an especially heavy price. Women have been
called on by politicians and the media to respond to the society's economic trauma by being more nationalistic than ever: they are being
urged to make more sacrifices, to lower their own economic expectations, to make their personal mission the support of their anxiety-
ridden husbands.[139] These are risky times, consequently, in which to
confront home-grown patriarchy. Economic crises can bolster the normalcy of masculinized militarism.

Thus it is that the internal patriarchal politics of anti-base, nationalist, and democracy movements help prolong public toleration of local
military prostitution. Korean feminists' ongoing development of an approach to nationalism, therefore, will be decisive in shaping their
strategies for addressing all forms of prostitution—past and present,
local and foreign, nonmilitarized and militarized.[140]

Korean and Asian American women filmmakers have begun to document the post–Cold War U.S. military prostitution system as it has
continued to play itself out in Korean women's lives.[141] It is not a simple story.

> There's beer and girls and food and clubs—everything a teenager could
> ask for.[142]

A young American male soldier here sums up his favorable impressions of serving in South Korea today. The impressions from the
"girls" are quite different. One Korean woman interviewed by filmmakers T. J. Takagi and Hye Jung Park for their documentary, *The
Women Outside,* said that she felt trapped not so much by coercion as
by debt. It was hard to quit a military brothel, she explained, when
your debts to the brothel owner kept mounting, given your salary of
$250 per month and your sense of obligation to your family, which
motivated you to send money home monthly. Then, too, you knew
that once out of the brothel you would still have to face ostracism
from many of your fellow Koreans. For many women, marrying an
American soldier has appeared to be the only way out of debt servi-
tude. Some American men sense this. "These days the GIs don't get
into deep relations with us." The speaker is a Korean woman who has
two children for whom she is the sole carer. Of the children's two
American soldier–fathers, "One was nice, the other was violent."

In the early 1990s, an estimated 1,200 South Korean women annu-
ally came to the United States as military wives. In acknowledgment of
this trend, the American military (through the USO) started to operate

a Brides School. A school administrator expresses pride as she addresses the visiting filmmakers. The school is helping Korean women to match the expectations of their American military husbands. Brides School instructors, for instance, introduce Korean women to American cooking: "[We start] with breakfast and go up to exotic desserts."

Todd, a young, white, American soldier admits to an interviewer that language and culture barriers are difficult to overcome: "It's hard to tell her about my job." He has heard of the many failed marriages; still, he says rather wistfully, "If two people love each other, it should be o.k." Todd's Korean fiancée has taken him home to meet her parents. It was awkward. But she too remains hopeful: "I trust him, I rely on him."

Once they have arrived in the United States as new military brides, Korean women face more challenges. Some find that other military wives, American-born women, don't accept them. Occasionally their husbands will confront those women on their apparent racism. This confrontation may not be easy to do if the offending woman is married to a man of more senior rank than is the husband of the Korean woman.

The Korean brides must also face the frequent ostracism meted out by other Korean Americans. Many are ashamed of these women, who they assume have worked as prostitutes before their marriages to American men.

Eighty percent of marriages between American male soldiers and Korean women have ended in divorce—often as a result of the husband's physical abuse.[143] The divorced women do not then disappear. Takagi and Park took their cameras to Jacksonville, Florida, an American military base town. They visited the seedy entertainment district outside the base. There they found Korean women. Some of the recently divorced Korean women had sought jobs in bars and massage parlors. Their lives were never demilitarized. The militarization simply continued to take on new shapes.

In 1995, the *New York Times* carried a feature article in its Metro section about the emergence of suburban prostitution.[144] In the shopping malls of affluent towns, in New York City's commuter suburbs such as Great Neck, Long Island, entrepreneurs were setting up brothels. Sometimes the brothels were camouflaged to look on the outside like barbershops or doctors' offices. "The trade—strip-mall brothels that accept Mastercard and offer reasonable rates—is expanding in the metropolitan area's upscale suburbs to convenient locations with plentiful parking."[145] The proprietors were recruiting women by placing advertisements in Korean American newspapers. Many of the women who came to staff these shopping mall brothels were "Korean women who share[d] a troubled history of broken marriages to American G.I.s and bleak job prospects as single women in this country."[146]

The ripple effects of militarized prostitution and militarized marriage do not halt at the gates of a military base.

PROSTITUTION AND PEACEKEEPING

When the Vietnamese troops withdrew from Cambodia, UN peacekeeping soldiers arrived. It was the task of the United Nations Transitional Authority in Cambodia (UNTAC) to restore peace and to create an environment for the democratization of Cambodia public life. A daunting mission. Yet along with land mines removal and voter education, UNTAC brought an upward spiraling of prostitution. UNTAC did not supply the pimps, but it did supply the customers. By 1994, an alliance of women and men working in the country for relief agencies and other nongovernmental organizations (NGOs) had concluded that senior UN officials were not taking responsibility for the sexually exploitative, "no rules, anything goes" behaviors of peacekeeping personnel. The newly formed Women's Development Association estimated that the number of women working in prostitution in Cambodia grew from 6,000 in 1992 to more than 25,000 in late 1994.[147] The NGO staff workers in Phnom Penh decided, therefore, to publish an open letter to the head of the UN mission in Cambodia:

> Cambodian and other Asian women are the victims of stereotyping and often are forced into subservient roles....
> Inappropriate behaviour by some male UNTAC personnel often leave women with a sense of powerlessness.... Women have little access to redress when they experience such behaviour.
> There has been a dramatic increase in prostitution since UNTAC's arrival and a noticeable absence of condoms and education about their use. It is not surprising that HIV has reached an "emergency" level of at least 75 percent among blood donors.[148]

Many of the women—and increasingly girls as young as twelve—recruited into Cambodia's prostitution industry have been ethnic Vietnamese, either members of Cambodia's long-resident Vietnamese minority community or migrant women drawn across the border from Vietnam by the chance to find work. Some Cambodian politicians tried to use ethnic Vietnamese women's visibility in the expanding prostitution trade as a basis for mobilizing a Cambodian brand of parochial nationalism. Despite the ongoing antagonism toward ethnic Vietnamese, this particular political ploy did not seem to meet with success.[149]

However, popular and international alarm at the prostitution industry's growth fueled by peacekeepers' presence did intensify. And, as so often has happened, once seeded by military consumers, the industry gained a foothold hard to dislodge, even when the foreign military's presence diminished. As the UN forces were reduced in the mid-1990s, a new influx of civilian men arrived in the impoverished, sexualized Cambodia. Some were drawn there by the Internet's "World Sex Guide," which in 1996 enthused, "a six-year-old is available for $3."[150]

Did the highly masculinized version of the UN presence in Cambodia foster the abuse of local women? UNTAC's presence did open up spaces for the UN's own women's advocates, staff members of UNIFEM, as well as for nongovernmental groups to extend support to Cambodian women and to nurture local women's own autonomous political organizing. Nonetheless, one report, authored by the UN Division for the Advancement of Women, noted that all fifteen of the UN Cambodian operation's civilian directorships were held by men and that, in general, "UNTAC was predominantly a male peace-keeping operation in which women held no decision-making positions."[151] Although "a few women" served in certain governments' military peace-keeping units—the Australian, Canadian, and Dutch—in May 1995 the proportion of women in the Cambodian peacekeeping mission was zero.[152]

Women activists inside the United Nations also argued that when peacekeeping was conceptualized as a *militarized* operation it became most masculinized. By contrast, when UN headquarters' officials see missions as not chiefly military operations (as was the case in the UN's 1989–90 operation in Namibia), not only are women more likely to gain posts with influence but also the entire UN field *modus operandi* becomes less masculinized.[153]

Many future military peacekeeping operations will look like the peacekeeping missions launched in Cambodia in 1992–1994, in Bosnia in 1996–1998, and in Kosovo in 1999: "victory" will be elusive; a variety of governments will contribute soldiers of their own, many of them trained to be combat troops; the UN Secretariat's own Peace Keeping Organization (UNPKO) will be able to run military training programs, but only for officers and only for those officers whose governments have the funds and the will to pay for their officers' UNPKO training; coordination between governments and the UN will be delicate; NATO will be directly involved; civilian businesses will win contracts to provide support services for the troops; humanitarian aid agencies will be trying to operate without being too reliant on militaries and too deeply sucked into militarized cultures; rival domestic politicians will be competing in the rearranged public arena; local residents will be trying to recover from war-produced trauma while at the same time creating political organizations to compete in the postwar public space; pro-democracy activists will be seeking lasting reforms. Each of these processes will be gendered, will be shaped by how femininity and masculinity are imagined and deployed.

There is nothing inherent in international peacekeeping operations as currently structured that makes their soldiers immune to the sort of sexism that has fueled military prostitution in wartime and peacetime. As in every other military operation conducted by every other government, the extent of future military peacekeeping operations' reliance on the prostitution of some women will be determined by decisions made at the top and in the middle of military organizations.

In January 1996, a group of human rights' and women's organizations sent a letter to the U.S. ambassador to the United Nations, Madeleine Albright. They called on her to press for UN human rights training of peacekeeping troops. Specifically, they called on troops to be formally trained to respect local women. These organizations wanted to ensure that the behavior of some peacekeepers toward Cambodian women was not repeated in Bosnia or in future sites of international peacekeeping.[154]

Child prostitution gained greater visibility inside the bureaucracy of the UN secretariat in late 1996. In a report to the UN secretary general written by Mozambique's education minister, Grace Machel, child prostitution was cited as a principal product of international peacekeeping not only in Cambodia, but in the former Yugoslavia, Mozambique, and Rwanda.[155] This report thereafter provided feminists working as officials in UNICEF, UNIFEM, and other UN agencies to take on the distorted genderings of peacekeeping as a topic within their own policy realms.[156]

The U.S. Defense Department also was nervous about its soldiers' peacekeeping behavior. In large part because the Pentagon defined its post-1995 Bosnian operation as "combat," 91 percent of the American troops assigned to Bosnia were men; only 9 percent were women—less than the 13 percent of women who made up all U.S. uniformed personnel when the operation began.[157] Given this predominance of male soldiers, the politics of masculinity thus would inform Defense Department officials' decisions. The Pentagon imposed no-alcohol and no-fraternization rules on American soldiers on duty in Bosnia. None of the other NATO governments who contributed soldiers to the Bosnia peacekeeping operation decided to impose such bans. Each of the alliance members, that is, were making their own calculations about the peacekeeping politics of their soldiers' gendered leisure and recreation. Such unusual bans, American officials believed, had worked well in Saudi Arabia during the Gulf War. Even though Muslims in Bosnia were far more secularized than were the Saudis and were not themselves teetotalers, Pentagon decision makers thought that the "Saudi Arabian model" was worth repeating.[158]

Washington saw its Bosnian operation as more like its Gulf War operation than like its South Korean maneuvers. One might imagine a map hanging in a Pentagon war room. Countries that were colored green, perhaps, would be those in which prostitution would be "bad for military success"; those tinted purple would be countries in which soldiers' ready access to women in prostitution was deemed "necessary for military success."

In fact, however, it was not clear to an outsider whether the Washington policy crafters were chiefly concerned that the mission would be jeopardized by American male soldiers' potential harassment of Bosnian women. Indications were, instead, that this nonfraternization policy stemmed from senior officials' worries about American voters. The no-alcohol, no-mingling-with-civilians rules seemed designed to ensure that no U.S. soldier deployed in Bosnia would get into any trouble that might ignite protest in a presidential election year among the already skeptical voters back home. American politicians imagined that voters were paying attention to their soldiers' behavior in Bosnia, although voters long ago had learned to ignore their soldiers' activities in South Korea—and Guam and Okinawa.

The politics of peacekeeping prostitution are played out not only in the actual conflict zone but in any country used as an operational launchpad. In late 1995, the people of the Hungarian town of Kaposvar just to the north of Bosnia were expecting to do their part in this prototype of a post–Cold War peacekeeping operation. Their region had been chosen by the U.S. Defense Department as the staging ground for American troops heading into Bosnia. The Americans would be the latest in a long line of foreign soldiers—Celts, Romans, Huns, Teutons, Goths, Slavs, Turks, and Soviets—to find the Kaposvar region a useful place in which to situate a military base. But the arrival of American soldiers held out the prospect of friendlier relations and, for some Hungarian post-communist entrepreneurs, perhaps a boost to business. Cafe and restaurant owners were stocking up on beer, installing french fry cookers, and equipping a night club called the Jolly Joker with a fountain, at the center of which would be a plaster statue of a nude goddess.[159]

> How are people in Kaposvar preparing to greet the Americans? "We're building the brothels right now," Zoltan Molnar, a waiter at a downtown pub, said with a smile.[160]

A year later, neither the fantasies nor the fears of Hungarians along the border had materialized. At any one time, 4,000 American soldiers, most of them men, were stationed in the Hungarian towns. But their Defense Department superiors had decided to extend their nonfraternization policy beyond Bosnia to Hungary as well. American troops were prohibited from leaving their base without special permission. They could drink beer but not off-base. Those soldiers who occasionally were allowed to venture outside the base were locally praised for their good behavior.[161]

The facts presented in this discussion seem to underscore the role of explicit policy decisions in determining when and if and how international peacekeeping fosters the commercial sexualization of local women.

AN OPPORTUNITY TO KICK THE "PROSTITUTION HABIT"

The seeds of political change sometimes can germinate in unlikely places. Apparently quite apart from the organizing being done by feminist human rights activists, by women attending the Beijing conference, and by women building networks of support for present and former military prostitutes, there began in 1995 a very modest process inside the U.S. Defense Department to make prostitution an issue at the senior levels of decision making. The initiators were mid-level civilian staffers, men and women. Their goal was to persuade their superior, Assistant Secretary of Defense Fred Pang—like them, also an appointee, also a civilian—to adopt and then to send down through the uniformed chain of command what they eventually decided to call "The Anti–Child Prostitution Effort."[162]

Seeds need soil and water in order to grow into full-fledged plants. Thus, although at first glance this handful of officials deep inside the Pentagon's maze appeared to be acting quite apart from any recognizable movement, they had tenuous connections to the global network of women who over the past decade had directed their attention to militarized prostitution: one American feminist who spoke with Asian feminists about the impact of American military bases on local women's lives; a nun who was active in an international campaign to end child prostitution; a handful of female U.S. military officers who wondered whether they were complicit in their male colleagues' promotion of prostitution; women outside the government who monitored persistent sexism in the military, including prostitution. Together, these women scarcely amounted to a campaign. Rather, they served as consciousness-raising resources and periodic sounding boards.

The Pentagon civil servants talked among themselves. They didn't know each other well, so the process was necessarily slow and cautious. They traded ideas and hunches about the Pentagon culture in which they worked every day. They knew that even getting prostitution acknowledged as an "issue" would be hard. They decided eventually that raising prostitution in general as an issue would not succeed in the current bureaucratic climate. It would be smarter, they concluded, to frame the issue in such a way that no one could object. Thus it was that *child* prostitution became their focus. Underlying this important choice was a presumption that while commercialized sex by American male soldiers with adult women would be written off as "natural" (and thus unstoppable), commercialized sex by male soldiers with children would shock because it was thought to be "unnatural."

The mid-level officials did their homework, learned more about the problem's international dimensions, found outside experts. Only then did they venture to raise the question formally with a senior official. He was impressed. He told them to proceed.

Their next step was to draft a memo to the civilian secretaries of the three armed services, both alerting them to the new issue of the military's relationship to child prostitution and asking them for their own suggestions as to how Defense officials should address this newly recognized issue. This step ensured that there would be no surprises. Everyone would have a say. The step also ensured that the issue would be dealt with on the inside. There would be no press releases, no congressional hearings. On the other hand, these senior officials had just lived their political lives through the years of 1992–1995, an era marked by the Tailhook scandal and the Okinawa rape. Stories of child prostitution had been featured on the front pages of the *New York Times*. These officials had had colleagues who had lost their jobs or had been compelled to take early retirements because they had acted as though misogyny could be ignored or even treated as a military resource.

The term *misogyny* did not appear in either this early memo or in those that followed. In fact, no recognizably feminist vocabulary was employed. These civilian officials realized that they were still dealing with the U.S. Defense Department. The language that they chose to use was the same language that had always been used when the military discussed male sexuality—the language of health, morality, discipline, diplomacy, and mission effectiveness. The threat of AIDS hovered over the correspondence. The focus of the memos remained child prostitution. Silence was maintained on the question of prostitution in general.

Several months went by. Responses were elicited and sifted. Options for action were weighed: what could a bureaucratic organization do? what was deemed doable?

Then in July 1996, a memo went out from the Assistant Secretary of Defense to the civilian Assistant Secretaries of the Army, Navy, and Air Force, with copies to the uniformed Deputy Chiefs of Staff for Personnel of the three services.[163] Action, it was decided, would take three forms. First, the Department of Defense, in this instance through the Assistant Secretary, would officially declare that "any use of child prostitutes is not only an egregious exploitation of children but, to the extent that there is a potential for involvement of US service members, is detrimental to the health and welfare of service members and the ability of US forces to carry out their mission."

The recently enacted civilian Violent Crime Control and Law Enforcement Act of 1994 (in whose congressional passage feminist groups played a major role) was cited by the Assistant Secretary, noting that the act made travel abroad for "the purpose of engaging in a sexual act with a person under 18 year of age" now a crime for American civilians and military personnel alike.

Second, the Department of Defense would send one of its own officials as a member of the U.S. delegation to the first World Congress against the Commercial Sexual Exploitation of Children to be held in Stockholm, Sweden, in August 1996, a conference sponsored by UNICEF and an NGO, End Child Prostitution in Asian Tourism (EC-PAT). The State Department voiced its approval of the Defense Department's decision to show its concern by attending; so too did officials in the Justice Department.

The Defense Department official selected to attend was Carolyn Becraft. Becraft had been a vocal civilian advocate for military wives and women in uniform before Bill Clinton appointed her Deputy Assistant Secretary of Defense for Personnel Support, Families, and Education.[164] By 1996, she had become a sophisticated inside operator and yet was still considered by the lower level bureaucratic initiators of the policy to be genuine in her commitment to stop American military complicity in child prostitution. The initiators hoped that eventually the administration of the new policy would be placed in "Carolyn's shop." As one of those civil servant activists observed, "She might *do* something on this!"[165] Their hopes were met: by 1997, responsibility for implementation of the anti–child prostitution policy had been assigned to Secretary Becraft's division.

Third, each of the armed services was instructed to begin its own program to "underscore ... the DOD's commitment to combating the child prostitution industry and ensuring that no DOD personnel knowingly or unknowingly support such activity."[166] In practice, those programs would take the form of training—of officers about to be sent abroad as commanders and deputy commanders of U.S. bases, of chaplains and health officers deployed to overseas bases. Base commanders and deputy base commanders were instructed on "strategies for combating child prostitution in areas around US facilities, including setting of off-limits establishments and coordination with the local business community to isolate and disestablish enterprises facilitating child prostitution."[167] The training did not delineate specific steps that base commanders and deputy base commanders—the colonels and would-be colonels—should take; specific implementation was seemingly left to their discretion.

This Anti–Child Prostitution Effort is not the first time that the U.S. military has devised a prostitution policy. The U.S. military, like the British, French, Japanese, and other militaries, has had prostitution policies for generations. Furthermore, those policies have never been static. They have been the subject of internal discussions, refinements, revisions.

What may be new in this small case is that a senior member of the military establishment was persuaded by members of his own staff to take explicit steps to reduce a particular form of prostitution for the well-being not only of the military but also of the prostitute, in this case a child.

As feminists have demonstrated, policy making can encounter countless slips between cup and lip. Implementation, enforcement, evaluation—these political processes are at least as crucial as initiation, formulation, and passage. The political process of altering American officers' and rank-and-file soldiers' relationships even just to children in prostitution has only begun. Every training session with base commanders and health officers will become a site where the politics (often racialized politics) of sexuality is conducted. Every meeting between base commanders and local chambers of commerce will be (as it already is) a site where the politics (often racialized politics) of sexuality is conducted.

The anti–child prostitution effort required many decisions to get to this point; it will require many more decisions to get to the next point—if the next point is achieved. Failure of this modest, though significant, initiative to reduce American soldiers' use of child prostitutes will not be due merely to the stubbornness of human nature or to the power of men's sexual drive or to the entrenchment of "the oldest profession." If this initiative fails, it will be because certain military decision makers decided not to make certain decisions after all.

4

WHEN SOLDIERS RAPE

Prostitution seems routine.

Rape can be shocking.

Prostitution can seem comforting to some. They imagine it to be "the oldest profession." Around a military camp prostitutes connote tradition, not rupture; leisure, not horror; ordinariness, not mayhem. To many, militarized prostitution thus becomes *un*newsworthy.

Rape, by contrast, shocks. It shocks, but then it loses its distinctiveness. Typically, when rape happens in the midst of war, no individual soldier-rapists are identified by the victims, by their senior command, or by the media (if there). The women who suffer rape in wartime usually remain faceless as well. They merge with the pockmarked landscape; they are put on the list of war damage along with gutted houses and mangled rail lines. Rape evokes the nightmarishness of war, but it becomes just an indistinguishable part of a poisonous wartime stew called "lootpillageandrape."

Thus when we try to increase the visibility of particular rapes committed by particular men as soldiers, we are engaging in a political act.[1] It is an act that must be undertaken with self-consciousness, for there are two traps. The first: women must be listened to, but with an awareness that their stories are likely to be complex. Atina Grossman, a researcher who has begun the tricky task of uncovering the murky but explosive history of the widespread rapes of German women chiefly (though not solely) by Soviet troops in 1945 and 1946, offers a caveat. To anyone who mistakenly imagines that it is a simple under-taking to reveal "the truth" about militarized rape, even brutal war-time rapes or mass-scale rapes, Atina Grossman warns: "Women's rape stories were framed in incredibly complicated ways, shaped by their audience and the motives behind their telling. Their experiences were ordered and given meaning within a complex grid of multiple images and discourses."[2]

The second trap: exposing militarized rapes does not automatically serve the cause of demilitarizing women's lives. Making visible those women raped by men as soldiers is usually a difficult task; but some-times it is a task made dangerously easy. A woman outside the military who has been raped by someone else's soldiers can be *re*militarized if her ordeal is made visible chiefly for the purpose of mobilizing her male compatriots to take up arms to avenge her—and their—allegedly lost honor. Today, long after the perpetration of their wartime rapes, Indian and Bangladeshi women are still trying to make adequate non-patriarchal sense of those rapes in the ongoing evolution of domestic and international politics of nations and states.[3] The challenge, there-fore, is to make visible women raped by men as soldiers *without* fur-ther militarizing those women in the process.

Militarized rape has gained visibility on the stage of international politics in recent years because of the incidence of mass rape that oc-curred in Bosnia during its 1992–1995 war and in Rwanda during its 1994 attempted genocide. Yet militarized rapes are far more diverse. Often, as in Haiti and Indonesia, action has been required through the organizing by women for women to uncover soldiers' systematic politi-cal uses of rape.[4] Rape perpetrated by men as soldiers has been experi-enced by women in a variety of forms:

rape by a male soldier of a woman he thinks of as a "foreigner"[5]

rape by an individual male soldier of a civilian woman of the same nationality while that soldier is "off duty"

rape by a male soldier of a woman soldier in the same army, per-haps because he resents her presence in a previously all-male unit or because he is angry at her for her unwillingness to date him or flirt with him[6]

rapes of women held in military prisons by male soldiers serving as guards; rapes perpetrated by a soldier acting as an interrogator with the apparent purpose of forcing the woman victim to give information rapes by a group of invading soldiers to force women of a different ethnicity or race to flee their home regions

rapes of captured women by soldiers of one communal or national group aimed principally at humiliating the men of an opposing group

rapes by men of one ethnicity, race, or nationality of men from the "enemy" group to make the latter feel humiliated because they have been, via rape, reduced to "mere women"[7]

rapes of women by men in accordance to male officers' system of morale-boosting rewards to their men after battle

rapes of women taking refuge in wartime refugee camps by men also taking refuge in those camps or by men who are assigned to protect women in those camps[8]

rapes of women by those men who are prostitution procurers, to "prepare" them for later service in a brothel organized for soldier clients

rapes of women in wartime by civilian men of their same ethnic or national community who are acting out a misogyny nurtured by and licensed by the militarized climate

rapes of women who publicly oppose militarization by men of their own supposed community who support militarization

This list may be exhausting, but it is not exhaustive.

There are as many different forms of militarized rape as there are subtle nuances in the relationships between militarized women and militarized men. Nonetheless, they share some important common features—features that will affect not only the rapist's sense of what he is doing and of what gives him license to do it but also the raped woman's responses to that assault. First, the male militarized rapist in some way imposes his understandings of "enemy," "soldiering," "victory," and "defeat" on both the woman to be raped and on the act of sexual assault. Second, consequently, the militarized rape is harder to privatize than nonmilitarized rape is, since it draws so much of its rationale from an imagining of societal conflict and/or the functions of a formal institution such as the state's national security or defense apparatus or an insurgency's military arm. Third, the woman who has endured militarized rape must devise her responses in the minutes, weeks, and years after that assault not only by weighing her relationships to the rapist and to her personal friends and relatives, to the prevailing norms of feminine respectability, and perhaps to the criminal justice system, but *in addition,* she must weigh her relationships to collective memory, collective notions of national destiny, and the very institutions of organized violence.

In this chapter I explore just three particular conditions under which rape has been militarized. These three forms seem especially important to understand because they have demanded so many feminists' attention in recent years: (1) "recreational rape" as the alleged outcome of not supplying male soldiers with "adequately accessible" militarized prostitution; (2) "national security rape" as an instrument for bolstering a nervous state; and (3) "systematic mass rape" as an instrument of open warfare.

SOLDIERS SEEKING RECREATION

Militarized rape and militarized prostitution are often treated by policy makers as if they were divided by a cultural Maginot Line. When they are, this division is marked less by cultural realities than by a fortified wall of ideas and practices built by nervous policy makers themselves. This imagined separation between militarized rape and militarized prostitution serves the interests of many patriarchal officials: it allows them to discuss rape and prostitution as if their perpetrators and their victims were entirely different. In actual practice, in the world of military policy making, officials think of rape and prostitution *together.* Providing organized prostitution to male soldiers is imagined to be a means of preventing those same soldiers from engaging in rape. It was this sort of thinking, connecting rape to prostitution, that informed the Japanese imperial government's 1930s and 1940s "comfort women" policy making. Strikingly similar thinking undergirds present-day British and American military sexual politics.[9] Take the Okinawa rape case of 1995.

Okinawa had been militarily occupied by the Japanese before World War II, but the militarization reached new heights during that conflict. That militarization process was both patriarchally gendered and sexualized. According to recently discovered documents, the imperial army created a total of 130 military brothels on Okinawa. The women forced to work in these establishments were both Okinawan and Korean.[10]

Okinawa suffered some of World War II's most devastating battles. More than one-fourth of the island's population—150,000 Oki-

nawans—were killed in June 1945. The Battle of Okinawa became the
Japanese and American forces' last major face-to-face engagement of
the war.[11] Every year, June 23 is marked by Okinawans as a day for
both memorializing the dead and recommitting themselves to peace.[12]
And yet Okinawa remains today one of the most thoroughly militarized places on earth. By agreements between officials in Washington
and in Tokyo, much of Okinawans' most fertile and commercially
valuable land has been given over to U.S. military installations. Five
years after the end of the Cold War Okinawans played host to 29,000
American troops.

The U.S. government created bases for its own military purposes (at
the peak of the Cold War there were 145 bases on the island). Okinawa became a linchpin in the American post–World War II Pacific defense strategy. In 1972, Okinawa was returned to Japanese control—
Okinawans refer to it as the "reversion"—but the American bases
remained. Reversion made Okinawans "Japanese," but the switch
from U.S. control to Japanese control did not reduce militarization. Although the island of Okinawa accounts for a mere 1 percent of Japan's
total territory, it has been host to 75 percent of the U.S. bases. By the
early 1990s, American bases took up 20 percent of Okinawans' land.[13]
Islanders found that their land, livelihoods, and environment were
shaped by U.S. military priorities that meshed well with mainland Japanese political leaders' strategy for cementing their own alliance with
the United States. Looking back on his island's history, one elderly Okinawan summed it up this way: "We were sacrificed ... Japan thought
that Okinawa was expendable, something it could leave behind, like
the tail of a lizard."[14]

Okinawans born after 1972 came to think of the U.S. bases as an
inevitable part of their local landscape. The thriving prostitution businesses around the bases scarcely seemed worth thinking about. They
were just there. In the mid-1990s, high school students told a Japanese
teacher who conducted annual opinion surveys that the presence of
American soldiers made the students feel as though they were more
"worldly" than their mainland Japanese peers. Teachers found it
difficult to teach classes with the roar of American fighters flying low
over the schools, but the children had learned to put their hands over
their ears.[15]

Some Okinawans saw the American troops as a source of commercial opportunity. Restaurants, souvenir shops, bars, tailor shops, tattoo
parlors, and prostitution businesses grew up around the American

bases. Their owners designed each enterprise to suit the tastes and desires of American military personnel. Local shopkeepers' livelihoods came to depend on the U.S.-Japanese military alliance. A tattoo parlor can be militarized. So can a tailor shop.

Other Okinawans, however, felt powerless in their own homeland, once an outpost for Japanese imperialism, thereafter a launchpad for Cold War rivalries. The best organized resisters were anti-bases landlords who petitioned to have their land returned. Other Okinawans' opposition was fueled by memories of past sexual assaults by U.S. military men on Okinawan nonprostitute women, for instance the infamous "Yumiko-chan incident," when in 1955 an American serviceman raped and killed a six-year-old girl named Yumiko; others could not forget the May 1993 rape of a nineteen-year-old woman by an American soldier, a man who was never brought to trial.[16] After this 1993 assault, six Okinawan women's groups launched a petition campaign. They called for a more thorough investigation of all forms of military violation of women's human rights "going back to the beginning." Moreover, they proposed "the initiation of counseling services for empowerment in order to restore the human dignity and bodies of women ravaged by both the Japanese and U.S. military."[17]

Even a decade earlier, in 1985, Okinawan feminists held a workshop on prostitution at the UN Decade on Women Conference in Nairobi. At home they had cast their coalition net widely. *Tapestry* was the metaphor the group's leaders chose to describe their alliance. The Unai (sisterhood) festival sponsored by Okinawa's women peace activists brought together a women's consumers' cooperative, a women managers association, women's peace and human rights groups, artists, and natural childbirth groups. According to Takazato Suzuyo, one of the island's most prominent elected officials and feminist peace activists, the ultimate aim of their organizing, of which critique of militarization was one part, was "women's autonomy, independence and networking."[18]

Thus when a twelve-year-old Okinawan schoolgirl from the village of Kin was abducted and raped in September 1995 by two American marines and an American sailor, some local residents were outraged but not surprised. Many more were shocked into a new consciousness altogether. Comments by Okinawan high school students capture the latter:

> I had taken the bases for granted till I came to know how frightening they are, but the fact that I have been ignorant frightens me more.

Till this happened, I had no fear nor any special feeling living in Okinawa with its bases. But through learning Okinawan history I came to
understand that the bases remain just like the scars of war.

I have had no previous doubts about the bases because they were already
here when I was born, but I have felt fear whenever I heard the planes
overhead.[19]

Many Okinawans' initial response to the rape was to call for basic
reforms in the Japan-U.S. Status of Forces Agreement (SOFA). As we
have seen in South Korea, ordinary citizens' lives are affected by the
fine print in the SOFA. Because militarization has been such a salient
issue in Japanese political life, criticism in the wake of the Okinawa
rape was aimed not only at American officials but at their Japanese
counterparts. Both were charged with fostering the militarization of
Okinawans' lives. Local critics accused Tokyo-based elected politicians
and civil servants of having reduced Okinawa to merely a convenient
card to be played in their foreign policy dealings.[20]

The 1995 rape of the schoolgirl thereby was added to a list that included loss of hearing and loss of land. Okinawan nationalists—and
their Japanese mainland male-led peace movement supporters—did
what some Philippine and South Korean anti-bases nonfeminist nationalist activists had done: they perceived the sexual exploitation of
local women by foreign soldiers as one more reason to reject the idea
that military bases were the currency of development and diplomacy.
These nationalists thought about colonialism and neocolonialism.
They thought about militarism. Most of these nonfeminist anti-bases
nationalists, however, did not think about misogyny. They did not
think about masculinity. They did not think about prostitution. They
did not think about violence against women in general.

It would take Okinawan feminists to challenge this anti-bases nationalist political myopia. But these women activists would find it hard
to redirect their nationalist and peace activist allies' attention from the
bases to the conditions of women.[21]

None of the three young American men charged with the rape of the
Okinawan sixth grader had had prior criminal records. The three were
African American men who had grown up in poor families in Texas
and Georgia; they had studied hard to pass the increasingly rigorous
U.S. military entrance exams and had looked to military service as a
vehicle for expanding their career opportunities.[22] The women in their
lives could not believe that these young men, whom they knew so inti-

mately, for whom they had held such high hopes, would violently assault another woman, much less a schoolgirl. The initial reaction of these mothers, sisters, and wives was to suspect the U.S. military of scapegoating, of using three young black soldiers as fodder for diplomatic wrangling between American and Japanese officials.[23] Given the long history of racism in the U.S. military, this presumption was not unreasonable.[24]

There were added reasons for skepticism about the motives driving the seeming willingness of the U.S. base commanders to hand the three soldier-suspects over to Japanese courts. An exhaustive exercise in investigatory journalism by two American reporters of the *Dayton Daily News* had revealed that the U.S. military's own criminal justice system for years had been systematically tolerating the behavior of military men accused of rape and other forms of sexual assault.[25] One civilian police detective, who had pursued numerous sexual assaults involving American navy personnel in his home state of Florida, had reached this conclusion: "It's like the military tries to keep it hush-hush and keep it in their own family ... I would hate for my wife or daughter to be in the military and be sexually assaulted and have them investigate. They don't have the expertise, the training, and sometimes, they don't have the heart."[26]

The mother of one of the three men accused in the Okinawa rape case did not want her son to enlist in the navy in the first place. On the other hand, Esther Gill did not want to be seen as the proverbial domineering mother. One role of the military in American gendered culture has been as a vehicle for young men's departure from the feminized home. Esther Gill felt the societal pressure to accept this cultural ritual: "I as a mother didn't want to sacrifice my son to the military ... But I had to cut the apron strings and the day he was leaving, the recruiting office van that came to the house to take him symbolized a hearse to me."[27]

It was hard for these women to hear the Japanese prosecutors' charges, which soon overlapped considerably with a friend's description and with their sons' own postarrest confessions of what they had done that day on leave:

> The three men [plus a fourth who later left] had discussed hiring prostitutes but ... Seaman Gill had said he had no money and proposed the rape instead. At first, the others thought he was joking, but then the discussion grew more serious. He said Private Harp, "didn't do anything to stop it. He just let things go."

[The] four servicemen rented a car. At some point, Seaman Gill, who was driving, began proposing a rape. The men went to a grocery store and Privates Harp and Ledet went in to buy tape and condoms. At that point, the fourth serviceman realized that his colleagues were serious about the rape and left ...

The men then drove around looking for a victim ... At about 8 p.m., they found the girl, stopped the car, and Private Ledet and Private Harp got out.

Private Harp acted as if he was going to ask directions. Private Ledet put his arm around the girl's neck from behind and Private Harp hit her in the face. Private Ledet shoved her into the car, the two Marines taped her eyes and mouth and tied her hands and feet. Seaman Gill drove to a remote farm road surrounded by sugar cane fields.

... The rape was over at about 8:20. The men drove away and left the girl, who went to a nearby home to call for help.[28]

There was a dispute among the three men over which of them attempted rape, which of them achieved penetration, and which of them participated in the kidnapping but did not attempt rape.[29]

These men's pretrial stories suggest that many soldiers think of prostitution as a routine recreational activity. Buying sexual services from a local woman has to be figured into a male soldier's weekly budget. Moreover, none of the personal accounts of war or the studies of U.S. military prostitution suggest that any particular racial group within the military rejects prostitution as a recreational activity. The only American racial characteristic of the discos and massage parlors around the U.S. bases in Okinawa that stands out is that Okinawa entertainment district's male clienteles are less racially segregated than those that patronize the bars that used to surround the U.S. bases in the Philippines and that still encircle the U.S. bases in South Korea.[30] In addition, while there have been heated debates among Japanese citizens in recent years about the prevalence of racism in Japanese culture, Japanese citizens reacting to the 1995 rape did not appear preoccupied with the particular race of the three American men charged. Rather, as long-time African American residents of Japan explained, what seemed to matter to most Japanese was that the three men accused of rape were foreigners and that they were representatives of the Washington-Tokyo security alliance.[31]

Right after the three enlisted men told their stories, a senior American officer, a middle-aged, male, white, four-star admiral, reiterated the military's well-worn distinction between—and connection between—military prostitution and military rape. He spoke as if he were saying the obvious. He did not speak as if he knew he was jeopardizing his entire career. He was.

Admiral Richard C. Macke, a thirty-five-year navy careerist, commander in chief of the U.S. Pacific Command, held a breakfast interview with reporters in Washington. It was November 1995. The Clinton administration was about to repeat its apology for the September rape to the Japanese government in the hope that this gesture would smooth the way toward delicate upcoming government-to-government renegotiations of the two countries' mutual security agreement. Admiral Macke had been carefully selected by the Secretary of Defense for this important Pacific command post after his predecessor, Admiral Stanley Arthur, had been asked to take early retirement in the wake of *his* mishandling of a naval sexual harassment case. As a result of the 1990s Tailhook scandal involving senior Pentagon officials as well as young navy pilots, skills in navigating the rapids of the navy's gender and sexual politics took on bureaucratic significance. At the breakfast on that November morning, it was thus not surprising that a journalist should ask Admiral Macke about the Okinawa rape. The admiral, who may have believed that he was speaking off the record, replied: "I think it was absolutely stupid, I've said several times. For the price they paid to rent the car, they could have had a girl."[32]

Feminists in Okinawa and the United States used rather different historical contexts to make sense of the admiral's remarks. For Okinawan feminists, the Okinawa rape of 1995 was the latest chapter in the story of Okinawa's militarized history and of Okinawan women's own distinctive experiences of that colonized history. By contrast, for American feminists, the Okinawa rape and Admiral Macke's response to it were the next chapters in a story much closer to home, the Tailhook saga. For many American women in public office, the admiral's prostitution-is-a-given attitude revealed a cause of American women soldiers' repeated experiences of sexual harassment: a military that tolerates (maybe even fosters) prostitution is a military that will breed male soldiers who feel hostile toward women soldiers who refuse to act like sex objects. Foreign civilian women assaulted by these male soldiers were not themselves of immediate interest to these American advocates of women's rights.

Senator Dianne Feinstein, one of California's two women senators and a member of the Senate Foreign Relations Committee, was among those women politicians quickest to respond Admiral Macke's breakfast comments: "I would say to Navy Secretary John Dalton, your guys

Figure 7 Baseball hats on sale in early 1990s Okinawa are decorated with logos designed to appeal to American male military consumers. Sentiments such as these, worn jauntily on the heads of American men, helped to create a culture in which rape and prostitution became mutually supportive. (Photographer: Saundra Sturdevant. "Hats and shirts displaying ... Okinawa," in *Let the Good Times Roll* by Saundra Sturdevant and Brenda Stoltzfus, The New Press, New York, 1992, p. 298.)

still don't get it ... Rape isn't about money and it isn't about sex. It's about power over women."[33]

Many American congresswomen had garnered a lesson from the Tailhook affair and, before that, from the Anita Hill–Clarence Thomas hearings: it was necessary to respond assertively to any government official's trivialization of sexual harassment and assault by their male subordinates. In fact, Secretary of the Navy John Dalton's own predecessor had been forced to resign when the navy's cover-up of the Tailhook Association's 1991 convention conduct was exposed.[34] In their turn, some American senior officials in the executive branch also had learned to act quickly, before chain of command sexism was translated into the prime-time media headlines. Thus Admiral Macke was soon persuaded by his Defense Department superiors to take early retirement with a demotion shortly after his undiplomatic, though revealing, breakfast statement. This rapid bureaucratic response had the hoped-for result: a manageable political wake. According to one middle-level Defense Department official, while the admiral's forced retirement did prompt "some ink" to flow along the Pentagon corridors, it did not provoke any serious reconsideration of the policy presumption that the military's facilitation of prostitution served to protect respectable women and girls from rape by U.S. male personnel.[35] That presumption was left standing even as Admiral Macke packed his bags.

Back in Okinawa, Japanese and Okinawan feminists were crafting their own political analysis of the schoolgirl rape. They took into account the fact that, by the 1980s, a change had taken place in the ethnic makeup of the women working in the bars around the U.S. bases in Okinawa. Before the 1972 return of Okinawa to Japanese control, most of the women were ethnic Okinawan; fifteen years later, however, most were Filipinas who had immigrated in search of work. Many of these Filipinas told of being deceived by Filipino labor contractors and Japanese organized crime syndicates into believing that they were to acquire jobs they deemed more legitimate than military prostitution.[36] By the mid-1990s, as the Japanese yen's value continued to outstrip that of the U.S. dollar, it became harder for the Filipinas working in the bars and discos to attract American soldier clients, the worth of whose spending money was shrinking in the local economy. The Filipinas who stayed working in the district were older than the women who worked there when military men had more money to spend on off-duty entertainment.[37]

Japanese feminists had been trying to create supportive alliances with feminists in the Philippines. The "comfort women" issue, the spread of sex tourism, the movement of American troops from one militarized entertainment district to another throughout Asia, U.S. military men's sexual assaults on local women—each issue was providing a basis for a new kind of international politics among Asian women. But Japanese women engaged in this work had become aware that, just as relations between Okinawan women and other Japanese women were fraught with distrust and inequality, so too were those between Japanese women and women of the Philippines, South Korea, Taiwan, Australia, and Thailand. Thus the efforts by Okinawan feminists to reach out to Filipinas living in Olongapo were seen as part of their wider reimagining of Japan's place in Asia and their own place among Asian women.

Filipina-Japanese feminist cooperation was lively by 1995. Activists from the two countries found common cause in their opposition to violence against women.[38] They had worked together to prepare for the

Fourth UN Conference on Women held in Beijing in September 1995. Still, it proved difficult to make that alliance the focal point for Japanese and Okinawan feminist responses to the 1995 rape by the American military men. The potency of Okinawans' own local autonomy concerns and the Japanese peace movement's marginalization of feminist analyses of militarism, together with many American women's short overseas attention span, have helped create a formidable obstacle on the road to a more genuinely international feminist-informed alliance. Suzuyo recalls what it was like trying to introduce a feminist perspective on the schoolgirl's rape in a crowded meeting of Okinawan peace activists, many of them men: "I remember walking into a large hall where the anti-bases activists were meeting. A man pointed his finger at me as I entered—'You! You always only raise the violence against women issue. That's not political. That's not what the U.S.-Japanese Security Treaty is about!' I just pointed my finger back at him and said, 'You know only one-half of what security means if you don't think military violence against women is part of this issue!'"[39]

Suzuyo and other Okinawan women had already organized, despite this multisided obstacle, to critique the impact of militarization of women's lives. Thus in the aftermath of the September rape, they could set in motion a series of actions to attempt, first, to ensure that the local and Japanese peace movement would not miss the connections between this rape and other patterns of violence against women and, second, to encourage women's groups in the United States to understand that this rape was not simply the act of three individual American men, but the product of their government's foreign policy design.[40] In the name of a group called Okinawan Women Act against Military Violence, Suzuyo and others held press conferences, lobbied the Okinawan governor (himself anti-bases but not necessarily sensitive to the wider issues of violence against women), and sent a delegation to Tokyo to deliver petitions to the prime minister and foreign minister that called for a reduction of U.S. bases on Okinawa. The group briefed other Asian women's groups and organized a women's speaking tour to five U.S. cities.[41]

In March 1996, the Japanese court handed down its verdict. Navy Seaman Marcus Gill and Marine Private Rodrico Harp were found guilty of abduction and rape and given a seven-year sentence. Marine Private Kendric Ledet was found guilty of a somewhat lesser charge and sentenced to a six-and-one-half-year term in jail. Barbara Cannon, mother of Kendric Ledet, held a press conference to criticize the sentences, saying they were longer than the usual sentences handed down by Japanese judges in rape cases.[42] Okinawan and Japanese feminists, on the other hand, told the press that these sentences, like the majority of sentences meted out by the Japanese justice system in rape cases, were far too lenient. The feminists accused the Japanese political system of being continuingly unwilling to take seriously all kinds of violence against women.[43]

With the trials over and diplomatic apologies made and accepted, officials in Washington and Tokyo went about reconfirming their commitment to a military alliance. One major concession made by the United States government was to return to Okinawans land occupied by Futenma Air Base. This changeover would not, however, entail any reduction in the overall number of U.S. military personnel on the island.[44] While American base commanders issued orders that soldiers had to leave the entertainment district by midnight, high-level governmental declarations made no public mention of ongoing prostitution policy or of violence against women inside or outside any of the military institutions involved.[45] Okinawans held local referenda in which a majority of voters expressed opposition to continued U.S. military presence. But the Japanese government in Tokyo applied formidable public relations and behind-the-scenes pressure on residents and their elected officials, ultimately paying little heed to the referenda outcomes.[46] Japanese officials simultaneously met with their Washington counterparts to decide Okinawans' gendered militarized future. While U.S. personnel were being reduced in the Pacific as a whole, those based in Okinawa were set to play a more vital role in strategic planning for the new century: American forces stationed in Okinawa were to become responsible for a region stretching from North Korea to Somalia; Japan's own Defense Force was due, under the new bilateral agreement, to play a more expansive role in supporting future U.S. military operations. The American forces based on Okinawa would continue to be overwhelmingly male. They would still have to have rest and recreation.

In Okinawa, local feminists continued to put out news bulletins to publicize incidents in which American military men—and former military men, since a number had taken up residence in Okinawa after leaving the service—assaulted local women.[47] Feminists were trying to make the point that it was routine for these incidents of militarized violence against women to occur. That is, the root causes of the violence were deeper than the distorted desires of particular men. Moreover,

feminists wanted to make the point that it wasn't only the rape of an
innocent young schoolgirl that should inspire Okinawan, Japanese,
and American citizens to think hard about the relationships of governments' national security doctrines and the masculinized sexualized violence wielded by men of any nationality. Unfortunately, their persistent
message often was greeted with derision: the bases were what mattered, not "normal" male violence toward women.[48]

At the same time that the declining value of the dollar against the
yen was keeping visits to local bars and discos too expensive for the
lowest paid American military personnel, Japanese young women
from the main islands were developing internationalized consumer
tastes and new ideas about "adventure." Some came to Okinawa to
have an "experience" with an American man. The American sailors
and marines, in turn, seemed to undergo a reconceptualization of
themselves; they made adjustments now to appear not just as commercial patrons but as potential boyfriends. In this new mode, single
men living on base successfully persuaded U.S. base commanders to
change their policies about guests: as of 1997, single men as well as
married men could invite nonmilitary guests to their rooms on the
base.[49] The particular dynamics of militarized sexuality, it seems,
change with the evolution of internationalized gendered consumerism
and with the fluctuations of the international currency markets.
When the dollar regains its competitive edge against the yen, the sexual politics of militarized sexuality on Okinawa is likely to shift once
more.

In the midst of intergovernmental alliance adjustments and shifts in
the sexualized relations between American soldiers and different
groups of Asian women, some Okinawan feminists active in the anti-
bases movement also sought to rethink what it meant to be an antimilitarist woman. They began to form a feminist critique of the standard
rituals of the male-led peace movement. They took the local referenda
campaigns as occasions to fashion a new style of activism, a style that
would be drained of what some women now began to see was the
mainstream peace movement's masculinized culture. Women began
meeting in small groups, voicing concerns about the bases and ideas of
security in their own terms. They were self-conscious about creating
and sharing skills, building their own and each other's sense of public
self-confidence. When they met, there weren't any speeches. The day
before the December 11, 1997, referendum in the Okinawan city of
Naga, all the small local groups of women came together to hold a

"walk"—not a "march." They decided ahead of time that there would
be none of the usual peace movement's chanting, there would be no
raised fists, no prominent women public figures would lead the demonstration, no one would wear uniforms, no one would carry banners an-
nouncing their own group. Every women would wear what suited her,
every woman would walk through the town only as herself.[50]

After the referendum and despite its being overridden by the Japanese government, women who had taken part in the walk decided to
form a new alliance to continue the consciousness raising and critiquing of militarism in Okinawan daily life. They chose as the name
of their alliance, "May Our Women's Voices Speak to Your Heart." In
one of their first post-referendum actions, women of the alliance presented the Okinawan governor with a washbasin full of letters written
individually by women, each expressing in her own words her opposition to the new navy heliport. In Japan, the washbasin symbolizes the
last stop in accountability: "the washbasin stops here."[51]

RAPE AS AN INSTRUMENT OF NATIONAL SECURITY

If we concentrate too exclusively on either "recreational," prostitution-
linked rape or on wartime rape, we risk missing how rape has been
used to militarize women under regimes preoccupied with what they
define sweepingly as threats to "national security."

Chile and Argentina in the 1970s

the Philippines in the 1980s

Guatemala in the 1970s and 1980s

Iraq, Israel, and India in the 1980s and 1990s

Haiti, Indonesia, Bhutan, Zaire, China, and Turkey in the 1980s
and 1990s

Government officials in each of these thirteen countries have been accused of systematically using rape and the threat of rape to ensure
what they thought to be national security.[52]

It is not inevitable that rape will be wielded by all regimes that see
internal political opposition through the prism of national security. For
instance, British feminist researcher Sarah Benton warns us to pose a
specific question about the uses of rape in any civil conflict—that is,
not to assume it. In researching the violent conflict in Ireland during

the period following the 1916 Easter Uprising, Benton found plentiful
evidence that British security forces used oppressive methods against
suspected Irish nationalists, including women suspects: women's hair
cut off in order to humiliate them, private homes burned, cooperative
dairy creameries destroyed. "The catalogue of the terrorism of the
forces of the Crown is still shocking to read today."[53] But in the numerous contemporary reports, including the Irish parliament's own
weekly accounts of military and police abuses, she did not find evidence of systematic rape. Reaching this conclusion does not lead Benton to adopt a rosy portrait of British security operations during
1916–1922 (or later); nor does she conclude that the 1920s conflict
was ungendered. Rather, she goes on to explore how Irish popular presumptions of widespread rape by British forces were used at the time
to mobilize Irish women in the nationalist cause and simultaneously to
sustain a disempowering image of the Irish woman as needing the protection of a "brotherhood" of Irish nationalist male combatants.[54]

The conditions that do seem especially likely to produce militarized
rapes in the name of national security are (1) when a regime is preoccupied with "national security"; (2) when a majority of civilians believe that security is best understood as a military problem; (3) when
national security policy making is left to a largely masculinized policy
elite; (4) when the police and military security apparatuses are male-
dominated; (5) when the definitions of *honor, loyalty,* and *treason* are
derived from the institutional cultures of the police and the military;
(6) when those prevailing institutional cultures are misogynous;
(7) when men seen as security threats are imagined by security officials
to be most vulnerable in their roles as fathers, lovers, and husbands;
and importantly, (8) when some local women are well enough organized in opposition to regime policies to become publicly visible. If the
first seven of these eight conditions are permitted to develop, then militarized rape becomes more probable, even when the country is not engaged in open warfare. By the late 1970s, all eight conditions had become entrenched in countries otherwise as dissimilar as the Philippines
and Chile.

The Philippines

The most thoroughly militarized period in Filipino history came to an
end in 1986. A combination of peasant and labor activists, women's
groups, the Catholic hierarchy, middle-class women, and middle-class

men, joined in the end by mutinous soldiers, forced President Ferdinand Marcos and his politically influential wife, Emelda Marcos, to flee the country.[55] Together, the anti-Marcos activists called their movement "People Power." The Philippines thus ended fourteen years of martial law. The United States government, nervous about the future of its large military bases in the Philippines, was slow to back the People Power movement and its presidential candidate, Corazon Aquino.

The new post-Marcos government of Corazon Aquino adopted an ambivalent stance toward militarization. It did end martial law, tried to put more distance between the police and the army, staved off several attempted military coups, revitalized the legislature, and restored democratic elections. Aquino herself took seriously the new constitution's ban on presidents succeeding themselves and stood down after just one term, creating a precedent that proved impossible for her successor to violate. On the other side of the militarization ledger, the Aquino administration continued military operations against the leftist insurgent New People's Army. One of the strongest members of Aquino's cabinet was Fidel Ramos, a graduate of West Point with close ties to the U.S. military. He would succeed Aquino as president after winning the 1998 nationwide election.

In its pursuit of insurgents, the Philippine army followed a military doctrine that had been fashioned by the American military in the 1980s especially for use by allied governments against dissident forces in Central America. Just like automobiles and sneakers, military doctrines have become products for international export and import. They arrive packaged together with trainers, aid, and blueprints. This American-exported anti-insurgency doctrine was labeled "Low Intensity Conflict" (LIC). The hallmarks of the LIC doctrine, taught in American military academies, war colleges, and training courses were (1) official denial of open warfare; (2) a view of rural development projects as instruments of national security; (3) a presumption that civilians can be as dangerous as uniformed armed guerrillas; (4) the imposition of the label "communist" to discredit a wide range of government critics; (5) a strategic emphasis on psychological pressure; (6) the selective removal of populations; (7) the organization of local militias; and (8) the refined use of sophisticated methods of surveillance and interrogation.[56] Each of these eight elements in the LIC doctrinal package had a gendered consequence for Filipinos in the late 1980s.[57]

The myth of the dichotomy between "home front" and "battle-front," a dichotomy that has been a pillar of military thinking about women and men, crumbles in the midst of an LIC military sweep. When he and his troops burst into a peasant home or a village clinic, the counterinsurgency strategist does not blame his military maneuver for this disintegration of boundaries between battlefront and home front. Rather, he points to the insubordinate woman. It is the woman herself who tears apart the social fabric—the safety barrier between battlefront and home front—when she begins to stretch the confines of feminized domestic space so that it includes organized action with other women. Thus a woman who helps organize a day care center, a health clinic, or a literacy class can be seen by military commanders and anticommunist vigilantes as doubly subversive: not only is she challenging the government to provide adequate services, she is questioning the very sexual divisions of labor on which the current political order rests. Even with their first woman president, many Filipino security elites found this alternative vision threatening.

Lourdes Ignacio
DATE OF INCIDENT: April 19, 1987
PLACE OF INCIDENT: Paco, Flora, Kaling-Apayao
PERPETRATORS: unidentified soldiers
CIRCUMSTANCES: Victim is a farmer suspected as an NPA.
Her body was already decomposing when discovered. She was raped.

Gina Isidro, Rosie Paner, Edna Velez, Susan Ubamos
DATE OF INCIDENT: April 26, 1987
PLACE OF INCIDENT: Sitio Munungka, Brgy. Celestino C. Villacin, Negros Occidental
PERPETRATORS: 57th and 61st IB-PA under Col. Pablo Sencil
CIRCUMSTANCES: Victims are teenage girls raped by their military captors. They were suspected NPAs. Col. Sencil denied any knowledge of his men's killings in Cadiz and EB Magalona. He said the deaths resulted from his men's battles with the NPA.

So reported Gabriela, a broad coalition of Philippine women's organizations, in 1987.[58] By 1988, *Philippines Human Rights Update* documented a total of 636 cases of torture of men as well as women.[59] Rape was subsumed under torture. But the motivations for each rape and each victim's responses to rape were gendered. Some women were too ashamed to talk publicly about their experiences in detention, afraid that they would be thereafter rejected as "tainted," as "soiled goods." Some women who had endured militarized rape felt they had no choice but to pursue a job in the prostitution industry. Those women who did press charges against their assailants often experienced dismissal by other male officials. As one former detainee told researcher Anne-Marie Hilsdon: "When I pressed charges, the military officer in question denied that rape had taken place because I was neither upset nor appeared physically harmed: I looked 'too happy.' When pressing charges you have to show your bruises; your history is scrutinized."[60]

So it is that patriarchal ideas about what constitutes a respectable woman—a woman who upholds the national security by her shunning of political activism and by guarding her sexual purity—are used twice by security officials: first, when a woman is selected for arrest and torture, and second, when a woman bringing charges of rape is deemed believable or unbelievable by law enforcement agencies.[61]

Why did rape become so integral to the Philippine army's counterinsurgency? If we leave this question unasked, we risk falling into the assumption that rape is inevitable in any military operation in any society at any time. This assumption shores up the (mistaken) belief that there is no policy choice being made, that there is no one responsible— in other words, that soldiers' behavior is universal and ahistorical, that soldier-perpetrated rape is nonpolitical, that rape is nonpolitical. A more analytically useful task is to look for the decisions and the policy makers behind these acts of rape.

In general terms, as Filipina feminists have demonstrated in their research, Filipino late-twentieth-century culture is full of patriarchal presumptions and practices. The Filipino officials who chose to adopt the LIC military doctrine were taking steps to bolster those cultural strains. By categorizing women activists as "communists" and "subversives," those officials were wrapping a local form of patriarchy in the flag of national security. Moreover, by deciding to create and develop a military institution that was 99 percent male, policy makers were binding masculinism to the state. And finally, by setting up armed vigilante groups in the 1980s as masculinized semipublic militaries to conduct counterinsurgency operations, Filipino political elites were giving yet another sector of actors the political resources with which to validate the narrow view of Christian feminine respectability.[62] That is, the widespread occurrence of national security rape in the Philippines in the late 1980s was not merely the result of amorphous, pre-political cultural tendencies. It was the product of decisions.

Even the creation of an intra-army reform movement played its part in institutionalizing national security rape in the Philippines. The movement was organized in 1982 by middle-ranking male officers, most of whom were graduates of the Philippines Military Academy, the "class of '71." These young officers called themselves the Reform the Army Movement, or RAM. In their drive to professionalize the army, to purge it of the corruption that had thrived in the "cronyist" political climate of the militarized Marcos years, RAM officers enlisted an ideology of masculinity that was hostile to anything they imagined to be feminine.[63] These men became colonels during the Aquino years. These officers saw decisive military defeat of the leftist insurgents as proof that the Philippine military was being purged of its weaknesses, was being successfully modernized and remasculinized. The evidence does not suggest that the misogynist culture of the RAM generation alone was sufficient for the use of rape as a weapon of counterinsurgency. What it does indicate, nonetheless, is that the politics of masculinity inside any military called upon to carry out a government's national security policy may be a significant factor in determining just how reliant that policy's success is on contempt for women.[64]

By 1993, the Philippine Human Rights Commission was reporting a drop in the number of, though far from an end to, government human rights violations. The decline appeared to reflect the move by the Philippine government to scale back its counterinsurgency operations.[65] On the other hand, Filipino women's groups continued to charge that even nonmilitarized rape was dealt with lightly by a male-dominated law enforcement establishment, an institution that had been central to the earlier counterinsurgency operations. These women's groups had reached the theoretical conclusion that misogynist counterinsurgency, sexualized foreign military bases, and the risks Filipinas faced when they migrated overseas for jobs were each part of a political economy that sustained national patriarchy. Their strategic decisions flowing from this analysis were that no one of these three factors should be prioritized over the others and that new women's advocacy institutions had to be created that would address all three simultaneously. Thus, for instance, Filipinas active in Manila's Women's Crisis Centre (established in 1989) declared that their task was to address all forms of violence against women—and the connections between them. The organization declared that "women's individual concerns and problems should not be viewed in isolation. In discussing individualised violence against women, the larger sociopolitical and cultural environment that reinforces oppressive conditions for women must be looked at."[66]

Chile

Militarized rape carried on by a government's male security personnel most often has served as a form of torture. One Canadian survey of twenty-eight former women prisoners who had fled Latin America—from Chile, Argentina, Uruguay, Brazil, El Salvador, Honduras, Guatemala—found that 64 percent had been sexually abused during their detention and 44 percent had been "violently raped."[67]

Chilean feminist anthropologist Ximena Bunster is one of the few scholars to have investigated in detail how torturers have used rape in the name of national security. From 1973 to 1988, during the years of the military junta headed by General Augusto Pinochet, Bunster decided to employ her ethnographic skills—and feminist curiosity—in order to understand how and why male torturers integrated sexual assault into their treatment of female political prisoners. She set out to reveal the cultural beliefs, symbols, and rituals that informed Chilean torturers' gendered profession. Ximena Bunster treated torturers as particular persons: they themselves were gendered; they were overwhelmingly male and masculinized; they were particular men who were part of a larger political system and yet who had to have developed views of femininity, masculinity, and the nation in order to make sense of their daily inflictions of pain. Torturers are trained—in military doctrine, chain of command, social psychology, and anatomies.[68]

What Bunster discovered from interviewing women who had survived the ordeal was that male torturers relied heavily on the sexist presumptions of the wider Chilean society—especially the notion of the *marianismo* model of idealized femininity drawn from Catholic teachings about the Virgin Mary as morally pure and maternally self-sacrificing. The torturers wove into this popular conception their own ideas about "enemies within"—especially communist enemies—along with their self-identities as militarized, masculinized protectors of the nation.[69]

"The woman prisoner is brought blindfolded and hooded to one of the many *casas de tortura* (torture houses) administered by the security forces ... The woman has already undergone the trauma of arrest ... She has been cut off from her family; or, if her arrest went unobserved by relatives, neighbors or passers-by, she has 'disappeared' ... Some victims captured on the streets start shouting their own names aloud so that the family will know they were dragged away."[70]

The military national security rapists employed by the Pinochet regime believed that a respectable Chilean woman was one who stayed home and devoted herself to servicing her husband and children. A woman who strayed from this model, who participated in all-women anti-Pinochet rallies, who organized soup kitchens in the urban shanty-towns, thereby surrendered her protective shield of respectability.[71] She deserved to be raped, to be treated by the government's men as a "whore." By choosing to discard her cloak of feminized respectability, she was "asking for it." At the same time, a woman arrested and tortured because she was the wife or lover of a man suspected of subversive activities was threatened with rape precisely because her military torturers imagined that she was merely the suspected man's faithful helpmate. Militarized patriarchy is no more immune from contradictions than is nonmilitarized patriarchy.[72]

Ximena Bunster takes us into the gendered world of a national security detention center. We see it through the eyes of a recently arrested woman:

> She is then taken to another room, where a group of men undress her, literally tear her clothing and start slapping and beating her up continuously ... During the course of this brutal battering, she is given orders to sit down—there is never a chair—so she falls to the floor ... In the meantime she is the target of crude verbal abuse and vile ridicule of her naked body. She becomes the pathetic jester who amuses her torturers ... Fun is made of the shape of the woman's breasts, her birthmarks, or the scars left on her abdomen after a cesarean birth ...
> As interrogations continue, sexual torture is increased.[73]

Rape is deliberately integrated into an elaborately sexualized scenario of verbal and physical abuse. The rapist's (and his superior's) ultimate purpose is to rob the woman prisoner of all sense of self-respect, even identity. The aftershocks can last for years, perhaps decades.[74] Military torturers investigated by Bunster appeared to believe that if they could take from the woman all sense that she could control her sexuality and thus all sense that she could protect her feminine respectability, she would be reduced in her own eyes to a nonperson. As a nonperson, she would do as she was told: she would tell them what they wanted to know; upon release (if she survived), she would return to her home and confine herself to playing a woman's "proper" role. As in the Philippines, national security rape in Chile was an authorized public act designed to push women back into their privatized societal roles.

As potent as the essentialist component was in the Chilean soldiers' view of women, these men nonetheless did draw class and race distinctions between women: "Proletarian women and women with markedly *mesizo* features—the fusion of European and Indian admixtures—have been even more brutalized than their lighter sisters coming from bourgeois families."[75]

Still, no woman was safe during the Pinochet era. If she were suspected of anti-regime activities on her own or if she were the relative or lover of a man suspected of such activities, she was branded by officials as a threat to national security and thus a potential object of rape torture.

At the same time that the military regime was wielding its notions of feminine respectability inside the *casas de tortura,* General Pinochet, seen by American policy makers at the time as a bulwark against communism, was maneuvering women outside to embrace this patriarchal ideology as their contribution to national security. Through the state's *Secretaria Nacional de la Mujer* (Women's National Secretariat) and its *Cema Chile* (Chilean Mothers' Centers), the regime mobilized thousands of women to spread among other women this maternalist, domesticated, politically passive model of respectable women's behavior.[76] In the Pinochet regime's overall national security scheme, these women's activities and the horrors of the torture houses were intended to be two mutually reinforcing cogs in the same militarizing system.

Many Chilean women were indeed lured by the regime's overt manipulation of feminine respectability. But other Chilean women developed their own feminist consciousness by considering the patriarchal presumptions and rationales lying at the core of the Pinochet national security project. By the mid-1980s, these women had produced both a feminist theory of militarism and a formidable nationwide women's movement. Acting through a variety of organizations and in cross-class and cross-party coalitions, these women were instrumental in forcing the military to relinquish power after fifteen years of rule. In the process, they created a new wave of Chilean feminism. One of the first bills that women delegates in the democratically elected legislature put forward in the early 1990s was for the punishment of perpetrators of domestic violence. According to leading women political activists, it had been the experiences of gendered militarized violence that had made many women talk explicitly for the first time about the prevailing gender ideology that had for generations kept women silent about abuse they endured at the hands of the men in their lives.[77]

Today Chilean feminist discussions of violence against women are more likely than those in many other societies (for instance, the United States and Britain) to include a conscious analysis of militarization.[78]

"LOOTPILLAGEANDRAPE": WAR, RAPE, FEMINISM, AND NATIONALISM

Doctors without Frontiers (*Medecins sans Frontieres*), the international humanitarian group, sent Dr. Catherine Bonnet to Rwanda to assess the impact of the devastating 1994 civil war on women and children. She concluded that "the scope of rape in Rwanda defies imagination ... It appears that every adult woman and every adolescent girl spared a massacre by militias was then raped."[79]

A majority of the Rwandan women chosen for rape were from families identified by the rapists as being Tutsi or as being of the Hutu intelligencia.[80] Many families in prewar Rwanda were formed by cross-ethnicity marriages; thus the rapists often made quite arbitrary choices. Most of the rapists were men who identified themselves as Hutu and who were members of paramilitary groups organized by the Hutu-dominated ruling party and trained by the government's regular military.[81]

The wartime rapes were carefully provoked during the prewar period. The regime used radio programs and newspapers to persuade Hutu Rwandan men and women that Tutsi women were both traitorous and seductive, both arrogant and sexually desirable. According to government propaganda, no genuinely patriotic Rwandan man—and certainly no Rwandan soldier—should choose a Tutsi woman for his wife because she would only use her wifely position to infiltrate and undermine the real nation. On the other hand, Tutsi women were portrayed as flaunting their physical attributes, tempting Hutu men to lust and Hutu women to resentment. In this politically ethnicized construction, Tutsi women were imagined by those Hutus in power to be women deserving of rape and worth raping.[82]

Yet few of the many news reports coming from Rwanda during the 1994 conflict evidenced a curiosity about the use of rape as an instrument of ethnically specific oppression or of generalized terror. This lack of attention was partly the consequence of the journalists' own insufficiently gendered political curiosity about the experiences of African women and partly the result of many women survivors choosing out of humiliation and fear not to tell strangers of their ordeals.

Yet many Rwandan women, like thousands of Chinese, Jewish, German, Italian, and Bangladeshi women before them, did not want to allow to come to term pregnancies that originated in their rapes by soldiers. Consequently, they often overcame their fear and shame in order to tell anyone who might be able to provide them with abortions, abortions frequently made illegal by their own governments.[83] In Rwanda, Bonnet found that "disclosure occurs mainly to doctors and gynecologist-obstetricians because of: 1) visible genital infections, whose violent origins are disclosed in confidence; 2) attempted abortions after discovery of rape pregnancy (abortion is not legal in Rwanda); 3) request for therapeutic abortion at a late stage of pregnancy; 4) requests for 'advice' about the future of the child when the pregnancy is nearing term ... Maternity clinics run by Tutsis are seeing a great deal more women pregnant by rape than Hutu-run clinics."[84]

Reporting particular sorts of violence is as much a gendered process as war waging itself. If the laws of society, such as those of prewar and postwar Rwanda, make women second-class citizens in realms such as marriage and ownership of land, then it is all the more dangerous for a woman to risk her respectability and family's support by telling of her experiences of sexual assault. Thus Shana Swiss and Joan Giller, each of whom has conducted scores of interviews with women in war zones, warn activists who are genuinely concerned about wartime rape not to let their own concern turn into the objectification of women as victims: "The very process of human rights documentation may conflict with the needs of the individual survivor. Recounting the details of a traumatic experience may trigger an intense reliving of the event and, along with it, feelings of extreme vulnerability, humiliation, and despair."[85] Swiss tells of visiting one woman refugee who had previously been questioned by twelve other interviewers.[86]

One of the success stories of the second wave of the women's movement is indeed that so many women in so many cultures have come to feel empowered enough to report when they have been raped. Another success story of feminism's second wave is that so many people in authority are now compelled to take sexual assaults seriously and to record those reports. Reporting and recording—each is a political act. For her international atlas that graphically displays the conditions of women around the world, feminist geographer Joni Seager created a map on global rape. This double-page full-color map of the world documents the locations of widespread rapes during militarized conflicts of the early and mid-1990s: Rwanda, Georgia, Afghanistan, Angola,

Mozambique, Cambodia, Peru, Djibouti, East Timor, Turkey, Sri Lanka, Burma, Kashmir (India), Kuwait, Liberia, Papua New Guinea, Somalia, Sudan, Bosnia, Haiti, Mexico.[87] To this list we can now add Kosovo.[88] Different cultures, different religions, different political ideologies, different foreign allies, different modes of warfare, different military-civilian relationships—but in each situation the rapes of women were by men who thought of themselves as soldiers.

The sheer variety of wartime rape sites may lure us into reducing the cause of wartime rape to raw primal misogyny. And yet succumbing to this understandable analytical temptation carries with it several political risks: the risk that mere maleness will be accepted as the sufficient cause for wartime rape; the risk that the operation of particular military hierarchies will be deemed not worth examining; the risk that feminists will decide that they can do nothing to call individual rapists and their superiors to account or even, perhaps, to prevent rape in the next war.

Assuming that such a diffuse and elemental misogyny is the sufficient cause of wartime rapes carries with it yet another risk: paying dangerously little attention to the war-waging objectives to which rape is put by strategists and to the specific gender division of labor undergirding the definition of those objectives. For instance, *if* military strategists (and their civilian allies or superiors) imagine that women provide the backbone of the enemy's culture, *if* they define women chiefly as breeders, *if* they define women as men's property and as the symbols of men's honor, *if* they imagine that residential communities rely on women's work—*if* any or all these beliefs about society's proper gendered division of labor are held by war-waging policy makers—they will be tempted to devise an overall military operation that includes their male soldiers' sexual assault of women.[89]

Rape was elevated to the status of a serious political issue (versus merely war's inevitable, natural side effect) during the 1991–1995 war in the former Yugoslavia. This elevation was caused by carefully garnered evidence suggesting that the rapes in this war were systematic.

For any string of occurrences to be "systematic" they must be found to be not random, not ad hoc. Occurrences that are systematic are those that fall into a pattern. That finding, in turn, suggests that those occurrences haven't been left to chance. They have been the subject of prior planning. Systematic rapes are *administered* rapes.

By contrast, the well-worn litany of "lootpillageandrape" implies that male soldiers rape women the way a tornado inhales barns and tractors: anything that comes in the path of warfare, it is imagined analogously, is susceptible to warfare's random violence. Men caught up in the fury of battle cannot be expected to be subject to rules of conduct, much less the fine print of memos. Grabbing a stray chicken or a stray woman—it is simply what male soldiers do as they sweep across the landscape.

This portrait of battle breeds complacency. It blots out all intentionality.

The 1991–1995 war in the former Yugoslavia rattled this complacency. Many reporters, diplomats, and television viewers found themselves confronting rape directly for the first time. They became outraged. Perhaps more radically, they became curious.

By August 1992, staff people of the United Nations High Commission on Refugees (UNHCR) had been hearing frequent stories of rape among the Muslim Bosnian women who were arriving from war-torn cities in central Bosnia: 49 women among 4,000 refugees from Travnik had been willing to speak about being raped.[90] Yet no officials were assigned to investigate the incidence of or uses of rape by soldiers and their commanders. By November 1992, more reports of rape had appeared in the press, yet still the officials of the UNHCR and the International Committee of the Red Cross held on to their shared beliefs that the rapes were random and that they were being perpetrated and experienced on all sides in the intensifying ethnic conflict. Officials of both organizations were not being simply crass or patriarchal. They were acting out of their own institutional ethos and assessment of priorities: they were committed to remaining neutral, working with all governments. They were also, by late 1992, stretched to their limits. No more issues, please.[91]

It was a combination of energetic journalism and organized pressure brought to bear by women in antiwar groups and human rights groups that eventually initiated serious and methodical international agency investigations of the scale of rape and its purposes in the Bosnian war. This two-pronged campaign prompted justices of the International War Crimes Tribunal eventually to announce on June 27, 1996 the indictment of eight male Bosnian Serb military and police officers on charges of raping Bosnian Muslim women. It was a historic day in the *re*gendering of international organizations. The announcement marked the first time in history that rape was treated separately as a crime of war. In past international war crime trials, rape had been included but always as part of a string of charges; it was not given legal distinction.

Christian Chartier, a spokesman for the court meeting in the Hague, described the change: "There is no precedent for this. It is of major legal significance because it illustrates the court's strategy to focus on gender-related crimes and give them their proper place in the prosecution of war crimes."[92]

International organizations—from the World Health Organization and NATO to the International Red Cross and the International Labor Organization—are as deeply gendered as a corporate law firm or an Olympic gymnastics team. Sometimes, especially since the end of the Cold War, all these agencies and their sponsors are clumped together and referred to as "the international community." The founders, the maintainers, and each international organization's chief constituencies—those citizens who have a conscious stake in using them and influencing their decisions—have particular ideas about what is "normal" for women to do, what is "proper" for men to do, what is unsurprising when it happens to women, what is expected when men do it. The politics of each of these institutions—and thus also of this nebulous entity called the "international community"—will only be fully understood when each is subjected to feminist analysis.[93]

The Hague International War Crimes Tribunal's first chief prosecutor, South Africa's anti-apartheid attorney Richard Goldstone, admitted to a journalist that "rape has never been the concern of the international community ... [Now, however] we have to deal openly with these abuses."[94]

Once this new understanding of rape is articulated, how deeply entrenched will it be in the workings and consciousness of all the actors who try to shape the war crimes tribunal, itself still a fledgling institution? Any international institution—the World Trade Organization, European Union, UN Rapporteur on Violence against Women, International War Crimes Tribunal—should be closely monitored in its early years to determine how and why its internal culture and its formal doctrines become imbued with feminized or masculinized assumptions.

Thus, while many feminist human rights activists were gratified by the Tribunal's acknowledgment that rape is a distinct form of internationally condemned war crime, they were learning just how risky it was for any woman who had been raped in the Bosnian war to come forward and testify. Court procedures would have to be reassessed and reformed in ways that would make it safe for a woman to appear as a witness—and to then return home—without risking her already very precarious social standing or indeed her life.[95]

Feminists attentive to the politics of the Tribunal also were wary when Goldstone resigned and was replaced by the prosecutorial post's second occupant. The person serving as the Tribunal prosecutor carried a heavy responsibility, overseeing not only the trials in the Hague but also those in Arusha, Tanzania, site of the second war crimes tribunal. This second tribunal was created by the UN Security Council to try those accused of war crimes during the 1994 Rwanda civil conflict. It was the Arusha Tribunal that in fact handed down the very first guilty verdict by an international court that included rape as a genocidal crime. In September 1998, the three-judge panel found Jean-Paul Akayesu, a civilian major in the Hutuist regime of Rwanda, guilty of overseeing the systematic rapes of Tutsi women in his town during the 1994 violence.[96]

Feminists who made the international war crimes tribunals the object of their political efforts had lobbied for the appointment of a woman to succeed Goldstone as chief prosecutor but had had no direct access to the appointment process. Their initial reaction, thus, was positive when the United Nations announced in 1996 that the person selected was a woman, Canadian Appeals Court Judge Louise Arbour. On second look, however, some feminist human rights activists were dismayed. During her time both as a private attorney and as a judge on the Canadian bench, Louise Arbour appeared more concerned about the rights of men accused of rape than the rights of women victims of rape. In particular, Arbour had argued against the rape shield law, which prohibited defense lawyers from questioning rape victims about their sexual histories. Moreover, Arbour had argued that an institution as fragile as the war crimes tribunal would be ensured of international credibility only if it adhered strictly to the rights of the accused.[97]

On the other hand, Arbour was taking over responsibility for a set of international institutions (both the Hague and the Arusha tribunals) that suffered chronic underfunding by major governments and that had to rely on very reluctant NATO forces and several authoritarian African regimes to arrest the tribunals' prime war crime indictees. The chief prosecutor's job was not an easy one. The uncertainty of the long-range future of both tribunals was made clear in mid-1998. Officials from around the world gathered in Rome to hammer out a carefully worded agreement to create a *permanent* international war crimes tribunal. The U.S. government was among the more reluctant participants; its Pentagon officials launched a campaign to weaken the International Criminal Court. Backed by Republican leaders in the

Senate, the Defense Department argued that such a tribunal would become a forum for accusations against American armed forces.[98] The
department pressured other governments' delegates to the Rome conference to draft the war crimes tribunal treaty in a way that would severely curtail the permanent court's prosecutorial powers. This American demand placed Chief Prosecutor Arbour directly at odds with the
late twentieth century's most powerful military.

It also put Arbour on the same diplomatic side as the NGO Coalition for an International Criminal Court. In the forefront of that coalition, in turn, was the Women's Caucus for Gender Justice in the International Criminal Court, headed by Alda Facio, a Latin American
feminist.[99] The Women's Caucus activists came to the Rome conference to press diplomats to include language in the treaty that would
ensure that the permanent tribunal had jurisdiction over rape and
forced prostitution when either was committed on a systematic basis
or on a large scale. The Caucus activists lobbied late into the night and
forged alliances with those government delegations, such as the one
from Canada, who sought a strong court. The activists also lobbied to
gain commitments that women be appointed to all the new tribunal's
departments.[100] In early July 1998, the delegates of 120 governments
signed the treaty document, which included language ensuring that
rape would be treated as a war crime by the future International Criminal Court (ICC). The curtailing amendments proposed by the U.S. delegation were defeated. Among the seven governments refusing to sign
the ICC treaty were the United States, China, and Israel.[101]

Meanwhile, back in the Hague and Arusha, Chief Prosecutor Arbour continued to oversee the trials of persons accused of war crimes
in Bosnia and Rwanda. Observers wondered how her complicated international administrative and prosecutorial strategizing would affect
her commitment to the prosecution of wartime rapists.[102] When open
warfare flared up in the Serbian-controlled province of Kosovo in
March 1999, Arbour took the initiative to press for the Tribunal's
gathering of credible evidence of war crimes committed against the region's ethnic Albanians. Her first indictments, handed down in May
1999, held Serbian President Slobodan Milosevic, along with four of
his top aides, personally responsible for war crimes in Kosovo. Rape,
however, was not explicitly mentioned among the crimes, suggesting
that more evidence would need to be collected by human rights investigators.[103]

The wars in the former Yugoslavia, like all wars, have taken place at a particular point in the ongoing development of women's theorizing and organizing. Rapes in the American Revolution, rapes in the Boer War, rapes in World War II—each were conceptualized and responded to (or ignored) in large measure depending on how publicly self-conscious women were at the time about the gendered causes of militarized violence against women. By the 1990s, women legal activists, together with grassroots antiviolence activists, had developed a coherent feminist interpretation of human rights and a cross-national lobbying network with which to press for the adoption of this interpretation by heretofore masculinized international agencies. Rape in peacetime and rape in wartime were made explicit in this new feminist human rights discourse.

"Women's rights are human rights" was, nonetheless, a theoretical assertion (and a basis for organizing) still subjected to continuing debate even among feminists. Some feminists worried that so much preoccupation with rights would foster too individualistic a focus for feminist activism. It had been liberal feminism that had provided the most comfortable bridge connecting women's movements and international human rights politics. Liberal feminists, in turn, usually invested their energies in pursuing individual claims of equality. Those women's advocates who had come to their activism through socialist feminism, anti-racist feminism, or anti-colonial feminism were made uneasy by such classic liberal unquestioning acceptance of individualism. Then, too, other feminists keeping track of the "women's rights are human rights" efforts expressed concern that the very inclusiveness of the language of human rights might blind its users to vital political, economic, and cultural differences among women. "Humanness" was real, but it was not adequate to express the diversity of women's conditions and aspirations—and the tough political work that was needed if women were to build alliances by confronting, not denying, this diversity and inequality. The gains that those activists employing a feminist interpretation of human rights made in a growing number of international political sites, consequently, were achieved in the midst of a lively and ever more broadly international feminist dialogue. How to think about what had happened to women in Bosnia became part of that lively dialogue.[104]

Thus it was not mere happenstance that between 1992 and 1999, investigators from the UN Secretariat, the European Union, Human

Rights Watch, Amnesty International, and the Organization for Security and Cooperation in Europe each were moved to launch investigations of wartime rape in the former Yugoslavia. These investigations
were a critical part of the campaign that led to the Hague justices' subsequent change of consciousness toward rape as a separate war crime.
By 1999, each of these international institutions had concluded that
soldiers from all three militaries operating in Bosnia—Croat, Bosnian,
and Serb—perpetrated rapes, but that the main perpetrators had been
Bosnian Serb militiamen. Furthermore, the investigators concluded, the
rapes of civilian women had been routinely used to terrorize people,
forcing many to leave their hometowns. Because of the gendered dynamics that make it hard for many women of all cultures to speak
about experiences of sexual assault, any numbers that were gathered
were only estimates, but the European Union's investigators calculated
that in 1992 alone, 20,000 Muslim Bosnian women and girls had been
raped by Bosnian Serb male combatants.[105] By the time of the ceasefire in late 1995, the number of women from all communities who had
endured wartime rape was estimated to be between 30,000 and
50,000.[106] The numerical uncertainty reflected the ongoing gendered
politics of silence and denial.

The first United Nations–commissioned investigation into rapes in
Bosnia was issued in February 1993 and was headed by the Rapporteur on Human Rights, Tadeusz Mazowiecki. (His successor in 1998
was Mary Robinson, former president of Ireland.) This team began to
note the patterns to the rapes that hinted at intentionality. Mazowiecki
reported:

> Rape has been used as one method to terrorize civilian populations in
> villages and forcing ethnic groups to leave. One example of this was de-
> scribed by a physician who interviewed several women from the region
> of Vukovar (Croatia). There Serb paramilitary units would enter a vil-
> lage. Several women would be raped in the presence of others so that
> word would spread throughout the village and a climate of fear was cre-
> ated. Several days later, Yugoslav Popular Army (NJA) officers would ar-
> rive at the village offering permission to the non-Serb population to
> leave the village. Those male villagers who had wanted to stay then de-
> cided to leave with their women and children in order to protect them
> from being raped.
>
> In one pattern that was reported in several Serb-controlled areas, par-
> ticularly in Bosnia and Herzegovina, local Serb forces in conjunction
> from outside the area would occupy a village and restrict movement of
> the local population. Often, men were deported or fled. Women were
> then often raped in their own homes or taken from their homes to an-

other location and raped, often by neighbors or people known to them....

Although the team of experts heard stories about individuals, Croats, Muslims and Serbs, who risked their own safety to try and help their threatened neighbors, they heard of no attempts made by anyone in a position of authority to try and stop the raping of women and girls. In fact, some of those in power actively participated in it. One example for this was given by a Muslim woman living in a Serb-occupied town. She reported being taken by an ethnic Serb policeman to a private home where she was presented with the words: "Here she is, Commander. I brought her!" She recognized the "Commander" as one of the strongest political figures in the region before the war. He told her to go into his office, which was his bedroom, where he raped her.[107]

Just as militarized prostitution is usually the product of particular relationships between particular groups of people, so too sometimes, this UN report reveals, is militarized wartime rape. The Mazowiecki team report implicated the following:

local Serbian policemen

local paramilitary militiamen

Serbian men from other militias

officers of the Serb-controlled, Belgrade-directed Yugoslav army, the JNA

local male politicians who took on military positions once war began

These different men's roles in the rapes of Bosnia's Muslim and Croat women were not identical. Yet these men appeared to have been known to one another, relied upon by one another; on occasion, they may even have coordinated their actions. Militarized rape rarely is a lonely or isolated act. It occurs within structured relationships. The woman who endures a militarized rape has more than one man to accuse. German journalist Alexandra Stiglmeyer has collected profiles of three Bosnian Serb men who admitted to raping Croat and Muslim women. Each told of acting in groups, of being conscious of operating within a chain of command, and of carrying out rapes for the sake of some alleged larger war-waging purpose.[108]

"Ethnic cleansing" became the phrase used to describe what appears to have been the overall objective of this intentional pattern of rapes conducted and permitted and relied upon by different groups of Bosnian Serb and Serb men. Cherif Bassiouni, director of a later UN investigation, offers this definition: "Considered in the context of the conflicts in the former Yugoslavia, 'ethnic cleansing' means rendering an area ethnically homogeneous by using force or intimidation to remove persons of given groups from the area. 'Ethnic cleansing' is contrary to international law."[109]

As in Rwanda, in the former Yugoslavia many women lived in mixed-ethnic marriages. Under the Titoist communist regime, this intermarriage rate was even the source of state pride: out of mixed marriages between Serbs and Croats, between Croats and Muslims, between Serbs and Muslims came children whose identity would be "Yugoslav." Feminists within the former Yugoslavia too have made a point of noting with pride the rates of mixed marriages before the civil war. In the year 1991, 34 percent of all new marriages in Sarajevo were between women and men of different ethnic backgrounds. Between 1981 and 1991 in all of Bosnia (rural villages, towns and cities), 18.6 percent of marriages were inter-ethnic.[110]

Yugoslav feminists pointed to these intermarriage rates throughout the country precisely because this reality made controlling women's identities and residences so frustrating to militant nationalists: the politics of marriage are always close to the center of any patriarchal nationalist movement. But not all patriarchal nationalists wage war and not all choose rape as a weapon for waging their patriarchal war. Despite their own celebration of cross-ethnic marriage, the architects of the Titoist Yugoslav state simultaneously celebrated the military—and male military service—as central to the country's identity. Thus while the nationalist politicians promoting the 1991 to 1995 breakup of Yugoslavia called for the jettisoning of Titoist marriage politics, they built upon the Titoist belief in militarized masculinity.[111] For those militaristic nationalists who were intent upon breaking up the former Yugoslavia, militarized rape became a means for responding to their demographically frustrating lack of control of women that had been produced by intermarriage. According to Serbian feminist Stasa Zajovic, "seven million Yugoslavs had at least one cousin belonging to some other nation." She adds, tellingly, "Nationalistic propaganda, however, labeled these marriages as 'factories of bastards,' ...[Thus] the female body as a spoil of war becomes a territory whose borders spread through 'birth of enemy sons.'"[112]

"Serbian feminist" has been treated as a nonentity, even an oxymoron. Much of the mainstream media coverage, even that responsible for making visible the scale and pattern of rapes in the war, was so pre-

Figure 8 A Bosnian woman who survived rape allowed herself to be photographed with her daughter. By 1993, they had become refugees and had to make difficult decisions amid scarce resources and myriad pressures. (Photographer: Nina Berman/SIPA Press.)

occupied with the Serb political officialdom in Belgrade or with the ethnic leadership of the Bosnian Serbs that journalists implied that Serbs were a monolithic community. Much of the media have portrayed all Serbs as having identical relationships to wartime rape. In actuality, among the most vocal groups criticizing Belgrade officials for their complicity in the Bosnian Serb militiamen's perpetration of rape were Serbian feminist groups in Belgrade, such as Women in Black and the SOS Hotline for Women and Children.[113]

Making visible and taking seriously the analyses of these Serbian feminist groups, many of which have roots going back more than a decade, helps us assess the intentionality behind the wartime rapes in Bosnia.[114] First, these women's very existence as dissidents challenges the assumption that the wartime rapes are being done by "Serbs" rather than by *particular* Serbs for *particular* purposes. That recognition, in turn, prompts us to ask *which* Serbs, why *them*, why *then*. Second, these women's critical investigations, while pushed to the margins of Serb political life, suggest that rape in war has been part of a deliberate *policy,* not just ethnicity-run-wild. Third, Serb feminists' distinctive monitoring of daily life in wartime Serbia reveals how much the wartime operations being conducted across the border in Bosnia depended on the manipulation of Serbian women's senses of their femininity. Serbian women had to be persuaded to see themselves chiefly as feminine members of a national community.

Thus it was that Serbian feminists active in Women in Black (*Zene u Crnom*), for instance, denied Serbian President Milosevic the right to claim that his policy of supporting Serbian Bosnian militias was a policy supported by and in the interest of women of the Serb "nation." The feminists chose dramatic silence as their mode of political expression. Starting in 1991, a core group of twenty women, often joined by others, organized a silent protest vigil in downtown Belgrade every Wednesday. Senka Knezevic, a member of the group, explained: "We manifest our opposition by not allowing the regime to speak in our name. One of our most important messages to the regime ... is 'Do not speak in our name—we will speak for ourselves!'"[115]

Paying close attention to Serbian feminists while trying to make sense of the Bosnian wartime rapes encourages us to be conscious of the specific relationship between the varieties of feminist and the accused soldier-rapist. To one feminist, the rapist-soldier may be her government's enemy; to another he is a minor character on a distant stage; while to still another feminist he may be a fellow citizen.

Feminists from many different countries and ethnic groups took actions in the years between 1992 and 1998 to ensure that the rapes of Bosnian women were made visible and treated as a distinct phenomenon with political import and to guarantee that those women who suffered rape by soldiers received effective and appropriate support. Serbian feminists, Croatian feminists, Bosnian feminists (of several ethnicities) all worked to make these things happen. So too did Spanish and Italian feminists, German, Canadian, American, and Algerian feminists. Together, they shared many concepts, explanations, and objectives. For instance, they commonly held that both militarism and nationalism were frequently informed by patriarchal values and that, consequently, both militarism and nationalism could deepen the privileging of men as a group and masculinity as an idea.

For all their diversity, those feminists from various countries who took up the issue of wartime rapes in Bosnia generally agreed that even the most patriarchal militarist and nationalist leaders needed to mobilize support among women for several reasons: to ensure that mothers urged their sons to enlist in the various militaries; to guarantee that household economies worked despite the scarcities imposed by war waging; to garner sufficient popular support for the war-waging regimes to claim that their leaders were legitimate; to "reproduce the race."[116]

Nevertheless, a Serb feminist, a Croatian feminist, and a Bosnian feminist faced quite dissimilar traps when each insisted that the mass rapes in the Bosnian conflict be acknowledged. When Serbian women launched a center in Belgrade to support women subjected to all forms of male violence, they believed it politically crucial to make clear that (1) they would welcome women subjected to all forms of violence, that is, not just violence perpetrated in the heat of war on the front lines, but also violence perpetrated by men in the living rooms and bedrooms on the allegedly safe national home front; and (2) that women of all ethnic groups and nationalities would be welcomed. Without these clarifying principles, they decided, even a women's rape crisis center could be militarized in 1990s Belgrade.[117]

The hostility faced by Serbian women participating in protests against the Serbian regime came not only from the government but from ordinary Serbian fellow-citizens who supported it. A Serbian woman who decided to join the Belgrade chapter of Women in Black at their weekly antiwar silent vigils could be subjected to a range of derisive innuendoes:

A man passing by their vigil taunted, "When will you go to Zagreb?"

A woman passerby said defensively, "We Serbs from Serbia are different from those from Bosnia."

Another man challenged, "You are wearing excellent clothes. Who pays you?"

A woman dismissed them with, "Again those bullshitists!"

A man exclaimed, "Fuck you, tarts!"

Another man asked rhetorically, "What do these lesbians want?"[118]

On the other hand, precisely because a majority of the rapes in Bosnia were the acts of men identified as Serbian, those Croatian and Bosnian women choosing to make such rapes a topic of organized concern risked being publicly embraced enthusiastically by their own Croatian or Bosnian war-waging governments. Some, like Dubravka Ugresic, soon left Croatia under pressure but continued from outside to write critical accounts of the new masculinized, militarized Croatian nationalism. For these women, "Yugoslav" remained an identity worth trying to hang on to.[119] Others stayed in Croatia and organized support groups for women opposing their new country's gendered march toward militarism. These women kept a long arm's length away from the state. Some joined with those Bosnian women now forced to live in Croatia who had themselves experienced systematic rape in Serbian-run camps, such as the infamous Omarska, but who were trying to turn those experiences not into shame or revenge or silence, but into public testimony. The challenge was two-sided: first, to avoid becoming mere fodder for the story-hungry foreign media intent on using women's ordeals for the entertainment of their own home audiences; and second, to avoid becoming fodder for those Croat militarists who wanted to publicize the rapes of "their" women for the sake of postwar nationalist politics and perhaps future wars of communal revenge. Women working in Zagreb-based groups such as the Croatian Division of the International Association of Human Rights and the Association of Women of Bosnia-Herzegovina sought to devise ways of working with women that could lead to personal renewal and to internationally imposed nonmilitarized justice. Their mission proved very difficult.[120]

In October 1995, another group of Croatian women, researchers at the University of Zagreb, held a scholarly international conference on the "(En)gendering of Violence." They received official support from Croatia's nationalist regime of Franco Tudjman as well as from independent overseas funds. These women were not mere tools of the regime's propaganda machine, however. They were determined to persuade a skeptical male-dominated Croatian academia of the significance of gender analysis, and they were eager to make known to the wider world the results of their own research based on ethnographic work with women in Croatia's war zones and with women who had become war refugees.[121] Nonetheless, because these women were situated quite differently vis-à-vis the majority of the accused rapists, that is, Serbian men, no nationalists in Zagreb called these women traitors, tarts, or lesbians. Just the opposite. These Croatian women faced the danger of being hugged too warmly by their own militarized government.[122]

Feminists inside and outside the former Yugoslavia sent up warning signals when the Peace Accords were signed late in 1995 by the male leaders of the governments of Serbia (now Yugoslavia), Croatia, and

Bosnia at the U.S. Air Force Base in Dayton, Ohio. Wars do not end so neatly. The women of Belgrade's Women in Black sent out an invitation to women from other countries to come join them in a conference to weigh the impacts on women of the peace accords. They began their invitation with a caution:

> The war in former Yugoslavia has allegedly ended. It no longer gets the top story in world news agencies and TV stations. The suffering of the civilian population is no longer "popular" and does not cause pity ...
>
> Those of us who live in this region know that the war continues. The environment in which we live is permeated with the practice and logic of war and militarism.... This is carried out with the state's nationalistic-militaristic ideology and propaganda, so that women endure patriarchal violence in both the private and public spheres."[123]

What the organization was calling attention to was that domestic violence had increased inside homes in Belgrade during the 1991–1995 war, and that increase was no mere coincidence. The official nationalistic-militaristic ideology that fueled rapes in the Bosnian war zone had also fueled the battering of women in their homes back in Belgrade. The Women in Black conference organizers also wanted to share the lessons they had learned from working with refugee camps.[124] Women in refugee camps who had suffered rape were being pressured to suppress their own subjective understandings of their experiences and to become fodder for the next war—a war that could be waged by their real and symbolic fathers and brothers to overcome "our national shame."[125] Homophobia had become increasingly politicized as a weapon with which to delegitimize women protesters and to divide activist women.[126] Military commanders coming to Bosnia under the NATO banner to enforce the peace accords had to be persuaded that, if their personnel were not explicitly trained in relating to women who had undergone wartime sexual abuse, they might entrench the marginalizing effects of that abuse. An ill-trained patriarchal peacekeeping soldier could act in ways that prolonged any individual woman's war.[127] In 1996, Belgrade's Women in Black activists saw all these forms of militarized patriarchy as connected and as being very much alive and well, the Dayton Peace Accords notwithstanding. The activists turned out to be farsighted.

During the cold and damp winter months of November 1996 to March 1997, thousands of Serbians turned out on the streets of Belgrade day after day to protest the Milosevic regime's efforts to deny opposition parties their victories in local elections. For a time, it

seemed as though the protest was broad enough and stubborn enough
to bring down the regime, which was now being blamed for the
wartime losses in Bosnia, for the economic hardships brought on by international sanctions, for the corruption in Milosevic's inner circle
(aside from Milosevic's wife, this circle consisted of men who exploited
those same sanctions in order to profit from smuggling), and for the
stifling of public dissent. Despite provocations, the demonstrators
maintained a code of nonviolence.[128] Many of the protesters were participating in their first venture into an openly defiant demonstration,
but many of the feminists had been out on the streets demonstrating
with Women in Black for five years. These feminists had developed
analyses of violence and skills of expression that would not provoke or
rely on militaristic forms of action. Thus Serbian feminists were among
those most active in persuading the 1996–97 demonstrators that nonviolence would enhance their political effectiveness. Some feminists
saw a critique of violence in all its forms as central to the protest. They
distributed whistles to be blown as expressions of resistance to all
forms of violence, including violence against women. Accompanying
the whistles was this pamphlet written by the Belgrade's Women's
Lobby:

Women, Let's Whistle!
Women whistlers and walkers
We are supporting protests on the streets of Belgrade and

- When I whistle I hear myself
- When I whistle the others hear me
- By whistling I protect myself
- By whistling I am stronger

Did you know

- That whistle is a traditional tool of women's self defense from those
  who are harassing, attacking and raping us.
- That in one suburb of Lima, in Peru, women have opposed violence
  of their husbands with whistles. Women have whistled when he intended to slap or hit her. The neighbors immediately responded and
  protected the women. In one week, violence against women ...
  drastically decreased.
- That organized whistling is a form of civil disobedience.

Whistling is courageous
Whistling is nice
Whistling is feminine

After the protest don't throw (away your) whistles
Let's whistle!
If somebody attacks you on the street, in the elevator, in the bus, in the
workplace, in your own bed.

With the whistle we are stronger.
Let's whistle without whistles as well! [129]

These whistle-blowing Serbian feminists, like feminists in Croatia, Bosnia, the Philippines, Japan, and Chile, have seen the logic in making visible and explicit the causal connections between militarism and all forms of violence against women. The feminists' evolving theorizing led them to a conviction that tackling one without tackling the other made neither theoretical nor strategic sense. Yet to many nonfeminist peace and antimilitarism activists—their best potential allies—the feminists' logic appeared distracting at best, threatening at worst. These critics became all the more dismissive when their antimilitarism derived from their own notions of nationalism. For them, the feminists' efforts to talk openly about men's violence against women—not just the violence wielded by the enemy's or foreigners' military men, but the violence perpetrated by civilian and military men of all communities—seemed divisive, alien, and perhaps even traitorous.

By the spring of 1997, Milosevic had outlasted the demonstrators. Their pro-democracy efforts were not taken seriously by those Western governments that had come to rely on Milosevic to implement the Dayton Peace Accords. Milosevic had made marginal concessions to the political party leaders, especially those who defined themselves as Serb nationalists, by offering them minor roles in his government and allowing them to take office in several of the cities that they had won electorally. At the same time, however, he starved them of funds with which to effectively govern. A certain brand of competitive party politics, according to some Serbian feminists, eventually overwhelmed a broader alliance. Party politics, even where a few women took on visible roles, also privileged a masculinized political style. Moreover, not all those demonstrators who had walked, sung, and faced down the police were consciously shedding militarized ideas of nationalism. As three Serbian feminists explained several months later to feminists in other countries, "We are not under the illusion that in Serbia, infected with the most bitter nationalist-militarist ideology in the past ten years, such [a] cultural mentality disappears overnight." [130]

A year later, their analysis seemed to be confirmed. Serbian feminists were having to direct their meager resources to challenge the militarization of neighboring Kosovo. This Belgrade-controlled province had only a small ethnic Serb minority, but had long been imagined by Serb nationalists to be a landscape saturated with patriotic meaning. It had been on the plains of Kosovo that Serbs had fought the soldiers of the Ottoman Empire. By 1998, the Milosevic regime's heavy-handed authoritarian rule over the mainly Albanian population had created a radicalized resentment throughout Kosovo. For months the principal Kosovar ethnic Albanian leadership had mobilized nonviolent resistance to Belgrade's silencing and Serb-privileging policies. But as the oppressiveness increased in the form of police raids of local citizens, that approach and the leadership who proposed it began to lose its appeal, especially among the province's ethnic Albanian younger men. A new Albanian group, espousing full independence for Kosovo, now argued that peaceful resistance had run its course, that the time had arrived for Albanian men to take up arms, to use violent means to confront Belgrade's police, army, and paramilitary forces. Spring 1998 appeared to be a significant moment in the gendered political history of all Yugoslavia's ethnic communities. While the Serbian government's militarized actions seemed to be on the brink of provoking a dramatic increase in the militarization of Kosovar Albanian masculinity, Belgrade's nationalist regime was having to rely on police units to conduct its militarized Kosovar operations because growing numbers of Serbian men were becoming disenchanted with soldiering away from home for the sake of a Greater Serbia.[131]

While Serbian feminists tried to resist Belgrade's nationalist appeals to Serbian women and tried to provide support for small groups of Kosovo women activists, Kosovar Albanian men were choosing between nonviolent action and enlistment in the newly formed Kosovo Liberation Army (KLA). As more men chose guerrilla warfare in the KLA, a force whose leaders exhibited little desire to give up any of the privileges of patriarchy, more ethnic Albanian women were having to decide how they would relate to the two expressions of Albanian masculinity and how they would respond to the devastating militarization of Belgrade's ethnocentric rule.[132]

As women in late-twentieth-century Northern Ireland, Sri Lanka, Chechnya, Rwanda, and the Sudan could testify, such dual processes of gendered militarization radically shrink the spaces available for women to craft their own domestic, national, and international politics against rape and other forms of violence against women. In May 1998, a full year before most of the world was paying any attention to the es-

calating militarism in Kosovo, Belgrade's women activists published a
warning that women activists elsewhere would find ominously familiar: if the militarization of masculinity is built upon the exclusion of
others and the painting of feminist critics as national traitors, the outcome in today's world is not likely to be a merely local conflict; it is
likely to be internationalized war. The Belgrade feminists began their
multilayered analytical caveat with this assertion: "We start from patriarchy."[133]

BRUTES, BOYS, AND GENTLEMEN

During imprisonment, the blindfold may have slipped, or it may have
been deliberately removed so she could witness pain inflicted on a husband or a child. Thus it is that a Chilean woman who survived imprisonment during Pinochet's rule might have imprinted on her memory
the faces of her abusers. In the months following the fall of the militarized national security regime, Chilean women report, they frequently
caught sight of their former torturer-rapists—on the street, in restaurants.

Women in Rwanda, Bosnia, and Kosovo have been urged by international aid agencies to return to their homes. There they, too, might
encounter a neighbor-turned-wartime-rapist.

Demilitarization in many countries has posed a dilemma: how to
entrench democracy, how to hold its opponents accountable and yet
not become so preoccupied with earlier atrocities that the past swal-
lows up the present and stymies the future. Women human rights advocates have invested considerable energy in resolving this puzzle.[134]
Practically, a resolution often has come down to determining who
should be tried and punished for their complicity in militarized rape-
as-torture. This determination, in turn, has required thinking about
military hierarchy. A feminist approach can prove useful in fashioning
a strategy for a demilitarizing justice.

One of the most distinguishing characteristics of any military institution is the explicitness of its hierarchy—its "chain of command." Even
a bureaucratized civil service doesn't require some officials to salute
others, or some officials to wear stripes while others are bedecked in
stars. But for a military, saluting and insignia are the telltale signs that
this institution is culturally committed to ensuring that inequality of
rank is never forgotten. The objective of a military's blatant and ritual-
ized inequality is to guarantee that authority is so crystal clear that it is

always—and quickly—obeyed. The other side of the military's coin should be that responsibility for decisions is transparent.

Class-differentiated notions about masculinity (frequently laced with racism) have been used by most militaries to reinforce this artificial ranking system. Thus, for instance, the officer is presumed to be a "gentleman." If he is not born one, then he must be taught to act like one. Male cadets at military academies—the next generation of officers—take lessons beyond map reading and engineering. If they can endure the dramatically *un*genteel initiation hazing, male cadets go on to learn how to dance a proper foxtrot with a lady, handle eating utensils properly in polite company, maybe even play golf. It is a gentlemanly officer, so the institutional presumption runs, who will command the respect of his less-polished rank-and-file soldiers. The latter's crude "boyishness" makes them valuable fighters but not suitable officers.

This class-dichotomized ideology of masculinities is woven into most military chains of command. It is an ideology of masculinities that serves to cloud the windows of transparency. It is an ideology of masculinities that can shield senior military officers from charges of rape or torture.

If the militarized rapist can be portrayed as a lower-class, lower-ranking brute-of-a-boy, then the upper-class, senior-ranking gentleman-of-an-officer acquires some protection. A gentlemanly officer may seduce; he does not, so the militarized gender mythology goes, rape. Still, the presumption of chain of command remains. Lower-ranking soldiers, even of a brutish variety, are only supposed to do what their superior officers order them to do. Consequently, an attempted defense for the officer charged with commanding (or performing) rape (as torture or as an instrument of war) must be a wobbly combination of classist masculinity and institutional inefficiency.

It is a combination not so far removed from that employed to protect the military senior command from charges of being the orchestrators of prostitution. The "boys will be boys" explanation for the inevitability of militarized prostitution is strikingly similar to the "rapists must be brutes" rationale for the inevitability of sexualized assault on battlefields and in military jails. Both rely on dichotomized masculinities among military men for the sake of distancing senior male officers from the sexualized abuse of women.

5

IF A WOMAN IS "MARRIED TO THE MILITARY," WHO IS THE HUSBAND?

The recent spate of feature films inspired by the novels of Jane Austen may seem an odd place to look for information on militaries. Most commentators note that Jane Austen herself, while acutely aware of the Napoleonic wars embroiling Britain and the nations of Europe during her lifetime, deliberately chose to keep her fictional lens angled away from the battlefield; she focused instead on the parlor.[1] But in her final novel, *Persuasion*, published in 1818, Jane Austen seemed intent on persuading her readers that marrying an officer in the Royal Navy was a very wise decision for a smart, spirited young woman of the landed (but precariously financed) English gentry. Earlier, in *Pride and Prejudice*, Austen had cautioned her readers that army officers on leave were only superficial in their appeal.[2] But perhaps having two brothers of her own in the King's navy disposed Jane Austen more favorably toward the seafaring branch of the military. Part of the attraction of a navy officer, Captain Wentworth, for *Persuasion*'s heroine, Anne Elliot, daughter of a small-minded, social-climbing, spendthrift father, was the chance he offered to Anne to belong to a community suffused with genuine camaraderie and meritocracy. Anne got a tantalizing taste of navy family life when she observed Captain Wentworth at ease with a fellow officer and his wife: "There was so much attachment to Captain Wentworth in all this, and such a bewitching charm in a degree of hospitality, so uncommon, so unlike the usual style of give-and-take invitations, and dinners of formality and display ... 'These would have been all my friends,' was her thought."[3]

Then too it was possible for a British navy captain during the Napoleonic wars to make a comfortable income capturing enemy ships and their cargoes. Finally, there was the opportunity for a senior officer's wife to make her life aboard her husband's ship. She could sail with her officer-husband far from the pleasant but-all-too-familiar green confines of southern England. Anne listened with envy as an admiral's wife described her mind-expanding, ocean-going military marriage: "In the fifteen years of my marriage ... I have crossed the Atlantic four times, and have been once to the East Indies, and back again ... besides being in different places about home—Cork, and Lisbon, and Gibraltar."[4]

In Austen's eyes, it was precisely because Anne Elliot was a woman of such lively intelligence, immune to petty considerations of rank, that her becoming a military wife—or, more specifically, the wife of a senior naval officer—seemed so liberating a prospect. If such a marriage was militarizing, then it seemed militarization would be emancipating.

Despite Jane Austen's own favorable assessment of marriage to a certain sort of military man, however, nineteenth-century Britain's male military planners, Captain Wentworth's superiors, developed quite mixed feelings about the institution of marriage. In general, marriage jeopardized a military's global effectiveness: "In short, it is evident that the presence of large numbers of women and children with a body of men intended for quick movements and for service in distant colonies, and for occasional fight is in the last degree inconvenient."[5]

Should military men marry? The concern of policy makers rarely was for the military wife. Even the well-being of the soldier-husband was of only secondary interest. What mattered to policy makers—and what still is uppermost in officials' minds—is the military's own institutional well-being. Thus a government's question is: what marriage strategy best serves the military? The answers have shifted over time and between cultures. But what seems striking is the persistent ambivalence. Patriarchal states of all brands—feudal, socialist, liberal, Stalinist, fascist, croneyist—have (at least in their rhetoric and their laws) promoted marriage.[6] But those same patriarchal states seem to have lost their assurance when they have come to their own soldiery. On the matter of whether male soldiers of the state should marry, states' principal attitude over time has been uncertainty.

Prior to the Crimean War, a generation after Austen's assessment, nineteenth-century British social opinion (and military official opinion as well) imagined the ordinary soldier as little more than a beast. Then in the late nineteenth century there emerged a new appreciation of the fighting man as a moral creature, a man who would fight all the better if his moral dimension were cultivated—by a woman, and especially by a loyal, respectable, patriotic wife. As one member of Parliament explained: "I believe that if there is a time when the home affections press most strongly upon [soldiers], it is not only in the heat of battle, but in the silence and loneliness of the wards of the hospital. Having lost everything but their kit and knapsack, they have produced to me, over and over again, from the linings of their coats, letters from the families whom they have left in England ... It is remarkable that every one of those letters which I saw, breathed the fondest affections; many of them expressed a woman's tenderness and a woman's fears; but not one of them invited the man to return home until the victory had been gained."[7]

And so a deliberate policy shift occurred. Henceforth, ordinary British soldiers would be allowed to marry. Perhaps, British officials thought, marriage—an institution arranged so that wives would provide material, spiritual, and sexual services to husbands—would make the military's men less indebted, more reliable, and less prone to disease.

Military wives long have been the subjects of shifting policy calculations. They still are.

Today, as Hollywood reacquaints today's moviegoers with Austen's witty comparisons of army and navy husbands, British and American military strategists are trying to refashion their organizations to fit the post–Cold War realities: (1) fewer soldiers; (2) fewer overseas bases and consequently more frequent, longer deployments away from home; and (3) dependence on professionalized volunteer soldiers. All three changes are requiring new marriage maneuvers. The current attitudes not only of military officials but of those women married to soldiers remain distinctly unsettled.

In many ways, a woman married to a soldier (or sailor or pilot) experiences pressures and obstacles common to *all* women who are wives. She is often presumed to be dependent on the man who is her husband, not simply for her financial well-being, but for her very identity; her social class or rank is derived from her husband's class or rank; she still is expected to adapt her own life to whatever uprootings her husband's job requires; she is pressed to see herself as the helpmate to her husband, regardless of her talents or waged employment; she typically is expected to be sexually available to her husband and to tolerate his occasional extramarital lapses.

However, on top of these demands, which all women-as-wives may experience (and try to defy), a woman married to a soldier has to cope with the demands peculiar to being a military wife: she is defined by society not only by her relationship to a particular man, but by her membership in a powerful state institution; she is seen not just as a particular soldier's wife, but as a military wife. Moreover, she lives in a social world often deliberately insulated from the "real world" (as many military people call the civilian world) and thus loses much of the potential support from women in that wider, less tightly controlled civilian world.[8]

Many of the elements of economic well-being in the military come in the form not of cash wages, but of privileges (e.g., access to the base store, to medical services); yet these privileges come to women solely by way of their soldier-husband's military status. Also, women married to soldiers are considered a part of an institution that to an extraordinary degree is infused with an explicitly masculine ethos. A woman's wifely femininity, as a result, is valued by military officials only insofar as it enhances militarized masculinity. Femininity and wifeliness must not be permitted to interfere with or dilute the male bonding that remains the preferred glue holding together military units.

Canadian military activist wife Lucie Laliberte and sociologist-researcher Deborah Harrison, after interviewing scores of Canadian soldiers and soldiers' wives, concluded that the present-day Canadian military establishment deemed male bonding so essential to the entire institution's combat mission that it lent its own authority to the wife-excluding practices of ordinary soldiers. Periodic wife-exclusion was not a maneuver designed to ban all forms of femininity from the military culture. Rather, wife exclusion was in part designed to permit the military command to preserve a space for another form of femininity, a form officials deemed to be more nurturing of a masculinized military culture:

> According to [Canadian] military folklore, any man whose wife enters or telephones the Mess [club] during TGIF is a "wimp" who cannot control her ... Men consequently develop ways of ensuring that their wives will not come to (or telephone) the Mess, and they erect a united phalanx against wives who disobey ...

> Even husbands' and wives' mutual affection is a problem for the military because conjugal intimacy is a threat to combat bonding. Military rules prohibit PDAs ("public displays of affection") under any circumstances. But no rules prohibit members from viewing sex shows ... because the women in these instances can be represented as the sexual property of all.[9]

Despite the Victorian shift in military familial calculations, many commanders seem most comfortable when they can treat their troops as if they were permanent bachelors: energetic adolescents or worldly Beau Brummells. Controlling their troops' sexual encounters with those women whom the military can categorize as prostitutes (because they are poor and/or are racial outsiders) is a nuisance. But at least, in many military commanders' eyes, those relationships are casual and commercial and—if effectively controlled by cooperative local authorities, military doctors, military police, and sometimes military chaplains—they can even prove useful in convincing their otherwise downtrodden male soldiers that they are "real men," heroes, and conquerors.

In contrast, when a male soldier seeks a more permanent and socially sanctioned relationship with a woman, military officials may get nervous. They may envision his loyalties being divided and his mobility obstructed. The military command foresees its own resources being diverted from military pay and weaponry to social workers, housing, and day-care centers. It visualizes an alien presence—civilian women and children—on base and "manly" soldiers transformed into uncombative "henpecked husbands."

Over the generations military commanders and their civilian political superiors have tried, nonetheless, to reconcile their worries with reality by finding militarized uses for those women who have married soldiers. But this reconciliation has required a lot of thinking. It has required the exercise of institutional control: only if those women can be socialized to *become* military wives can they perhaps further some of the military's own goals. For instance, in times of war, a properly socialized officer's wife can be mobilized to calm the anxieties of the wives of enlisted men. Women as military wives can help win civilian support and sympathy for the military by making it seem a less brutal or insulated institution. Military wives can—if they do find their own militarized lives satisfying—persuade their husbands to reenlist. Finally, military wives can—if properly controlled—give male soldiers emotional support and incentives to "act like men" in battle.

So much hinges on whether a woman married to a soldier will invest her talents and aspirations—and her pride and satisfaction—in the militarized career of her husband. An African American woman, once married to a soldier, offered this explanation to her daughter: "If your husband is in the military, everyone [in the family] is in the military; it is the only way to survive and advance in the military. The military base is its own community. Everything is on base ... These types of social activities can help in the advancement of your husband, because the more visual you are, the more people know who you are, the more you get ... The general's son may be on the same [little league baseball] team as the corporal's son, so sometimes kids can be used to help advancement."[10]

This explanation is not offered by a woman who sees herself as having been a pawn. Looking back, she still believes she was advancing her entire family's welfare by directing her energies toward ensuring the promotion of her soldier-husband. Thanks in part to her militarized wifely efforts, this woman's husband achieved the rank of a senior noncommissioned officer.

THE MILITARY WIFE AS A POLITICAL "PROBLEM"

In the early 1990s, the commandant of the U.S. marine corps could not contain his frustration with the "problem" of wives any longer. In the summer of 1993, the commandant issued a unilateral order: he instructed his subordinates to start phasing out the enlistment of any recruits who were married. Unfortunately for Commandant Carl Mundy, he had forgotten to obtain approval for his radical policy from his own superiors, the secretary of defense and the president. Both disagreed. The commandant's order was quickly rescinded.[11] But his frustration was not just the product of one man's idiosyncratic quirk. It had historical roots reaching deep down into the history of masculinized militaries' ambivalence toward marriage:

Historian Myna Trustram describes Britain's military marriage debate between 1850 and 1880, a time during which the British military expanded its imperial responsibilities. Not coincidentally, this expansion took place at the same time as the more celebrated controversy over the Contagious Diseases Acts.[12] Women as wives and women as prostitutes then, as now, are connected in military policies. But the connection is militarily effective only if its existence as a conscious policy can be denied. In mid-nineteenth-century Britain, officials believed that *as long as* male soldiers' morale and reenlistment could be ensured without taking responsibility for wives and children, it made sense to discourage troops from marrying. Recruiting officers who traveled from town to town in Britain in fact enticed young men to join the army as a way to escape their wives: "If any gentleman, soldiers or others have a mind to serve Her Majesty, and pull down the French King; if any prentices have severe masters, any children have undutiful parents; if any servants have too little wages, or any husband too much wife, let them repair to the noble Sergeant Kite, at the sign of the Raven in this good town of Shrewsbury."[13]

In 1871, only 1.5 percent of the British army's rank-and-file soldiers aged twenty to twenty-four were married, as contrasted to 23.03 percent of British male civilians at the time. Among older soldiers, aged thirty to thirty-four, the marriage rate rose to 25 percent, but this rate was still far below the male civilian marriage rate of 75 percent.[14] By 1971, a century later, one-third of British male soldiers had wives and/or children, and by 1979 two-thirds of male soldiers were married. It was a slow process by which the British army accepted the necessity not only of allowing soldiers to marry, but of providing soldiers' wives with decent living conditions and soldiers with pay adequate to support a family.

Permitting marriage became more imperative as the tours of duty to which British soldiers committed themselves were shortened and thus reenlistment decisions came more frequently in the life of any soldier. In the 1860s and 1870s, additionally, the British army came under political pressure to conform to Victorian social morality and ensure that soldiers were orderly, moral men civilized by domestic ties. This conformity, in turn, meant that women relating to soldiers should be made into "angels of the house," providing their husbands with comfort and moral uplift. For military commanders who had thought of soldiers' wives as "useless sloths ... miserable drabs who are seen sauntering and smoking in the yard," this new approach required a radical change in gender ideology.[15]

It was not until 1960, nevertheless, that the British army surrendered its cherished pay concept of the single soldier. Only then did the military salary structure finally repeal the disincentives for ordinary soldiers to marry. But with this change came the military's increased control of women who were married to soldiers.[16]

In 1942 the U.S. Congress passed a law that provided some obstetric care and minimal family allowances to American military wives.

And according to military social workers, it was only in the years following the Vietnam War that the American military establishment took the matter of military families seriously.[17] Whereas in 1953, in the midst of the Korean War, less than 38 percent of American military personnel were married, by 1982, in the post-Vietnam, post-draft military, 51 percent were married.[18]

In recent decades a major transformation of the American military has come in the form of more and more enlisted personnel choosing to marry.[19] The marital inclinations of enlisted men have brought into "the military family" thousands of young military wives, women in their late teens and early twenties who never have lived away from home before and often have little experience in household management or waged work.

The U.S. military enters the new century with a less certain mission—torn between war waging and peacekeeping—but its marital profile is becoming more stable. In 1995, 60.1 percent of all military personnel were married—the highest marriage rate in this military's history. Nonetheless, marriage inclinations still varied by rank and by branch of the military. While 73.5 percent of all American officers were married in the mid-nineties, only 57.3 percent of all enlisted personnel were married.[20] The very lowest ranking men were least likely to combine marriage with soldiering, but it was especially the lower ranking marines who seemed to practice marriage-avoidance: in 1995, only 27.8 percent of marines at the four lowest ranks (E1–E4) were married. By contrast, 47.9 percent of their lower-ranking counterparts among the air force's enlisted personnel were married. Achieving senior officer rank, on the other hand, had the effect of enhancing marriage's attractiveness across all four branches: 87.2 percent of senior naval officers and 92 percent of senior marine corps officers were married.[21] These differences in marriage rates between the services once again suggests that there may be quite dissimilar militarism-masculinity-marriage ideologies being played out inside any military.

American military officials have appeared more ready than their British counterparts to mobilize public resources to try to solve—or perhaps absorb—family problems. They have awarded Defense Department contracts to civilian social scientists to study everything from military youth problems to family budgets. Scores of civilian sociologists and psychologists have found in the Pentagon's embrace of social science and social work a source of research funding, captive subjects to study, and an attentive audience for their conclusions. Perhaps the explanation for the differences between British and American policy attitudes lies in the latter's lack of a comprehensive welfare state— whittled down even further in the late 1990s—to draw on to solve those problems; the American military's officials have had to create their own solution. Perhaps, too, the difference stems from the two countries' distinct locations during the Cold War. Between 1945 and 1989, the U.S. military vastly expanded its global mission (often taking over from the British military in areas like East Africa and the Indian Ocean). While the postimperial British forces continued to have personnel based in Germany, Hong Kong, and Belize, it was their American allies who were hardest pressed to guarantee that, despite the strains imposed on wives by overseas deployments, soldiers signed up for second, third, and fourth voluntary tours.

In the late twentieth century, it would take a subtle and complex formula to maneuver women into conforming to the model of the Good Military Wife. For women living the lives of military wives, there is a chasm between the institution's rhetoric, which asserts that "the military is a family," and the daily isolation the wives often experience. Their husbands are an integral part of an institution that is defined as essential to the meaning of manhood and that is deemed crucial to the nation's security. Military wives, on the other hand, are fundamentally marginal, at least to the publicly articulated meaning of the military, even while they are integral to that same institution's day-to-day maintenance.

Despite their real and apparent privilege, even those women married to senior military officers can feel alienated. Researcher Doreen Lehr interviewed U.S. air force officers' wives during the early 1990s. They voiced concern about not doing anything that might hurt their husbands' careers. A 1988 Defense Department directive—brought about in large measure by concerted lobbying by military wives—made wives' involuntary volunteering illegal. The major policy change was brought about by those military wives who lobbied women members of Congress, who, in turn, brought their influence to bear on Pentagon male officials. Yet the pressure on officers' wives to volunteer persisted. Thus, even if their own husbands did not push them into doing unpaid volunteer work on the base, the women themselves told Lehr that they still felt they should. Refusing to volunteer might look bad in the eyes of the people whose evaluations would determine their husbands' chances for promotion: the base commander and the commander's wife.[22]

And the stakes had become higher in the 1990s American military. With the end of the Cold War, the government was cutting the number of military personnel. That meant fewer senior officers, fewer promotions, more competition for the fewer promotions available. But this intensifying pressure was coming at a time in the history of American marriage when more women, including those married to soldiers, expected marriage to be a partnership between equals and also presumed that an adult woman should have a waged job of her own. Doreen Lehr herself had been a military officer's wife. She listened between the lines as these women worried out loud about the escalating strains shaping their lives as militarized wives. In their late-twentieth-century American heads they carried a list of risky behaviors: "A military wife's refusal to comply with the military system; their housekeeping ability; their appearance; their civilian employment; reporting domestic abuse; offending a senior officer or his wife; or living by their own rather than military standards."[23]

THE MODEL MILITARY WIFE

Every institution that relies on employees who are married is prone to send out messages about what the ideal spouse should be. The "ideal" is measured in terms of what attitudes and behavior enhance their partner's contribution to the objectives of that institution. Colonial plantation companies, universities, diplomatic corps, law firms, major league baseball teams, secret services, elected legislatures—and militaries—each of these institutions have distinct notions about what sort of spouse is best suited to the institution's own well-being and what those spouses should be doing to maximize their value to the organization. What is distinctive about militaries is how clear and how patriarchally feminized that message is. It is spelled out in rituals, in memos, in orders, and in handbooks written by military wives themselves.[24]

The Model Military Wife in the twentieth-century modern military might include the following features:

She has come to her own conclusion that the most important thing for her own and her family's well-being is that her husband perform his military job well.

She feels as though not only her husband but she herself is an integral part of what she thinks of as "the military family."

Being a supportive military wife gives her a genuine sense that she is doing her "patriotic duty."

She realizes that she has to accept a number of restrictions, but she views those restrictions as a logical and crucial building block in "national security."

The material benefits that are accorded her as a military wife are, in her eyes, a source of security and satisfaction.

She is a good mother; her children do not get into trouble, or if they do, she does not burden her husband unduly with these maternal worries.

This list is just the beginning, perhaps the toes-to-knees part of the profile of a Model Military Wife for the contemporary era. There's more:

She has become a very competent occasional single parent and head of household when her soldier-husband is off on a training tour or deployed to a war zone. She knows how to handle the checkbook, fix the plumbing, renew the car insurance.

Still, she does not take inordinate pride in her competence. The weeks when he is away are, to her, an inevitable but "unnormal" time; a happy, "normal" time resumes when he returns. She is pleased to relinquish the head-of-household mantel when her husband is home.[25]

She accepts that waging war—or keeping the militarized peace—is a high-stress occupation, and so she makes allowances for her husband's moodiness, short temper, and impatience in the weeks and months following his deployment to a conflict zone.

She acknowledges the hard work generated by her husband's constant transfers (packing up, unpacking, getting the children adjusted to new schools), but mainly she sees these moves as chances to make new friends and explore new places.

If she and her husband come from ethnic or racial groups that are subjected to discrimination in the civilian world, this model military wife is grateful to the military for providing a special opportunity for acquiring income, training, and public respect.

She is quite comfortable with social relations based on rank: they seem natural; they provide an aura of order in an otherwise uncertain world.

As she rises along with her husband through the ranks, she gains a sense of expanded authority and responsibility by helping younger wives learn—and accept—the military ropes.

She enjoys unpaid volunteer work; it helps her husband's career and it makes her feel a useful member of the military community.

She is sexually faithful.

She accepts that soldier-husbands do not tell their wives everything, so she would think it neither worthwhile nor appropriate to ask her husband about clandestine missions or about any sexual activity he might engage in while away from home.

She takes pride in her son, or nowadays perhaps even her daughter, following in her husband's footsteps by deciding as a teenager to join the military.

The increasing likelihood that her husband will now have female military colleagues on the job does not cause her anxiety.

She does not feel much need to express herself politically beyond the periodic marking of a ballot.

She is prepared to remain militarized in her wifely dedication long after her husband's departure from actual service, supporting him in his interpretations of the meanings of his military actions, sometimes in the face of the public's critical reassessment of those actions.[26]

Few women in reality manage to squeeze themselves into this snug, idealized mold. But many try. Some women reap genuine rewards from trying. Women who are married to senior officers in those militaries that enjoy social and economic privileges may be particularly prone to struggling to live up to the ideal. The wives of senior officers in 1970s Chile, Guatemala, the Soviet Union, Argentina, Taiwan, and South Korea (before those countries' pro-democracy movements reduced some of each military's privileges), wives of ambitious senior officers in 1990s Indonesia, Burma, China, Mexico, Iraq, and Nigeria—all these women might find living up to the expectations of a model military wife more than worth the effort.[27] We would know a great deal more

about exactly how military politics (and economics) work in each of
these twelve countries if we devoted energy to learning more about the
lives and thoughts of the military wives.

In May 1998 a spate of news stories described the Indonesian military. It long had been the single most influential institution in that
country's political system, but it took the emergence of a pro-
democracy movement led by students and urban poor residents to attract most journalists' attention. Indonesian women married to officers
were among that country's most privileged women. The military had
been the bastion of the "New Order" Suharto-led regime from 1965 to
1998. The decisive factor in compelling Suharto to resign from the
presidency was the decision by senior military officers to join the reformers in pressing Suharto, to whom they had been deeply loyal for
three decades, to resign. Men in military's upper reaches had the opportunity to become partners in lucrative businesses while still on active duty. Increasingly, it was young men from the country's growing
middle class who were seeking careers in the military. The military,
perhaps even more so since some of its officers sided with reformers in
calling for less authoritarianism and less corruption, had about it the
aura not only of nationalist pride but of economic opportunity. These
men's wives continued to enjoy privileged lives. In exchange, the government expected them to perform certain duties: "Each service has a
wives' organization that all spouses are expected to join and which are
chaired at each level by the senior officer's wife. The role of these organizations is to provide a venue for social interaction, to promote social
solidarity within the armed forces and loyalty to the regime, and to do
charity work."[28]

During the mounting protests against Suharto's rule that occurred
during April and early May 1998, there was some speculation concerning how aware military officers—being called on by Suharto to suppress the dissidents—were about the depths of alienation among the
civilian population, alienation that had been rising since the economic
crisis rippled its way through the lives of ordinary Indonesians. Were
military men out of touch? An advisor to Megawati Sukarnoputri, the
most prominent woman in the pro-reform alliance, hoped out loud
that the military was aware of the people's hardships and thus would
be wise enough to use restraint against the demonstrators: "Even the
soldiers are affected by the pain ... Their wives are calling to ask them
where the money is."[29] In this crisis, the possibility that wives of soldiers were *not* isolated, were not cocooned inside a militarized social

world, may have helped the military keep its legitimacy in the eyes of the public.[30]

Within days after Suharto's resignation, Defense Minister General Wiranto, thought to have been a critical player in the withdrawal of military support from the president, announced that his wife would be resigning her seat in the Consultative Assembly.[31] Her resignation, announced by her husband, not by herself, suggested that Suharto as president had placed the wives of important inner circle male loyalists in public positions. Maybe an Indonesian feminist will soon conduct a study of the role of wives and of marriage in the politics maintaining the New Order regime for thirty years.[32]

MILITARIZING CHAPLAINS, PSYCHOLOGISTS, AND SOCIAL WORKERS

Precisely because the ideal is so hard to obtain—or sustain—some militaries today have had to hire specialists to plaster over the gaps between actual lives and that militarized ideal. In the British and American forces today, these specialists' jobs are harder than ever and more crucial to the military than ever precisely because so many of the current pressures are working in directions opposite to that ideal of the Model Military Wife.

The British military has depended on the volunteers, nurses, and social workers (mostly women) of the Soldiers, Sailors, and Air Force Association (SSAFA), which was founded in 1885 in the wake of marriage being more positively assessed for male soldiering and in response to the late Victorians' "rediscovery of the poor, among whom were most women married to rank-and-file soldiers."[33] Paralleling SSAFA have been four groups of mostly male military specialists: chaplains, psychiatrists, medical officers, and family officers. Together, their mission has been to cope with the problems posed by the militarization of family life. Most of these social service personnel have operated at the local base level and have been subject to the base commander's authority, which has limited their autonomy and influence. The British military, unlike its American counterpart, has been slow to directly employ professional social workers.[34]

Among the earliest recruits to do SSAFA's work were the wives of military officers. Officers' wives were thought to be especially well equipped to provide these services because they were women, because they were middle class, and because they were uniquely familiar with the problems posed by military life. This sort of unpaid work also kept an officer's wife attached to her husband's regiment while he was abroad, thus perpetuating the notion of the regiment as a community. On the eve of the Thatcher government's 1982 Falklands War, it was still routine for the SSAFA garrison committee to be headed by the wife of the base commanding officer.[35]

In the 1980s, in reaction to the growing proportion of young male soldiers who were marrying and having children and to the civilian consciousness of violence within families of all sorts, SSAFA created a child abuse register, but since SSAFA nurses and social workers had no powers and were subject to military rule and law, the ultimate decision on any child abuse case remained in the hands of the base commander.[36] The British military establishment, especially the army, has been wary of social workers and generally has kept the services that deal with military wives as peripheral as it has the wives themselves. This detachment represented a mixed blessing. On the one hand, military wives' needs were often neglected. On the other hand, Britain's social workers were not fully militarized. The military seemed to resist, give in, waffle, then retrench on the question of whether the military itself should provide social service to military families; but what remained constant was the criterion against which any given scheme is tested: the military's own effectiveness and the maximization of its own capacity for mobility, discipline, and strategic force.

Nevertheless, the 1990s pressures on the government to reduce Britain's military personnel exacerbated the social stress experienced not only by soldiers but also their spouses. So the SSAFA was called upon to make "downsizing" palatable. When, in 1993, six thousand army personnel received a brown envelope containing their redundancy notices, among the soldiers'—and their wives'—first worries was where they were going to live: they had lost not only their income, but their housing. The Conservative government became nervous about its slide in the public opinion polls and saw homeless soldiers as something less than a vote-winner, so it joined SSAFA with the Ministry of Defence's Armed Forces Financial Advisory Services and a savings bank in Birmingham to launch a scheme that would provide low-cost civilian housing to soldiers and their families while they looked for new jobs.[37] It is one thing for professional military men to eschew what they dismiss as social work responsibilities; it is quite another, however, for a governing party to leave itself exposed to civilian anger for being insensitive to the needs of soldiers and their families.

The U.S. military has been far less reluctant to use social scientists and social workers in its efforts to devise strategies to socialize women into being contented military wives and thereby to reduce family problems that might undermine military readiness and reenlistment. Today every branch of the armed forces has an elaborate family services unit that works with the military's medical services and its chaplaincy. By the late 1990s, the Defense Department's family service specialists were expected to cope with more than two million American military spouses and their children. Already by 1995, there were more U.S. military children and spouses than there were U.S. uniformed personnel.[38]

Militaries move. Mobility is one of the hallmarks of a military. The Pentagon's social science advisors are supposed to help the military—and the military families—make those moves. Wives enhance a military to the extent that they assist soldiers' mobility. Wives are a problem to the extent that they are a drag on soldiers' mobility. For a military wife, a transfer order means taking the children out of school and surrendering a hard-to-get, even if low-paid, job. Once transferred, she must again try to make often shabby housing livable, help the children readjust, make new friends, find a new job. One daughter of a military wife recalls longing out loud after one move that she wished she could go home. Her mother replied, "You are home." The family moved eleven times while this young woman was growing up. Her mother, a successful military wife, rehung a sign in each new kitchen: "Home is where the army sends you."[39]

Being told by their own social workers and by outside social science consultants that these strains are hurting their soldiers' morale and cutting into reenlistments, Pentagon officials began in the 1980s to take more seriously the strains of moving. By the mid-1990s, the military family services offered by military social workers had become elaborate. The Defense Department's own "Military Family" newsletter contained articles about seminars on child abuse, workshops on domestic violence, plans for new youth programs, profiles of male soldiers who were learning to be better fathers, job data banks for military spouses. These articles continue today to be directed less to military wives themselves than to the social service professionals whose job it is to ensure that family members do not jeopardize the U.S. military's post–Cold War global missions.[40]

Chaplains support the work of military social workers. In the U.S. military, chaplains act as family officers, although they identify most closely with the soldiers themselves. The Vietnam War prompted many army chaplains to question the idea that they were an instrument in the hands of commanders designed to keep up the troops' morale. Because chaplains are inside the regular military structure and depend on a commander's evaluation for their own promotion, they have been understandably reluctant to act on their own skepticism.[41]

Whether their post–Vietnam era questioning could overcome their own personal investments in the military hierarchy determined how much effective assistance they could provide to women on base. After all, providing that assistance—say, to a woman being battered by her officer-husband—could arouse the irritation of the chaplain's military superior. That, in turn, could endanger the chaplain's own military career. A military chaplain is embedded in the military's hierarchical chain of command. Although there are some women chaplains, most are male. It is not clear how or whether they attempt to provide an alternative form of militarized masculinity to male soldiers—or whether they succeed if they try.

Some of the contradictions faced by military social workers are identical to those experienced by civilian social workers employed by state welfare bureaucracies: they may be motivated by the desire to help individuals, but they depend on the authority of a state that is suspicious of or hostile to those individuals. But the military social worker is part of an even tighter chain of command and has less access to those civilian political support groups—feminists or a progressive party organization—trying to monitor and transform the welfare system in which the social worker plays so instrumental a role. The military social worker works within an establishment that sees women-as-wives not just as a potential financial drain (a theme certainly familiar to civilian social workers) but as a threat to its mobility and fighting capacity.

In addition to chaplains and social workers, the U.S. military has mobilized psychiatrists and social scientists to fine-tune its personnel. As recently revealed by historian Ellen Herman, the U.S. military has drawn into its fold more-than-willing psychiatrists to keep its soldiers psychologically fit to fight, while it simultaneously has used chaplains and social workers to keep soldiers' wives supportive of their husbands' combat readiness.[42] The American military establishment also contracts out many of its social service functions commercially. Scores of academically affiliated sociologists have agreed to conduct research for the Department of Defense—on housing, spouse employment, recreation, child abuse, and dual career families. As funds for social science research from civilian agencies have become scarcer and as the Defense Department has become more worried about fashioning a policy on military wives that will serve its reenlistment and readiness needs, some American academics and their university administrations are likely to be more tempted to compete for Defense Department research contracts.

WHEN DIVORCE BECOMES AN ISSUE OF NATIONAL SECURITY

As the American military prepares for the new century, an era when it will have fewer permanent overseas bases but still a global vision of its mission, the political knot between military wives and military operational effectiveness has been tightened another notch. Shipping soldiers in an all-volunteer, largely married military at short notice to operations in the Persian Gulf, Haiti, Somalia, Bosnia, or Kosovo has become dependent on effective management of soldiers' spouses and their children. "In the three-month period when most of the troops returned home, divorce rates have surged from 37 percent to as high as 56 percent over a year ago in communities near three large Army bases that sent troops to the gulf."[43]

News that divorce rates among U.S. soldiers went up after the Gulf War sent tremors down those corridors of the Pentagon. The Gulf War, after all, had been a short war; it had been a "successful" war. It was supposed to have been the war that finally dispelled Americans' post–Vietnam War malaise. On the American side, the Gulf conflict was also a war fought with sophisticated family policies. There were support groups not only for military wives, but for military girlfriends. There were telephone hot lines and crisis centers and special communications hookups between the U.S. and sand-swept Saudi Arabia. No government's war-waging strategy ever had incorporated such elaborate and deliberate use of social science and social work professionalism.

Still, by the end of the short Gulf War, many American military marriages had come unglued. Not only were divorces spiraling, but social workers were alarmed at the number of reported cases of child abuse in the homes of returning soldiers. Military mental health workers noted that many American soldiers sent to the Middle East in 1991—60 percent of them—were much more likely to be married and have children than had been their fathers and uncles drafted in the 1960s and 1970s to fight America's war in Southeast Asia. And though more American women soldiers were deployed in the Gulf War than in the earlier Vietnam War, 93 percent of all the U.S. soldiers sent to the Gulf were male. While the "military husband" made news, it was military wives who were the problem in the eyes of the military:

American troops lived in searing desert camps, isolated from the Saudi people and fearful of Scud missile attacks. Hours of boredom were punctuated by alarms warning of possible poison gas attacks.

Bottled up during the war, these anxieties are now being uncorked at home and mixed with concerns like financial hardships or a child's slipping school grades.[44]

It would be a mistake to imagine that all the actions taken to ensure that American military wives—and girlfriends—stayed loyal to their soldier-husbands and their military mission were actions crafted along the pentagonal corridors of the Defense Department. Militarization does not always require such total control. Especially if militarized beliefs and values already are rooted in a society, the military itself may only have to provide legitimation, an encouraging nudge here, a supportive nudge there. Thus many members of the American society in 1990 and 1991 seemed quite self-propelled to motivate women close to male soldiers to express their loyalty to these men and their mission. The most notable form such actions took was the making, displaying, and wearing of the now-familiar yellow ribbon.[45] While the yellow ribbon phenomenon did crop up occasionally in Britain and in Canada, both of whose governments also sent troops to fight the Iraqi forces in the Gulf, the ribbons were nowhere nearly as prevalent in either of these countries. We have yet to conduct detailed ethnographies to determine the gendered origins and gendered stages of the American yellow ribbon phenomenon, but as so often now happens in American militarized social eras, individual initiatives came to be mixed with commercial campaigns and governmental interventions to create a heady cultural brew. The anthropologist Nina Browne observed the ways in which television producers of one program, *The Home Show,* sought to manipulate the yellow ribbon expression: "Women who had written to [U.S.] soldiers in the Gulf to find their pen-pal efforts paid off in a wedding engagement were interviewed more than once. One day in March [1991] the show presented (with much hurried excitement and romance) the work of a woman fashion designer: a line of wedding gowns for patriotic brides which 'tastefully' incorporated yellow, red, white and blue ribbons, hawked as perfect for brides whose grooms might be shipped off at any moment."[46]

The blossoming of yellow ribbons in sites that ranged from secretarial in-trays to officials' lapels and daytime television shows allowed very little public space for any American military wife or fiancée to oppose the Gulf War waging policy. But some women found other ways to express their dissent, if not from government policy, at least from their own wifely participation in its implementation. In the years subsequent to the Gulf War evidence continued to mount that militarized social services had failed to keep up with the problems faced by American soldiers and their families in the 1990s. In 1995, *New York Times* defense correspondent Eric Schmitt reported that "Gulf veterans are experiencing higher rates of unemployment, divorce and alcohol abuse than Vietnam-era vets."[47]

The increasing frequency of deployments has continued to create what one reporter called "psychic holes" in the fabric of military family life.[48] At Fort Drum in upstate New York, home of the Army's 10th Mountain Division, soldiers had been to Somalia and then to Haiti. The base's social support professionals, together with volunteers, had attempted to create a safety net: classes in stress management, informational meetings, spiritual support, legal services, tips on car maintenance. Yet the strain showed. Some children felt distant from their soldier-fathers and acted out at school; some soldiers' wives suffered depression. Other wives found that they learned new skills while their husbands were away and that they were proud of their newly sensed independence. But this independence in turn caused stress between those women and their returning husbands. Sergeant Ed Sigmund was candid in his confusion when he returned from his 1995 peacekeeping tour in Haiti to find that his wife did not want to "go back to normal": "When you are away, they have to take care of everything. When you first come back, you have got to take it easy."[49]

It was not clear that the sergeant's newly confident wife would want to turn back the clock in their relationship after just a few weeks of readjustment. Furthermore, the 10th Mountain Division had its own brand of militarized masculinity that was generating other stresses. It was a light infantry unit, one whose male soldiers typically went into warfare as part of a second wave after the first-strike forces. The men who had chosen the 10th Mountain Division did not expect that they would be doing peacekeeping; they had looked forward to traditional war waging, not mere policing. Thus in the 1990s, the soldier-husbands of the 10th Mountain were trying to handle simultaneously two assaults on their manliness: peacekeeping instead of war waging and equality in marriage instead of playing the manly head of household. It was not surprising, perhaps, that the number of divorces among the families stationed at Fort Drum was going up after each recent deployment.[50]

It was the Clinton administration that placed a new institutional emphasis on coping with the strains posed by less-than-fully-militarized military wives. President Clinton appointed Carolyn Becraft to the crucial position of Deputy Assistant Secretary of Defense for Personnel Support, Families, and Education. Becraft had been a familiar figure in congressional committee hearings for a decade, working as an independent advocate for the rights of both women in the military and military wives, first through the Women's Equity Action League and then through the Women's Research and Educational Institute. Lobbying from the outside, she had been one of the prime movers in persuading the Defense Department to issue its 1988 ruling prohibiting senior commanders from requiring that the wives of senior officers give up full-time paid employment in order to perform all the volunteer duties expected of a senior officer's wife.[51]

In the years following the Gulf War, the principal ideological weapon in the hands of Becraft and her family-advocate insider colleagues remained the concept of military "readiness." Its bureaucratic beauty derived from its malleability: readiness could be used to refer to everything—from the state of truck repair to the quality of troops' training. Readiness requires, wives' advocates contended, that a wife's depression or impoverishment not make a soldier reluctant to board ship. Readiness requires that a male soldier be sure enough of his wife's sexual fidelity back home that he can give his primary attention to following orders in battle. Paradoxically, in the discourse of readiness—a militarized policy discourse that had its origins in the Reagan years—the needs of wives are attended to today in order to ensure that a male soldier's first loyalty is to the military.

A Pentagon task force issued a mid-1990s report on the military's working and living conditions. The report was especially critical of the state of military housing. Thirty-three percent of American military families worldwide lived in housing provided by the government, while the remaining 67 percent had to find housing in the private civilian housing sector, using allowances paid by the government.[52] The authors paid special attention to the impacts of family conditions because, the report's authors argued, neglecting spouses and children could undermine the performance of soldiers: "forces satisfied with their quality of life are motivated to fight—this is the 'iron law of readiness.'"[53]

Readiness is closely tied to retention. Even in the post–Cold War era, when the U.S. military has been shedding manpower, an armed force needs to pay close attention to retaining personnel. A military is falling short of a full state of readiness if it cannot recruit the new personnel it requires or if it cannot retain the seasoned soldiers it already has (expensively) trained. A 1993 study of the army confirmed a belief already widely held among military personnel specialists: the opinions of a soldier's spouse are critical when that soldier comes to decide whether to reenlist or quit. In fact, concluded researchers Mady Segal and Jesse Harris, in the 1990s the "spouse's attitude sometimes has more influence on the soldier's actual reenlistment behavior than the soldier's own predilection."[54]

An American army wife's encouraging her husband to reenlist is dependent on whether she believes her uniformed husband is gaining satisfaction from his military work; whether she values the financial security afforded by her spouse's military job; and whether she is looking forward to enjoying the military's generous retirement benefits.[55]

Further down the list of factors affecting an army wife's decision to urge her husband to sign up for another tour of duty are whether she believes that the military is a good place to raise children; whether she is convinced that senior defense officials genuinely care about families; whether she thinks the military is sending her husband away more and more often without provision for her to accompany him; and whether she finds that she can obtain a satisfying, well-paying job for herself.[56]

The U.S. military's 20,000-soldier peacekeeping operation in Bosnia, following the 1995 Dayton Peace Accord, provided a chance for the Defense Department to put into practice the lessons it derived from the Gulf War. It introduced its own page on the World Wide Web. "Bosnia Link," it was hoped, would not only circumvent the media, giving the Pentagon direct access to the computerized public, but also enable the Defense Department to have an immediate communications link to military spouses and children.[57] But the Web could not dispel all military wives' concerns. "We are suddenly all going to be single parents," Nancy Carlisle reminded an inquiring journalist.[58] She was thirty-two, living on a U.S. base in Baumholder, Germany, and pregnant with her second child. She planned to have the birth filmed on video. Married to an infantry captain, Carlisle worked as a volunteer in a military family support group to help other wives solve family problems during the Bosnia deployment. She and her colleague, a woman married to a staff sergeant, worried especially about the younger wives married to enlisted men: some of these women seemed uncertain about why their husbands joined the military or what they did; some were not confident in dealing with routine family finances, such as banking their husbands' paychecks. The Defense Department agreed to fly back to the United States those younger wives who were most at a loss.[59]

Special attention was devoted to Christmas celebrations on U.S. bases in Germany, from which so many of the soldiers were deployed. Amid the holiday wrappings and new Barbie doll accessories, several military wives described what it was like to be an occasional single parent this time around. Pat Sullivan grew up in an American military family during the Vietnam War era. Her entire life had been a series of separations. She and her friend Hazel Camardelle now counted on each other's support. They had had "a few boo-hoo sessions," but now felt ready to cope with the stresses of separation: "Before Phil left, he told me he felt he was just doing his job ... He told me, 'I signed the papers. I said I was ready to do whatever my country needed me to do. Now there's a job to do, and I'm going to do it.'"[60]

Sullivan and Camardelle admitted to a reporter that they did harbor some reservations of their own about the wisdom of sending U.S. troops to Bosnia. But hearing their husbands' convictions, combined with reaching their own understandings of what damage had been done to civilians in Bosnia, they pushed aside their preliminary doubts: "I can't imagine living in the conditions those people are living in. If [American soldiers] can help, that's great."

The wives left behind on bases in Germany might also have calculated what impact their wifely resistance to the deployment might have on their husbands' future careers. The Bosnia operation came at a moment when armed forces downsizing remained a source of anxiety for many American military careerists. Any soldier who voiced reluctance to accept a battlefield deployment would jeopardize his chances for promotion in this increasingly competitive, insecure army. Such an action would have financial consequences for their wives, especially since their wives themselves had such an uncertain toehold on the civilian job market.

All the persuasion and organized support mounted by Becraft and her staff in the Defense Department before and during the Bosnia peacekeeping operation would be judged in terms of how well it translated into soldiers' performance in Bosnia and into their willingness to reenlist when their current tours were done. Among the male peacekeeping soldiers themselves, mail from home was one measure employed. Another was the cheerfulness of the woman's voice on the

Figure 9 At the outset of the peacekeeping mission in Croatia and Bosnia, officials of the U.S. Defense Department tried to lessen tensions emerging inside military families by installing field phones with which soldiers, such as Sergeant Jeffrey Hunter of Cleveland, Ohio, could call home. (Reuters; *New York Times*, 26 December 1995.)

other end of the telephone line. In the 1990s, the telephone began to push aside the traditional mail call. The AT&T tent became a central part of an American military's base, the company having won a very lucrative contract to supply phone services for homesick soldiers. The militarization of one company, AT&T, could be assessed in terms both of the profits made from its military base telephones and of its opportunity to sell phone service to civilian customers through images of the homesick soldier calling home.

The more uncertain, however, any relationship was between a male peacekeeper and his wife or girlfriend, the higher the soldier's phone bill and the more likelihood of debt. Just as it did a century ago in Victorian Britain, soldiers' indebtedness now worried their commanders. For a young American soldier earning $2,000 per month while on duty in Bosnia, a not untypical monthly phone bill of $650 could be staggering.[61] Military marriage, as originally imagined by nineteenth-century military planners, was supposed to keep the government's male soldier out of debt, not bury him more deeply into it.

Even in this era of the phone card, Defense Department officials still urge mothers, wives, and girlfriends to write to soldiers, but to write only upbeat letters, missives full of affection and reassurance. Thus officials back in Washington might have been particularly pleased with the letter that enlisted man Jim Allen, twenty-three, received from his wife while he was on duty in Bosnia: she had been to see a lawyer, she wrote, and had decided not to divorce him after all.[62] On the other hand, in one U.S. infantry unit, a platoon of Charlie Company, the mail in mid-1996 was bringing with it a steady stream of wifely discontent. After seven months of service in Bosnia, there were six divorces pending among the platoon's thirty men.[63] One soldier, despairing amidst a crumbling marriage, had taken up a machine gun to attempt suicide. The unit's chaplain, Captain Clark Carr, estimated that for about two months he was seeing "a dozen people a day about serious marital problems."[64]

The marital news coming from American male troops in Bosnia reflected many women's incomplete militarization: they were unable or unwilling to put their husband-soldier's military duty first or to gain sufficient pride or satisfaction from their own handling of the stresses of military wifedom to sustain their marriages. Simultaneously, the news from Charlie Company suggested that the extraordinary attempts in the 1990s by the Defense Department to craft a policy designed to sustain a military wife's loyalty to her husband and his employer fell short of meeting the institution's goals.[65]

The incomplete militarization of spouses was even more notable among those women—and men—married to soldiers in the U.S. National Guard and Reserve units. To compensate for the shrinkage in numbers of regular duty personnel, the Defense Department had begun to routinely call up National Guard and Reserve units for tours in places such as Bosnia. Such tours were not what most women expected when their husbands decided, in addition to their civilian jobs, to earn extra pay by signing up for some weekend soldiering. The Defense Department admitted that marital problems were part of the cost of its new personnel formula.[66] Those marital problems, in turn, were a reflection that at least some women married to part-time soldiers refused to take on the identities of military wives.

The news from the U.S. Air Force's most elite, most highly paid officers (with salaries of more than $65,000 annually) was not any more reassuring to Pentagon policy makers. In 1996, 498 pilots had taken early retirements from the air force. In 1997, officials expected more than 700 pilots to resign. In 1994 the air force had retained 81 percent of its top pilots, but now the retention rate was dropping down to 30 percent.[67] The most obvious cause: the lure of civilian piloting jobs. Expanding American commercial airlines were offering annual salaries as high as $180,000 to these experienced military pilots. However, below the surface, underneath the salary appeals, were two gendered dynamics. The first dynamic was the militarized, masculinized definition of excitement. Many American male fighter pilots who had reached the pinnacle of their military professions expected to fly combat missions against well-defined enemies and to enjoy deserved off-duty pleasures when on the ground. Yet in the 1990s, before U.S. pilots were deployed to drop bombs on Serbia, these men were being deployed to fly patrolling missions over the so-called no flight zone of Northern Iraq. They had to fly over the same terrain day after day. And when they returned to the ground they endured the frustrations of American life in Saudi Arabia—cramped quarters, little entertainment, and no alcohol. As one air force major, the pilot of an F-15 E fighter jet, explained, "There is no upside to a mission in Saudi Arabia ... You're in effect in prison over there."[68] It is not clear whether the two-month NATO bombing mission over Serbia served to persuade more American air force pilots to reenlist.

The second factor is the new gendered dynamics of air force marriages. Observers note that many men entering today's jet pilot fighter ranks are less willing than their predecessors to accept the military culture's convention of masculinized sexual bravado. That convention has been an institutional culture in which "divorce was common, and womanizing among male pilots was legendary."[69] On the brink of the new century, more male U.S. Air Force pilots were expressing an unwillingness to put military flying above their wives and children. This reluctance, in turn, was in large measure, Defense Department commentators speculated, because more pilots' *wives* were refusing to stay in marriages bound by the existing norms of a militarized, masculinity-privileging subculture. Thus men who were turning in their F-15 fighter cockpits for 747 civilian cockpits were doing so, they said, in order to bring more homebound predictability and transparency into their marital lives.

WORKING WIVES AS MILITARY WIVES

When soldiers' wives go off base for waged jobs, they pose a problem for officialdom. On the one hand, those military wives who are able to get decently paying civilian jobs on their own reduce the demoralizing poverty of soldiers' families and lessen the pressure for military pay raises. On the other hand, military commanders lose some of their control over those more independent women. The military also has more difficulty moving the soldier-husband because his wife has increased her economic stake in staying where she has found civilian employment. Furthermore, as more officers' wives as well as women married to rank-and-file soldiers obtain off-base jobs, the myth of the single-minded, devoted military family cracks. The military family thereafter has to be recognized as the household of women and men and children with differing powers and differing needs that in fact it always has been.

The American military, with its current penchant for contracting social science investigations into issues, already has produced scores of studies of the "problems" posed by this new generation of working wives in the military.[70] The air force, the service that has prided itself on being in the vanguard of services recognizing and responding to new social problems, took the initiative in the early 1980s to establish a Military Spouse Skills and Resource Center near Washington, D.C., to provide job information for the thousands of military wives who move in and out of the Washington area every year. The more possible it has become for military wives to obtain paid jobs, the more they have pressed the Pentagon to supply on-base child care. Inside the Pentagon and the Congress, there was resistance. Child care expenditures were harder to feel passionate about than weapons expenditures were. Furthermore, wives with jobs of their own might be less available to do unpaid volunteer work, the sort of support work that the military needs now that it is sending soldiers off on long-distance rapid deployments more often. Deputy Assistant Secretary of Defense Becraft supported military wives in their desire to be able to have paid employment, but she had to couch her advocacy in terms of the military's own need to keep soldiers' families satisfied so that morale would be bolstered and reenlistments would continue. She spoke to members of Congress in the shared language of military readiness: "We have become dual income families. And the fact is, working spouses do have an impact on readiness."[71]

Her approach was effective. Congress authorized a significant infusion of funds to be channeled into military base child care. American soldiering parents in the late 1990s have more access to child care than do most American civilian parents. Most politicians have not conceptualized publicly funded child care for the ordinary American parent as a matter of national security. Militarizing some family's needs has enabled them to get publicly funded care for their children.

Taking the long historical view, what is new in the military today is not that there are working wives but that they are working for pay, working off-base, and working in jobs to which they are developing some career aspirations of their own. Military policy makers do not feel threatened by a woman's labor; they rely on that labor to keep military base communities and military households running smoothly. But they do feel threatened by a woman's commitment to paid labor and its personal rewards: is the military wife with a paid job neglecting her duties as a loyal military wife? Is a woman married to a soldier becoming herself a careerist in a way that is making her a liability to her husband's upwardly mobile career?

For centuries soldiering has had appeal for many men because not only did it confirm their sometimes-shaky purchase on manliness, but it provided shelter, pay, and regular meals. Many women in poor countries see marriage to an military officer as a route out of ungratifying paid work. Becoming a full-time housewife—married to a military or a civilian man whose salary is sufficient to support an entire household—is seen as reasonable aspiration.

Nonetheless, soldiering and poverty are not uncommon bedfellows. Militaries often do not keep their pay scales in line either with the cost of daily necessities or with their soldiers' material expectations. More than one coup d'état has been hatched by soldiers who felt they—and their wives and children—were being underfed and underpaid.

The breakup of the Soviet Union in 1991, together with the end of the Warsaw Pact, meant the withdrawal of 500,000 Soviet military personnel and 700,000 Soviet civilians from various corners of Eastern Europe. Among them were thousands of Russian military wives. Russian politicians in the post–Cold War years have had good reason to be nervous during these withdrawals of Russian forces from East Germany and the Baltics. Russian military wives stationed there with their Red Army husbands had enjoyed amenities that they knew they would not have back home: decent housing, access to consumer goods. There were grumblings by not only soldiers but their military wives when word began to trickle down that military families were likely to be living in tents when they returned to Russia.[72] A soldier who simultaneously is a husband may feel his manliness doubly jeopardized if he thinks he is being put in a position in which he cannot ensure the wellbeing of his wife and children. Thus the politics of newly impoverished military wives, while rarely treated seriously by international relations commentators, is indeed a topic worthy of concentrated analytical attention.

In post–Cold War Canada, the declining living standards of sol-diers' families emerged as a political issue in 1998 when it was made a cover story of *Maclean's,* Canada's premier news weekly. Canadian readers read stories of senior policy makers apparently out of touch with the realities of military wives trying to support themselves and their children in dingy housing while their husbands are deployed more and more frequently on international peacekeeping missions, for which the Canadian military has earned an esteemed reputation[73] The story broke, as any military story does, at a very particular moment in the history of Canadian military politics. It followed close on the heels of revelations of a group of Canadian peacekeeping troops torturing and murdering a young Somalian prisoner, revelations that set off a nation-wide reassessment of the culture and role of the country's armed forces. Soon after *Maclean's* carried its feature on the shabby economic conditions endured by many enlisted soldiers and their families, the magazine carried yet another cover story on the military, this one about Canadian male soldiers raping women colleagues while their su-periors systematically looked the other way.[74] Public discussions about military rates of pay, the living conditions of military families, and the right of military wives to pursue well-paid jobs of their own always oc-cur in specific historical moments—in the evolution of any given soci-ety and in the evolution of the militarization of the international politi-cal system. The Canadian military's relationship to both the rest of Canada's citizenry and to post–Cold War international politics is not the same as either the Russian or the American. Even a woman mar-ried to a low-paid soldier is operating in particular state and interstate cultures and structures when she protests her miserable living condi-tions.

In 1992, 3 percent of American military personnel qualified for fed-eral food stamps; 1 percent had actually applied for and received them.[75] Soldiers at bases from Hawaii to Florida were finding it impos-sible to live what they and their spouses considered a "decent life" on military pay, as the gap between military and civilian pay was widen-ing. For instance, Beth Edwards, twenty-two and based in Hawaii, de-scribed how she coped with her airman husband's $1,330 monthly salary: "whenever I want to cook something with ham, I substitute Spam."[76] Most of the military families slipping into poverty in the mid-1990s were young and at the lower ranks. In the majority of the militarized poor, the wife did not have a paid job.[77]

The very embarrassment that this news provoked provided U.S. military family advocates with an opening to press Congress and the

Clinton White House to allocate more public funds for military pay raises. The reports had a second effect: they allowed more military wives to argue in favor of their right to work for pay in full-time jobs, even if their doing so reduced the military's ability to monopolize their loyalties and their attention. After their electoral victory in 1994, Republican congressional representatives made a point of voicing their support for military families and of criticizing the Clinton administration for imposing budget cuts that hurt armed forces personnel and their spouses. On the other hand, the Republican leadership was so eager to pass legislation that would reduce federal expenditures on what they believed were wasteful welfare programs that in March 1995 they voted for a package of cuts that included the elimination of school lunch subsidies for the children of low-income soldiers. At Camp Lejeune, North Carolina, 55 percent of the 3,400 children enrolled at that army base's eight schools received meals for free or at the reduced price of 40 cents.[78] Political commitments to military strength and to a shrunken social safety net often are imagined to be part and parcel of the same conservative ideological platform. The two planks are at odds, however, if many soldiers' pay is low and their wives have a hard time gaining decently paid employment.[79]

WHEN THE MILITARY WIFE IS A MAN

All military strategy designed to control soldiers' spouses has been rooted in the assumption that a soldier—or sailor or pilot—is a man and that, if a soldier is allowed to marry, the soldier's spouse is a woman. The military spouse will be a wife. A wife is feminine; a wife is auxiliary; a wife is dependent. A wife, in other words, is not a husband.

The benefits as well as dangers allegedly flowing from the military spouse are defined by military officials in terms of gender, not mere spousehood. The military spouse is presumed to be an effective morale booster or a comforter of the wounded partner because the spouse is a woman doing what a woman "naturally" does so well. Likewise, commanders for generations have tried to reduce any danger the military spouse poses to military readiness by reinforcing the gender ideology that claims that men decide where a family will reside and how it will make a livelihood. Ideas about gender, not just about spousehood, have led to the belief that the military spouse can jeopardize military readiness because she is a woman, and as a woman, as a "feminine" creature, she naturally puts emotional attachments and loyalty to her children ahead of her husband's professional occupation or the abstract notion of patriotism.

The post-1970s increase in volunteer women professional soldiers—in Britain, the United States, Canada, New Zealand, Australia, and most recently, Russia—has created something quite new in gendered military culture: the male military spouse.

Their numbers are not high: in the early 1990s, for instance, only about 2,000 of the U.S. Army's 11,000 women officers had chosen to marry. That proportion drops among women army officers who aspired to make their careers in the service's combat branches.[80] Still, it is less their numbers than their ideological awkwardness that makes military husbands politically significant. The military husband is not expected to play the same helping, nurturing, soothing role for the military as his female counterpart is. He is not expected to quit his job and move every time his soldier-wife is transferred. He is not expected to be as deferential either to the general's wife or to the general as his female counterpart is. And he cannot be expected to provide unpaid or cheap labor to make the base a community.

Some of the ideological hazards produced by the emergence of the military husband are diluted in the United States, however, because so many of today's military husbands are themselves soldiers. In the 1980s, a decade after the U.S. military began recruiting women volunteers in earnest, there were 55,293 dual military career families in the American forces.[81] Today, if military men married to military women are not kept happy, the Pentagon risks losing not one, but two trained soldiers: the wife and the husband. In American bureaucratic language, when one heterosexual soldier marries another heterosexual soldier, they are creating a "joint service family." But it has been women in uniform who have been more likely than their male counterparts to choose other soldiers as their spouses. In 1995, the percentage of U.S. male and female members in "joint service marriages" was 3.9 percent and 23.2 percent respectively.[82]

RACE AND MARRIAGE: THE EXPERIENCES OF MILITARY WIVES

Scratch a military, and one is likely to find an ethnic or racial hierarchy. Officer corps are more likely than not to have different ethnic or racial profiles than do the rank and file. Air forces are frequently quite unlike either navies or armies in their ethnic and racial compositions.

This difference is true not just in apartheid-era South Africa or pre-1948 United States. It is a common characteristic of militaries in Belgium, Canada, Kenya, Peru, Pakistan, Iran, Malaysia, India, and contemporary United States. And the causes are not simply the cultural proclivities of men of different communities toward ocean travel or even their differential access to the civilian job markets. Any military's racial and ethnic divisions of labor and ranking differentials have been caused in large part by a history of conscious policy calculations.[83]

One result of this history is that in scores of militaries, the women who marry ordinary soldiers, not surprisingly, have different ethnic and racial identities than those women who marry officers. The racialized or ethnicized hierarchies can divide military wives from one another as much as do the stratifications of rank and social class. The popular belief in 1870s Britain, for instance, was that a large proportion of rank-and-file soldiers' wives were Irish and that Irish and Scottish women "were the backbone of the slatternly class of soldiers' wives."[84]

African American women have been American military wives since the Civil War. But it has been between the 1970s and 1990s, especially with the end of the draft and the rise in black males as a significant proportion of all male volunteers, that black military wives have grown in number. By 1995, African American spouses were 17 percent of all American military spouses; Hispanic spouses were 6 percent. All together, Asian American, Native American, and Pacific Islander spouses constituted 8 percent of military spouses.[85]

The U.S. military's long history of institutionalized racism suggests that Asian, Latino, African American, and Native American women married to American soldiers have had to cope with those problems confronting white military wives but in an exaggerated form. On the other hand, when the military has moved—if, belatedly—ahead of many other American institutions (e.g., schools, the press, banking) in dismantling racist structures, these women may find military living less marred by daily encounters with racism than is civilian living. This comparative experience could increase their willingness to meet the institution's expectations for military wives. That is, we should not assume, in the United States or in any country, that the wives of soldiers who come from groups marginalized in the larger society will automatically be the most alienated of military wives.

Many children around the world grow up not just in families but on the margins of institutional cultures—on plantations, in company towns, in university towns, in the families of elected politicians, in diplomatic communities. By the mid-1990s, there were 1.4 million military children in the United States.[86] Although this scale is new, the phenomenon is not. For generations girls and boys have been growing up in households in which the father was a military man, a man often soldiering in a racialized world.[87] Charlayne Hunter-Gault, today a prominent television and radio news journalist, may be even better known as the first African American woman to attend the previously all-white University of Georgia. What is less well known is that she grew up as the daughter of an army chaplain. Hunter-Gault was a "military brat." Like all military children, her childhood was shaped not simply by raw militarism, but by the particular quality of the military institution during those formative years—how often were its troops (her own and other children's military parents) deployed abroad? How good was the military pay? How strict were the racial and class lines of stratification? Were wives pressured to reproduce the hierarchies of class, race, and rank among themselves?

Hunter-Gault lived as a military daughter inside the 1950s U.S. military, a military just starting to shed its devotion to racial segregation, a military designed to fight globally in the name of fending off a Cold War super-rival, a military that held women soldiers to a quota of 2 percent, and a military that presumed that military spouses would be wives and that wives did not have, or need to have, lives of their own. What is striking about Hunter-Gault's experience is that it was so detached from the military. Her mother made that low level of childhood militarization possible. She decided not to move with her military chaplain husband from assignment to assignment. In so doing, she may have jeopardized her husband's chances for promotion, but she also preserved some of her own autonomy. Only in 1954, when he was transferred to Alaska, did Hunter-Gault's mother agree to join her husband. Thus the militarization of her daughter's life took the form of a largely absent father, an all-female household, a brief but memorable taste of life in a reluctantly desegregating U.S. army. Hunter-Gault recalls entering the military base school and meeting for the first time military children whose more thoroughly militarized upbringings had turned them into old hands at moving from place to place. But these children were parochial Americans nonetheless: "I assumed that this meant that as world travelers they had broad exposure to all races, classes and creeds. Little did I know that most of them lived in sheltered American enclaves, attending post or on-base schools, with limited contact with non-military and/or foreign students ... In Alaska, my father was the only Black chaplain, and one of only a handful of Black officers. And as I was to learn in the coming months, the white students were affected by the same sometimes subtle, sometimes overt dynamics that existed in an army not yet fully desegregated or comfortable with the idea."[88]

If a military changes—whether in the levels of its institutionalized sexism, racism, or homophobia, in the degree of its reliance on volunteer soldiers, in its access to overseas bases, in its willingness to take part in multinational peacekeeping, in its dependence on wives' unpaid labor, in its acknowledgment of domestic violence in its midst—so too will change the experience of militarized childhood. Thus, for instance, two decades after Hunter-Gault navigated her way through the militarized parochialism of her army schoolmates, another African American military daughter experienced a rather different childhood. Georgie's (not her real name) mother was far more willing to engage in the military life than Hunter-Gault's mother had been. As a young black woman, she had wanted to enlist herself, and so, in compensation, accompanied Georgie's army father on his overseas deployment to Germany. It was the mid-1970s. The U.S. military, due less to its own internal momentum than to the pressures exerted by black civil rights groups, had become a less racially stratified and segregated institution than it had been in the mid-1950s. Moreover, the mid-1970s American military was a post-draft military, now wholly dependent on volunteer enlistments and reenlistments and thus compelled to devote far more attention and resources to families' needs. On the other hand, the Cold War was still in full swing, making "national security" the overriding criterion for measuring any military policy, and the U.S. women's movement's second wave had as yet barely penetrated the insulated lives of the military family.

For Georgie, the life of an African American military brat is remembered with fondness. Even today she recalls it as a more secure way of life than the civilian life she lived thereafter in her economically depressed, racially fragmented hometown in western Massachusetts: "It was a happy time, a more safe time, living on the base. You could stay out late playing. Everything was very big, we had brick duplexes with a kitchen and a half bath with a washer and dryer ... We each had our own room. Everybody [on the base] had the same. You knew all the kids and you all went to the same school. The majority were white, but there were Blacks and Hispanics, the housing was all mixed. I hung out with Black kids, but at eight, issues of race were not important yet—just a little about being cool."[89]

Empire building is one of the processes that can transform the politics of race and marriage among military wives. Each phase, for instance, of Americans' historical military expansion—to Panama, Cuba, Japan, South Korea, the Philippines, Thailand, Vietnam, Germany, and Britain—has produced marriages of local women to American soldiers. Looking at a mural portrait of U.S. military wives consequently is like looking at a map of American global military doctrine. Over the last half century, American military wives have become a more culturally and racially diverse group.

During the American military's years in Germany as a post–World War II army of occupation, there ran a constant undercurrent of sexualized anxiety. Many Americans and Germans complained that it was difficult, albeit important, to distinguish who among the German women was a promiscuous, opportunist camp follower, who was a professional prostitute, and who was a legitimate fiancée. In the interactions between the victorious soldiers and the defeated civilians, the gendered politics of respectability became militarized, ethnicized, and racialized. By 1952, the first of the mixed-race children, born of liaisons between white German women and black American soldiers (and also French African soldiers), began entering German schools. They were defined by German education authorities as a "problem," just as, earlier in World War II, children born of African American soldiers and white British women had been defined as a "problem."[90]

This discourse, however, was part of a wider popular questioning among Germans: how could they overcome their collective Nazi past, so deeply informed by racism, and yet also construct a postwar national propriety? A variety of actors had a stake in the direction of this postwar conversation. First were the so-called veronikas, German women impoverished by war who saw relationships with occupation troops as a means of economic survival. Among them were young German women who saw black American soldiers as embodying "the modern." These women were compatriots of German men who saw their country's wartime defeat as a personal humiliation. Further up the ladder of authority were postwar German leaders who believed that German men now needed to be returned to their status of respected family heads if the postwar, post-Nazi nation were to be rebuilt on a healthy social foundation.[91] Also trying to direct this fraught postwar sexualized discourse was the U.S. military occupation command. Its members wished American troops to be accepted enough and satisfied enough to perform their difficult occupation duties effectively, and thus attempted to control which soldiers would marry and whom.[92] Entering the dance of discourse too were the U.S. male troops themselves, men of a variety of ethnicities and races in a still racially segregated American military. At the end of a brutal war, many of these soldiers sought leisure and solace and possibly long-term partnerships where they had been taught such partnerships were most readily available—in the company of local civilian women.[93] The intricate minuet between these expectations and anxieties shaped the American military occupation and the crucial first stage of post-Nazi German democratization.

Postwar militarized marriages also played a part in the refashioning of U.S.-Asian international politics. Between 1945 and 1990, more than 200,000 Asian and Pacific Island women married American soldiers overseas. Most of these women immigrated back to the United States after their husbands' tours of duty were completed.[94]

With the emergence of the second wave of the American women's movement, some American male soldiers saw Asian women as an appealing contrast to what they perceived as the increasingly assertive American women back home. Needing to find a validation of their own beliefs about natural femininity, these men imagined Asian women to be docile and subservient, part innocent, part "Susie Wong," eager to please their men.[95] Men nurturing such caricatures have rarely imagined that Asian forms of femininity are just as historically dynamic as their American counterparts. Nor have most of these American men taken notice of feminist movements in Korea, Japan, the Philippines, or Thailand. In a sense, these American military husbands have shared with the civilian men of the Asian countries where they were based a conventional vision of Asian femininity as existing outside of history and a vision of feminist politics as merely a foreign import.

Asian American women social workers reported that the Asian wives of American soldiers face awesome problems, magnifying the isolation, marginalization, and violence that so many military wives experience. In 1976, a coalition of women's groups, the military Chaplain's Office, and the American Red Cross came together to form the National Committee Concerned with Asian Wives of U.S. Servicemen. Their principal concern was the high incidence of physical abuse suffered by Asian military wives at the hands of their soldier or veteran husbands.[96]

MILITARIZING DOMESTIC VIOLENCE: A REDUNDANCY?

It took almost a decade for the challenges of the second wave of American feminism to penetrate the walls surrounding that country's military's bureaucracy. It was only the 1979 U.S. Inspector General's report that addressed domestic violence: "Social workers and other persons working with battered women in [American] military families agree that military service is probably more conducive to violence at home than at any other occupation because of the military's authoritarianism, its use of physical force in training and the stress produced by perpetual moves and separations. In addition, those men in the civilian population most likely to physically abuse the women with whom they live are men who have had prior military service."[97]

For generations, U.S. military officials had refused to admit that widespread domestic violence occurred under their commands or to take any responsibility for the "exceptional" incidents that did get reported. Military social workers, chaplains, police, psychiatrists, and doctors had joined with base commanders to weave a curtain of silence around military domestic violence.

The silence about violence inside military families was partly shattered in the 1980s by a convergence of civilian women's shelter movements in the United States and military manpower officials' own need to be more candid about the factors that were frustrating their efforts to persuade higher percentages of their volunteer soldiers to stay in the military. In spite of the advances in turning domestic violence inside the military into an issue, there remain motivations for a woman in a militarized marriage to try to cope on her own. Often it is the very character of military life that intensifies a woman's reliance on her soldier-husband, even if he is abusive. On the basis of interviews with twelve U.S. Air Force wives in 1991, at the height of the Gulf War, researcher Doreen Lehr concluded: "In the mobile and uncertain military world the relationship between husband and wife can be more important than in civilian life as this may be the military wife's only constant relationship ... The military wife may go to extreme lengths to avoid threatening this primary relationship, her main source of support."[98]

According to the Defense Department's own records, the number of confirmed spouse abuse cases in 1988 was 12 per thousand military households, but in 1993 that number climbed to 18.1 per thousand.[99] Those American military family advocates who were trying to set off bureaucratic alarm bells translated the numbers into a startling statistic: "an average of one child or spouse dies each week at the hands of a relative in uniform."[100]

The causes for this upward trend have been contested. Some officials have taken comfort in concluding that the incidence of military family violence has not been on the rise; just public consciousness and women's reporting of that brand of violence are rising. This argument implies, however, that 18.1 violent husbands per thousand has been the incidence for decades. Not a reassuring portrait of contemporary military life. Advocates inside and outside the Defense Department have pointed to structural changes in the post–Cold War American armed forces—especially the escalating anxieties derived from downsizing and the strains flowing from longer overseas deployments—that were making soldiering (and the task of supporting of a soldier domestically) increasingly stressful. For instance, Peter McNelis, himself a military veteran and head of the Military Family Institute at Pennsylvania's Marywood College, observed regarding military personnel and their spouses, "You can't talk to anyone without getting the sense they're tense and feel that the system is letting them down."[101]

Most official attention is directed toward young male soldiers in the lowest enlisted ranks. It is, again, somewhat soothing bureaucratically to imagine that wife battering (and child abuse) are confined to those soldiers who are living away from hometown relatives and friends just when they learning how to cope with the added responsibilities of marriage. Yet anecdotal evidence collected by people working in violence prevention programs implies a less sanguine story. The head of a civilian advocacy program in Cumberland County, North Carolina, a program that attempts to support personnel from nearby Fort Bragg, warned, "We see people of all ranks because family violence crosses all lines ... It's an equal opportunity plague on our society."[102]

One possible cause for the high rates of violence in military families is rarely discussed in policy-making sessions. Something inherent in the process of militarizing a man's sense of his own masculinity makes him not only more capable of shooting at an enemy, but less able to resist resorting to violence when tensions escalate inside his own home. Tackling this possible cause would compel any military to dig deeper than the stresses of downsizing, deeper than the geographic separation of young male soldiers from their aunts and uncles. Seriously weighing this possible cause—the nature of militarized masculinity—would entail confronting the potential incompatibility between a social role intended to nurture and sustain another human being and a profession designed to wield violence in the name of the state.

In 1996, the U.S. Congress passed a new law intended to reduce, if not the nationwide incidence of domestic violence, at least its severity. A person convicted of a domestic abuse charge would be prohibited under the new law from legally possessing a gun. Congressional representatives, however, as has been the custom in American politics, gave in to Defense Department officials' insistence that the military be treated under the law as a special case and granted the military thirteen extra months in which to make its personnel comply with the law.[103] At the end of 1997, Pentagon officials reportedly were still not in compliance and had not even attempted to conduct a survey to estimate what percentage of uniformed personnel had records of domestic abuse conviction. They had decided instead to rely on a questionnaire asking each soldier to tell truthfully whether he or she had such a record. All soldiers who answered in the positive would thereafter be required to hand over their handguns and rifles. Those soldiers, nevertheless, would still be able to operate deadly weaponry in the course of their military duties.

The very militarization of the issue of domestic violence may be undermining those genuine efforts to try to reduce it: the ultimate criterion for measuring the success of the new policy of domestic violence prevention remains its value to the military's own operation. The rights of women married to violent soldiers are secondary. Linda Smith, a senior Pentagon official in its Family Policy Directorate, spelled out the department's institutional rationale: "The proactive programs provided by military help Service members and families get their personal lives in order, which in turn, of course, allows them and their supervisors to concentrate on getting their missions accomplished."[104]

A study of the Canadian military's recent practice—as versus formal policy—concerning the punishment of soldiers who abuse their wives sheds light on the ramifications of the militarization of the issue of domestic violence: "When the [armed forces] member is valued by his unit, the military does not want to know how he behaves during his hours off the job and has ways of ensuring that it never finds out."[105]

FEMINISTS AND MILITANT MILITARY WIVES

Many American women's advocates saw the military's begrudging admission of the problem of domestic violence as an opportunity to make some inroads in this powerful state institution. American feminists, more than their British antiviolence counterparts, appeared willing to enter into quasi-insider relationships with military policy makers for the sake of getting domestic violence prevention on the agendas of the Pentagon and of local base commanders. British women active in the battered women's shelter movement were less trusting of the state, more concerned about the risks of co-optation. These differences are one more signal that feminists' estimations of the costs, rewards, and risks of engaging with a still-patriarchal state can vary remarkably between countries—and among feminists active in the same country. Although the strategic solutions vary, what are common are the intense debates that women's advocates have had and still have with each other over when and how to engage with the state. Providing support for women married to the state's soldiers is one more site for that ongoing feminist debate.

As the contradictions in the military's attitudes and policies toward military wives have become more acute, space has opened up for some military wives to assert their autonomy and to begin to organize politically. Often they have done so without making any explicit connections with organized civilian feminists. The relationships between the two groups of women in most countries is uneasy at best. Military wives often believe that most civilian feminists see them as so integral to the military that they must be complicit in militarism and thus in the very patriarchy that many feminists are committed to overturn. For their part, most civilian feminists either do not even "see" military wives as a political category, or they imagine women married to soldiers to be too politically isolated or too lacking in political consciousness to be worthy of organized support.

Among those military wives who have led the way in political organizing are, perhaps not surprisingly, those enjoying the greatest cultural and bureaucratic distance from the military—the widows of soldiers and the divorced wives of soldiers. Their complaints and their organizing cannot hurt their current husbands' military careers, and thus they are less constrained by how senior officers define marriage's "fit" in the military mission. Yet space for action provides no assurance of success.

For instance, the widows of three Australian pilots criticized the insensitivity of their husbands' superiors. Following the 1993 crash of their husbands' 707, these widows contended that the military establishment communicated with them in an insensitive and confusing manner. There was little support for the widows: "It was almost as though it appeared that once [our husbands] were buried, they were out of sight, out of mind."[106] What is significant in this small story is not that three military wives were critical of the military's attitude toward them, but that the wives made their displeasure known to the national media. They challenged the legitimacy of their country's military.

Military widowhood can be an ideological boon to militarism, but it can also be a liability to the military itself. Widows can be used to symbolize the "supreme sacrifice." By encouraging all women in the country to identify with each military widow or grieving mother, a government can try to turn the government's soldiers into "our boys," deserving of all women's support. In World War I–era Canada, the all-male government bestowed the right to vote on women relatives of soldiers in 1917 while continuing to deny the franchise to all other Canadian women. A year later, the all-male Belgian government, also trying to mobilize women in its own war-waging effort, gave the vote to those women whose husbands or sons had been killed in battle. A generation later, Mussolini's Italian fascist regime elevated the widows and mothers of dead soldiers to a special status. Israel's government has bestowed special state pensions on women who have lost either husbands or sons in its wars.[107]

At the same time, military widows are expensive and often politically awkward. In the 1980s the Argentinean military regime was embarrassed by its Falkland war widows. The regime hoped that the widows and the surviving veterans would stay discreetly out of public view.[108] In the aftermath of their Falklands victory, Britons set up a private South Atlantic Fund for the widows of 247 servicemen and merchant seamen killed in the conflict. The fund was testimony not only to British militarist pride but to the inadequacy of the military pension scheme. Its creation also raised questions about inadequacy and inequities of compensation for widows of British soldiers killed in Northern Ireland.[109] Are the women widowed in some wars less worthy than women widowed in other wars?

Closely related to activist military widows are women who feel betrayed after their husbands (or sons) have been damaged by their soldiering but have been left by the military to cope on their own—or, more frequently, to be cared for by the women in their families. Thus in the wake of the Gulf War, when scores of American soldiers found that they were debilitated by myriad health problems that appeared to be connected to their participation in the Middle East conflict, it was women who led many of what came to be called the "Gulf War syndrome" activist organizations. They raised money, attracted media attention, testified before congressional and Veterans Administration hearings, and gathered scientific information. They were explicit in mobilizing women relatives of soldiers, and they provided advice so that those women could become agents rather than victims of the American military policy-making process.[110]

Other women who have organized to criticize the military are ex-wives. EXPOSE (Ex-spouses of Servicemen [women] for Equality) was formed in May 1980 to "alert members of congress to the need for laws to correct injustices to ex-military spouses caused by the loss of military benefits in event of divorce—especially of long marriages"—and to educate "past, present, and future military spouses to what happens to spouse benefits in event of divorce from a member of the Uniformed Services."[111] In the past, divorce was frowned upon by the American military establishment. By the Reagan era, these women resentfully observed, "all the top brass are divorcing—even three and four star generals."[112] The women spearheading EXPOSE's mobilizing and lobbying efforts were heartened by their group's growth from a dozen women in 1980 to more than 3,000 women in mid-1982. One ex-wife of a general explained that the catalyst was the U.S. Supreme Court's 1980 *McCarty* decision. The Court declared that a man with military retirement benefits (pensions, PX privileges, health care) had total control over those benefits and did not have to share them with his ex-wife in any divorce settlement. Since retirement benefits constitute the chief property of a military careerist, this decision left military ex-wives essentially with no alimony.[113] The angriest women were those who had been married to their husbands during most of the men's twenty years of preretirement service. They had worked to promote their husbands' careers; they had staffed on-base volunteer services; they had "kept the home fires burning" while their husbands were off fighting the government's wars. Did all that work mean nothing? One woman explained her activism: "I'd always been shy, keeping the home going when we moved, doing the entertaining required of an officer's wife. My husband retired as a brigadier general. I was never active, I was a helper. Then after thirty-one years of service, my husband divorced me and married a younger woman he'd known for two months. Now she gets all his benefits. I resented it and so I'll fight to the grave for this. Other women, too, who've felt all alone, divorced, stripped of benefits we deserved—now we feel part of a group."[114]

Developing their congressional lobbying skills and gaining the support of the Washington-based Women's Equity Action League, ex-wives persuaded the Democratic majorities on the House and Senate Armed Services Committees that they had made a contribution not just to their husbands' careers but to the military itself and that they deserved some portion of their soldier-husbands' military benefits upon divorce. Representative Patricia Schroeder of Colorado played a key role in this 1980s political victory, just as she did later in the congressional debates over military sexual harassment and women's access to combat jobs. The lobbying done by the ex-wives is credited with not only reversing the *McCarty* decision but making the Defense Department substitute "military family member" for "military dependent" when referring to the spouses and children of armed forces personnel. During the same decade of activism, military wives and ex-wives persuaded the Pentagon to drop the section of military personnel evaluation reports that specifically called on superiors to weigh the behavior of military spouses and, closely related, to compel the Defense Department to issue formal directives calling on commanders to halt their usual practice of insisting that male military officers' wives quit any full-time job before her husband could be considered for the post of a base commander.[115] The mentality and the practices toward military wives did not change radically because of these victories, but the military's very resistance to making even superficial changes in its stance toward wives suggests that these achievements were not merely hollow.

One of the most outspoken and publicly visible military wives' organizations to develop in the 1980s was created by a small group of Canadian military wives. Its founders were politicized by learning almost by accident that they did not have the rights accorded other Canadian civilian citizens. Because their husbands were in the military, their husbands' base commander informed them, they could not conduct such ordinary civic actions as carrying a petition from door to door calling for better dental services. By the time these women came together to form a formal organization and to raise their issues with the national ministry, through the national press if necessary, they had decided on a name with an acronymic message: Organizational Society of Spouses of Military Members—OSSOMM—pronounced by its members as "awesome."[116]

Like so many efforts to change a military's policies toward women, activism involved more intimate engagement with the military establishment. The Canadian military, similar to its American counterpart, initially tried to ignore the wives' challenges, then tried to take from them ideas that could be fashioned into a policy that would not disturb the masculinized military culture. Thus, a study of OSSOMM's actions on one military base in New Brunswick found that while several of the group's ideas were adopted, OSSOMM's own members were gradually frozen out of participation in the implementation of those ideas. More-over, no wider civic space was created in which military wives could engage in ongoing political discourse. Co-optation took the form of bureaucratization. Those women unwilling to be co-opted were left on the outside.[117]

Most of these newly militant military wives, ex-wives, and widows have not yet questioned the role of the military in society. That is, most of these women have stopped short of analyzing militarism. Rather, they are challenging the militaristic idea that women deserve attention, protection, counseling, or pensions only *insofar* as they enhance male soldiers' military effectiveness. Their activism has stemmed from a new understanding: if a choice is ever posed between the military's own needs and military wives' needs, the latter will be treated as expend-able—not only expendable, but as a threat to the male soldiers' per-formance and ultimately to the mission of the entire military establish-ment. For many women, coming to this understanding has been a painful process.

Feminists in many countries have cut their political teeth by chew-ing on the thorny problem of women accepting—and pressing for—state-administered social welfare. Theoretical and strategic lessons learned in this arena could provide feminists an avenue for thinking more clearly about military wives. Military wives are very similar to women reliant on state welfare programs: their housing, schooling, medical care, often their food, and even their recreation flows from the government. In fact, fresh research by Theda Skocpol reveals that the origins of the U.S. welfare system lie in programs intended to distribute benefits to Revolutionary War and Civil War veterans.[118] So it would be a mistake to juxtapose military wives and women on welfare as somehow opposites. Feminists in many countries have learned to be skeptical of state welfare programs that extend state control over women; yet in the midst of the government-shrinking 1990s, many ac-tivist women have found it wise to protest those welfare cuts that would shred the public safety net on which so many women depend for daily survival.[119] If feminists do press their own country's military establishment to pay *more* attention to and provide *more* services to military wives, will that effort serve only to more deeply entrench the militarization of women married to soldiers?

Those civilian women activists who have made antimilitarism (for-eign and local varieties) integral to their feminist politics will not find alliances with military wives easy to create or sustain, however. The experiences of married life can shape a woman's ideological view if her husband is deeply invested in an institution with a sharply edged world outlook and if that woman has developed her own stake in her husband's career success inside that institution. Thus, many women married to soldiers do adopt the beliefs of the military as their own. They do begin to see some citizens, including feminists active in peace movements, as both threatening to the country's national security and insulting to their husbands and perhaps even themselves as military wives. One British woman, Susan, married to an army private, saw the women at the 1980s Greenham peace encampment as something less than "sisters." Her husband had just returned from maneuvers in Wales. Susan had been looking forward to the two of them going off and having some time together. Suddenly his unit was deployed to keep order at Greenham. Susan's anger at the Greenham women activists was multilayered. Susan's story, on the other hand, also suggests the limits of an antifeminist military wife's capacity to live her life as a full citizen:

> They do honestly, they really drive me spitting mad all those selfish bitches at Greenham Common ... Some of us [military wives] were even thinking of hiring a coach privately among ourselves and going down there for the day and telling them what we thought about them ... We got as far as booking the coach, but then one of the sergeant's wives came round us all and said it would be better if we didn't get ourselves involved, it'd look bad in the newspapers if soldiers' wives went there and had their own demonstration. So after a bit of arguing between ourselves we decided not to. That's one of the things of being an Army wife, you're not free to do what you want like everyone else: it's always gotten to be taken into account what effect it's going to have on the Army.[120]

At the heart of the politics of women married to soldiers is everyone's—the state's, the husband's, the wife's, and the feminists'—murky answer to the question: who is the military wife married *to?* Researcher Doreen Lehr's discovery is telling. During the Clinton administration, officials in the Women's Bureau of the U.S. Department of Labor were surprisingly uninterested when she spelled out the employment problems faced by military wives. One woman civil servant told her, "We let the military take care of their own." Lehr recalls: "She seemed surprised when I explained that the vast majority of military wives were civilians."[121]

NURSING THE MILITARY

The Imperfect Management of Respectability

Every few years we need to take a long, questioning look at figures whom we routinely deploy as collective reference points and about whom we assume we know all we need to know: Sojourner Truth, for example, or Mary Wollstonecraft, or Sappho, or Florence Nightingale. I have been forced to do some serious reimagining of Florence Nightingale recently. Ten years ago I thought I knew what I needed to know about the Victorian nursing pioneer. Now I'm not so sure.

The image of Florence Nightingale that comes to mind must be from a picture book I once saw. Florence Nightingale in the Crimea, ladylike in her long Victorian dress, carrying her lantern as she moves calmly and competently from one wounded soldier to another. You can almost hear the reassuring swoosh of her skirts while artillery guns echo in the distance. Some of the young men are up and about, un-shaven, wearing torn uniforms, talking with their comrades. Yet they have fresh bandages around their foreheads or newly folded slings holding up their shattered limbs. Other soldiers seem in a more desper-ate condition, lying on cots or leaning up against the walls of this makeshift hospital. They are waiting patiently for the woman with the lantern.

The childhood image that so many of us carry in our heads is of a woman who is daring but proper. She is no man's wife, but neither is she a commercialized sex object nor a victim to be pitied. She is a pio-neer woman among men. Yet she remains a Victorian lady for all that.

Florence Nightingale's military nursing appears brave without seeming revolutionary.

In this iconographic image that has been passed down to us so carefully, military nursing sustains a particular conventional notion of femininity; it doesn't upset it. Insofar as we each still accept this image of Nightingale-the-icon as authentic, we each continue to validate a pallid vision of the politics of nursing and to legitimate a military's utilization of different women in different ways for its own multiple ends, ends that include waging war in a fashion that ultimately maintains the patriarchal multilayered arrangement of masculinities and femininities.[1]

FROM CAMP FOLLOWERS TO THE CRIMEA

Medical care long has been a part of military planning and wartime operations. It would be intolerably expensive for commanders and military politicians to discharge every wounded soldier or to let men trained and fed at military expense simply die on the battlefield for lack of care. Before the mid-nineteenth century, however, women who performed the military's nursing duties remained invisible because they came from poorer social classes and thus were lumped together with the "masses" swooped up in any wartime: they were deemed mere camp followers. Furthermore, nursing then was not yet a job done by specially designated individuals, let alone individuals formally trained and organized into a profession; nurses were imagined perched on a rung below chambermaids. Ironically, while these two popular presumptions made women's contribution to warfare invisible and unrewarded, it also meant that women's provision of health care was somewhat more independent of military organization and authority than it is today. Progress for women in military nursing has taken the form of increasing visibility, increasing professionalization, *and* increasing military control. Some nursing leaders thus have wholeheartedly embraced militarization, seeing it as a process through which women as nurses could achieve full respect—and professional rewards—from male officials and from the general public as well.[2]

"Progress," as always, has had a complicated relationship to women's militarization.

NIGHTINGALE'S CRIMEAN MANEUVERS

General Robert Venables, commanding the British forces in the West Indies campaign of 1656, argued afterward that his operation would have been more successful had he been allowed to bring soldiers' wives along to nurse his men: "[There was the] necessity of having that sex with an army to attend upon and help the sick and wounded, which men are unfit for. Had more women gone, I suppose that many had not perished as they did for want of care and attendance."[3]

A century later, one British soldier, noting the unkempt colonial soldiery he faced during the American Revolution, attributed the rebels' uncleanness to the fact that they didn't have their women with them: "When at home, their female relations put them upon washing their hands and faces, and keeping themselves neat and clean; but being absent from such monitors, through an indolent, heedless turn of mind, they have neglected the means of health, have grown filthy, and poisoned their constitution by nastiness."[4]

The Crimean War in the mid-1800s became a turning point in many Western military men's thinking about how to organize their forces. The frustrations and failures on all sides—widely publicized in the contemporary press—prompted many European armies to craft new regulations concerning venereal disease, prostitution, marriage, and careers. The lessons derived from this war also produced a marked change in the class composition and bureaucratic status of women military nurses. For many—not all—military officials, one of the lessons of the Crimean War was that medical care was so critical to military effectiveness that it had to be brought under tight military control; it could no longer be left to mere—and annoyingly independent— camp followers.

This lesson was not learned easily by many military officers. It was taught to them by a crusading reformer, Florence Nightingale. She aimed her criticisms chiefly at what she saw as the backward and arrogant male military and medical elites. But simultaneously, she dismissed as inadequate those lower-class women whose foresisters, without formal credentials, had done so much of the hard military and civilian medical work earlier in eighteenth- and nineteenth-century Europe.[5]

Nightingale, the determined campaigner, was not just the "lady with the lantern," so comforting to children's book editors and military historians. She was both more crafty and more complex. Nightingale broke barriers—and provoked patriarchal hostility. But she was herself an insider. She came from one of Britain's well-to-do English families. She and her sisters went to parties at large country houses and traveled to the continent and, at the age of thirteen, even to Egypt.[6] Her refusal to marry, one of the early signs of her rebellious inclina-

tions, may have made her seem rather odd in the eyes of her social
peers, but she was far from an outcast. She knew men in high places, in
Parliament and the Cabinet and along the bureaucratic corridors of
Whitehall. When the Crimean War broke out, Nightingale already was
superintendent of a charitable nursing home on London's Harley
Street, the address of Britain's most fashionable male physicians. She
offered her services to the War Office. In the same day's post came a
letter from Sidney Herbert, a senior official in the War Office, a member of the Cabinet, and Nightingale's close friend. Impressed with her
dedication to Christian virtue, her charitable work, and her administrative capacities, Herbert was asking for her assistance in waging the
Crimean War. She would have an official appointment. According to
one of her earliest biographers, Lytton Strachey, when Nightingale and
her thirty-eight handpicked women nurses set off for Constantinople,
she had behind her both public authority and "popular enthusiasm."[7]

Despite her avowed Christian devotion, Nightingale did not see her
objective to be the reduction of militarism; rather, she sought to make
militarism more efficient and humane. She did not question Britain's
attempts to use its military might to expand its empire. Nor did she
doubt either the natural fit between masculinity and soldiering or between femininity and caring.[8] What Nightingale did challenge—with
energetic persistence and the strategic acumen of a consummate political insider—was (1) the authority of male military surgeons; (2) their
prevailing assumption that hygiene, nutrition, and administrative order
were irrelevant to wounded and ill soldiers' recovery; (3) the common
notion held by military surgeons and their civilian male superiors that
ordinary male soldiers had virtually no intellectual or spiritual needs of
their own; and finally, (4) the twinned patriarchal beliefs that only easily marginalized women, women contemptuously relegated to the status of camp followers, should be allowed near a battlefield and that,
therefore, women with a specialized training that gave them authority
had no place and no value among militarized men. These entrenched
beliefs would not be easily dislodged. They were fundamental elements
in the Victorian military culture of the day. The presence of professionalized women military nurses in the famed MASH tents on the Korean
battlefields one hundred years later testifies to Florence Nightingale's
success in partially dismantling that military culture. She accomplished
this feat using well-honed bureaucratic skills.

Nightingale and her contingent of nurses, mostly unmarried young
women from the English middle class, arrived at Scutari on Novem-

ber 4, 1854. Not among them was Mary Seacole. Mary Seacole, a Jamaican woman who was born in 1805 to a free black woman and a Scottish army officer, had already nursed men in the gold mining camps of Panama when she sailed to London to offer her services to the British army in its Crimean campaign. Seacole was first turned down in the War Office, then at the home of Elizabeth Herbert, wife of the War Office official and herself the organizer of women nursing volunteers after Nightingale had departed for the Crimea. Finally, when she was turned down by one of Nightingale's own close colleagues, Seacole began to suspect that the same racism that afflicted the Americans she had known also afflicted these Britons, whose sons she was offering to nurse. Upon being told by Nightingale's associate that there were no more places in the Crimea-bound nursing contingent, Seacole reflected, "I read in her face the fact that had there been a vacancy, I should not had been chosen to fill it."[9]

Seacole, nonetheless, was determined to nurse the men in the British regiments, men she had known when they served in Jamaica. So she set sail to the Crimea under her own agency to establish a hotel there for wounded soldiers.[10]

The British army had set up its hospitals in a suburb of Constantinople. It was here, upon Nightingale's arrival in 1854, that a second wartime front was about to be established: a struggle not just for control of military medicine but also for control of the meanings of *femininity* and *masculinity.*

What the newly arrived nurses found upon their arrival was chaos. The hospital was full to overflowing. Wounded men were arriving aboard ships after as long as three weeks afloat with minimal care, inadequate rations, and scarcely sufficient water. Once arrived in Scutari, the men were typically left to lie in their soiled uniforms, their bed linens and bandages rarely changed: "Hell yawned. Want, neglect, confusion, misery ... filled the endless Corridors ... The very building itself was radically defective. Huge sewers underlay it, and cesspools loaded with filth wafted their poison into the upper rooms ... here there was no ventilation. The stench was indescribable ... There were no basins, no towels, no soap, no brooms, no mops, no trays, no plates ... Stretchers, splints, bandages—all were lacking."[11]

Such was the operation of the British imperial army. Nightingale had brought supplies with her, not trusting the reassurances from officials in London that she would find all she needed in Scutari. With the aid of British journalists covering the war, she also began soliciting donations from ordinary citizens back home. Simultaneously, she launched a formidable stream of letters and reports to Herbert in the War Office, detailing the horrors and incompetencies she found and naming names up and down the British chain of command. Nightingale knew the power of public revelation. She would turn Scutari into a "scandal." When members of the civil service or the cabinet dragged their feet in responding to her proposals, she threatened to share her devastating field reports with her supporters in the press.[12] What the illustrator of my childhood book had left out was Florence Nightingale's sharp pen nib.

Simultaneously, Nightingale and her volunteers launched an assault on the male medical surgeons' authority. She insisted that these men conduct their profession differently. She responded to their initial hostility with tact, common sense, and goodwill. According to Strachey, who was writing about Nightingale in the midst of a later military horror, World War I, and who himself was no admirer of military men's intellect, Nightingale brought hope by "impos[ing] her personality upon the susceptible, overwrought, discouraged, and helpless men in authority who surrounded her."

One of her major reforms was to rethink the character—and thus the needs and potentials—of ordinary male soldiers. Contrary to their male superiors, who saw them as possessing little moral worth and even less spiritual capacity, Nightingale saw in these men an appreciation of dignity and social responsibility. She thus instituted a combination of hygienic and social innovations. She opened up the dank corridors to outside ventilation. But she also introduced knives and forks and ordered thousands of new shirts. She got the boilers repaired and employed British soldiers' wives as laundresses so that bed linens and bandages could be washed and replaced. When she insisted that a reading room be created and that a lecture series be started, she was accused by some officers of "spoiling the brutes."[13] She set up a system by which soldiers could send home part of their pay to their parents and wives.

Of all her innovations, the latter reform evoked the most scorn from her male superiors, one of whom pronounced, "it will do no good ... The British soldier is not a remitting animal."[14] Although she herself had eschewed marriage, Nightingale conceptualized the ordinary soldier as a social creature, a man self-consciously embedded in familial relationships. This concept was a radical ideological shift, one at which many militaries today still balk. Initially, she herself acted as the soldiers' banker, sending money home on their behalf. Eventually, though reluctantly, the British government set up its own machinery to collect and distribute soldiers' remittances.[15]

While occupied with redesigning hospital architecture and the very machinery of government, Nightingale made it a practice of being, with her woman nurses, constantly visible on the wards. One of her volunteers recalled:

> Two days after my arrival, Miss Nightingale sent for me to go with her round the hospital ... it seemed an endless walk, and it was not easily forgotten ... Miss Nightingale carried her lantern, which she would set down before she bent down over any of the patients. I much admired Miss Nightingale's manner to the men; it was so tender and kind ... The hospital was crowded to its fullest extent ... The building, which has since been reckoned to hold with comfort seventeen hundred men, then held between three and four thousand ...
>
> Whether in the strain of overwork, or the steady fulfillment of our arduous duty, there was one bright ray ever shed over it—one thing that made labour light and sweet; and this was the respect, affection and gratitude of the men ... Familiar as we were to become to them, though we were in and out of the wards day and night, they never forgot the respect due to our sex and position ... where stood groups of soldiers smoking and idling, the moment we approached all coarseness was hushed.[16]

In the postwar years that followed, as Nightingale continued in her campaign to change the public policy and entire outlook of the British War Office, many of the men, now veterans, who had witnessed and benefited from her work in the Crimea, became among her most important public supporters in her lobbying efforts. Among the international policies she opposed was the creation of an International Red Cross. She argued instead for medical services being tightly integrated into military institutions. Nightingale believed that if governments and their war ministries did not have to pay the direct medical costs of military operations they launched, officials would be tempted to go to war more frequently than they already did. She was opposed to reducing the governmental costs of war.[17] The Nightingale proposition: the militarization of medical services for soldiers could reduce wars.

The Crimean War provided more public access for women in the other war-waging countries as well. Russian middle-class women, like their British counterparts, thought of wartime service in terms of class. They perceived the chance to serve the military not as destitute and despised camp followers but as professionalized, formally integrated

military nurses. Together, Nikolai Pirogov, a noted Russian surgeon
and educator, and Elana Pavlovna, sister-in-law of the Czar, persuaded
the Russian government to solve its increasingly acute personnel shortages in the Crimea by sending female nurses to the front. Pavlovna, as
a court liberal and a friend of Russian social reformers, was convinced
that creating even an "auxiliary" nursing corps not only would save
men's lives but would allow women to play a larger role throughout
Russian public life. She didn't believe that such a unit could be commanded by a woman, however, so she urged her ally, Pirogov, to super-
vise the new nurses' corps. Pirogov agreed with her: Russian society
was backward partly because of its wasteful treatment of women. It
was the state, he believed, that ultimately suffered from such wasteful-
ness. Thus women should be educated and no longer "treated in an ar-
chaic and inane way ... women must take a role in society more nearly
corresponding to their human worth and mental capacities."[18]

The resultant Russian nurses' corps, the Sisters of Mercy of the Society of the Exultation of the Cross, mobilized 163 women volunteers.
Of the total, 110 were from ethnic Russian (i.e., Russian-speaking)
privileged sectors—wives, widows, and daughters of officials and
landowners. Another 24 came from the Russian petty bourgeoisie; and
about 5 came from the families of clergy. Five were nuns, two were do-
mestics, and one entered the auxiliary after already having worked as a
nurse. In his *Sevastopol Tales*, Tolstoy describes the Russian military
nurses on the Crimea as "sisters with peaceful faces and with the expression not of futile female lachrymose pity, but of active useful participation, stepping here and there among the wounded."[19]

The French forces also introduced women into formal military roles
in order to carry on their Crimean operations. Every French regiment
had its "Mademoiselle Courage," its *cantiniere*. Many of the *cantinieres* were wives of sergeants and other noncommissioned officers.[20]
Unlike earlier French camp followers, these *cantinieres* were sufficiently "on base" to be assigned specially designed, feminized military
uniforms: brass buttoned, tight-fitting military tunics and baggy
Zouave trousers beneath voluminous skirts. They carried little barrels
of brandy from which they sold drinks to the French troops and were
considered important to the health and morale of French troops serving in the disease-infested Crimea. But it wasn't until 1886 that the
French army's health services explicitly relied on women as health professionals, in the form of the private agency the Societé Secours aux
Blessés Militaires. This organization later became the Red Cross. In

France's war with Russia during the 1870s and in its 1907 war in Morocco, French women served in military hospitals and in the evacuation of the wounded from the front lines. Gertrude Stein and Alice B. Toklas, serving as ambulance drivers for the French military in the First World War, thus had joined a procession of women that could be traced back to "Mademoiselle Courage" in the Crimea.[21]

During the decades between 1860 and 1880, some War Office officials claimed that such widespread employment of women nurses to tend wounded or diseased men violated society's sense of propriety, especially since so many of the ill soldiers were suffering from sexually related diseases.[22] Britain's Army Nursing Service, nevertheless, was founded in 1881. For the next twenty years British army nurses served in a succession of colonial wars in South Africa, Sudan, and Egypt. In the Boer War alone, 1,400 British women served as army nurses. Their units were given names of royal patronesses in order to raise the social status of military nursing and attract more middle-class women: Princess Christian's Army Nursing Service Reserve, Queen Alexandra's Imperial Military Nursing Service, and later, Princess Mary's Royal Air Force Nursing Service.[23] Women in these royally sponsored, militarily deployed units were nursing male soldiers. They also were nursing British imperialism.

The decades between 1860 and 1880 were the same postwar decades in which British male officials debated the pros and cons of military wives. These decades were also the ones in which British male officials attempted to impose the Contagious Diseases Acts on any women they deemed to be prostitutes. These actions were not mere coincidence. While these several groups of women usually had little contact with each other and rarely sat down to strategize about a response to the government's militarizing maneuvers, they nonetheless were being connected to one another by postwar male policy makers. Josephine Butler, the anti-CD-acts campaigner, and Florence Nightingale both challenged the contemporary cultural construction of feminine respectability. Both women revealed in their writings and in their actions that the British Victorian military-political establishment was extending its imperial reach, and success in that enterprise required the establishment's control of gendered respectability.

THE "OTHER" CIVIL WAR

American officials always have kept an eye on British military practice. Exchange of information and lessons—about how best to use women as well as about the latest weapons technology—between governments is one of the chief functions of today's expanding NATO alliance. But the internationalization of military innovation began long before the creation of the North Atlantic alliance. Even without benefit of NATO's elaborate alliance structure, nineteenth-century American officers were watching Britain's medical innovations in the Crimea. When the American Civil War broke out in the 1860s, they had a chance to put some of those innovations into military practice. Like the Crimean War, the American Civil War produced male manpower shortages and an escalating carnage that demanded the expansion of medical services and the more calculated military use of women.

As in Britain, this change in military needs came at a time when middle-class white women were beginning to assert that they had a public role to play. In the eyes of the young Louisa May Alcott, a thirty-year-old white middle-class "spinster" who wanted to "do something" in 1862, the choices before her were quite limited. Her friends and family in Concord, Massachusetts, offered suggestions: "Write a book"; "Try teaching again"; "Take a husband ... and fulfill your mission"; "Turn actress, and immortalize your name." But then one relative proposed, "Go nurse the soldiers." Upon hearing the last, Alcott declared, "I will."[24] She was responding to a deliberate Union recruiting campaign aimed at young women. In all, an estimated 3,200 women provided nursing services to both the Union and Confederate armies during the Civil War. Most received no pay.[25]

It is always a difficult moment in the evolution of women's liberation when women's desire to break out of the airless domestic sphere crystallizes at the same time that their government's military commanders decide they can make use—selective, limited, and controlled use—of a number of women in military roles previously closed to women. At times like these—1852, 1862, 1914, 1942, 1973, 2000—it is easy to mistake women's militarization for women's liberation.

Of all the women who offered their services to the Union Army, widows and "spinsters," such as Alcott, were deemed by male officials to be the most acceptable. Single, young, marriageable, white women who volunteered faced popular suspicions that their motivations were less patriotic than sexual.[26] This attitude supplied part of the motivation for War Department male officials to select Dorothea Dix to take charge of the women nurses. Many of her male superiors expressed distaste for Dix, for her strong opinions and lack of feminine graces, but, they believed, she would control the young women nurses in a rigidly moralistic fashion that would allay public fears about what those young women were doing away from home, living amid male soldiers.[27] This situation would not be the last time that men in government would select a particular kind of woman—particular in the respectability of her racial, class, and generational positions, particular in her public presentation of feminine morality, particular in her gendered organizational philosophy—to control those women that the military wanted to use without risking their own loss of popular legitimacy.

In the 1860s, Clara Barton, disagreeing not only with Dix but with Nightingale, took a more arms-length approach to wartime nursing. Initially a schoolteacher and then one of the first female clerks in the U.S. Patent Office, Barton chose to do her nursing of Civil War soldiers outside the governmental establishment. After the war ended, Barton accepted a government post leading the new Missing Soldiers Office, an agency that tracked down 22,000 missing soldiers, thereby becoming the first woman to head a bureau of the U.S. federal government. Like Nightingale, she continued to weigh the risks and benefits of placing wartime nursing inside or outside the state. Ultimately, Barton chose a political strategy different from Nightingale's, and in 1881 she founded the American Red Cross.[28]

Civil War nursing challenged American popular dictates about what a young white woman could do in public and yet hold on to her reputation as a respectable woman. But Civil War nursing also revealed divisions even among white pro-Union women. Thus some young women riled against Dix's rigidly feminized routines, seeing them as diminishing their ability to develop their talents to the fullest. Other women nurses directed their anger against those upper-class northern white women who behaved as though grisly battles were mere entertainment to enliven a Sunday afternoon picnic. According to historian Elizabeth Leonard, the male doctors seemed to enjoy these elite women's visits and their gifts of strawberries and other delicacies. By contrast, middle-class nurse Mary von Olnhausen vented in a letter home the nurses' common contempt : "A lot of women came in to-day just as I was dressing [a soldier's] wound. One of them, as she saw it, just gave a stagger and fell up against the wall ... All the women crowded around, and one young one said, 'Oh, I always thought I should so like to be a nurse.' She looked about as much account as a yellow cat."[29]

The prevailing ideology of femininity for white women in the 1860s American South presented even greater obstacles for those women wanting to enlist as military nurses and for the Confederate strategists who wanted to put them to use. One woman, Kate Cumming, was especially bemused by her brother-in-law's opposition to her volunteering. When he contended that no "refined lady" would want to place herself among ordinary soldiers, she reminded him that his own mother and sister only a few years earlier had traveled to Scutari to serve with Florence Nightingale. His response: the women serving with Nightingale were supported by a stronger government than that of the Confederacy. That is, a woman's respectability required the protection of a robust state. Unpersuaded, Cumming enlisted.[30]

In both the Confederacy and the Union, debates between women and men over how to best make use of both white and black women's skills and enthusiasm without jeopardizing conventional notions of manliness and of a racialized social order in general raged throughout the five years of war and into the decades of postwar reconstruction.[31] African American women were used by both sides in the Civil War, but without any formal recognition of their skills or contributions. Rather than acknowledging them as nurses, white male military strategists saw these women chiefly as camp followers—camp followers who enhanced the sanitation and nutrition of soldiers' living conditions, yet camp followers nonetheless. They were not to be recognized as integral members of a white-run masculinized military institution. Consequently, racism combined with sexism set limits on the extent of these women's militarization. Full militarization might have risked full acknowledgment.

When the Union forces reached as far south as Vicksburg and Natchez, Mississippi, in 1863, many newly freed black men chose to enlist in the Union army and many newly freed black women chose to follow them. Those African American women from Mississippi worked as military cooks, laundresses, and nurses. During the last years of the war, many of them married black soldiers, for the first time in their lives having access to legalized marriage. Union commanders swung from side to side in their policies toward the black women who joined their camps: sometimes appreciating how their services improved their soldiers' health, other times trying to eject them on the grounds that they were a corrupting influence on their men.[32] Therefore, while white women in the 1860s were making inroads into the masculinized notions of militarized femininity, most African American women continued to be relegated to the position of camp followers.

FROM THE SPANISH-AMERICAN WAR TO WORLD WAR I:
RACE, GENDER, "OPPORTUNITY"

All-black male units fought for the U.S. military in the ten-week Spanish-American War of 1898.[33] They required medical care, but who would nurse these men? This question had to be answered if the U.S. military were to play their part in expanding the reach of American imperial power.

Alarmed at the rates at which Caribbean tropical diseases were decimating U.S. forces, the Surgeon General, George M. Sternberg, called for the mobilization of women as military nurses, not only white women but black women as well. Thirty-two women volunteered for what was the U.S. military's first black women's nursing corps and were sent to Georgia's Camp Thomas to treat black male soldiers.[34] At the same time, civilian white women were pressed to offer their nursing skills to the war effort. With Congress's authorization, a system of contract nurses was created in 1898, overseen by the newly created Nurse Corps Division. The nurses themselves were not allowed, however, to be assigned military ranks. They were kept just outside the military. They were militarized, yet not so militarized as to earn the rewards bestowed by a militarized public and its government on those it deemed "real" soldiers. As earlier, when the Union male strategists chose Dorothea Dix, here too the American military command chose an elite civilian woman to serve as its mediator—and gatekeeper. During the Spanish-American War this ambiguous role—as both controller of and advocate for women—was played by Dr. Anita Newcomb McGee. A white woman, a doctor, and vice president of the Daughters of the American Revolution, McGee created admissions standards for these quasi-militarized white nurses by collecting endorsements from their training schools and reading letters of reference to ensure that each woman was a "lady." McGee played her part inside the state with great efficiency. By September 1898 the army had 1,158 women serving as contract nurses.[35]

Confirming McGee's confidence, the chief surgeon of the U.S. volunteers wrote: "During the four trips I made on the hospital ship relief, to and from Cuba and Puerto Rico, I had ample opportunity to compare the work of the male and female nurses and I have no hesitation in speaking in decided terms in favor of the latter. Nursing is women's special sphere ... She is endowed with all the qualifications, mentally and physically, to take care of the sick. Her sweet smile and gentle touch are often of more benefit to the patient than the medicine she administers ... Her sense of duty and devotion to those placed under her care seldom is equaled by men."[36]

The list of military outposts to which women were deployed in the years following the Spanish-American War reads like a chart of American imperialist ambition: Cuba, Puerto Rico, Hawaii, China, Japan, and the Philippines. As recent feminist historians of American nursing have acknowledged, those white women who saw nursing as a way to serve their country, gain valuable technical experience, and "see the world" facilitated—wittingly or unwittingly—the international dissemination of their government's presumptions about gendered culture and racialized gender.[37]

The men in Congress were impressed with women nurses' contribution to the military campaigns in both the Spanish-American War and the Philippines. They thus authorized the establishment of the Army Nurse Corps in 1901 and the Navy Nurse Corps in 1908. But they created each as a white-only corps. During World War I the American Red Cross agreed to admit black nurses, but the Surgeon General vetoed the plan. He had the support of President Woodrow Wilson, himself a white southerner and advocate of racial segregation. Wilson had *re*segregated bathrooms and eating areas in federal office buildings, but this move did not stop African American men from volunteering for military service. Many black women who had graduated from newly established black nursing schools in the previous twenty years also wanted to enlist. According to historian Darlene Clark Hine, these women saw military nursing as an entrée to wider professional opportunities at a time when the all-white American Nurses' Association joined with other white medical institutions to confine black nurses to the hospitals' lowest positions. The white leadership of the American Red Cross did little to press for the opening up of the military nursing corps to African American women.[38] Not until the country was on the verge of peace, an influenza epidemic had created a massive demand for nurses, and African American women's groups had undertaken intense lobbying did the federal government in July 1918, after having already given 21,000 white women nurses the opportunity to gain military experience, finally allow twenty-four black nurses to be appointed to the Army Nurse Corps.[39]

It was only after World War I, in those postwar years during which the gender politics of the war are reassessed, that the still all-male U.S. Congress acknowledged the contributions and sacrifices that American military nurses made (260 had died during the war, mostly from diseases) by integrating the nursing corps more fully into the regular armed services. That is, militarization was made a *reward*. By passing the National Defense Act in 1920—just months before the women's suffrage amendment was ratified—the Congressmen permitted women as nurses to attain officer ranks as high as major and to apply for military retirement benefits.

A certain brand of respectable femininity remained salient in these masculinized legislative calculations: a woman who nursed for the military would be dishonorably discharged if she became pregnant outside of marriage *or* if she married while in the military.[40]

When World War I broke out in Europe in 1914, race was also on many Briton's minds. On the one hand, British imperial enthusiasts had for decades seen their country's acquisition of colonies as a natural extension of the British, and more broadly, white race's global civilizing mission. On the other hand, each setback or defeat experienced while traveling along the imperial road provoked official and popular anxiety about the actual vitality of the British/white race. Just what place imperial visions held in the imaginations of each British woman who volunteered for military nursing in the late nineteenth century, however, should be considered carefully. Florence Nightingale seems to have seen women's progress, their spiritual virtue, and the imperial project all of a piece. Yet historian Anne Summers warns us not to imagine that all British women who went into nursing were inspired by Nightingale's imperialist religious pursuit of virtue.[41] Evidence suggests that during the decade prior to the outbreak of World War I, many middle-class British women had come to see nursing in India or Africa as a means to express not their spirituality but their own earthly individualism. One British nurse working in South Africa wrote home: "An English nurse ... seeks her fortunes in South African hospitals, as her brother seeks it in the mines of Kimberley or in far-off Rhodesia."[42]

To many British nurses, World War I appeared initially as yet another opportunity—to gain professional experience, to assert their individual identities, to have an adventure, to demonstrate their patriotism, and to prove women's collective value to the nation and its male-only governing elite.

World War I broke out, as does any war anywhere, at a very particular moment in the political evolution of relations between men and women and between the meanings of masculinity and femininity. In Australia, all adult women of European ancestry had won the right to

vote in national elections in 1902. Yet even a decade later only single
women were eligible for the Australian Army Nurses Service. Australia's male policy makers rather naively classed the nurses as officers,
not so that the nurses could wield authority but so that their feminine
respectability might be maintained; their pay rate was set at that of enlisted men.[43] In Canada, women who served as Army nurses during
World War I were the first women on whom that country's all-male
parliament, acting in wartime 1917, bestowed national voting rights.[44]
This legislative action was perhaps the first time that women's suffrage
was militarized—the first but not the last.

In Germany at the outbreak of World War I, concerns about nurses'
respectability were similar to those in Australia, though German
women were still five years away from winning their own right to vote.
German Red Cross leaders, working closely with the Patriotic
Women's Association, strove to recruit middle-class women into military nursing.[45] The German women who volunteered did so, however,
not just out of nationalist loyalty but, as their letters and diaries reveal,
out of a desire to break out of the contemporary confines of bourgeois
domesticity. No home front genteel voluntarism for these women.
They wanted to be on the battlefront. Wrote Emmy von Rudgisch in
her diary: "The impatience with which we [nurses of the Baden Red
Cross] await that great moment when we are called to the area behind
the lines is indescribable."[46] And another German woman similarly recalled: "My heart was thumping ... it was a day of honour for us all:
the F2 was the first hospital train off to the front ... into the line of
fire ... Our faces were positively transfigured, all petty concerns forgotten."[47]

Even this cursory journey—from the United States to Britain, Australia, Canada, and on to Germany—should give us pause. The comparisons suggest that our understanding of what World War I was—
what it took to wage, what meanings its participants drew from it,
what lessons were drawn and shared internationally among military
men and civilian elites—will be incomplete (and thus unreliable) if we
treat women's nursing on all sides as if it were either inevitable or
natural. It was neither.

World War I is still remembered by Europeans today as "the Great
War." What was "great" was the scale of suffering. More than any other
war, this war's prolonged length, its muddy terrain, its rival military doctrines, and its new technology—especially poison gas and the machine
gun—combined to make medical policy making a crucial element in

commanders' war waging.[48] The result was a convergence: many middle-class women's picture of nursing, especially nursing abroad, as a multisided opportunity peaked at the same moment that male policy makers realized that they faced an escalating military need that certain women, if properly selected and properly controlled, could fill.

What continued to be of political concern was maintaining feminized respectability. Somehow this ferociously fought war would have to be waged without violating conventional notions of the "respectable woman." The military maneuver designed to address this political requirement was to mobilize women of middle-class backgrounds who were blessed with native-born parents, young women whose virtuous character could be vouched for by at least one "lady." Vera Brittain, among other British applicants, found the consequent examination humiliating: "I stood ... all through the interview, and know now how a servant feels when she is being engaged."[49]

Still today, World War I stands as a high-water mark of human brutality. At the Battle of the Somme, fought between July and November of 1916 on French soil—mud, really—more than one million soldiers were killed and thousands more were injured.[50] One million soldiers— twice the number killed at the Battle of Gettysburg fifty years earlier, twice the number of Americans killed in the Vietnam War five decades later. Despite the horrors that they witnessed and the consequences of those horrors that they tried to repair, many British women who served as military nurses were reluctant to return to civilian life in 1918. It appeared to them that their vistas were about to shrink.

The British writer Radclyffe Hall, famous for her novel *The Well of Loneliness* with its explicitly lesbian heroine, crafted a story in the postwar years that sought to capture some British women's sense of postwar shrinkage. They had won the vote, but somehow, with the coming of peacetime, they had lost their hard-won freedom. The heroine of Hall's "Miss Ogilvy Finds Herself" had spent World War I on the battlefields of France, leading an all-women's ambulance unit. Now, at the war's end, she watched her battered ambulance being lifted aboard a ship to return home. This, Radclyffe Hall imagines, was the vehicle that had "set Miss Ogilvy free."[51] Miss Ogilvy stands there, "her hands thrust deep into her pockets ... as though she were still standing firm under fire while the wounded were placed in her ambulance." Her reverie is broken by the voices of the younger women in her ambulance corps. She had been their officer. They had been her community. "'It's rotten!' Miss Ogilvy heard someone saying. 'It's rotten, this breaking up of our Unit!'" She scarcely trusted herself to respond. Soon she herself would be across the Channel and on a train heading home. Out of the windows she would watch "small homesteads, small churches, small pastures, small lanes with small hedges; all small like England itself, all small like Miss Ogilvy's future."[52]

WORLD WAR II: RACIALIZED MILITARY NURSING COMES OF AGE

Helen Pon Onyett was one of the Chinese American women who volunteered for the Army Nurses Corps in 1942 during the aftermath of the Japanese air attack on Pearl Harbor. She was already a trained nurse; until the Pearl Harbor attack, however, she had not felt compelled to offer her skills to the military. Then one day she was visiting New York's Chinatown and joined a group of people discussing the newspaper headlines detailing the attack on Hawaii. Everyone, she remembers, was "so excited and up in arms." Like many Chinese Americans, Helen Pon Onyett joined the military out of a combination of American patriotism, Chinese nationalism, and a sense that the armed forces might provide a space in which she could be judged by other Americans on the basis of her skills, not her race. For her, this hope was fulfilled: "I was treated as a nurse, not an Oriental somebody."[53]

The managers of the 1940s U.S. war effort were far less ambivalent about using women as military nurses than had been their World War I predecessors. They brought into the armed forces 350,000 women volunteers, comprising at their peak 2 per cent of the total American military's personnel.[54] Still, these policy makers, which included a number of prominent white women, would not abandon either their gendered or their racialist presumptions. Thus the great majority of American women uniformed personnel were channeled into office work, communications, and health care. Thus, too, women were assigned to units according to white policy makers' notions of both propriety and threat.[55] Helen Pon Onyett and other Chinese American women and men were assigned to racially integrated units—that is, units that included small numbers of Puerto Ricans, Native Americans, and other Chinese Americans. These units were deployed to both Europe and the Pacific. By contrast, white officials, presuming that all Japanese Americans posed a security threat, placed Japanese American men and women, including nurses, in all-Japanese American units. These units were sent to Europe but were not allowed to serve in the Pacific.

Exploring the diversity of these wartime experiences should make observers wary of using the category "women" or even the category "Asian American women" alone when trying to make sense of the militarization of women's lives and of the nursing profession. Both "women" and "Asian American" do indeed serve to shed light on the gendered processes of militarization, but when used just by themselves these gross categories may not be sufficient to reveal how and why the U.S. military's officialdom has crafted its gendered maneuvers.

African American women, like Japanese American women, were assigned to racially segregated military units during World War II. The white official thinking derived less from an assumption that black volunteers would collude with one of the Axis powers than from two still-prevalent beliefs: (1) that black woman nurses were not as skilled as their white counterparts and (2) that the white American public would not tolerate "their" white troops being ministered to by black nurses. In 1941, Army General George Marshall replied to a black official in the War Department who had been urging that racial quotas and segregation be abolished: "The War Department cannot ignore the social relationships between negro and white which have been established by the American people through custom and habit ... Either through lack of opportunity or other causes, the level of intelligence and occupational skill of the negro population is considerably below that of whites ... such a social experiment would only bring a danger of efficiency, discipline and morale."[56]

At the outset of World War II, therefore, the number of black nurses allowed to volunteer was restricted by a quota, and black nurses were assigned solely to care for black male soldiers. Only after the war had dragged on for year after year and only after officials had begun to predict that white women would need to be drafted did President Franklin Roosevelt relent. He ordered, for the first time in the gendered, racialized evolution of the U.S. military, that black nurses be permitted to nurse *all* American personnel.

Yet we should not over-determine (depoliticize) our explanation for such a change in the gendered, racialized structure of American militarized thinking. This policy turnaround would not have occurred had it not been for the political lobbying by black nursing leaders such as Mabel K. Staupers of the National Association of Colored Graduate Nurses (NACGN).[57] It was Staupers who had pressed the white-only American Nurses' Association (ANA) to allow black nurses to join and to add its considerable influence to the effort to break down segregation in military nursing. It was Staupers who, in 1944, as Congress was beginning to discuss the unpleasant prospect of a white women's draft to fill the military's escalating nursing needs, arranged a meeting with Eleanor Roosevelt and persuaded her to urge the president to change the existing racialized nursing policy. It was Staupers who posed the rhetorical question to white officials and to the general public, "If nurses are needed so desperately why isn't the Army using colored nurses?"[58]

Consequently, when on January 20, 1945, the U.S. government lifted the lid on its quotas of black women nurses and allowed black women nurses to be assigned throughout the nursing corps, it was not proof of history as inevitable "progress." It was not proof that wars naturally shake up existing racialized gendered structures. It was not even convincing evidence that when wars are prolonged, even racist officials will be compelled by the logic of war waging to surrender at least a few of their racialized practices, though this often is a factor. Rather, the story of African American military nurses in World War II suggests that it takes a particular kind of warfare (long, bloody, geographically dispersed), a policy elite's intense fear of violating public cultural expectations (e.g., the exclusion of white women from the draft), and a significant level of preexisting civilian political organizing (e.g., the NACGN), together with the potential for a strategic alliance between certain women on the outside and certain women on the inside of the state structure (e.g., Mabel Staupers and Eleanor Roosevelt) for change to occur. Even then, the reform was launched only when the war was almost over.[59]

WAR AS ROMANCE

During World War II at least one million Soviet women served in their country's military, often under brutalizing conditions. Women were fighter pilots, artillery gunners, snipers, and surgeons. Thousands of Soviet women served as medics and nurses, often on the front lines. Some women who were conscripted as nurses later in the war persuaded their male commanders to give them weapons training and transfer them to gunnery posts.[60] Nevertheless, after the war, government officials seemed determined to re-feminize Soviet womanhood. Part of this campaign was their adoption of a policy to promote the idea of the Soviet woman as a mother first. Another part of the government's effort was to recategorize those women who had served as com-

bat troops: thousands of women who had fought as gunners and
snipers retroactively would be listed officially as medics and nurses—
as if this historical reassigning could preserve an orthodox version of
Soviet femininity for the next generation.[61] According to historian
Reina Pennington, even that campaign of feminizing revisionism was
not judged sufficient. Moscow's postwar officials enlisted Soviet filmmakers to help drain World War II military nursing of its more unappealing (i.e., unfeminine) attributes. In the hands of film directors, Soviet women nurses had to be reconstructed as romantic figures. One
Soviet nursing veteran reacted to the postwar screen image with in-
credulity: "There are films about the war in which one sees a nurse at
the front line. There she goes, so neat and clean, wearing a skirt, not
padded trousers, and with a side cap perched on top of an attractive
hairdo. It is just not true. Could we have hauled wounded men dressed
like that?"[62] Postwar years in all countries are a time of continued gendered war waging. But now the battle is not to take the next hill. It is
to capture the collective memory.

By the end of World War II, the U.S. government had mobilized
69,000 women to serve as military nurses. It had also steadily militarized them, drawing them ever more tightly into the entire military
structure. Many women nurses and their civilian supporters viewed
this process with satisfaction; being militarized meant being made integral to the pay, rank, and deployment structures of the military establishment. To be militarized, to them, stood as proof of women's skill
and value.

At the war's end, being militarized also meant that thousands of
women were eligible for the new G.I. Bill, Congress's "thank you"
package of housing, health, and education benefits for returning veterans. In 1947, Congress also passed the Army-Navy Nurses Act,
thereby establishing the Army and Navy Nurse Corps as permanent
units of the armed services.[63]

The U.S. military, along with most of the other militaries that came
out of World War II intact, nonetheless remained an overwhelmingly
male and masculinized institution. War was still legitimized as a masculine activity: women were meant to be the rationale for, not the actors in, war waging. A woman who was nursing soldiers, even a
woman of respectable class background, even a woman officered by a
woman superior of rigid moral outlook, remained a woman among
men. A respectable woman among men remained a woman whose
feminine propriety, presumably, was being placed at risk. A respectable

woman among men whose propriety was jeopardized could cast doubt
on the legitimacy of the entire military enterprise. Male military planners—and their women allies in any war effort—continued to care
most about military legitimacy. A war waged with slipping public belief in the military's legitimacy was a war-waging effort in trouble.

Several ideological strategies have been employed simultaneously to
preserve the feminine propriety of feminized military nursing and so
too the public's confidence in the military as a whole. These strategies
have involved the manipulation of images and of women themselves.
One strategy has been to discourage women from speaking about
wartime nursing experiences that might taint their military's image.
Often the woman who remained silent, however, was led to believe
that what her silence was protecting was not the military's image but
her own "good name."

The multiple strategies for sustaining shaky notions of militarized
feminine respectability have not always been compatible. They could
be divided into two categories: the "Dorothea Dix strategy" and the
"Nurse as Ideal Soldier's Girlfriend strategy." The first strategy has em-
phasized moral rectitude, middle-class origins, and policies to ensure
that military nurses cultivated angelic asexuality along with professional competence. The second strategy has seemed to place value on
innocence, emotional generosity, and perhaps, availability, as if a
wounded male soldier would recover more quickly if he could fanta-
size about his nurse. Both these formulas have elicited awkward questions about marriage.

The married woman would have loyalties other than to the military.
Her propriety might be thrown into doubt if she chose to leave her
husband in order to care for other men. And how could soldiers in the
wards innocently daydream about their nurses if those women wore
wedding bands with their uniforms? Perhaps the problem of dealing
with married nurses has made U.S. military strategists' policy making
so hesitant. At the end of World War I, even as Congress was insinuat-
ing female nurses more integrally into the regular military bureaucracy,
it retained the ban on married women as nurses. That ban was in place
at the start of World War II. But the army soon relented and allowed
married women nurses to volunteer in 1942. The navy's officials were
more reluctant to give up their single-women-only rule. Not until they
faced squarely the fact that they were losing so many valuable nurses
to forced resignation upon marriage that they too, in 1944, abandoned
their restriction.[64]

Marriage, femininity, military function, and romance—all these factors have been routinely woven together in the fabric of militarized women's lives. Nurses have been no exception. Yet the bundle of presumptions about nurses and nursing has made ideas about militarized romance particularly salient.

The "Dorothea Dix strategy" might have been especially appealing to some male strategists and many women advocates and it might have been reassuring to large portions of the public, but it was not very appealing to the mass media. And the media's importance to war-waging officials had grown steadily since Nightingale's strategic use of journalists in the 1850s. By the 1940s in Britain and the United States (and also in Japan, Italy, and Germany), the war-shaping media included the movie industry, radio stations, and the publishers of books, newspapers, and magazines—including comic books.

Many reporters and commentators did not find that the morally pure, above-all-reproach angel made as good a "story" as the heroine of a hospital romance. Nightingale's self-conscious use of press reporters covering the Crimean War had helped create British popular support for her nurses and thus, in turn, for her efforts to reverse male military surgeons' conventional practices. But ninety years later, the nurses had much less capacity to control how they were to be portrayed. And the military saw that the nurse-soldier romance, while it violated previous Victorian feminine conventions and still carried with it political risks (it would *not* do for stories to reach back home of married soldiers being seduced in the wards by lustful nurses; it would *not* do for moviegoers on the home front to be fed images of innocent patriotic girls being harassed by army doctors), could bolster wartime male morale and feminine orthodoxy.

After all, by the mid-twentieth century, there existed in both Britain and the United States a well-entrenched notion that women's natures were romantic, heterosexually romantic. Military nurses could be portrayed by writers and directors, therefore, as experiencing not warfare, the preserve of manly men, but romance, the natural arena of feminine women. In the life of the female military nurse, war thereby became adventure; care was converted into romantic love.

Publishing executives have been happy to comply. Patricia L. Walsh wrote an autobiographically based novel derived from the fourteen months she spent nursing Vietnamese and American war casualties in the late 1960s. Walsh used the novel to expose in uncompromising detail the burns from napalm, the black-market and gray-market selling of medical supplies, and the cynicism of American military personnel, who called the victims "crispy critters." Her publishers, however, decided that to guarantee display on the grocery store and newsstand racks, Walsh's novel should be packaged as a romantic tale. Thus they gave it a suitably romantic paperback cover and teased the reader with the question, "She was fighting to save lives, but at what cost to her own?" Inside, they imposed a subtitle: "Their War-Torn Love."[65]

The crafters of recent military advertising images have waffled. Sometimes they have portrayed the woman nurse as the fully militarized professional. Other times they have reinforced this media-constructed image of the demilitarized, romanticized military nurse. Over the last two decades advertisements in both the United States and Britain have offered a mixture of upward mobility via paid training on the one hand, and social life and adventure on the other. Queen Alexandra's Army Nursing Corps' 1981 glossy brochure, for example, described the nurse as a woman whose job and social life reflect some of the new as well as the old gender conditions of the British military. It also laid out the British military's Cold War and only partially postimperial global view:

> On Duty: You'll work in up-to-date hospitals with modern equipment nursing servicewomen as well as soldiers, their wives and children, and civilians. Your career in the QAs will normally bring fresh posting every two years, perhaps to Hong Kong, Nepal, West Germany, Cyprus, Northern Ireland ... wherever you go, you may have the opportunity to use any specialist qualifications you may possess, and plenty of time to be a good nurse. And except in the rare emergency, you will never find yourself with too many patients.
> Off Duty: Comfortable accommodation is provided for everybody ... you are well looked after in the modern army ...
> You can join in with other serving men and women in dramatic and folksinging clubs. Your social life—in effect—can be as active and varied as you like.[66]

The precariousness of the dual-strategy approach makes any news of sexual harassment of nurses especially damaging. "Romance" in the military hospital ward only works politically for a military command if the soldier-boyfriend can be portrayed as innocent. But his innocence must be made compatible with his militarized manliness. His wounds, his immobility, his isolation from society, and his battlefield sacrifice all can lend themselves to this portrayal of innocence masculinized. With this image in place, the woman as military nurse then can be portrayed as a competent maternal sister who gradually—it must be gradual—

Figure 10 Hollywood studios have produced scores of films in which military nurses have found problematic love on the battlefield. *Flight Nurse* was released by Republic Pictures in 1953, during the Korean War. ("Flight Nurse," Republic Pictures, 1953; reproduced in a postcard collection called "Career Girls," Pantheon Books (New York), edited by Michael Barson, copyrighted by Michael Barson, 1989.)

discovers something appealing and individual behind this soldier-patient's bandages and manly diffidence. Her maternal emotions are transformed into feelings more sexualized.

But military nurses' experiences in reality frequently have failed to match the myths of the paperback and silver screen romantic scenarios. LaVonne Camp waited five decades before succeeding to get her

own real-life story of World War II army nursing into print. She had
written a memoir long ago, but it had stayed buried in a dresser
drawer. Now, writing to the editors of the New York Times, Camp expressed a desire finally to clear up a misunderstanding about that war,
a misunderstanding that, she believed, was being perpetrated in the
war's fiftieth anniversary commemorations.[67] Camp had been an
American army nurse in that war's China-Burma-India theater. She had
nursed both American and Chinese soldiers on a troopship, in
makeshift jungle hospitals, and in a large Calcutta hospital. She had
met a soldier, an American pilot, and had fallen in love. He took her
along on his missions, flying "over the hump" into China. After the
war, they married. Fifty years later, they were still married. At this
point the orthodox tale of militarized romance would end. This point
is where most officials would like it to end. But Camp had a more
complicated story of military nursing to tell: "I found that the perils of
preserving my virtue in a testosterone-laden world were just as con-
suming as worrying about a Japanese submarine torpedoing our troopship. Those were the days before sexual harassment was considered an
issue ... I saw splendid professional people succumb to alcohol abuse
and sexual profligacy, probably not for the duration, but that behavior,
too, becomes a memory."[68]

NURSES UNDER FIRE

The term combat has been so infused with patriarchal understandings
of masculinity (that is, of what femininity is not) that debates over the
definition of the term have shaped—and today continue to shape—
every official effort to mobilize women for military purposes. Nurses,
in practice, have served in combat regardless of official prohibitions
banning their presence there. They have served in combat not because
of unusual individual bravery—the stuff of nursing romances—but
because they have been part of a military structure that has needed
their skills near combat. Nonetheless, to close the gap between myth
and reality would require military officials to resolve their own ideological gender contradictions, something many are loathe to do. Instead, those officials, often with the help of journalists, leave the public
naive and leave the military nurses coping privately with the psychological strains of such a gap.

   These elite contradictions may help explain the American public's
own ideological confusion. A decade after the Vietnam War, pollsters
asked a sampling of Americans which sort of military roles they found

most acceptable and least acceptable for women in the U.S. military.[69]
This poll took place when the second wave of the American women's
movement was prompting popular debates about the meanings of femininity and masculinity, when the percentages of women in uniform
were rising, and when the Pentagon needed a significant number of
women in uniform to make up for the male conscripts they lost with
the ending of the draft:

> "Do you approve of a woman working as a typist in the Pentagon?"
> Answering in the positive was 97 percent of the respondents.

> "How about a woman flying a jet fighter plane [a military job that,
> at the time of the polling, the Congress banned women from hold-
> ing]?" A surprising 62 percent of the public sampled said that they
> found this possibility acceptable.

> A woman serving as a "soldier in hand-to-hand combat"? The pub-
> lic's acceptance rate plummeted. Only one-third of the respondents
> could accept that scenario.

Now, where in this range—from an acceptance high of 97 percent to
a low of 31 percent—would you expect these post–Vietnam War,
Reagan-era Americans to set the acceptance rating for "nurse in a
combat zone"? The response was 94 *percent.*

That is, nursing had become so deeply feminized in the American
culture by the 1980s that even putting a nurse in a place where a respectable woman ideologically is not "supposed" to be—in a combat
zone—did almost nothing to reduce Americans' willingness to accept
her there. In an American cultural contest between the feminization of
military nursing and the masculinization of militarized combat, the
feminization of militarized nurses was winning hands down. This success rate was good news for U.S. military policy makers. They could
continue to deploy women as military nurses wherever those nurses
were needed. The general public back home, these same officials
hoped, would continue to see those women as doing what feminine
creatures are supposed to do.[70]

FROM MARGIN TO MONUMENT

Today, more than two decades after its end, we are starting to fully understand the genderings of the Vietnam War. Only now, for instance,
are many Vietnamese women who fought with the North's military be-

ginning to tell their own story outside official channels. An estimated
1.5 million women in North Vietnam served in various military capacities during the war against the United States and its allied regime in
Saigon. Some 100,000 of those North Vietnamese women veterans are
still alive today.[71]

Many of these women, now approaching old age, are feeling quite
abandoned. Despite the Vietnamese culture's validation of warrior
women defending the nation—against first the Chinese, then the
French, then the Americans—and despite museums and town square
monuments memorializing women's wartime achievements, the real
women living real postwar lives are an embarrassment if they come out
of the last war too injured to attract husbands and bear children. Thus
many of those living warrior women harbor a sense that they have
been treated with disrespect and neglect.

Among these women are those who served as nurses in the Hanoi-
commanded military. Some, like Le Thi Than, have become Buddhist
nuns.[72] Le Thi Than was a medical assistant in the North's army in the
1960s and early 1970s. She ended the war partially disabled. Her parents urged her to return to their village to settle down, get married,
have children. But she refused. She felt she could not marry given the
wounds that left her unable to bear a child. It would be unfair to a
husband. And, as she explained to a Vietnamese journalist two decades
after the war, she could not forget all those she had bandaged, all those
who had died while she had survived. As a nun, she felt, she could be
more free to seek a kind of postwar harmony. Two decades after the
war's end, this military nursing veteran rises at three in the morning,
prays to Buddha, works in the fields all day, helps care for an old
homeless woman, and ends her day in prayer.

Karen Turner, an American historian, has joined with Vietnamese
writer Phan Thanh Hao to publish an independent account of Vietnamese women who fought for the North. From her interviews, Turner
discovered that most women, no matter what their official duties, included nursing among their wartime responsibilities—as if merely being a woman qualified one to nurse wounded male comrades.[73] And
always with a smile. Smiling, Turner came to understand, served complex functions for Vietnamese military women. Nonetheless, Turner
warns, we who today look back at those wartime smiles, captured in
perpetuity on celluloid, scarcely understand the multiple functions of
those smiles.[74] The women who smiled amid napalm and carnage are
themselves still working to decipher their earlier smiles.

On the other side of the war, there also is an ongoing effort to make women's military nursing in Vietnam visible—both in popular and in bureaucratic cultures. When it used the term *Vietnam veterans,* the U.S. Veterans Administration (VA) usually meant male veterans. It took a decade of political lobbying by women nursing veterans to compel the VA to revise their linguistic—and medical—procedures. Only in 1984 did the VA begin offering gynecological services to veterans at its hospitals around the country. Gynecology was not simply a new service; it amounted to a new bureaucratic definition of *veteran.* And it came as a result of intense pressure by women veterans who, after decades of accepting invisibility, began in the 1980s to organize.[75]

Deborah Joiner, who was discharged from the air force in 1972, described twenty-five years later the government's attitude toward women veterans: "We got no briefing when we left. When you're discharged, you're dumped."[76] Her assessment was echoed by Ruth Schairer, a veteran from the 1950s: "We were sort of tossed in like popcorn with all the men ... You just accepted it. This was the way of the VA. They care for the male vets."[77] That is, when officials of the Veterans Administration, one of the American government's biggest agencies and today the country's largest public health care institution, heard the word *soldiers,* they thought *men.*

This thought process implies a paradox that government officials—civilian and military—constantly engage in when they think about women and about femininity. Women and femininity—a sector of the population and an idea: together they offer officials war-waging opportunities but yet provoke anxiety. Women and femininity: if a military's mission is to be accomplished, each has to be managed—carefully.

So how is it possible for a major military institution such as the Veterans Administration to forget about so many women veterans? The paradox perhaps can be unraveled if we keep in mind that military strategists have tried to use women for military purposes only in those ways that will not unsettle the military's masculinized status. That is, what officials have found so worrisome is that if they actually integrate women into the military structure—that is, not keep women at arm's length as mere camp followers—they might unwittingly undermine one of the chief pillars holding up their military's political legitimacy: its association with manliness. Thus during the postwar eras of the 1950s and of the 1970s to the 1980s, VA officials were implementing precisely the policy that made possible the simultaneous utilization of women and maintenance of the military's masculinized image and practice: pretend all veterans were male, or only treat as "real" veterans those women veterans willing to act as if their medical problems were identical to those of men.

Looking at the process of women's militarization from this analytical vantage point, the introduction of gynecological services at a VA hospital in any city takes on significance. Insofar as a veterans' medical facility has to make women's health care needs explicit—in its budget, in its hiring of physicians and nurses—that medical facility is helping destabilize the twentieth century's standard military gender formula. But essential to that destabilizing has been the activism of women veterans. They have had to lobby for inclusion. They themselves have had to learn that their invisibility is not a natural part of the feminine experience.

Joiner and Schairer, veterans of two different American militarized eras, were being interviewed in Syracuse, New York, in 1995. Journalists were publicizing the women's views on the occasion of another step toward demasculinizing the Veterans Administration: the opening of a Women's Health Center as a separate wing of the local VA Medical Center. Schairer, then 70 years old, was among the woman organizers who for years had been pushing the VA to make women veterans' health needs visible in their operations. Simply having gynecological services available within the male-oriented VA hospital was not, she had decided, enough. She wanted a freestanding clinic to address women veteran's distinct needs. Thus, according to the clinic's director, the new facility would focus not only on gynecological care but on post-traumatic stress disorder (PTSD)—a special problem for women who have served as battle front nurses—and would offer cancer screening, wellness education, and sexual abuse counseling. The last was deemed an important service for the VA to offer, because sexual harassment had been integral to the military experiences of many nurses and other women veterans.[78]

Many men who served in Vietnam for the American military have protested at the way they were treated by the VA as well as by their families, neighbors, and potential employers when they returned from that unpopular war. But the men have been visible, if not well served. By contrast, American women who served in the U.S. military in Vietnam were scarcely acknowledged to exist. The campaign to create a women's Vietnam war memorial in Washington and the network television series *China Beach* (featuring American women nurses, Red Cross volunteers, and entertainers and employing women veterans as script

Figure 11 Sculptor Glenna Goodacre (seated in front) is pictured here with the women who in 1993 posed for the Vietnam Women's Memorial, America's first memorial dedicated specifically to women veterans. (Photographer: Dirk Halstead/Gamma Liaison.)

consultants) each served to make American women's Vietnam War nursing somewhat more visible.[79] The high point of the visibility campaign was the commissioning and installation of the Vietnam Women's Memorial in Washington, D.C., in 1993. Now sightseers who visit the famed "Wall" will see nearby the memorial to American women who served in the military during the same war. The memorial, designed by a woman sculptor, shows four figures, three women in rumpled fatigues and a male figure outstretched in agony. It is the form of a classic pietà. The male figure, a wounded soldier, lies across the legs of one of the women nurses. The image is one of feminine caring, though here it is represented as a professional, militarized feminine caring.[80]

Despite changes achieved in the Veterans Administration and the installation of a public memorial, it has taken constant surveillance and organized pressure by women veterans to prevent the American portrayal of the Vietnam War from being remasculinized in the offices of government and in the memories of ordinary civilians. Only 2.3 percent of American Vietnam veterans at the end of the twentieth century are women. But of all the American women who served in the U.S.

military in the Vietnam War, 80 percent were nurses. They were all volunteers.

NURSES AND PROSTITUTES: A MISSING ALLIANCE

Women experience military nursing through ideas about class and race
as well as through ideas about gender—their own ideas, those of the
male soldiers they tend, those of the military institution both serve,
those of their formal adversaries, and those of the publics upon whose
support they rely. The majority of American women who nursed soldiers during the Vietnam War were white. But not all. Lily Lee Adams
was Asian American; Karen Johnson was African American. Both
Adams and Johnson came out of the Vietnam War thinking about military prostitution and about their own personal relationships to prostitution.

Yet prostitutes were supposed to be far removed from nurses—ideologically distant, if not physically so. In the conventionally patriarchal
formula of twentieth-century gendered militarization, a feminized
nurse should be the respectable woman, though able occasionally to
mix maternal sisterhood with innocent romance. By contrast, the feminized prostitute should be hardened enough to survive in a commercialized, often violent milieu, yet be professionally skilled enough to offer war-weary male customers brief solace between battles. The
woman nurse and the woman prostitute were not supposed to know,
much less ally with, each other. In fact, the conventional formula historically has worked best if women in military nursing and women in
military prostitution perceived one another with skepticism, even hostility. After all, the woman military nurse's day-to-day status among
her military peers (and her fellow citizens back home) depended on her
being respected; and that respect presumably would be jeopardized if
she were thought to be promiscuous.

Lily Lee Adams was born in New York City of an Italian mother
and Chinese father. She had wanted to be a ballet dancer. Instead, she
enrolled in the nursing program at the Mount Vernon Hospital. When
an army recruiter came to the school and showed a movie about being
an army nurse, Adams was persuaded. The army would pay the rest of
her nursing school tuition. Moreover, it was 1967. She could still remember President John Kennedy's inspiring call: "Ask not what your
country can do for you, ask what you can do for your country." Two

years later Adams was stationed at the 12th Evacuation Hospital in Cu
Chi, Vietnam.[81] A decade after returning from Vietnam, she tried to
provide a journalist with a taste of the complexities that added up to
her nursing experiences there:

> So then I'd go back to the officers' club, where it was cool and I could
> have a coke or get talked into a card game. Well, I'd play cards and
> they'd treat me as an equal, but once the card game was over, they'd
> start coming on to me ... the officers really were the worst ones ...
>
> What I see is a typical patient: a double amp ... No legs, the bones
> and muscles and everything showing ... Ten people are doing ten thou-
> sand things ... they were cutting the uniform off, looking to see where
> the wounds were, making the assessment, getting the IV in, asking him
> to give his name, rank and serial number ...
>
> So I'd had it with that ward. I wanted to go someplace where I didn't
> have to know all the stories. I just could not take one more story about a
> guy who was supposed to get married when he got home in May, only
> he had no legs, and he couldn't tell his girlfriend ... So I put in for a
> transfer ... "Get me to triage." ... What I didn't know till I got to triage
> was that you could nurse somebody for five minutes and still get very at-
> tached.[82]

Adams's story confirms many American women's wartime nursing stories. But most of them didn't look Vietnamese in the eyes of American
male soldiers.

> As far as the issue about my looking Asian, when I was in civilian
> clothes and walking around the compound with a guy, the other guys
> would assume I was a whore. The Army used to truck in whores all the
> time. Guys would say all kinds of things to me—interesting things—
> that only whores get to hear. That used to bother me. I used to feel like
> telling them, "You guys don't even know that if you came into my hospi-
> tal I'd be taking care of you—giving you everything I have just to keep
> you alive." It made me angry. It made me very angry. Only it wasn't a
> personal thing; I was more angry because I was thinking, "So that's how
> you treat Vietnamese women."[83]

Karen Johnson is an African American woman and a former air
force nurse. She served on a U.S. air base in northern Thailand in the
early 1970s. She cared for the men who flew bombing missions over
Cambodia and Vietnam. There were only fourteen women nurses—
and 5,000 American men. Johnson was the sole black nurse. She came
to this air base already well equipped to handle certain forms of
racism. She had been only the second African American student at her
nursing school. At the large San Antonio hospital where she had

worked, only nine of the three hundred nurses were black and the institutional climate was less than welcoming. Yet, today when she thinks back and tries to understand what had led her to do the sort of work she is now doing, she concludes that it was there, on an American air force base in northern Thailand in 1972, that she had a radicalizing experience, an experience that would redirect her career. She calls it an "epiphany."[84]

The air force base, Johnson recalls, had a "highly sexualized atmosphere." The presumption that commercial objectification of local Thai women was acceptable was underscored by the widely believed rumor that the American base commander himself had a Thai mistress. Prostitution on the base, moreover, was not a casual matter. Like the air force bomber operation itself, prostitution here was explicitly organized. Outside the base gates Johnson and other nurses could see American male officers actively engaged in bargaining with women working in prostitution. To "rent" a Thai woman for a day cost $1.00. This arrangement was labeled a "teafuck." Nurses routinely witnessed several dozen American men standing in lines in front of the air force's own venereal disease clinics. The men in line were from enlisted ranks. Male officers, Johnson explains, went to private doctors, paying them under the table. A list of approved bars was publicly posted on the base bulletin board. Some bars were designated for black soldiers, others for white. All the women who were made sexually available in the bars were Thai.

The racialized dynamics in this sexualized wartime setting were difficult for a young black American nurse to negotiate. Johnson was a professional. She was a lieutenant, a low-ranking officer, but an officer. She was a devout Christian. She was an institutional subordinate. She was an American. She was at war. It was the early 1970s, and the civil rights movement at home was turning more militant; the second wave of the American women's movement had barely begun to make ripples and had not yet addressed the interactions of sexism and racism.

The first American military man on the base who propositioned her was white. The second was one of the base's Christian chaplains. Black enlisted men would call out to her, "Hey, baby," ignoring her superior rank. Every day she watched the officers and the enlisted men, white men and black men, treat local Thai women as if they were products to be purchased, like bottles of cola or tubes of toothpaste: "That's when I became a feminist. I realized that as a woman and as a black woman, I wasn't treated as a full human being."[85]

Three years later, with the rank of colonel and stationed at a U.S. base in Spain, Johnson joined the National Organization for Women (NOW). The wife of the base chaplain had started a chapter. In the mid-1990s, Johnson, a veteran, was elected vice president of NOW. In 1997, during a period of successive American military sexual scandals, she became NOW's chief Washington spokesperson on the issues of military sexual harassment.

MILITARY NURSES AMONG OTHER MILITARIZED WOMEN

Women serving as military nurses were deployed in the U.S. military invasions of Grenada and Panama in the 1980s and in the Gulf War of 1990–91; nurses have been integral to U.S. militarized peacekeeping operations in Somalia, Haiti, Croatia, and Bosnia. Twenty-five years after the Vietnam War and two decades after the officially fostered increase in the proportion of the U.S. military that is female, most American women in uniform are not nurses. This fact represents a significant change in U.S. official gender doctrine.

On the other hand, nursing and health care in general remain far and away the dominant role among American military women of officer rank. In 1995, for instance, the Defense Department's own figures show that women in health care jobs accounted for 46.2 percent of all U.S. women military officers.[86] The second most common posting for an American woman military officer was in administration.[87] But as the shrinking post–Cold War military was reducing its openings for administrative officers, opportunities in its medical services were expanding. Among Hispanic and African American military women, nursing remained the single most promising path to officer rank: in 1993, 45 percent of Hispanic women of officer rank were in the medical services; 44 percent of black women officers were in the medical services.[88]

Journalists looking for a story, members of Congress worried about national security, and women's advocacy groups lobbying for equity—each have preferred in the 1990s to focus their own attentions on military women flying jets and helicopters, repairing armored vehicles, and operating ships' radar. These women seem to be breaking new ground, challenging masculine privilege. But those postings are not where most uniformed women—of all ranks—are living their militarized lives. The sexual division of labor has remained alive, if not entirely well, in the 1990s U.S. military.

At the start of the new century, the heterosexual female military nurse may appear to be the patriarchal military's most comforting woman: she supplies needed labor for the military without controlling policy; she can be seen to embody conventional respectability, the self-sacrificing, benignly romantic angel against which the behavior of all other women in a militarized society can be measured; she is resourceful without claiming the badge of heroism; her very presence sustains the masculinization of "real" soldiering. The stories in the media today about women in the military are not about women who are nurses but women who are fighter pilots and infantry troops, women who are breaking conventional codes of femininity. The very appearance of these stories seems to entrench the presumption that military nurses are the patriarchal official's boon. But, as the historical record demonstrates, this facile portrayal is seriously flawed.

First, the presumption that women as military nurses are totally compatible with militarized masculinity is ahistorical. It overlooks the long series of sometimes fierce controversies about whether any women should be allowed to become so integral to military operations—and if so, which women and with what constraints. Florence Nightingale was in reality no mere quintessential Victorian angel-in-the-house. She was a bureaucratic infighter par excellence. African American military nurses today tend to the wounds of injured white soldiers not because of the unchangingness of racialized patriarchy but because of the political astuteness of Mabel Staupers. The monument commemorating American women nurses who volunteered to serve U.S. military needs in Vietnam does not stand in the Washington Mall because the architects of male privilege deemed it a clever device to sustain militarized femininity. It is a testimony to hundreds of women veterans' legislative lobbying and fund-raising. The Veterans Administration's newly offered rape counseling is not one more in a list of medical services; it is, rather, a service whose very offering makes once-invisible women politically visible.[89]

It is politically risky, however, to picture feminized military nurses in isolation, even when they are pressing for deserved recognition. The conventional military nurse represents only one kind of femininity among the varieties of femininity that most patriarchal military strategists think they need. To the degree that any real, living woman serving in her country's military manages to fulfill her government's nursing ideal, she—usually without intending to—helps sustain the other sorts of femininity that the military needs if it is to perpetuate its masculine privilege. That is, to the extent that any military nurse is both competent and the object of soldier-patients' romantic fantasies *without* crossing the line into unprofessional promiscuity, she is doing her part to sustain two complementary militarily useful notions: the hardened military prostitute and the loyal military wife. Most militaries have acted as if they require women in all three roles but need to contain those women carrying out each role within their own separate militarized compartment.

FILLING THE RANKS

*Militarizing Women as Mothers, Soldiers,
Feminists, and Fashion Designers*

Militaries can have a hard time getting all the "manpower" they think
they need. This fact may come as a surprise. It is surprising to those
who imagine that all men, at all times, naturally want to soldier. They
don't. Many men may be loathe to *admit* that they want to avoid soldiering. That, however, is a different matter, a contingent story of individual men negotiating with society over the norms of masculinity.[1]

Masculinity has been intimately tied to militarism, yet the two sets
of ideas are not inseparable. Masculinity and militarism might be pictured as two knitting needles; wielded together, they can knit a sturdy
institutional sock. But even such a sturdy sock—the military—is not
immune to holes. When darning is required, military planners try to
wield their two needles in a way that knits new narratives sustaining
both militarism and masculinity. For this maneuver to succeed, for the
military to obtain and keep the number and kind of men in the ranks
that officials think they need, military policy makers have to control
not only men but women. If very particular concepts of motherhood
and femininity—and at times, the concept of the liberated woman—
are not sustained, the sock may unravel.

I often think back to several years ago when I spent a day with a
rather forlorn British army recruiter. I was visiting him at his office in
Aberdeen, Scotland. He was having a hard time filling his monthly
quota. It was the late 1970s, and young Scottish men at the time were
not all that keen on enlisting in the British Army. Compulsory military

service for young British males had been abolished; the only men joining were volunteers. As postcolonial British soldiers, they would face
the unappealing prospect of serving in Northern Ireland. Even the association of this army recruiter's regiment with a local Scottish clan
could not provide sufficient allure. The young men of Aberdeen could
confirm their manliness, as well as earn a livable wage, by working for
one of the big oil companies. They could operate the giant offshore
rigs, sitting like great ocean insects out in the stormy North Sea. On
the day of my visit, consequently, this army recruiter was spending
hours trying to convince one rural Scottish woman that she should persuade her son to enlist. It was a tough sell.

Watching—with a feminist curiosity—any state attempting to fill
its military's ranks yields two valuable political lessons. First, states
have to think more consciously about masculinities and femininities
than nonfeminist observers realize and than most state officials care to
admit. Second, states have to expend more energy and resources in trying to shape their citizens' ideas about what constitutes an acceptable
form of masculinity and an acceptable form of femininity than nonfeminist observers realize and than most state officials care to admit.

On the eve of a new century, several developments are worrying
military manpower planners and their civilian superiors. In the United
States, Russia, Canada, and Israel, the appeal of military service, even
for young men eager to prove their manliness, has been diminished by
controversial operations, revelations about the abuse of soldiers, or
simply uncompetitive pay scales. In the United States, public opinion
surveyors have found that the military was the second most popular
agency of the U.S. government (the Postal Service ranked first).[2] Yet
that high ranking does not guarantee that recruiters will meet their
monthly enlistment quotas. Military service was being tarnished by reports such as the one in mid-1997 that revealed that accidents had become the most common cause of American soldiers' deaths. Suicides
were second.[3] Some American observers noted that the popularity of
both the Postal Service and the military—bureaucracies with quite dissimilar relationships not only to the state, but also to violence and to
masculinity—might be explained less by their public actions than by
the size of their advertising budgets. Lieutenant Colonel James Sullivan, the U.S. Army's chief of marketing and advertising, objected to
any suggestion, however, that the military sought to win citizens' favor
via television ads. He explained to reporters that his own 1998 advertising budget of $86 million was devoted solely to recruitment.[4] Filling

the ranks with volunteers at the end of the century was proving to be a costly operation.

In those countries with compulsory male military service requirements, the end of the Cold War has raised questions about the need for conscription. Enlisting conscripts is one way for a military to fill its ranks with the numbers of men it thinks it needs. Another means has been to deliberately create among men of certain racial and ethnic groups a sense that volunteer soldiering is somehow integral to their particular masculine identity. If this call is aimed at the young men—and their parents—of an ethnic or racial group that is marginalized politically or economically, the appeal can weave together communal notions of manliness with desperate hopes for "first class citizenship" and career opportunities. This maneuver might be called the Gurkha formula after the famed soldiers of Nepal on whom the British and Indian manpower recruiters relied for more than a century. It could just as well be labeled the African American formula, the Israeli Druze formula, or the Scottish formula. If, alternatively (or sometimes simultaneously), ethnicized military recruiters aim their message at the young men—and their parents—of ethnic or racial communities that already enjoy either political or economic privileges under the status quo, then the siren call of recruiters can couple communal notions of manliness to communal presumptions of cultural superiority and national leadership. This second recruitment formula might be thought of as the Javanese formula or the white British formula—or the Jewish Israeli formula or the Afro-Guyanese formula.[5]

A third strategy for filling the ranks is to contract out military missions to civilian public and private agencies. These organizations, while civilian, can be militarized if they will pursue those goals set by the military. A fourth strategy for supplying a military with a sufficient number of men has been to hire foreign male mercenaries. A fifth strategy has been to kidnap boy children.

No matter which personnel strategy officials choose to employ, however, they must win over and then sustain at least the passive cooperation of women who are the mothers of these men. The militarization of mothers—and of the very idea of motherhood—has been crucial for any successful manpower formula.

When those officials still committed to a masculinized military decide to travel down a sixth recruitment path—deliberately enlisting women into the ranks—they proceed as if they were performing a political high wire act. They are. For they believe that they need to recruit

and deploy women in only those ways that will not subvert the fundamentally masculinized culture of the military. To surrender its masculinized culture might result in few young men joining the ranks at
all. Somehow, that is, the military that enlists women must remain, it is
thought, a military that is appealing to men. These strategists never in-
tend that women provide the majority—or even a third—of the military's manpower. Moreover, not too many women should achieve high
rank. And women recruits should not deprive men of the chance to
serve in those posts held most precious to masculinity-seeking men. Finally, women soldiers who experience sexism should be discouraged
from allying themselves with other militarized women—soldiers'
wives, for instance, or military rape survivors, or military prostitutes.

To accomplish the delicately controlled enlistment of a certain number of women, military planners frequently seek the help of some civilian women: women as social scientists, women as legislators and lobbyists, women as fashion designers. These women see younger
women's entry into the ranks of the state's soldiery as a step toward all
women gaining "first-class citizenship." They are willing to work inside the most militarized corridors of government to advance what
they believe is women's cause. They don't see themselves as being militarized by the state; they are exercising women's political agency.

AFTER CONSCRIPTION: MILITARIZED
CIVILIANS, MERCENARIES, AND CHILD SOLDIERS

In a growing number of countries today, male conscription laws either
have been terminated altogether or are being subjected to public debate.[6] Between the end of World War II and the early 1970s, Japan,
Canada, the United States, Australia, and Britain eliminated the male
draft. Now, in post–Cold War Belgium and the Netherlands militaries
have become newly reliant on volunteers—women and men. Dutch
military recruiters put Dutch women in telltale blue peacekeepers' hel-
mets on their 1990s recruiting billboards. These post-conscription recruiters are soon to have more company: in France, male conscription,
for generations a symbol of republican (masculinized) citizenship, is to
be ended by the start of the new century; the post-apartheid constitution of South Africa has eliminated conscription, which until 1994
shaped the lives of white males; many governments in Eastern Europe,
where military service still is tainted by its association with the era of
Soviet domination, are seriously weighing the end to compulsory male

service. In Russia, President Boris Yeltsin campaigned in the 1996 presidential campaign on a promise to end the increasingly unpopular compulsory male military service. Yeltsin, however, faced strong opposition from his own senior officer corps and from many civilian nationalists, who still envisioned soldiering as essential for the preservation of Russian masculinized nationhood. Given Yeltsin's subsequent pledge not to seek reelection in the 2000 presidential campaign and given the front-runners' opposition to ending the draft despite its unpopularity, it seems unlikely that conscription will end soon in Russia.[7] Military recruiters and the courts, the parliament, and eighteen-year-old Russian men and their parents each are left to make their own decisions about how to implement conscription and to respond to it in the face of growing resistance.

In 1993, the twentieth anniversary of the end of U.S. military conscription ("the draft") and the creation of the country's all-volunteer armed services, the Pentagon called a formal meeting of military personnel officials and several dozen civilian social scientists who work for the Defense Department under contract. Looking back, the participants agreed that the 1970s had been a difficult decade for manpower planners. Back then, in the aftermath of the Vietnam War and the early days of the all-volunteer force, they recalled, they could not enlist enough men—and a few women—with the educational credentials that military strategists believed had become essential for their "post-Vietnam" military. Yet, after several years of trial and error, a large advertising budget (based on the now-famous slogan, "Be All You Can Be"), two pro-military presidents (Ronald Reagan and George Bush), and two much-publicized successful invasions (Grenada and Panama), the all-volunteer formula finally had been deemed a success. The 1991 victory in the Gulf War was, in the eyes of these Defense Department officials and their social science associates, the high-water mark of a post-Vietnam, post-draft, rehabilitated, all-volunteer American military.[8]

By 1993, nonetheless, as these participants gathered together to look toward the future, worrisome developments were clouding the recruiters' horizon. One particular statistic sent tremors through the assembly: teenage American boys and young men (sixteen- to twenty-one-year-olds) of all races, but particularly white youths, were expressing less inclination (the Defense Department specialists call this "propensity") to consider future enlistment in the military than their older brothers had just three years earlier.[9] The mandate given to the conference attendees was to explore which conditions in American

society and the American military might be jeopardizing the recruitment and retention of soldiers. Women as potential and actual soldiers
were mentioned now and then during the two days of discussions, but
the priority was to make sense of the inclinations and motivations of
young men.

The U.S. victory in the Gulf War elicited yellow ribbons, homecom-
ing parades, and a short-term spurt in teenage male enthusiasm of soldiering. Now, the khaki-tinted rose was wilting. In the longer term, the
Persian Gulf battlefield success had not made young men more favorably disposed toward soldiering: in the 1991 afterglow of the Gulf operation, 34 percent of the young American men aged sixteen to twenty-
one who were polled said they were inclined to consider enlisting in
the military; by 1993, the number had dropped to 29 percent; in the
post-conference 1994 Pentagon propensity survey, the rate continued
to slide, to 26 percent.[10]

Some of the conference speakers discussed these worrisome survey
results in terms of the revived economy. Declining unemployment
figures can be a depressing sight for the military recruiter; expanding
civilian job opportunities lure male volunteers away from the recruiting office in droves. Other participants pointed to the spread of demoralizing news stories about the military's shrinking manpower levels
and, with them, forced early retirements—before a soldier reached the
magic twenty-year mark that triggered eligibility for an attractive
package of retirement benefits. Several conference speakers, among
them senior uniformed officers, laid the blame for the declining male
enthusiasm for soldiering elsewhere. Soldiering, they opined, is about
making war, not peace. They speculated that the U.S. government's
foreign policy of increasing American involvement in peacekeeping
was reducing the appeal of soldiering among American male youths.
Soldiering in Somalia or Bosnia (sometimes during the conference pronounced "somaliabosnia") in the name of peace was not, they concluded, how a healthy American boy expected to earn his claim to
manliness. And manliness was, as it had been for generations, a central
component in military recruiting success. To meet recruiting quotas
called for a certain *kind* of military mission, these conferees argued, a
mission that allowed male soldiers to prove and then repeatedly reconfirm their shaky masculinity. Had Irish, Canadian, Fijian, Finnish,
or Ghanaian military recruiters been in the audience—recruiters from
militaries that had made international peacekeeping a principal professional mission—this strategic assessment would have been met with

disagreement. The American relationship between masculinity, soldiering, and military peacekeeping does not have global applicability. Six years after the recruiters' conference, the Pentagon continued to experience shortfalls in its military recruitment efforts. The civilian economy in mid-1999 was continuing to generate jobs, and most young American men continued to find peacekeeping, now in places like Kosovo, an activity unlikely to confirm their manliness.[11]

Military manpower strategists have a range of options for overcoming the current shortages in recruitment. The most obvious is to drastically cut back the size of the military. This cutback would entail a basic rethinking of national security and of military doctrine. If, however, civilian and military officials are reluctant to replace militarized perceptions of threat with, for instance, ideas of environmental or social concepts of security, then other measures will be undertaken to compensate for the military's diminished luster and the consequent drying up of male conscripts. Military planners might press legislative and treasury decision makers to increase the military's budgetary allocations, especially in the areas of pay, housing, and pensions. Failing this, military policy makers might convert more military jobs into civilian jobs, turning those jobs over to the government's civil servants or contracting them out to private firms such as McDonalds or Marriott (both of which in the 1990s earn corporate profits from Defense contracts). These newly "civilianized" jobs will thereafter not turn up in the statistics on "military personnel," although the jobs themselves, and thus the women and men performing those jobs, will be militarized. A cafeteria worker serving up cheeseburgers can be militarized. So can a civilian employee working in a large industrial laundry or a secretary typing classified memos. Few would think to compare these workers to an eighteenth-century camp follower. But such a comparison might be useful.

In a postwar era, even these civilian employees of militaries might be subjected to layoffs. Between 1993 and 1996, the U.S. Department of Defense cut 21.3 percent of its civilian workforce. American advocates for women in government, Federally Employed Women Inc., nonetheless were pleased. Through attentive monitoring and sophisticated lobbying, these women operating inside the state had managed to prevent the common masculinizing result of defense downsizing, a process that targets people at the bottom of the bureaucratic ladder and people without the protection of military veterans' hiring preference. Thanks to these women civil servants' insider activism, women and racial minority civilian employees during this downsizing were proportionately *less* likely to have been fired or forced to take early retirement than were white men in the Department's mid-level civilian management posts.[12] Women acting inside the state protected militarized women by ensuring that they kept the benefits that accrued with employment militarization. This political process was going on inside the Pentagon at the same time that recruiters were surveying American society, trying to fill the uniformed ranks.

Some anxious government officials, faced with a shortage of male recruits—men they consider not only competent but trustworthy—have turned to paid foreign mercenaries. The governments of Sierra Leone and Papua New Guinea are among those that have signed contracts in the 1990s with overseas professional soldiers. Both governments hired armed troops from the South Africa–based company Executive Outcomes. Mining and oil drilling executives today also have found Executive Outcomes' services attractive when they have felt that they could not rely on the local state's own soldiers for their security.[13] The founders and managers of these new militaries-for-hire are men. Their gendered construction of their commercial product is masculinized: the tough, battle-hardened, technologically sophisticated, mission-driven, mobile man, a man unencumbered by wives and children (even if they, in fact, have either). Yet making a profit from mercenary operations today is not guaranteed. In late 1998, Executive Outcomes director Nico Palm announced that his company would no longer make fighting African governments' wars part of its business operation, though he said he was proud of the work done by Executive Outcomes' soldiers in both Angola and Sierra Leone.[14]

When they are desperately short of the adult male soldiers they imagine they need, some military recruiters turn their gaze toward children. American manpower strategists today discuss programs—such as Junior ROTC, which can be launched in the early grades of schools, and the Young Marines, which operates outside of schools but brings in girls and boys as young as eight—that socialize children to look upon soldiering as an attractive career prospect.[15] In dire conditions, other countries' militaries have enlisted children directly into the ranks of the military. In Liberia, Angola, Sudan, and Mozambique, children, chiefly boys, have been lured or coerced into joining insurgent militias and into besieged state militaries. Often the mothers and fathers of these children have become displaced or are refugees; sometimes the parents have been killed. To the eight-year-old or the twelve-year-old

Figure 12 During Sierra Leone's 1990s civil war, foreign mercenaries not only fought but also served as trainers of child soldiers recruited by local commanders. (Photographer: P. Strudsholm/Polfoto.)

boy, the army is offered up as a surrogate family, a provider of food and protection; a rifle is presented as his new sibling. Football games have been turned into recruiting grounds. During the Liberian civil war in the 1980s and early 1990s, a local term was created just to describe the process of press gangs' forced conscription of young boys: *afesa,* "sweeping up."[16]

In the mid-1990s, United Nations officials in UNICEF estimated that worldwide some 50,000 children were being used as armed com-

batants.[17] The campaign to persuade more governments to sign the
UN Convention on the Rights of the Child, an international agreement
that at least espouses the principle that children should not be drafted
into armed forces, has been spearheaded by those women working inside international agencies and independent human rights organizations. (At the end of the century, UNICEF is a new site in which to do
antimilitarist feminist work.) To date, the governments of Somalia and
the United States have refused to sign this UN convention.[18] The U.S.
government's signing of such a treaty might throw into question the
Defense Department's successful Junior ROTC program, now established in hundreds of American high schools.

MASCULINIZING CITIZENSHIP, MILITARIZING MOTHERHOOD

Malathi de Alwis is a Sri Lankan feminist who has developed a respect
for the political power of literature. She has revealed her own Sinhala-
dominated government's manipulation of the image of the ancient queen
mother Vihara Maha Devi for the sake of waging its present fifteen-year-
old war against ethnic Tamil rebels in the country's north. The government's education policy makers adopted a policy, de Alwis found, of encouraging schoolchildren to identify with Vihara Maha Devi, a woman
who, according to legend, inspired her reluctant son to wage war. At the
same time, in the Sri Lanka's north, Tamil insurgents inspired their
troops with tales of women warriors.[19] In neighboring India and Pakistan, the 1998 escalation of nuclear threats were fueled in part by the
manipulations of motherhood on both sides. Pakistan's former prime
minister, Benazir Bhutto, once hailed by Westerners as a South Asian
feminist, reacted to the Indian Hindu nationalist regime's provocative
nuclear weapons test by chastising her political successor for not being
manly enough to respond in kind. To make her point, she sent him feminine bangles. Bhutto evoked the myth of the mother inspiring her reluctant son to demonstrate his manliness by going to war.[20]

Mothers of male soldiers and women as soldiers can converge in the
minds of male military manpower planners. These two groups of
women rarely talk directly to each other; they rarely get together in
any country to jointly weigh their prospects, their values, their shared
womanly concerns. The very indirection of their "convergence" makes
it harder for women playing each of these two roles to see the common
patriarchal presumptions fueling their respective militarizations. Long
before manpower strategists think about women as soldiers, they think

about women as the mothers of sons. In a militarized society, mothers of boys choosing to resist their sons' volunteering for the military or answering the conscription call affect the lives of young women. During those periods when holes are worn in the myths of militarized motherhood, young women may be envisioned by military strategists as inconvenient but necessary soldiering substitutes. A demilitarized mother of a son inadvertently may broaden the opportunities for young women to become soldiers.

These two groups of women come to affect one another because of the ambivalence of sons. If maleness, masculinity, and militarism *were* inevitably bound together, militaries would always have all the soldiers they believed they required. Military manpower politics then would merely be a matter of administering the ample flow. The history of international emigration, however, suggests otherwise: for generations, emigration's tale has been in no small part a history of men leaving home in order to travel beyond the clutches of the recruiting officer. Young men who hear stories from older brothers of brutal hazing, arrogant officers, and inedible rations often associate soldiering less with warrior-hood and heroism than with humiliation and slavery. There is a reason that so many states in the world have implemented military conscription laws for young men: most of those men would not join the state's military if it were left up to them to choose.[21]

For conscription to become politically palatable, however, it has had to be assigned a meaning that resonates as the opposite of slavery. A soldier in the state's military must not be perceived as an emasculated, downtrodden serf, but as a free, manly citizen of a nation performing a manly citizen's duty. When a military manpower planner hears a new conscript referring to his forthcoming compulsory tour as "in the service of my country," he is heartened.

It has been the very success of this welding of citizenship to military service that has prompted so many twentieth-century women's advocates to press for women's "right" to serve in the state's military. Nira Yuval-Davis has been among those feminist theorists who have shed light on the political and cultural processes that define citizenship in such a way that a manly man can slip most comfortably into the cloak of "citizen" and that a man who has served in the state's military wears that privileging cloak most comfortably of all.[22] Yet seeing military service as the path to full citizenship status, as some feminists have pointed out, leaves unexamined the militarization of "first-class citizenship" itself.[23]

Turkish feminist researcher Ayse Girl Karayazgan has undertaken
the task of trying to understand exactly how it is that the Turkish state
has managed to enforce military conscription on approximately
200,000 young Turkish men every year. Military service in Turkey is
low-paid. It entails waging war against other Turkish citizens, members of the country's Kurdish minority. Does the solution to her puzzle
lie partly in the image of the Turkish military as the bastion of the nation's secular political culture? Is it perhaps the prestige that comes
from soldiering in a military that is a member of NATO, the alliance
that has become the symbol of "modernity" in the eyes of many
Europeans? Alternatively, Karayazgan suggests, the widespread conscription compliance is the product of an interaction in Turkish contemporary culture between three ideas: soldiering, citizenship, and
masculinity: "Serving in the military has been one of the major practices of identity construction in the lives of young Turkish males, sig-
naling a passage to both citizenship and manhood. The Turkish Constitution (Article 72) defines this obligation as 'the right and duty of
every Turk,' yet only men serve ... Women cannot become a part of
the 'army nation' and do not have the 'right and duty' to serve for the
homeland."[24]

In the mid-1980s, the Turkish armed forces permitted a few women
to enlist as volunteers. While officials hesitated to provide actual numbers, they reassured their NATO colleagues that the previous policy of
allowing women to enlist only as officers, a policy that restricted applicants to those women with university education, was being relaxed;
women hereafter would be accepted "in principle" as noncommissioned officers, that is, as sergeants.[25] Nearing the end of its first half
century, NATO had begun to define militarized modernity partly in
terms of its state members allowing at least a token number of women
to serve in uniform. To insist on having an all-male military, in NATO
eyes, was to be a not-quite-fully-modern military. Still, the Turkish
military, like those other NATO forces who are reliant on conscription
to fill their ranks (France, Germany, Italy), continues to depend on
male-only conscription, thereby preserving a masculinized hold on its
conception of militarized national citizenship. A Turkish young man
may not look forward to his tour of military service, and his sister may
be relieved that she can get on with her schooling or paid civilian work
without having to endure military service, but that military tour will
have its rewards—not only for individual men, but for all those men
who reap advantage in political life from the privileging of masculinity.

Yoking citizenship to military service has been a deliberate political enterprise. In the United States this enterprise began during the Revolutionary War and was consolidated in the years after that war.[26] This deliberate political project gives military veterans a special public status. In countries such as Israel, Russia, and the United States, it enhances the electability of male politicians to public office. Yoking citizenship to military service (real or just potential service) also allows men to dominate conversations about foreign policy in parliament and over supper.

Although the ideological yoking strategy has proved highly successful, there still are times when not enough men willingly don the state's uniform. Recruit-hungry government officials have thus needed to wield more than the idea of masculinized, militarized citizenship. They have needed to craft and deploy a specially honed concept of motherhood. Designing militarized motherhood, however, also requires marginalizing or suppressing alternative notions of motherhood:

> In the autumn of 1991 women in Sarajevo protested against the war. "We are women—not nationalists, generals, or murders!" they shouted ... A few days later hundreds of women from Croatia and Bosnia set off for Belgrade, where they were to be met by women from Serbia. They were all supposed to go together to the Headquarters of the (by then already former) Yugoslav People's Army. The women had only one weapon in their hands: little photographs of their sons. The generals, realizing for the first time that women after all amounted to half the population, roughly prevented them from meeting ...
>
> The very next day Serbian [state-controlled] television showed pictures of weeping Serbian mothers joyfully sending their sons into the army. "This is the happiest day of my life," said one of them, wiping away her tears.
>
> On the third day other men, Croats, convinced their wives that they had no choice but to send their sons "to defend the homeland."[27]

That sense of resignation among women as mothers in the former Yugoslavia didn't last for even a decade. During the spring of 1999, reports began to surface that Serb women—as wives and mothers—were organizing open protests to demand that Belgrade's male elite stop sending their husbands and sons over the nearby border into wartorn Kosovo.[28]

The very ambivalence with which many young men weigh the prospect of military service has made military manpower officials approach the mothers of sons with a mixture of warmth and wariness. During World War I, Canadian and Belgian male legislators, desperate to sustain popular support for male enlistment, awarded women who were mothers of soldiers with the right to vote before most other women (in Canada, only military nurses preceded mothers of soldiers in gaining the vote; most Belgian women did not gain suffrage until forty years later).[29] During the period leading up to World War II, the fascist policy makers in both Germany and Italy took conscious steps to persuade women that militarized mothering could earn them public respect.[30]

Militarizing motherhood often starts with conceptualizing the womb as a recruiting station. Government officials who have adopted a pro-natalist policy—using state resources to press women (especially those women of "trusted" ethnic or racial groups) to have more children—frequently have cast that policy in militarized terms. That is, a woman who has more children—sons, preferably—is a woman who is contributing to "national security." Giving birth to sons is giving birth to the next generation of the state's soldiery. French republicans, German fascists, Soviet communists, Croatian nationalists—each have sought to militarize women's fertility. But women have not always been compliant.[31]

Sudanese anthropologist Jok Madut Jok, for instance, discovered a startling pattern among ethnic Dinka women in today's war-torn southern Sudan. Facing daily life that has become saturated with military violence, devoid of both prenatal health care and economic opportunities and infused with male soldiers' sexual claims, many Dinka women have resorted to abortion—secretly. Clandestine pregnancy terminations appear to have been rising in tandem with both Dinka male leaders' escalating pressure on "their" women to bear more children and Dinka male soldiers' increasing insistence that their wives submit to intercourse whenever they are home on leave. In the midst of a three-sided masculinized war (the Northern regime versus the Southern insurgents, and in the South, the Nuer militias versus the Dinka militias), women have crafted their own reproductive strategies: they have complied with the men's demands that they have intercourse and become pregnant; but they have devised ways to ensure that those pregnancies do not come to term. When political leaders and husbands' relatives have inquired, these Dinka women have blamed their miscarriages on a new illness, one they call *duony kou,* "broken back." Women in these most extreme wartime conditions have only a sliver of space for agency. But in that space left to them, they have strategized.[32]

Contested maneuvers to militarize motherhood do not occur just in preparation for and during wars; they continue for years after wars.

Thus in the era after the last of their successive twentieth-century wars—against the Japanese, the French, the Americans, the Chinese, and most recently, Cambodia's Pol Pot regime—Vietnam's male leadership authorized the building of a Woman's Museum. The officially connected Women's Union raised the funds. This recognition came at a time when the male leadership had yet to appoint a woman to the Politburo, the senior body of the ruling Communist Party. The first woman would gain entrance into that most powerful political body only in 1996, a year after the women's museum was inaugurated.[33] In 1995, the new Women's Museum opened its doors in Hanoi. The overarching theme of the museum is motherhood—Vietnamese women as Mothers of the Nation. Museum-goer and feminist historian Karen Turner summarized her impressions: "A tour of its displays shows that the ideal Vietnamese woman is a juggler, who can raise and nurture soldier sons, fight like a man in times of war, and act like a peacemaker when the wars end."[34]

The problem is that many of the Vietnamese women who actually served as combatants in the war against the Americans survived that war physically unable to bear children. "Childless war veteran" is a notion that provokes profound discomfort among many postwar Vietnamese women and men.

Things that cause discomfort usually are shoved away, out of sight. The Women's Museum is caringly designed to make some women—for instance, childless war veterans—invisible. Feminist researchers and activists in many countries have conducted oral histories, restored old photographs, written stories and novels, directed documentary films, all with the intent of making visible those dimensions of war waging—and the postwar costs of war waging—that people equipped with a more conventional masculinized mindset forget, never think to record, or deliberately delete. Mothers have been assigned a central role in patriarchically inspired war stories. These stories have been inspirational. Thus, among the projects of some feminist researchers has been the publishing of women's poetry, fiction, and firsthand accounts that tell quite different versions of the "war story." These stories radically complicate the meanings of militarized motherhood.[35]

Motherhood rarely serves as a firewall protecting women from militarization. In Latin America today, in the aftermath of successful popular campaigns to rid their societies of the most extreme forms of militarism, the subject of women's mothering of soldiers to fulfill the needs of militarized states remains fraught. Anthropologist Nancy Scheper-

Hughes draws a caveat from her own experiences of living among very poor women in a Brazilian urban neighborhood. She warns us that women in their roles as mothers do not automatically— "naturally"— resist giving up their children to externally imposed risk: "I learned how the frequent experience of child death in impoverished shanty towns shapes maternal thinking in a way that extinguishes maternal grief over premature death. Instead it summons another dimension of maternal thinking—one more congenial to military thinking: the notion of inevitable, acceptable, and meaningful death."[36]

Across the Andes, in the poor neighborhoods of La Paz, the current Bolivian government has encouraged a particular maternal military manpower lesson: military service will help mothers turn their boys into men, into marriageable men. Bolivian women with meager resources find it reasonable today to calculate that through army experience their sons will become mature. Their sons, because they have endured what most Bolivians agree is a hard, even brutal conscript's life, will have proven to their own mothers that they are truly "adult" men. They will thereby become men that other women will want their daughters to marry.[37] In many countries, when mothers of daughters assess a military, they often have marriage in mind: does the government's military produce young men who will provide the sorts of husbands best suited for their daughters? A mother of a daughter is militarized to the extent that she judges the military to do just that.

Outside observers watched intently in the 1970s as Nicaragua's rebel Sandinista movement became a magnet for discontented men— and women. Many women as mothers came to agree with the rebels' goal of toppling the corrupt and oppressive American-backed regime of Anastazio Somoza. Supporting their children's enlistment in the insurgent army was to many Nicaraguan women an act of political engagement. Many of these same outside commentators, a decade later, had turned their attention elsewhere. They had stopped being curious about how the now-governing Sandinistas were enlisting their soldiers, raising troops to withstand the armed challenge of the American-equipped Contra forces. But Nicaraguan women as mothers were not standing still. They continued to assess and reassess their political relationships to the Sandinista military, a military that now had become the government's military.

Many Nicaraguan mothers, it appears, had cooled in their enthusiasm to support the military with their own children. In the 1980s, the Sandinista-led state military had become a force based on a new male-only conscription law, much to the consternation of many Sandinista women. Women continued to volunteer for military service, but women's advocates interpreted the regime's enactment of a male-only conscription policy as a step toward remasculinizing the state's military.[38] At the end of the insurgency the Sandinista army had been 30 percent female; by 1988, women had slipped to 20 percent of the regular army, few being deployed to the battlefront.[39] Young men of draftable age during the 1980s were propelled toward military service not only by the conscription law, but also by a desire to be seen as manly and by the fear of being seen by others as one of the *cochones*, "faggots."[40] But many young Nicaraguan men, faced with their conscription notices, could claim that their draft avoidance was not a sign of compromised manliness but instead was motivated simply by filial loyalty to their mothers. It was their mothers, they could insist, who could not stand the prospect of their sons going off to war. And it was women in their public roles as mothers who, in practice, did organize the few open antidraft demonstrations in Nicaragua during the war with the Contras. The mothers' demonstrations set off political alarm bells. In response, the Sandinista government launched a campaign designed to allay mothers' fears and to remind them of their maternal patriotic duties: "One long-playing television ad repeated the refrain, 'Nicaraguan Mother, a Heroic Mother.' Mother's Day became a government extravaganza ... And whenever cohorts of inductees completed their military service and were demobilized, giant homecomings were held ... 'They went out cubs, they came back lions', read the posters ... but most of the propaganda showed pictures of young men coming home to their mothers."[41]

Among the reasons that the Sandinistas ultimately agreed to a ceasefire—followed by multiparty elections in 1990 that they lost—was that the persistent armed conflict with the Washington-supplied Contras was steadily gnawing away at the regime's popular support. The candidate who defeated the Sandinistas at the presidential polls in 1990 was a woman, Violeta Chamorro, a conservative who constructed a maternal campaign persona: as mother of the nation, she would bring peace, she would return sons to their mothers.[42] The Sandinistas had lost control of the popular culture's narrative of wartime motherhood.

In neighboring Guatemala, impoverished Mayan Indian women spent the 1970s and 1980s making excruciating calculations about what purposes were served by their sons answering or resisting the

government military recruiter's call. No single answer seemed to ensure
security. The calculations that they and their sons made would haunt
them both for years. Many Mayan mothers saw army conscription
sweeps as just one more form of anti-Indian violence. Other women,
however, were grateful for that portion of their soldier-sons' paychecks
that the Guatemalan military sent home to their families. Still, having a
son in the military did not provide women protection against militarized violence: "Dona Margarita ... is a widow whose husband and
youngest son were killed at the hands of the Guatemalan military,
while her oldest son was a member of the Kaibil special forces, the elite
counterinsurgency unit of the Guatemalan military, self-described as
'messengers of death.'"[43]

Postwar eras are suffused with the politics of motherhood. Motherhood is not simply and always a bond between women; it can divide
them. In postwar Nicaragua and Guatemala—and postwar Northern
Ireland, Angola, South Africa, Sudan, Rwanda, Bosnia, Serbia, and
Croatia—those women who have resisted their sons' military enlistment and those women who have accepted, perhaps even encouraged,
their sons' soldiering have had to find ways to reconcile their contra-
dictory approaches to mothering for the sake of creating a lasting postwar peace. It is not an automatic discovery.[44]

When conscription ends and is replaced by an all-volunteer, professionalized military, it takes a convergence of personal, societal, and
state expectations to achieve the militarization of motherhood. There
are some American women whose hopes for their children are filtered
through what they think will make their husbands happy. A woman
who believes that the sharp edges of her husband's disappointment
with his own unfulfilled life may be blunted if he can acquire reflected
pride from his son's military adventures is a woman likely to militarize
her motherhood out of a sense of wifely duty.[45] Other American
women in recent years have seen their country's all-volunteer military
as an ally in the complex, often frustrating project of mothering. With
the help of the military recruiter, these women believe, it will be possible for them to get their directionless teenage sons "off the couch and
out of the house."[46] Veronica Calvo, a young mother in Virginia, explained to a reporter why she had encouraged her son, an elementary
school boy, to join the Young Marines. He suffered from attention
deficit disorder and was having trouble in school. She hoped that taking part in the drills and group activities offered by the Young Marines
would bolster his self-esteem: "He wanted to do it, and it's given him a

lot of self-confidence. Once he got the uniform, he thought it was the coolest thing."[47]

All these enticements notwithstanding, it is a rare woman who totally satisfies a military's own mothering ideal. The profile of the fully militarized mother might look something like this:

> She is a woman who will find it reasonable that a government would urge its female citizens, especially those from the politically dominant racial and ethnic group, to have more children for the sake of ensuring the nation's future security.
>
> She is a woman who sees the mothering of her sons as different from the mothering of her daughters.
>
> She is a woman who imagines that, by being a good mother in the eyes of the state, she is helping to confirm her own status as a citizen of the nation.
>
> She is a woman who accepts unquestioningly the phrase "patriotic mother."

A military usually does not require the ideal. The internalization of a few simple militarized maternal beliefs often may be sufficient to provide the military with the manpower it thinks it needs. Moreover, a woman who has become a militarized mother is not a mere puppet. She is likely to be a thinking woman. She will engage in what at times is a complicated calculus. Thus militarizing a mother may entail a military's appreciating that

> She is a woman who needs a portion of her son's paycheck to support the household.
>
> She is a woman who believes that if she voices reluctance to her son about his answering the conscription order or the recruiter's call for volunteers, she will be subverting his pursuit of full manhood.
>
> She is a woman who hopes that through military service her son will become a responsible adult.
>
> She is a woman who is grateful that her husband takes fatherly pride, and perhaps vicarious pleasure, in his son's military success.
>
> She is a woman who sees as an extension of her mothering the caring for her soldier-son's morale—with reassuring letters, food packages, upbeat phone calls.

She is a woman who gives the photograph of her son in his uniform pride of place at home, a representation of him that is worthy of special public attention.

Living up to the militarized maternal ideal requires a woman to relate to her soldier-son in certain ways and to create relationships with others that will continue to sustain the military's legitimacy and perpetuate the appeal of soldiering in the eyes of other mothers of sons:

> She will become a woman who doesn't ask too many questions about the on-duty and off-duty activities of her soldier-son.
>
> She is a woman who, if her son marries, will take pride in her new daughter-in-law's military wifely coping skills and encourage her not to complain.
>
> She is a woman who will offer solace and physical care if her son is released from the military wounded or ill.
>
> She is a woman who learns to trust the military; when the military informs her of her son's death, she will find its explanation credible.

Although the totally militarized mother is a rarity, it is a rare mother of a son who can resist absorbing several parts of the ideal into her own maternal values. Few women who have borne sons and raised them to the age of potential military service have been able to escape the pressures that are generated by these militarized expectations of motherhood.[48] Those pressures may be particularly hard to withstand if they come not only from the government, but from husbands, fathers, neighbors, friends, ethnic community leaders. In fact, if just government officials alone articulated these militarized maternalist expectation, a mother may not find it all that hard to resist them. It is the confluence of militarized family dynamics, a militarized popular culture, and a militarized state that makes the myths of militarized motherhood so potent.

The consequences of such a confluence have been experienced in recent years by Israeli Jewish women and by Russian women. They have not responded identically. As we will see, a majority of Israeli Jewish women have cooperated with the militarization of their sons, whereas a growing number of Russian women have been turning motherhood into a platform from which to launch public critiques of their government's military uses of their sons.

Figure 13 In Israel, women creating antimilitarism alliances on different sides of the militarized conflict and of class, religious and ethnic divides have had to overcome political pressures to think of themselves as patriotic mothers of soldiers. (Photographer: Sarit Uziely.)

Women strategizing as mothers and the politics of motherhood each has been a significant process during the 1990s conflict between Palestinians and Jewish Israelis. On both sides women have had to consider and reconsider their understandings of mothering's relationships to militarism, to children, to nationalism, and to the state and the would-be state.[49] Israel is one of the few countries today in which the government's conscription law applies to women as well as to men — that is, to Jewish Israeli women and men. Neither male nor female Palestinian Israeli citizens are subject to or eligible for the draft. But even among the country's Jewish citizens, military service is unequal. The rules of conscription are designed to sustain the military's masculinized character. Thus Israeli women comprise in the late 1990s just 32 percent of the present military's conscripts and only 13 percent of its career officers.[50] In post-Oslo Accord Israel, the militarization of motherhood more than girlhood sustains that country's war-waging culture.

Rela Mazali was one of those Israeli Jewish women who had accepted compulsory military service when she was young. But more recently, as a mother, Mazali was compelled by her sons' coming of age to think new, hard thoughts about militarized mothering. In her life as a contemporary Israeli Jewish woman and as a mother-of-sons, she was surrounded by friends, colleagues, media, and officials who all placed a premium on nationalist militarized mothering. Together, they constructed the good Jewish Israeli woman as a woman who, by carrying out her duties as a militarized mother, fulfilled her responsibilities to the nation and thus secured for herself the status of a patriotic citizen. This milieu did not welcome a radical reassessment of a woman's mothering values. If Mazali urged her sons to avoid military service or to end their tours of duty early, would she be undermining their chances for later civilian employment? Would she also be depriving them of the opportunity of experiencing life within one of the country's most ethnically diverse institutions, made up of Jews from both Ashkenazi and Sephardic backgrounds? If she argued with her soldier-sons about their political views, would she be threatening military morale? If she spoke out publicly against soldiers' treatment of Palestinian civilians in the Occupied Territories, would she be branded unpatriotic? If she questioned the wisdom of other women pampering their soldier-sons, excusing them from domestic chores when they come home on weekend leave, would she be labeled a bad mother? Mazali has chosen to take all five risks: in so doing, she remains in a distinct minority among Israeli Jewish mothers.[51]

In November 1997, Mazali and a small number of Jewish Israeli women formed a new group that they called "Women and Mothers for Peace." They decided to mount vigils every Friday, holding signs declaring, "We don't have children for futile wars" and "We'll raise our children to live." Most of the women in the little group came from backgrounds that were middle class and Ashkenazi (that is, Jews whose heritage is eastern European, not Sephardic). They committed themselves, according to Mazali, to trying to "actively subvert militarization." They chose as their starting point a fresh look at life inside their own homes. In their informal group conversations they would ask each other, "Where and how can we actually start poking sticks through the spokes of the wheels?" These women had a sense that in the late 1990s, as women on whom the Israeli government depended to maintain its high degree of military mobilization, they might possess real power: "We just have to learn how to exercise it—mainly by undermining the brainwashing all of us and our children are subject to."[52]

Senior policy makers of the Israeli Defense Force (IDF) had not always been eager to draw women as mothers into the military's folds. In the past, the IDF had wanted mothers' sons (and a few daughters), but not their "maternal meddling." Sociologist Hanna Herzog found that it was only in the early 1980s that the military's strategic attitude toward mothers' involvement changed.[53] Between 1948 and 1982, the bureaucratic inclination had been to keep both mothers and fathers of soldiers at institutional arm's length; after 1982, the tendency was to embrace each in separate institutional bear hugs. The turning point, Herzog discovered, was the IDF's invasion of neighboring Lebanon, an operation that sparked a new willingness in many Israeli civilians to publicly criticize their military. Many of those who became vocally opposed to the military's Lebanon operation were mothers and fathers of active-duty soldiers, sons eligible to be sent into combat in Lebanon. This stream of protest continued in the late 1980s when male Israeli soldier-sons were deployed in the Occupied Territories to quash the Palestinian uprising, the Intafada.

In reaction to this newly critical parental stance, the IDF began welcoming parents' involvement in their sons' and daughters' military lives. Parents began to be invited to visit bases on weekends; the military created radio shows aimed at parents; parents were encouraged to telephone their offspring's commander. Yet, as Herzog explains, "parents" were not treated undifferentially. Fathers were encouraged by IDF officials to bond with their soldier-sons as men—as fatherly men who themselves had undergone military service, as fatherly men who "naturally" understood military technical matters. Mothers, on the other hand, were seen by these same policy makers as politically naive: mothers were best encouraged to see themselves as maternal cooks, caring laundresses. Making up a picnic basket can be militarized if it is packed with the intention of keeping up the morale of a soldier. Doing laundry for a son home on leave becomes militarized when the mother's washing is undertaken in recognition that a soldier on leave deserves to be relieved of annoying household chores.

In Russia, and throughout Eastern Europe, constructing mothers as patriotic figures to pressure women to make sacrifices for the sake of achieving state objectives has been common but not easy.[54] Contemporary Russian officials have encountered firsthand the limits of nationally portrayed, statist control of motherhood.

During Moscow's unsuccessful attempt in the mid-1990s to suppress a separatist armed rebellion in Russia's southern province of Chechnya, the regime of President Boris Yeltsin and his military commanders had to contend not only with stubborn male Chechen

fighters, who were rapidly militarizing the meaning of Chechen masculinity, but also with bold ethnic Russian mothers-of-soldiers. In February 1995, the *New York Times* published a photograph that would
spike the anxiety level of any military's personnel director.[55] The black
and white photo shows a Russian male officer, bulkily clad in his
padded camouflage fatigues, boots, gloves, and fur cap, sitting on the
hood of a tank out on an open plain. He is pointing off into the distance. Kneeling next to the officer, there on the wintry battlefield, is a
middle-aged woman. She is bundled up against the cold in a white
scarf and a heavy civilian coat. In her ungloved hand is a document.
She is leaning forward, listening intently. This photograph illustrates a
serious wartime exchange. The woman has traveled to the front to find
her soldier-son. Once she has found him, she plans to take him home.
Few commanders dare to stop her. She is not alone. She has arrived in
the Chechnya war zone on a bus filled with other Russian mothers, a
bus chartered by the Committee of Soldiers' Mothers. This woman is
part of a growing grassroots movement, one of the concrete expressions of post-Soviet civil society.[56]

The political mobilization of Russian women in their identities as
mothers of conscripted soldier-sons started during the 1980s Afghanistan war, a war that ended in a humiliating defeat for the Soviet Red
Army. The meaning of motherhood, once the bulwark of patriotic Russian military service, was being transposed.

Mobilization of mothers to critique the military escalated in the late
1980s as more women began hearing reports of brutal hazing, suspicious "accidental" deaths, and suicides among the troops. Being a
"good mother" was beginning to require, in the minds of many Russian women, a direct challenge to the Red Army. These protests were
an important factor in what became the dismantlement of the Soviet
state.[57]

Today, under the new Russian state, military conscription remains a
subject of heated popular debate. Even with the post–Cold War downsizing of the military, it has proved hard to fill the ranks because of
rampant draft avoidance and desertion by young Russian men. A mid-
1998 Russian public opinion poll revealed that 82 percent of young
men did not want to serve in the military.[58] Even the understandably
defensive officials of the Russian Defense Ministry put the number of
men who have deserted their military posts between 1994 and 1998 at
20,000. Valentina Melnikova of the Committee of Soldiers' Mothers
estimated the number of deserters at twice that.[59]

In this political milieu, the women in the Committee of Soldiers'
Mothers began to extend their political reach. According to Canadian
researcher Valeria Zawilski, some of the committee's activists (especially those in the Moscow group's office; less so those associated with
the St. Petersburg branch) began challenging the very idea of the carefully constructed and culturally hallowed long-suffering Russian
mother so cherished by male Russian nationalists.[60] These women also
have reached out to Chechens, a people widely scorned by ethnic Russians. Drawing on their experiences of negotiating with Chechens for
the release of their captured sons, they developed proposals for creating a process of peace and reconciliation. For the women who became
activists in the Committee of Soldiers' Mothers, what began as a private concern about their own sons was becoming a public citizen's
concern about the very structure of militarized gender and ethnic politics in the new Russia.[61] In the post-Chechnya war era of the late
1990s, participants in the committee began to concentrate on the conscription process itself. Activists organized meetings at which sympathetic officers and lawyers tutored mothers—and wives and girlfriends
and young men—on how to avoid compulsory male military service:
(1) how to keep copies of a young man's medical records (draft boards
were notorious for deliberately losing them); (2) how, if necessary, to
bring court suits against the Red Army in case the young man is injured—or dies—in uniform due to military negligence; (3) how to
"buy" their son an assignment in one of the army's better units.[62] The
women disagree with activists in another military-focused dissenting
organization, the Antimilitaristic Radical Association, who concentrate
their current efforts on teaching young men how to gain the status of
conscientious objector (a status only legitimized in the new 1993 Russian constitution). Instead, Melnikova says that her group has a more
ambitious goal: "The fact that you don't support that kind of military
service is also a kind of social action ... If the state doesn't want to
change the way its military is run, maybe if we get enough people involved, we can make them do it."[63]

Women as mothers of draft-age sons and young women as job seekers are politically connected to each other in state policy maneuvers,
even if they are not necessarily conscious of that connection. In response to the plummeting credibility of the military among young Russian men and their mothers, Moscow policy makers set their sights on
that "other" group of young citizens, young Russian women. Officials
in the 1990s began to recruit significant numbers of women as volun-

teer soldiers. This recruitment was a significant change in state policy.
The Red Army had demobilized almost all its women personnel at the
end of World War II. Today, though, soldiering is being offered by
troop-short officials as an attractive option for young Russian women,
women who are finding the new post-communist market economy in-
hospitable to women employees. In 1980, in the heat of the Cold War,
the massive Soviet military included a mere 10,000 volunteer women
in uniform.[64] By the mid-1990s, the now-shrunken and demoralized
Russian military had become increasingly dependent on 160,000 post-
Soviet, post–Cold War Russian women volunteer soldiers.[65] The patriarchal character of the market economy can work quite harmoniously
with the daily work of the *man*power-short military recruiter.

As the experiences of women in both Israel and Russia reveal, mothering as a series of daily acts and motherhood as an idea about what
those acts together should stand for each have long political histories.
It is hard to make sense of any state, past or present, without taking seriously that state's attempts to craft ideas about motherhood that pressure women as mothers to do certain things judged useful for the state.
But because it is such a demanding role in practice and such a potent
package of notions in people's minds, mothering and motherhood also
have been occasional sites of women's efforts to resist the state or
shape the priorities of civil movements.

Consequently, during the final decade of the Cold War, two of the
most dramatic and successful movements challenging state-sponsored
militarization were initially propelled by women participants' ideas
about mothering and motherhood: The Greenham Common Peace
Camp in Britain and the Mothers of the Plaza de Mayo in Argentina.
Each group self-consciously wielded the concept of mother to contest
its respective state elite's own uses of mothering to further militaristic
ends. As each movement evolved, however, discussions grew among
women activists about the varieties of maternal values, about the patriarchal risks in relying on motherhood as a political idea, and about the
limits of building a broad women's movement on a maternal role that
not all women can or want to assume.[66] Thus, on the one hand, there
is the contest between statist (often nationalist statist) and anti-statist
efforts to promote specific ideas about what women as mothers should
be and do. On the other hand, there may be simultaneous discussions
going on among feminists about whether motherhood really is the best
site from which to launch resistance to state militarism.

WHICH SOLDIERS SHOULD WEAR HIGH HEELS?

The uniform. Commercial airline pilots' uniforms are designed to give them an aura of authority associated with navy captains. Behind them, in the passenger cabin, women flight attendants have been required to wear costumes that sometimes have made them look like disco dancers, sometimes like figments of Orientalist imaginings, and sometimes like corporate lawyers. Civilian nurses in many countries have debated with each other over the designs of hats, capes, and pants: which ones will best allow them to do their jobs, which will preserve their feminine identities, which will make it clear that they have a higher professional status than those nursing women lacking formal credentials? Olympic athletes are attired in ways designed to capture some essence of their national versions of manliness and femininity, straw hats for some, cowboy hats for others. IBM male executives pressured to accept the blue Oxford shirt as their global uniform, American Catholic schoolgirls issued plaid pleated skirts to encourage a sober form of young femininity, court justices donning a version of choir robes in order to speak on behalf of the state—each is engaged in the gendered politics of the uniform.

No uniform, no matter how humble, has materialized out of the blue. Every uniform has been designed. Every one is the product of conscious thought, about the nature of the institution being represented, about the meanings of femininity and masculinity when associated with that institution's services and authority. Every uniform, consequently, has a history, has a politics. Usually it is a contested politics. Delve into the history of air stewardesses' union organizing. Listen to Japanese "office ladies" complain about their corporate uniforms.[67] Watch schoolgirls roll up the waistbands of their standardized skirts.

Investigating the confusion over what a woman soldier should wear can expose deeper anxieties over what a woman soldier is supposed to do and to be in a masculinized institution.

At the end of the twentieth century, we are digging more deeply than ever into the subtle ways in which power shapes fashion—and fashion shapes power. The power dynamics operating in the politics of military uniform design have their own distinctiveness. There is little room here for individual women's agency in fashioning or even altering the semiotics of attire. Few women soldiers would dare to roll up the waistbands of their standard-issue khaki skirts. The arena in which a military woman dons her wardrobe is not the same arena in which an Australian or Japanese civilian girl toys with her hairline or hemline to experiment with her identities; it is not the same fashion arena in which an American woman lawyer decides what to wrap around her neck as a surrogate tie when she appears in court. This arena of military fashion is even more constrained than the arena in which Iran's urban women shop for suggestive lingerie to wear underneath their prescribed chadors. In the arena of military uniform fashion the state is deciding the hemlines and hairlines. An entire bureaucracy is charged with determining whether women's waists should be visible or invisible. Official memos fly back and forth debating the best color of women's lips and the correct arch of their eyebrows. In this arena, the need to maintain soldiering's masculine image will dictate how high should be the heel on the woman soldier's shoe.

This is not to say that designing uniforms for male soldiers is a process free of contest and confusion. Most of the world's militaries have created formal bureaucratic committees to resolve disputes provoked by such sticky questions as: Is a beret manly? Do enlisted men in the navy or coast guard feel demeaned by having no pockets in their form-fitting, bell-bottomed trousers? How high can a leather parade boot reach before an image of disciplined masculinity slips over into one of masculinized fascism?

America in the late 1990s is facing the unresolved, long-standing debate about the threat to militarized masculinity posed by the umbrella. The umbrella. Such a seemingly humble functional accessory. Yet in the late 1980s and again in 1997 the controversy over the umbrella spawned memos, letters, official declarations. The U.S. Air Force and the U.S. Navy commands already had determined that both male and female uniformed service personnel could carry umbrellas without subverting the authority represented by their uniforms. Their counterparts in the U.S. Army and U.S. Marine Corps disagreed, often adamantly.[68] In May 1997, army and marine senior commanders reiterated their earlier official policy: male officers were prohibited from carrying umbrellas; women officers were permitted to carry umbrellas; male officers could take cover under an umbrella if it was carried by a woman officer. Trying to stay dry on a rainy day as they dashed from the far end of the parking lot to their Pentagon offices, women and men of the U.S. Army, Marines, Navy, and Air Force were running a politically gendered course. Any male army or marine officer taking cover under his own umbrella would be charged with denigrating his uniform and be subject to formal discipline. Army Chief of Staff General Dennis Reimer refused to reconsider the existing ban. Marine Corps Commandant Charles C. Krulak went so far as to reject the advice of the Marine Corps Uniform Board, which, after formal deliberation, had advised that male marines be allowed to carry umbrellas.[69]

In Britain, Ministry of Defence officials saw the umbrella as unthreatening not only to navy and air force masculinity but to army masculinity as well. All officers of both genders, the ministry declared, could and should carry umbrellas in order to stay dry.[70] Thus when NATO meets on a drizzly day at its Brussels headquarters, the student of gendered militarization might take notes on which of its member countries' uniformed officers turn up wet.

Fashioning a uniform for women in the military has been a process even more tangled with ambivalence and contradiction. Policy makers eager to use women selectively for soldiering have not wanted to create Amazons; nor have they wanted to validate cross-dressing. Quite the opposite. Most government policy makers have wanted to use women as soldiers only in those ways that simultaneously would serve the military's own operational goals and sustain the culture of militarized masculinity. That policy has meant using women in ways that have perpetuated a respectable brand of femininity.

Women in the military must not be mistaken in public for soldiering men. Neither, however, should women in military uniform be mistaken for bar waitresses or flight attendants. Women soldiers must look like representatives of the state's military. Women soldiers must be attired in a manner that enables them to do their job effectively for that military. This four-sided fashion mandate has not been easy to satisfy.

For the officials responsible for sorting out these competing requirements of women's military uniform design, the opposite of "feminine" has not been "masculine," it has been "mannish."

To be "mannish" is to be a freak, a defiler of femininity, an offender of both respectable women's and respectable men's sensibilities. In short, a mannish woman is a threat to the proper order of things. Attiring a woman's shoulders and hips can be politically fraught indeed. In the militarizing 1930s leading up to its launching of an actual military offensive, for instance, the Nazi regime in Berlin cautioned leaders of its own paramilitary women's organizations to avoid adopting any uniform designs that might give their women wearers a mannish appearance, features "such as narrow hips and broad shoulders."[71] These German planners saw any fashion that blurred lines between the sexes as something that "alien" designers (Jewish, Parisian, British) subversively encouraged. If such styles caught on in Nazi Germany, Nazis predicted, it would jeopardize the race itself.[72]

Shoes. How high should the heel be? Hats. Should women soldiers' dress hats come with visors? And then there is the perpetual pants problem. Under what conditions, if ever, should pants be issued to women? Should pants be issued to enlisted women, yet denied to officer women? Official debates often square off at the breast pocket: should women's uniforms have them or not? British officials pioneering the recruitment of women into the regular forces during World War I were confused by the breast pocket quandary. *Without* breast pockets, women's uniforms would not be identical to men's, thus violating the military principle of uniformity. With such pockets, however, a woman wearer's breasts might become alarmingly pronounced, thus jeopardizing her status as a respectable woman. In the end British officials decided to sacrifice military uniformity for the sake of understating militarized women's anatomy. The resultant policy: no breast pockets.[73]

In the realm of women's dress, as in most areas of women's lives, the state may be powerful and may have its own ideas about the models to which women should conform, but neither factor guarantees that any state bureaucracy will be immune from external considerations, including women's own aspirations and tastes. Worldwide, because most women enlisted by male officials must be recruited as volunteers, a significant factor in the politics of women's uniform design has been notions about how potential recruits—civilian women—would assess the state's preferred design. This factor has offered a crack through which some meager women's agency might creep, though the potential recruit is left still contending with the likely patriarchal fashion perceptions of her family and friends. It is no easy thing to voluntarily don a uniform that friends or the media judge "dowdy" at best, "mannish" at the alleged worst.

Male filmmakers and magazine publishers in the fully mobilized wartime of 1940s Britain seemed preoccupied with women's attire— not only with the wardrobes of women soldiers but also with those of women conscripted into factories and into the women's farming corps, the Land Army. Although the Land Army was being portrayed by writer Vita Sackville-West as British women's pathway to postwar professional agriculture, male media image creators expressed anxiety.[74] They went to considerable lengths to reassure a nervous public that, underneath the overalls and khaki, women's bodies remained essentially female and feminine. When the war was won, the media predicted, women surely would give up masculine jobs, mannish pants, pitchforks, riveting guns, and code-breaking machines and once again would take up nylon stockings, lipstick tubes, and hair curlers. Film historian Antonia Lant describes British director Leslie Howard's 1940s film *The Gentle Sex*: "Most of the first reel of 'The Gentle Sex' concerns the reorganization and training of the seven female recruits into a disciplined and controlled unit, able to drive trucks and ambulances and spot enemy aircraft. The process of removing their civilian clothes, and replacing them with standard issue, is documented through several scenes, so that camp training is presented almost entirely in terms of undressing and dressing for action. It is as if Howard needs to assert over and over again the presence of a female body beneath the uniform."[75]

Fashion anxieties were trans-Atlantic. In each instance, the political arena included state officials (who often didn't agree with each other), the media, potential women recruits, and their parents and friends. Historian Ruth Pierson has revealed the Canadian military's worries about civilian perceptions of women soldiers during World War II. This war broke out in an era of consumerism. Government designers had to produce a uniform for women that would not violate potential volunteers' and their parents' and their boyfriends' senses of the feminine and the fashionable. At the same time, the Canadian government wanted to support Britain under attack from Germany (with as yet no American military support), enlist more women into the services, and still silence the rumors that women in uniform were either lesbians or heterosexually promiscuous. There was considerable pride among Canadian Women's Army Corps officials, consequently, when after early uncertainties and retailoring the CWAC finally produced a women's uniform that was deemed "smart."[76]

The CWAC's successful uniform was created through the collective effort of Canada's National Defence Minister, his wife, the Master-General of Ordnance, a Toronto dress designer, and in the final stage, a committee from the National Defense ministry. The final uniform produced in this political atmosphere by these political actors was a two-piece khaki ensemble, each element designed with several goals and multiple audiences in mind:

a gored, slightly flared skirt

two hip pockets on the skirt

a single-breasted tunic—with one breast pocket

brown epaulets and CWAC and Canadian badges on the shoulders
and arms of the tunic

a khaki shirt and brown tie

a khaki peaked hat

khaki hose and brown oxford shoes

Pierson tells of one Canadian woman who recalls that this uniform
design helped her decide to enlist in the army rather than the royal air
force or the navy: "Perhaps if I had big baby blue eyes, I might have
considered the blue uniforms of the R.C.A.F. or the Navy, but be that
as it may, not only did the khaki match my brown eyes (used for coyly
rolling and flirting in those days, besides the less use of just plain seeing); the trim, fitted tunic and the A-line skirt of the CWACs was
known to be the most attractive of the three services."[77]

South of the border, World War II (when the U.S. government did
enter it) set off similar uniform fashion controversies. Leisa Meyer has
documented the competing concerns that percolated through the U.S.
Women's Army Corps during the early 1940s.[78] The formidable Texas
journalist Olveta Culp Hobby along with other women leaders of, and
advocates for, the WACs were determined that the women enlisted into
their corps would appear "respectable." Once again, war waging and
feminized respectability would be tightly interwoven in a country's political process. Feminized respectability, Hobby and her associates
strategized, was the only sure guarantor of popular legitimacy for the
1940s American woman soldier. These women chose to operate inside
the wartime state. They were following in the footsteps of other professional women reformers who, in the wake of the success of the
women's suffrage movement, had entered the American state as civilian policy makers and administrators under the New Deal administration of Franklin Roosevelt.

Throughout World War II the American WAC leaders, like their
Canadian counterparts, had to combat a highly charged rumor mill
that, tinged with amazonian anxieties, portrayed WACs as loose or lesbian. The source of most of the rumors—which were intended to undermine the legitimacy of the WACs among both the general command
and the civilian public—turned out, upon investigation, to be rank-

and-file male soldiers. These militarized men felt threatened as WACs increasingly demonstrated capacities that enabled them to take over many tasks previously assigned to men.[79]

In Hobby's view, the respectable woman was a patriot who put her country's interests above her own. The respectable feminine patriot would not volunteer to wear the WAC uniform out of a desire for "glamour." Glamour, Meyer shows, was thought by Hobby to be too closely associated with sexual promiscuity. Yet while eschewing glamour, the uniforms, that is, the public representation of the WAC, should not suggest that the women's corps was a den of lesbians. Lesbian purges (among black as well as white women in the racially segregated WACs) and confusion over uniform design became two prongs of the leadership's effort to refute male soldiers' slander campaigns, senior male officers' reluctance to accept women as genuine soldiers, and the general public's patriarchal misgivings.[80] In this countercampaign, shoes, stockings, pockets, and ties all became sexually and politically loaded.

In America, it was the WAVES—the U.S. Navy's women's corps—that won the public's fashion endorsement. Whereas the WAC uniform was designed by the Philadelphia Quartermaster's Depot (using male patterns and sizes), the leaders of the WAVES decided to contract with civilian fashion designers. Furthermore, WAVES' uniforms could be purchased during the war at women's clothing stores and be individually fitted.[81] The WAVES leaders kept one calculating eye on the feminine tastes of the consumerist young women recruits; the other eye was trained on the elite men in Congress and the War Department who would decide whether or not women would be fully militarized in the regular armed forces. These strategically minded women inside the war-waging state, like the nursing leaders in Britain, defined success as achieving full militarization for their women. The opposite of militarization, they believed, was not demilitarization. The opposite was wartime marginalization. These women took deliberate steps to be sure that their WAVES would not be marginalized because any man in Congress or the War Department deemed them less than respectably feminine. To that end, leaders of the WAVES installed Elizabeth Arden beauty salons on WAVES bases.

The WACs and WAVES contesting fashion calculations were part of a larger militarized gender strategy that deployed American sexual, class, and race biases to the WAVES' political advantage: during the years of World War II, the WAVES remained an all-white women's corps, employing black women as cleaning staff to serve WAVES officers. By contrast, the WACs, though segregated and with a white leadership that was often clearly racially ambivalent, did make it their policy to admit thousands of African American, Asian, and Native American women. The WAVES, furthermore, accepted only women volunteers with at least a high school diploma, favoring those women with college degrees. The WACs were a more open and broadly based institution. Whereas most WACs were trained on Army bases, the WAVES' leaders selected as their training grounds the campuses of prestigious schools such as Smith College. Thus, when a 1944 Gallup poll revealed that 70 percent of American civilian women surveyed said that they would choose to join the WAVES rather than the WACs, perceptions of more than the navy women's fashionable uniforms were at work.[82]

The array of strategic moves made to protect the WAVES from the sexualized rumors that bedeviled the WACs did not allow the WAVES leadership to relax. They felt compelled to keep up their guard against lesbians in their smartly tailored, all-white ranks. Even a lesbian herself, attired in a designer-created, custom-outfitted midnight blue uniform, could be guided by fear of exposure—by either her women peers or women superiors—as she went about her wartime military duties. WAVES veteran and writer Mary Meigs recalls:

> After light-out I heard a stealthy sound as some of my roommates climbed into upper bunks, or occupants of upper bunks climbed down. The sounds of giggles and cautious movements was accompanied by the whispered confidences of straight WAVES who had changed bunks in order to talk ... I, too, climbed up to Preston's welcoming arms one night ... I had conjured up the specter of an officer on-watch bursting in, and of our subsequent dishonorable discharge ... It was standard practice for lesbians to hint at male lovers in their lives or claim to be mourning a lover who had been killed in the war.[83]

After the war, the U.S. War Department—soon to be renamed the Defense Department—demobilized most military women. In the 1950s, the American military, like the militaries of the Soviet Union, Britain, and Canada, was remasculinized. Remasculinization was one of the patriarchal rewards of a victorious peacetime. Peace meant normalcy. Normalcy meant soldiers would be male; only an almost invisible 2 percent of the uniformed American military would be women. But as new feminist historiography is revealing, the years in American society between the mid-1940s and the early 1960s, while dominated by domesticated, white, suburban, middle-class ideals, were not years without gendered subversion and open protest.[84]

The tiny minority of women who remained in the U.S. military after World War II are of particular interest. In keeping their stubborn purchase on militarization, they were resisters. They chose not to marry when all around them more women than ever before in the country's history were embracing marriage. They remained in a military that was being consciously remasculinized. These women were to become the senior generation of officers during the early decades of the military's Cold War era. They would become commanders and role models for the trickle of women who entered the American armed forces during the 1950s and 1960s.

Donna Dean, a working-class Cherokee woman, enlisted in the WAVES in 1963 in pursuit of a way out of her family's grinding poverty. Still today she remembers the lessons that the World War II generation of WAVES instilled in younger women like herself: "Never disgrace your uniform, don't lie when the going gets rough, and never forget who you are and what the uniform you wear represents."[85] The WAVES meant "uniform" not only symbolically, but literally. To be a WAVE in 1960s America meant to act and dress like a lady, at least in public. It was public visibility that posed dangers for any woman in the peacetime, Cold War, remasculinized American military: "We never went outside without gloves and hats, we never played baseball, and we never swore. We always wore girdles and firmly engineered brassieres so there would be no unseemly jiggle. Pantyhose were believed to herald the beginning of the end of morality and right thinking, as there were no seams to keep straight."[86]

Girdles can be militarized.

It would be tempting to portray these older women officers, with their obsession with girdles and ladylike respectability, as antediluvian prudes. And, in fact, that image is how they frequently were characterized. But this portrayal, I think, is a mistake. These military women of the World War II generation were trying to devise a strategy that would leave open inside a remasculinized military institutional culture a small but secure space for themselves and for younger women. Girdles and seamed nylons were a means to an end: remaining active in a place in which American women in a Cold War militarized peacetime were not supposed to be—soldiering for the state.

In more recent years, as the American all-male draft ended in 1973 and as the Defense Department searched for ways to use women to compensate for the loss of white, middle-class, young men, ambivalence about the meaning of women-as-soldiers continued to plague military uniform and cosmetic designers. Preserving visible signs of women soldiers' femininity became a bureaucratic campaign, though one marked by contradiction. Army officers instructed a woman soldier to keep her hair short enough so that it reached just the collar of her uniform, but not so short as to appear "unfeminine." Women in the U.S. Marine Corps were required to tweeze their eyebrows in a regulation arch. An early 1980s army recruiting brochure suggests the military's ambivalence and institutional nervousness: below a color photo of a pretty woman smiling out from under a camouflaged combat helmet is the caption: "Some of the best soldiers wear lipstick."[87]

During the most recent era of militarized fashion maneuvers, some of the most tortuous fashion gymnastics of the post-draft era were staged at the country's national military academies. Although the U.S. Coast Guard Academy admitted women as cadets as early as the 1940s, not until 1976 did Congress order the U.S. Military Academy at West Point, the U.S. Naval Academy at Annapolis, and the U.S. Air Force Academy at Colorado Springs each to break with their all-male student traditions.[88] At each of the three academies, women's uniforms had to be designed for the new female cadets. As always, this mandate proved a complex political task.

Elizabeth Hillman has provided us with one of the most detailed investigations of gendered military uniform design politics in her study of the academies' decision making.[89] She tells of the anxiety provoked when women cadets initially were issued the sort of visored hats worn by male air force academy cadets. It proved quite disconcerting to male officers not to be able to see women's eyes. Male cadets' eyes being shadowed by the glossy visors somehow gave them an aura of strength and authority. Female cadets' eyes cast under a similar shadow made them, apparently, inscrutable. Women's visored caps were withdrawn.

Hillman relates the air force academy's struggle over the proper length for a woman cadet's dress jacket. What jacket design would be properly militaristic, suitably feminine, and yet not provocative? Should the woman cadet's jacket be short or long? Should it cover her buttocks or leave them exposed? The latter was deemed fashionably militaristic for male cadets, but too provocative when donned by the women marching on the parade grounds in front of them. The men's minds might wander. Then there was the problem of underwear. Even unseen garments, it was officially concluded, should be the objects of formal policy—a decision that suggests the depths of nervousness touched·by introducing women into a previously masculinized institutional culture. The academy decision makers' worry seemed to be that, even if unseen by others, the very act of wearing a half-bra might make the woman cadet think unsuitably racy thoughts or, perhaps even more alarming, might inspire sexualized imaginings among the general public or her male peers, who were encouraged to have such thoughts, but only of other women, not their officer peers. Thus, after visiting the U.S. Merchant Marine Academy (which became coeducational one year earlier than did the three major academies), a navy official, aware that Annapolis would soon have its own cadets to attire, wrote this memo in 1975: "the Merchant Marine Academy issues standard type underwear (Panty hose, panties, bras and half slips) although the items are not normally viewed by the public, I think the issue of all these items are necessary to standardize the uniforms, and would eliminate the wear of fancy panties and half-bras."[90]

All these memos, trial runs, and U-turns might appear designed less for national security than for stand-up comedy; but something serious is going on here. Figuring out exactly which hat, which jacket, and which bra a woman should be officially issued as she entered into a masculinized, militarized enclave of the state was thought necessary if that woman's entry was to sustain a militarized version of national security, not subvert it. And this maneuver was difficult—and thus often confusing and even rather comical, at least to outsiders—precisely because militarizing women always has been pursued for the sake of controlling women in ways that maintain the sorts of masculinity that enhance militarism. It is, in reality, no more trivial to watch officials puzzling over a hat style or an eyebrow arch than to watch them debating whether to create different brothels for male officers and enlisted men. Both sets of puzzlings, both processes of policy making, are part of a larger attempt to control women for the sake of controlling men for the sake of achieving the desired level of militarization.

Once again, however, we need to be careful not to imagine that just because state officials try to micromanage women's militarization, they always or fully succeed. Two questions, instead, need to be added to our investigatory list: first, where and when do women, individually or collectively, manage to exercise some agency? and second, at what point does women's effective agency, paradoxically, not roll back militarization but integrate women ever more thoroughly into a militarized culture?

In the late 1990s, a young American woman stationed as a peace-keeping soldier in Bosnia offered her own interpretation of the historical trends in the politics of military cosmetics. In the 1970s, she explains, during the increased recruitment of women into the U.S. military, the military itself enthused over its women volunteers' femininity: these women were the sort who wanted to wear lipstick. In the late 1980s, however, women soldiers were calling for the chance to be assigned to male-only posts. In this era, our peacekeeping soldier explained, women were encouraged to discard their facial cosmetics, to draw less attention to their "otherness." Ten years later, the politics of militarized cosmetics had taken yet another turn. Now this American peacekeeper and her fellow American women soldiers felt more confident as military personnel. They were members of the third generation of post-conscription women soldiery. They were the beneficiaries of three decades of Congressional and women's movement advocacy. One result: these women soldiers were making more of their own fashion decisions in those few areas in which individual taste was permitted. Military Policewoman Marcy Perry, one of seven hundred women deployed to Bosnia (ten percent of the total U.S. peacekeeping contingent), was showing a visiting woman journalist the women's tent: "A few years ago, Private Marcy Perry said, women would not have dared to point out those 'other differences,' as she calls them, between males and females. Nor would they have thought mascara was appropriate to wear with fatigues. But the 24-year-old MP says that female soldiers have proven they can perform in the military. Now, Perry says, they feel more comfortable just being themselves."[91]

Two analytical temptations lie in wait here. The first is to imagine that the militarized history of cosmetics has reached its apogee and it has come to a natural standstill in the late 1990s with American women soldiers feeling free to apply mascara. The second temptation is to imagine that the 1990s American formulation of a gendered military is everyone else's future: in a few years (or decades) the Australian, Japanese, and South African women soldiers also will feel free to wear mascara with their combat fatigues, and then history really will stop. The lessons derived from the larger exploration of women and militarism, however, strongly suggest that in any country, the relationship of femininity to women's soldiering in the state's military remains unstable. It will be analytically necessary, therefore, to go on monitoring just how that instability is dealt with in military decisions on umbrellas, shoes, eyebrow arches, and mascara.

FEMINISTS THINKING ABOUT THE STATE'S WOMEN SOLDIERS

It is a bright springtime morning. From the windows of the Metro you can see Washington's famed cherry trees in full bloom. Federal bureaucrats are out in shorts and t-shirts, taking noontime jogs along the banks of the Potomac. Soon the train descends underground. Its second stop is designated simply "Pentagon." On disembarking, you are surrounded by gift shops and fast food outlets. Workers on their lunch breaks are rushing about doing errands. You scarcely feel as though you are walking into "the belly of the beast."

"The state"—or "the State"—has become ever more central to feminists' thinking. There is not yet agreement on whether the term *the state* reveals or exaggerates the cohesiveness of patriarchal power. While Korean, French, and Egyptian political cultures encourage us to think of the state as a coherent single-minded force, American political culture (and to some extent the political cultures of Canada and Britain as well) prompts us to think of the state as a collection of constantly shifting institutional alliances: some days the White House sides with the Department of Agriculture, other days it backs the Treasury; on some issues the Defense Department and the CIA agree, while on others the two agencies are locked in fierce battle.

The American portrayal is a liberal conception of the state. It allows for considerable optimism. Even though sexism may be pervasive, an incohesive state always allows cracks and niches into which a feminist might wiggle and from which she might exert some influence on some policy decisions some of the time. On the other hand, a feminist is left feeling less sanguine when faced with a European and Asian philosophical tradition that portrays the state not only as patriarchal in its outlook and its interests but also as a cohesive, unconfused structure— a structure whose cracks run only skin deep. Feminists' capacity to effectively shape even some state policy some of the time in this structure will look less like a genuine opportunity and more like a mirage. A mirage that, in itself, may be a wily patriarchal construction.

Feminist theorists and activists both have had to tackle a fundamental question: is male privilege so tightly woven into any sovereign public authority—a state—that the phrase "nonpatriarchal state" should be considered an oxymoron? There is a package of attributes that— when they exist simultaneously—distinguishes a state: publicness, authority, exclusiveness, sovereignty, and the capacity for coercion. Wrapped together, these attributes appear worrisomely (or, to some nonfeminists, comfortingly) similar to that condition that privileges masculinity in a patriarchal society. If a state, any state, is *intrinsically* patriarchal, then it would appear rather futile, naive, or maybe downright dangerous for feminists to seek entrance into the state in the hope of defusing its sexist actions from the inside.[92]

The U.S. Pentagon may seem to be the perfect materialization of those theories of the state that treat the state as, if not monolithic, at least coherent, potent, and patriarchal. From a distance—the vantage point from which most feminists have to view it—the state as represented by the Pentagon exudes solidity, authority, rationalism, exclusivism, secrecy, hierarchy, and masculinity. So it comes as a bit of a surprise to enter "the belly of the beast" and see its mundane dailiness up close.

To enter the Pentagon itself, those geometrically designed offices of the U.S. Defense Department, you must have an official pass or be escorted by someone who does. Waiting for an escort to arrive, you can watch a bit of American political culture in motion. It is easy to see why most Americans adopt the liberal view of the state, that is, the state as porous, as merely "government."

The Pentagon is a popular destination for American tourists. School classes and family groups sign up to take tours through the hallways of the Defense Department. American citizens dressed in an assortment of logo-embossed baseball caps, sneakers, cotton dresses, and plaid open-necked shirts are led into the Pentagon by straight-backed, handsomely uniformed, young military personnel, most of whom are male. When they set off, the tourists appear a bit apprehensive. By the end of the tour, they seem eager to have the approval of their military guide. In the school groups, boys especially cluster admiringly at the front to be near the uniformed soldier-guide. He may not be more than a few years older than they are, but he is the man, they are the boys.

Once admitted through the security entrance, a non-tourist visitor begins a trek down geometric corridors. The corridors aren't so different from the hallways of any other civil service bureaucracy. You see civilians as well as people in uniform carrying telltale file folders, the stuff of governance. Office doors are marked by acronyms. A robot scoots along the floor delivering mail. Then you turn a corner into a corridor with a glass display case filled with photos and memorabilia recalling women's roles in the military. Nearby is a small auditorium. A meeting is about to begin.

Several dozen civilian women and men from academia as well as advocacy groups have gathered to talk with a small group of civilian officials and uniformed women and men of the Defense Department. The discussion is to be about women's roles in the American military at the end of the twentieth century.[93] Here amid polite, even cordial, conversation, the state does not appear monolithic; the state's patriarchal inclinations seem open for negotiation. A navy woman commander acerbically describes male officers' sexist faxes with which she routinely has to contend; an army captain declares her commitment to conducting a thorough investigation of sexual harassment. Each of these women talks in terms and tones that sound as genuinely feminist as those used by any of the outsider women's advocates in the room. Furthermore, both the commander and the captain are attending this meeting with the approval of their Pentagon superiors; neither is speaking in cautious whispers.

This meeting seemed to many women's advocates inside and outside the American state to be a good forum for trying to reform those state policies (both written and unwritten) that continued to foster and maintain sexism within one of that country's most powerful institutions, the U.S. military. First, in spring 1997, the ripples from the navy's 1991–1993 Tailhook scandal (in which young naval flying officers, with the apparent toleration of their older superiors, systematically sexually harassed both civilian and military women at the Las Vegas Hilton during the post–Gulf War 1991 annual convention of the Tailhook Association) were, five years later, still inspiring deliberate policy reforms to prevent the navy from having to endure a repeat of such a sexualized and publicized embarrassment. The Tailhook scandal was an institutional embarrassment that navy women and their feminist allies believed they could put to good use. In the American state structure (unlike, for instance, the Canadian), different branches of the military, while all clustered under the Defense Department's unified civilian leadership, had plenty of room in which to carry on lively, sometimes ferocious intramilitary bureaucratic rivalries. The navy's Tailhook disaster, therefore, became the air force's and the army's opportunity to gloat.[94] Briefly. By the spring of 1997, the women and men gathered in that small Pentagon auditorium were determined to translate both of those rival branches' more recent brushes with gendered, sexualized scandal into opportunities for reform. "Aberdeen" had become almost as much of a public household term as "Tailhook."

Following close behind was "Kelly Flinn." Aberdeen was an army training ground in Maryland where a number of male drill sergeants had been accused of systematic sexual harassment of young female trainees, while "Kelly Flinn" (a story that broke shortly after the feminist gathering at the Pentagon) referred to the first air force woman officer to be allowed to pilot one of that service's principal weapons, the B-52 bomber. Her male commander's decision to threaten her with a court martial after the revelation of her affair with a married man, while he and other senior officers turned a blind eye to the seemingly routine involvement of both married and unmarried air force men in such affairs and in commercial prostitution, provoked public and congressional ridicule and cries of "double standard."[95] All three scandals—Tailhook, Aberdeen, and Kelly Flinn—were seen in 1997 by feminist lobbyists and state officials both as confirmations of the military elite's failure to implement their past pledges to rid the military of its deeply masculinized, even misogynist, institutional culture and as a chance for feminists to intervene effectively in the state's military policy processes.

A second factor was on the minds of the gathering's participants that spring. These women's advocates felt a sense of worried urgency when they considered the structure of the American state. The divisions within that state structure—the constitutional reality that inspired an optimistic liberal theorizing about even a patriarchal state—also meant that successful intervention in one sector of the state could be undone by formal opposition in another sector of the state. In 1997, that constitutional division was reinforced by partisan electoral politics. There was a partisan split between the executive and the legislature (something that cannot happen in a democratic parliamentary state system such as Britain's or Japan's or in an authoritarian centralized state system such as Croatia's or Nigeria's). The American presidency was held by Democrat Bill Clinton, who not only was favorably disposed to women's expanded role in the military but also had appointed to top posts in the Defense Department a number of civilian officials who shared this policy position. Further up Pennsylvania Avenue, the Congress was controlled by the Republicans, many of whom, especially in the House of Representatives, espoused a conservative ideology that not only opposed women's expanded military roles but interpreted that expansion as emblematic of an unraveling of the country's entire social fabric. In this same system, the military was under

the authority of the Democratic presidency but depended for its appro-
priations and to some extent its foreign mission mandate on the
Republican-controlled legislature. Women's advocates believed that,
given the persistent potency of soldiering in American popular imagination and given this divided state structure and the current partisan
reality and despite the recent scandals' opening up of political opportunities, they, as feminists, would have to join together in an insider-outsider alliance to bring executive, media, popular, and legislative pressure to bear if those antisexist reforms making their way up the
Defense hierarchy were not to be reversed in the Congress.[96]

In every country, the understandings of particular feminists about
the conditions that make focusing on women in the military and engaging with the state from the inside as well as the outside promising
or frustrating or risky will vary—depending on the particular structure
of the state (in law and in practice), the degree to which the popular
culture is open to new ideas about gendered militarism, and the level
of partisan regime cohesiveness. As political scientist Mary Katzenstein
has wisely warned us, such efforts as the gathering in the Pentagon auditorium in spring 1997 should be looked upon *neither* as proof that
the liberal feminists' theory of the state is universally valid *nor* as validation of an argument that feminists everywhere have made the best
strategic choice when they mustered their scarce energies to fight for
the rights of women as soldiers.[97] What the spring 1997 Washington
gathering, however, does suggest is that under certain political conditions such a feminist intervention can prove useful. As always, the
question to be rigorously investigated is "under what conditions?" It is
when that question is left unposed or is casually pursued that the perpetuation of patriarchal military culture *and* the militarization of feminists are most likely to occur.

Feminist activists in many countries are trying to sort out their relationships to governments and, more generally, to the state. As long ago
as the 1850s, when Florence Nightingale used her considerable political skills to change the British state's policy, advocates of women's
rights have searched for ways to exert influence on government decisions. Most women did not have Nightingale's upper-class male insider
connections to state authority; they were compelled instead to work on
the state from the outside, either devising individual strategies or, more
ambitiously, organizing to exert collective pressure. There were many
more Josephine Butlers than Florence Nightingales. The Victorian

British state was thoroughly masculinized; the denial of women's right to vote was only the most obvious sign. Judging, policing, soldiering, legislating, negotiating with foreign regimes, setting tax rates, managing public roads and ports and the post—all were presumed to require attitudes and capacities possessed only by humans innately equipped with masculinity. In most societies women (with the exception of the occasional queen or empress) were deemed to be incapable of managing the state's affairs; moreover, women, due to their allegedly feminine natures, were commonly thought to be in need of the protection and control not only of their fathers and husbands but of the masculinized state as well. How could those humans who were considered the state's wards be allowed to make state policy?

Thus, merely the gathering in the Pentagon on that day in 1997 suggests a genuine change in the nature of the state. Some of the women participating in the meeting still operated from outside the state—as academics, as lobbyists. Yet other women in attendance were invited because they were civil servants and military officers: they were acting from inside the state. Women outside the state were talking with women inside the state about the gendered implications of state military policy. On the surface, the patriarchal pillars of at least this state seemed to be wobbling.

But what was going on underneath? Was the presence of women in those state policy-making rooms, where decisions were being made about women as soldiers, convincing proof that the state was being truly transformed? Or was their presence perhaps just the newest form of patriarchy? And how could you tell?

American late-twentieth-century feminists were not the first to pose these important theoretical questions. They also were not the first to see the significance of their answers for activist strategizing. The first generation of Egyptian feminists began lobbying in the 1920s and 1930s to have more women appointed to state posts; they succeeded. They saw women's entrée into the ministries of education and public health not just as a chance for individual women to gain professional career opportunities but for women as advocates of all Egyptian women's advancement to increase their leverage on public policy.[98] Fifty years later Australian women became determined to take advantage of their state's increasing apparent porousness in order to work for women's advancement from within the offices of the state. They coined the term "femocrats."[99] Today, in political systems as different as those of Chile, Britain, Jamaica, Norway, Costa Rica, South Africa, Japan, France, and Ireland, women with conscious feminist goals have made headway in gaining access to official state positions—not only in elected legislatures, where they are most visible (though not necessarily the most influential), but also in executive departments of justice, immigration, trade, transportation, welfare, public health, and foreign affairs. Working in these executive sectors of the state, feminist civil servants may attract little public attention, but they wield significant influence over specific areas of public policy.[100]

This apparent expansion of self-conscious feminist participation inside state structures, however, has not occurred without feminist debate. How can a woman hold on to her feminist values once she becomes an official of a still-patriarchal institution? If she owes her appointment to the political party currently in power, how will she react when that party's male leadership declares that the time for feminist reforms is "not now, later"? How should grassroots women's groups operating outside the state relate to an insider femocrat: as "one of us" or as "one of them"? Are femocrats transforming the state or being co-opted by it?

How a woman answers these questions will shape both her theory and her strategy. If her theory is mistaken, her strategy is likely to produce results she didn't count on. Putting strategy into practice, however, is one of the best ways to test and eventually refine a theory—if a woman has the courage to do a full accounting of the results of strategic practice. The intimacy between theory and practice is nowhere more clearly revealed than in the experiences of feminists attempting to shape state policies regarding women as soldiers.[101] But devising measures of assessment is a difficult task. Should increasing the proportion of women in any military be counted as proof of joint feminist insider-outsider cooperation's success? Or alternatively, should the upward trend on the gender graph be seen as evidence that the patriarchal military policy makers are succeeding in militarizing women without surrendering any real power of their own? Experiences in a number of countries suggest that the line separating the militarization of women from the liberation of women can be reed-thin.

The difficulty in determining on which side of this line women's soldiering—and efforts to expand it—falls is due in part to patriarchal governments having their own, nonfeminist reasons for introducing women into their militaries or for expanding the numbers and roles of women as soldiers. Here is the beginning of what probably should be a longer list of statist *non*feminist reasons for increasing the numbers and roles of women soldiers:

To make up for the young men who are avoiding conscription

To make up for the shortfalls in male volunteers when the civilian job market is good for young men

To look "modern" and "democratic" in the state's patriarchal eyes

To look "modern" and "democratic" in the eyes of the state's principal international allies

To free men from the military's necessary secretarial, medical, and communications tasks so they can perform "real" military duties

To avoid having to enlist men from those ethnic and racial groups that the current regime does not trust

To enhance women's patriotic mobilization during wartime

To gain the educational skills women occasionally have in greater proportion than men (or than those men most likely to consider military enlistment an option)

During the Vietnam War era, women comprised a mere 2 percent of the total U.S. military's personnel. Most were white women; most were assigned to the nursing corps. Yet, by mid-1997, women made up 13 percent of the U.S. uniformed military personnel. African American women had become a prominent (if still scarcely visible politically) segment of the military: one-third of all women in uniform, while only 12 percent of all American women nationally. Latina and Asian American women in the military by 1997 numbered in the thousands. All but a few military posts—those in combat infantry units and armored divisions and on submarines—had been opened to women. Most daily operations of the U.S. military by the end of the century had come to depend on women's skills and labor. The U.S. Air Force had become 17.2 percent female.[102] A year later, women's proportion of all U.S. uniformed personnel had risen again—to 14 percent.[103]

Not all of these changes have been brought about simply by patriarchal male officials pursuing their own statist goals. Some of these increases have been the result of the contemporary descendants of Olveta Culp Hobby, women like those gathered in the Pentagon in the spring of 1997, women who have systematically pressured the Pentagon from the inside and the outside to demasculinize the military's institutional culture, a culture that, they believe, has fueled witch-hunts of suspected lesbians, given license for military men to sexually harass their female colleagues, and permitted senior officers to turn a blind eye to the persistence of both. These same feminists operating inside and outside the American state—as lobbyists, academic researchers, military officers, members of Congress, journalists, and civil servants—also have acted in alliance to lower sexist barriers that have kept the number of uniformed women under 20 percent and that have kept the jobs that serve as launchpads to senior rank promotions—"combat" posts—a masculine preserve. The following figures, therefore, should not be read simply as proof of the patriarchal state's maneuvers in successfully achieving the patriarchal state's own self-defined ends. Something else more complex is going on in the late-twentieth-century American state. According to April 1997 data from the U.S. Department of Defense:[104]

Number of American women in all the active duty branches of the military	192,140
Women as the percentage of all uniformed military	13.5%
Proportion of all military women who are white	57.2%
Proportion of all military women who are black	31.1%
Proportion of all military women who are Hispanic	6.1%
Proportion of all women in the military who are "other" (including Native American, Asian American, Pacific Islander)	5.5%

To whose agency do these figures testify? Who is co-opting whom? Perhaps part of the answer will lie in who gets to tell the public story of soldiering in the next generation.

The story, in its multiple versions, of American women's soldiering is not the only story of women in the uniformed ranks of a state. To make feminist sense—in other words, realistic, sophisticated sense—of women's ongoing relationships to statist soldiering, we need to resist the parochial temptation to monitor only American developments. Today, states with distinctly (if varied) patriarchal policies and authoritarian structures have enlisted small numbers of women into their militaries: Croatia, Mexico, Jordan, Argentina, Chile, Japan, South Korea, Kuwait. In countries with democratically structured states and histo-

Figure 14 During the war that fragmented the former Yugoslavia, the new Bosnian government created its own army in 1994 that included women, many of whom were Muslim, here
undergoing training. In the highly charged post–Dayton Accord political climate of the late
1990s, policies about women's roles inside and outside the region's several armies have
continued to be debated and refashioned. (Photographer: Agence France-Presse.)

ries of organized women's activism, women's prominence in the state's
armed forces sometimes is due to pressure deliberately exerted inside
and outside the state by strategically sophisticated feminists, sometimes due to masculinized elites simply pursing their own militarized
ends.

Of all the states in NATO, only one, Italy, has had no women at all
in its military. In 1998, however, the Italian government, now led by a
center-left coalition, introduced a bill that would for the first time allow women to volunteer to soldier in the Italian military.[105] Italian
feminists have not been not quite certain whether this is a good thing
or a bad thing for Italian women. Women, who had been confined to
posts in the medical corps, are becoming more evident in the ranks of
the German military at a time when the German government is shedding some of its post–World War II reticence and asking to be accepted
as an equal partner in Europe's military joint policy making.[106] The
French military, with 7 percent women, looks forward to the prospect
of filling its ranks with more women once male conscription is ended

after 2000.[107] Austria lifted its ban on women as volunteer soldiers on the eve of its joining the European Union (EU).[108] Until recently, leaders of the EU did not envision the organization as a military alliance; however, significant areas of coordination between the EU and NATO are developing, most visibly in the realm of intervention in Balkan civil strife. Barring women totally from the military's ranks appears to be taken today as evidence of a state's unreadiness to join the community of Euro-American "modern," "democratic" states.

By the late 1990s, the Canadian military, for instance, had become 11 percent female. One woman, Kim Campbell, had served, if briefly, as the civilian cabinet minister in charge of the Department of National Defence, something still unheard of in late-twentieth-century America. Canadian lawmakers and judges also had outpaced their counterparts south of the border by compelling the military to lift its ban on lesbians and gay men serving in the armed forces and by opening up combat units to women. On the other hand, a spate of press reports in spring 1998 documenting Canadian enlisted men's and male officer's perpetration of, and toleration of, rapes and other forms of sexual harassment of Canadian women soldiers suggested that these political reforms were meeting significant resistance from inside an institutional culture informed by both masculinization and militarism.[109] In response to the revelations—revelations that followed on the heels of investigations into some Canadian peacekeeping troops' torture and murder of a man detained in Somalia—the Canadian army's commander, Lieutenant General Bill Leach, held a press conference. He announced that the army now would intensify its efforts to recruit even more women, especially into combat units.[110] His conviction was that only by increasing the ratios of women to men in combat units would men's sexist attitudes and behaviors be modified.[111] There were few calls by any influential politicians for reading these revelations as evidence that the Canadian military needed to be remasculinized. In this, too, Canada's military politics seemed to differ from its American counterpart.

At almost the same time, Britain's Ministry of Defence announced that it too would launch a major campaign to recruit more women into the army. Another explicit goal of that campaign was to increase the number of black and Asian British recruits.[112] This policy decision came at a time when women comprised 7 percent of all uniformed military personnel. And while Afro-Caribbean, African, and Asian

British soldiers together comprised 6 percent of all Britons, they were less than 1 percent of all British soldiers of officer rank.[113] The Ministry of Defence was not facing an organized lobbying alliance of British feminists inside and outside the state making women in the military its priority, but ministry officials had been embarrassed in recent months, first, by losses in several civilian court cases in which judges decided in favor of women soldiers who had brought charges of sex discrimination and, second, by evidence of racial discrimination made public by an Asian member of Parliament, an MP speaking now from the government benches of the newly ascendant Labour Party. The ministry's recruiters expressed optimism about reaching their goal of increasing the proportion of women. One woman recruiter, Major Sarah License, explained: "Our research shows that a lot of young women simply aren't aware of the career opportunities the army offers, and that is something we need to address ... The more women we recruit, the easier it gets."[114]

In South Africa, the radical shift in racial and constitutional systems that occurred after 1994 had profound implications both for the level of militarization in people's everyday lives and for the proportions of the state's military that were female. It had been the politics of sustaining apartheid that had pushed the formerly white, deeply patriarchal regime to recruit more women as soldiers. As anti-apartheid activist and sociologist Jacklyn Cock demonstrated in the late 1980s, the apartheid regime had become so reliant on militarism to maintain the racist system and had by then run so short of white male conscripts to sustain that high level of militarization that not only did it have to enlist growing numbers of black and mixed-race males into its military but it also had to contradict its own Calvinist patriarchal values in order to recruit significant numbers of white women. By the end of the apartheid era, the South African Defense Force was 11 percent women, the same proportion as the U.S. military at the time. This result did not come from either feminist lobbying or femocrat strategizing.[115]

When, following the dismantlement of the apartheid political system and the democratization of the state, the South African government reorganized its military, officials self-consciously did it in a way that ensured no rollback in the proportion of women, although now more of those women soldiering for the state would be black women. State officials were being pressed to do so by both white women career officers and black women who had fought in the anti-apartheid guerrilla forces. Had the decision been left up to the men at the top of the post-1994 administration of President Nelson Mandela, the new military's profile might have been remasculinized. This process of remasculinization is what had happened in Nicaragua after its revolution, in Zimbabwe after its revolution, in Eritrea, Vietnam, Algeria, and China after their revolutions. The prominent roles of women as armed combatants in insurgent armies has been no bulwark against the masculinization of the new post-revolution state military.[116]

In the wake of the dismantlement of the apartheid political economy and the continuing intraracial and interracial violence that frightened local citizens and foreign investors, the men at the top of the Mandela administration were less concerned about women being integrated into the military than they were about not alienating the largely white Afrikaner male officer corps while simultaneously absorbing the potentially disruptive (and armed) unemployed young men of the now-disbanded insurgent forces. Only a small contingent of women activists joined with the white women officers and the women ex-guerrillas to pressure the new government not to totally remasculinize the renamed South African National Defence Force (SANDF). By late 1997, three years after the fall of apartheid and the ending of the state policy of militarized security, women comprised 8,000 of the force's 76,000 uniformed personnel. This figure amounted to 11 percent, about the same proportion of women to men at the end of the military's apartheid era. But of all the women soldiers in the SANDF, 38 percent now were black women, an increase over their representation under the former political system.[117] The political priority of many South African feminists, however, has not been to ensure women a place in the state's reformed military but to marginalize the military's role in the country's political life altogether.

Patriarchy has survived because of its facile adaptiveness, not because of its rigidity. Perhaps many women, once they are in uniform, have found satisfaction indeed in being so directly militarized: the military offers "adventure," travel, camaraderie, physical fitness, skill training, college scholarships, the chance for leadership, equal pay, child care for their children, pensions. Some women have expended considerable political energy to ensure that women serving in the military were more, not less, fully militarized as soldiers. Militarization has meant integration. Less-than-full militarization has meant marginalization. A woman serving in a masculinized institution is likely to be marginalized. Thus pushed to the institution's margins, she is less likely to be promoted, taken seriously, or awarded a pension; she is more likely to be sexually harassed and less likely to be able to speak out about that harassment. Women who have pursued full militarization have felt as though they are participating in a feminist endeavor because they have been called on to think hard about the nature of their state's patriarchal assumptions and to endure misogynist ridicule.

Yet this militarizing endeavor usually has been conducted without creating alliances with those feminists working with wartime rape victims, with military prostitutes, with women refugees, or even with women living as military wives. Most American feminists who responded to the proliferating military scandals of the 1990s did see gay and lesbian activists as natural allies. Together they were working to roll back state-sanctioned homophobia, a brand of sexism that had been wielded against any woman who challenged the military's masculinized heterosexualized institutional culture. Thus, feminists focusing on women's right to hold combat positions could join with gay and lesbian activists critical of the "don't ask, don't tell, don't pursue" policy in a sense of victory when Under Secretary of Defense Edwin Dorn, having been briefed on the homophobic abuses of the current policy by the Servicemembers Legal Defense Network, decided to issue the following memorandum just before the spring 1997 Pentagon gathering:

> This guidance is issued because of information we have received that some service members have been threatened with being reported as homosexual after they have rebuffed or themselves reported acts of sexual misconduct ...
> The fact that a service member reports being threatened because he or she is said or is perceived to be a homosexual shall not by itself constitute credible information justifying the initiation of an investigation of the threatened service member. The report of such a threat should result in the prompt investigation of the threat itself.[118]

In other words: stop lesbian baiting.

By contrast, the American feminists active in exposing and dismantling what, by the late 1990s, was increasingly theorized as a masculinized military "culture" did not form political alliances with those civilian women regularly hired to perform as strippers at military men's gatherings, or with those civilian girls and women who lived around American bases in Okinawa and Korea, or with black and white military wives who remained loyally quiet when their military husbands were charged with sexual harassment.

This omission is not so surprising. Not just in the United States but in any country, for women soldiers' advocates to create effective political alliances with any or all of these other militarized women would necessitate theorizing about, and thus building a strategy upon ideas about, *militarism*. But publicly challenging militarism has not been a successful strategy for getting generals, cabinet ministers, and powerful legislators to pay attention to the concerns of women as soldiers. If the fully militarized integration of women as soldiers is achieved, however, via a strategy that requires certain sophisticated feminists to remain silent on the character and consequences of militarism, then might not the success of that integration send the roots of militarism even deeper down into the soil of a nation's political culture?

On the other hand (when feminists engage with any state, there is always another hand) should feminists adopt either a theory that argues that soldiering is so "naturally" masculine that any alternative gendering is impossible or a theory that asserts that the masculinization of their state's military is so trivial in the larger scheme of things that it is not worth expending strategic resources on? There is also the possibility that patriarchal state elites have initiated something they cannot control. That is, it could be that while patriarchal state officials initially bring women into the military merely to fill the ranks, not transform them, in the longer run those elites may find they are unable to keep firm control over the gendered political processes that they too-confidentially set into motion. Although the presence of women as soldiers alone is not a reliable indicator of declining state masculinization, under certain conditions the presence of those women in the ranks may provide a platform from which feminists can raise fresh questions about the legitimacy of state-sanctioned masculine privilege. The rape of a female soldier by a male soldier and the subsequent cover-up by the rapist's commander can tear away the legitimizing camouflage that has sustained that military as a symbol of national pride and security. News of the rape and the official cover-up can make that military appear to many citizens for the first time to be little more than a men's club. Under such special political conditions, state officials who believe they need women in the ranks for their own militarized objectives may become confused. Although state confusion is not as invigorating to witness as state transformation, it can be revealing. And revelation can alter consciousness.

Conclusion:
Decisions, Decisions, Decisions

I first read Virginia Woolf's classic antiwar essay, *Three Guineas,* back in the early eighties, at about the time I was carrying the can of Star Wars tomato soup home from Great Britain in my knapsack.[1] Woolf had finished writing that book in the year I was born. But it took me decades to get to the point where I could read it and absorb what she was saying. I didn't want others to have to wait so long, so I began making it an integral part of a seminar on women and militarization. With different groups of students, I have by now read *Three Guineas* perhaps eight times. I have worn out my original paperback copy and have almost filled up a second copy with inky marginal mullings. With each reading and with each new group of students—from the United States, Nepal, Japan, Mali, Korea, Bulgaria—Woolf's spiraling paragraphs have shed new light on the subtly gendered processes of militarization.

Virginia Woolf was certain that most of her friends among London's famous Bloomsbury intellectual circle would not like her essay. Even though it was 1938 and everyone was talking about the horrors of the Spanish Civil War (in which Woolf had lost a beloved nephew) and worrying anxiously about the imminent outbreak of another world war, what Woolf was determined to reveal, she predicted, would scarcely be greeted with applause.[2] For, after painstaking research (her notes make as startling reading as the essay itself), Woolf had come to the conclusion that war had causal roots that insinuated themselves into those very institutions and cultural inclinations that many Britons proudly imagined were the centerpieces of their democratic civilization: the law, universities, civil service, and middle-class refinement. Woven into each, she had found, were the sorts of presumptions and rituals that nurtured hierarchy, rivalry, and the privileging of masculinity—the Holy Trinity of militarism.

I still find reading *Three Guineas* unsettling. In it Woolf not only points to the continuing masculinized culture of the government's civil service, for instance, but warns readers that even supporting women's colleges or backing efforts to promote women in law and medicine could serve to make women complicit actors in militarism *if* those young women adopted uncritically those professions' masculinized norms of hierarchy and competitiveness.

The research that has informed the present book underscores Woolf's double message: militarization does not occur simply in the obvious places but can transform the meanings and uses of people, things, and ideas located far from bombs or camouflaged fatigues; militarization may privilege masculinity, but it does so by manipulating the meanings of both femininity and masculinity. Evidence collected here suggests in addition that militarization does not just happen: it requires decisions, many decisions, decisions made by both civilians and people in uniform. And though their decisions usually are quite self-conscious, militarizing decision makers are not just machines of logic and interest. They can be afflicted with confusion and ambivalence; they often do not reap the results intended. Readers of these chapters who found themselves at any point smiling, even chuckling—perhaps over an umbrella debate—could take that reaction as a sign that militarizing can be a process fraught with contradiction.

Woolf's radical analysis led her to a radical strategy: women should move toward a profound detachment from all those processes fostering militarization. The preceding chapters here, however, show women as feminists choosing a variety of strategies to engage with the militarizers inside and outside the state, taking on the complex risks that those engagements necessarily entail.

With their acute consciousness of the recently devastating Great War and ominous Spanish Civil War and their memories of the Crimean and Boer wars, Woolf's contemporaries were quite aware that some things were routinely prone to militarization. Sixty years later, we, Woolf's offspring, still are trying to understand exactly why and how and with what consequences these things become militarized:

nationalism

masculinity

racism

motherhood

heroism

women's suffrage movements

prostitution

government budgets

women's desire for good industrial jobs

secrecy

venereal disease

On the other hand, the full range of things that can be militarized has been uncovered only recently, and we barely comprehend their militarizations today:

laundry

umbrellas

girdles

domestic violence prevention

feminine respectability

mascara

democracy

scientific research

marriage

fashion

security

first-class citizenship

town pride

homophobia

anti-homophobia

And, at the dawn of a new century, the list of what can be militarized extends even further:

upward social mobility

liberation

rape

humanitarian aid

peacekeeping

AIDS and AIDS prevention

civilian judges

children's toy manufacture

cinema scriptwriters

electoral campaigning

femininity

sneakers

There is nothing automatic about militarization. None of the items listed here will inevitably be militarized. Militarization is the step-by-step process by which something becomes *controlled by, dependent on,* or *derives its value from* the military as an institution or militaristic criteria. What has been militarized can be demilitarized. What has been demilitarized can be remilitarized. Thus a pair of sneakers is militarized to the extent that the women who are sewing those sneakers (in China, Indonesia, or Vietnam) have their wages kept low because major brand corporations and their factory contractors hire former military men as their managers, call on local militarized security forces to suppress workers' organizing, or ally with governments who define the absence of women workers' independent organizing as necessary for "national security." To the extent that a sneaker company gives up any of these management techniques, the sneakers carrying its brand name may be partially demilitarized.

Several more examples. A marriage becomes militarized to the extent that the woman who as the wife depends for her sense of public or domestic security, as well as for her housing and medical care, on a man who as her husband defines himself as a soldier. To the extent that any woman married to a soldier-husband (or a veteran-husband)

comes to see herself as having rights of her own and as being an autonomous public actor in her country's political affairs, and has a paid
job of her own that can be pursued as a career without concern for her
husband's commander's values, that woman is demilitarizing her marriage. Or take international humanitarian aid. More and more frequently, according to staff people working for agencies such as the International Red Cross and UNICEF, aid workers today are having to
request NATO military convoys and to make difficult deals with local
commanders in order to ensure that their relief supplies reach those
people displaced by acts of war. These staff people worry that their aid
operations, maybe even their institutional cultures, are becoming militarized. They feel they are sacrificing demilitarization and, thereby, the
very integrity of their professions and thus the trust of those people
victimized by violent conflict.[3]

The step-by-step militarizing process usually moves forward because
of decisions that are made, decisions made by specific people. As we
have seen, those decision makers are not all generals and admirals.
Some of them are colonels in their roles as local military base commanders; others are military chaplains, physicians, psychologists, and
recruiters. The decision makers whose choices will determine whether
or not a wife, a hemline, or a relief operation will be militarized also
include people who have never worn khaki and never pointed a gun at
anyone. Digging into the past and present workings of militarization
makes clear that among those nonmilitary decision makers are mayors,
fashion designers, legislators, social scientists, moviemakers, toy manu-
facturers, journalists, UN officials, ethnic community leaders, and advertising executives.

Even leaders of movements opposed to militaristic regimes can become militarized, making decisions that militarize their movements in
ways that privilege masculinity and thereby marginalize some men and
most women. When an authoritarian regime calls out its militarized
riot police to confront a spreading popular opposition, do the leaders
of that opposition choose to meet it with a militarized response of their
own in the form of a front line of bold, brick-carrying, masculinity-
wielding men? If they do, where are the women? The women are usually pushed to the back, into the feminized roles of supporters for and
admirers of the men in the front lines. When a regime calls out its riot
police, it can be hard for pro-democracy women to spot the decisions
that are militarizing the movement into which they are pouring so
much energy. Some women under these conditions, nonetheless, do
manage to weigh the likely outcomes of militarized pro-democracy an-

timilitarism and devise less militarized forms of opposition, innovative forms that keep the spaces open for women's voices. Such opposition is one of the significant features of the whistles handed out by the Belgrade Women in Black and of the decision by the Okinawan women activists to "walk" rather than "march." For many women active in pro-democracy protests, however, it is only months or even years later, when they try to sort out the reasons for the resultant reforms or the new, male-dominated electoral parties, that they realize earlier decisions made in the heat of protest have held long-range masculinizing implications.[4]

Militarization is not a simple process; it is not an easy process. It takes a lot of decisions to propel and sustain militarization. Some of the decisions integral to militarizing women are decisions of omission: senior officers' decision not to rein in younger officers who make strippers central to their squadron parties; senior officers' decision to turn a blind eye to their male subordinates' acts of sexual harassment of female colleagues; civilian politicians' decisions not make their own government's military prostitution policies a topic of explicit consideration. One of the reasons that militarization is often so hard to monitor is that it is caused by a combination of decisions of commission and omission.

Women thinking and acting as feminists have been responsible for revealing how dependent any militarization process is on certain ideas about femininity and on the labor and emotions of women. Most conventional commentators discussing the causes of war treat femininity and women as sideshows. The main event, presumably, is the performance of masculinity and the public choices made by elite men. In narrowing their analytical stage, these observers underestimate the number and quality of calculations made by leaders both of governments and of political movements. That is, by largely ignoring the decisions that maneuver women into those positions where they can smooth the processes of militarization, these conventional (nonfeminist) political commentators underestimate the working of political power. They write as if the American, Russian, and South Korean policy makers never crafted policies on military prostitution. They analyze the Rwandan genocide without thinking to ask how so many men were persuaded to rape their fellow countrywomen. They construct their commentaries on military affairs as if all women married to soldiers were "naturally" obedient wives. They talk as if Serbia's Milosevic could launch a military campaign on the province of Kosovo without thinking about the politics of motherhood.

Feminists have exercised their broader curiosities to widen the stage of political observation. They have asked, "Where are the women?" To this basic query, they have added three other questions: "Which women are there?" "How did those women get there?" and "What do those women think about being there?" The "theres" are varied. "There" may be a silent protest in a Tel Aviv traffic intersection, or it might be a disco just outside a military base, or it could be a bedside in an army hospital. That is, wielding a feminist curiosity prompts an analyst to ask: What maneuverings does it take to position certain women in any society to support their governments in certain ways when those governments rank public priorities so that they bestow superior value on the military as an institution and on soldiering as a public activity? Among these feminist analysts' discoveries have been that governments and political leaders have invested a great deal of time and resources into shaping what it means to be a loyal wife, a patriotic mother, a modern woman, a professional nurse, a healthy prostitute, an ashamed rape victim, an understanding girlfriend. Militarizers may want men to make up the majority of soldiers, they may trust only men to craft the doctrines of war waging, they may believe that male party operatives hold the key to ensuring legislative support for military expenditures. Nonetheless, according to feminists' findings, all these factors do not add up to militarizers not caring about women. They do.

Principally, militarizers seem to believe that if women cannot be controlled effectively, men's participation in the militarizing enterprise cannot be guaranteed. Thus women and the very ideas about feminine respectability, feminine duty, feminine sexuality, and feminine skills will have to be, they decide, the objects of policy and persuasion. Decisions about women will have to be made not just in the midst of that conflict, but in the years preceding any anticipated conflict and in the years following that conflict. Having made this discovery, feminists concerned about the masculinized privileging effects of militarization on society have become convinced that monitoring and responding to the militarization of women and of femininity are necessary activities during even what looks on the surface to be peacetime, or "the postwar era."

In the past two decades feminist thinkers and activists in many societies have paid more explicit attention than ever to the differences among women. Indian feminists have been investing intellectual energy in understanding the different values and circumstances of Indian Muslim and Indian Hindu women. Mexican mestizo urban middle-class

feminists have been seeking to chart the ways in which indigenous rural women and urban factory women cope with everyday demands
that they only barely fathom. Northern Irish Catholic and Protestant
women have developed fresh analyses of their country's problems in
order to create effective cross-communal groups that can contribute to
building a new civil society.[5] In each instance, feminists have been motivated by their analytical sense that the perpetuation of differences
among women has allowed women to be militarized and thus has been
a crucial factor in fueling militarized violence, even if the most visible
perpetrators of that violence have been men.

This feminist awareness of the differences among women is not totally new. It is a mistake to portray women's advocates in 1880s
Britain, Germany, or the United States, or their counterparts in 1920s
Vietnam, India, Egypt, Japan, or Brazil, as blind naïfs who imagined
"sisterhood" to be automatic, who thought of women as homogenous.
These early activists wrote and argued about the divisions between
women of different ethnicities and races, between women of unequal
social classes, between women of different and often hostile religious
traditions, between women adhering to rival political ideologies, between women who lived in the cities versus those who lived in rural
villages. Being conscious of such differences, however, did not mean
these early advocates for women always made theoretical and strategic
choices that overcame the differences and the distrust that was generated (often with the help of male officials and party leaders) by these
differences. Women activists often did not dig deeply enough. They often shrank from the personal and strategic implications of their awareness. And the processes of militarization frequently were oiled by the
failures of women activists to create cross-sector alliances, to lower
those barriers separating women. At the opening of a new century, militarization continues to rely on women located in different social, economic, ideological, and cultural locations remaining uninformed
about, unconnected to, or even hostile to one another. The experiences
of fragmentation have provided an incentive for some current feminists
to expend more intellectual and organizing energy in understanding
those differences and reducing the hostilities they can foment.

Women are militarized in different ways and to fulfill different militarizing functions. Women militarized as nurses, for example, are usually
from quite different economic, cultural, and even national backgrounds
than those militarized as prostitutes, and they develop a stake in being
clearly distinguished from those militarized women commonly deemed
less respectable. Women militarized as wives of enlisted men usually

come from both different ethnic and different economic backgrounds than those women militarized as wives of senior officers. Women militarized as refugees may see themselves as living lives totally unlike the lives of those subtly militarized women working for humanitarian aid agencies. Moreover, the very experience of being militarized in these disparate ways can serve to raise the barriers between women who already were divided from each other by ideology, class, or ethnicity.

Having noted this disparity, however, is not to argue that there is no such thing as "women," that women comprise an analytical category as insubstantial as cotton candy. There indeed does not exist any such mythically monolithic creature as "Woman." But that assertion is quite a separate matter.[6] Most decision makers who have attempted to maneuver women into locations in which their self-perceptions and their labors serve to make militarization possible have acted according to two assumptions, held simultaneously: first, these decision makers have believed that there are such people as "women" and, no matter how varied they are from one another, they share a common "womanhood"; and second, they have believed that women are diverse and thus should be treated in policy making according to their specific sociocultural locations. Women in virtually every society have experienced militarization, consequently, quite unlike the experiences of even those men with whom they share ethnic and religious identities, geographic residence, historical generation, and economic class position. A Bolivian woman of Indian descent living in a poor urban neighborhood in 1990s La Paz has much in common with her husband and very little in common with the Bolivian woman who has had the resources to attend a university and gain a professional career. And yet the Bolivian government officials who believe that their country's—and their regime's—security depends on conscription of young men, especially young men from poor neighborhoods, into the ranks of the state's military will not approach that indigenous woman and her husband in identical ways. The government needs different things from each of them. Because she is a woman and is presumed, as a woman, to assign primacy to her role as a mother, she must be encouraged to keep seeing young men who have done their army service as manly, mature, and marriageable. Likewise, those women made into refugees by militaristic armed forces and those women with a secure roof over their heads in part because they are married to the men soldiering in the armed forces appear to have little in common. And yet militarizers need both of those groups to be sexually available as women, whether to male refugee camp guards or to male soldiers home on leave. These two sets of women may never have the chance to sit down and exchange impressions and, even if they were in the same room together, they might refuse to speak to one another. But if they did find a way to have such an exchange, they would probably discover that, together, they could build a sophisticated theory of women's militarized sexuality.

To avoid seeing all women as natural allies simply because they are women, then, is crucial for building reliable causal analyses and for crafting effective strategies. However, arriving at this conclusion does not require a person to lose all confidence in the belief that "women" is an authentic political category useful in making sense of the causes and consequences of militarization.

While never simple, the most successful efforts to create cross-sector alliances among women who have experienced militarization have been alliances among women who have believed that they have been victimized by that experience and alliances among the feminists who have devoted their political activism to support women as victims of militarization. Thus cross-national and cross-class and cross-ethnicity campaigns have developed to make systematic wartime rape an internationally recognized and prosecuted "crime against humanity" in the Hague and Arusha UN tribunals. Thus, too, Japanese, Korean, Taiwanese, and Filipino feminists, despite their different locations in today's global political economy, have created a fragile but workable political alliance to press the Japanese government to take official responsibility for compensating the elderly women who survived the former Japanese regime's "comfort women" prostitution system.

Yet many women who experience militarization do not see themselves as victims of that process. While still politically marginalized as women—and perhaps *because* they have been politically marginalized as women—these women perceive militarization as offering them opportunities they otherwise might not have: the opportunity to achieve upward mobility through their soldier-husband's promotions; the opportunity to delay marriage and also get training in "nontraditional" fields through enlisting in the military; the chance to earn patriotic credits by doing ordinary household chores efficiently in a time of war; the chance to play a political role by speaking out publicly as a representative of "the nation's mothers" in a militarizing nationalist movement.

If militarization were oppressive for all women in all situations, militarization would not be so potent a political process. It is precisely be-

cause militarization holds out such advantages to some women some
of the time that it has been difficult to see the maneuvers of decision
makers and difficult to detect militarization's fundamentally patriarchal consequences. Moreover, the advantages that some women in any
society garner from the militarization of femininity makes it challenging to create broad-based feminist alliances to slow down or roll back
militarization. Those women—as weapons factory workers, as military nurses, as girls in school cadet corps, as those girls' proud mothers, as political lobbyists pressing militaries to take seriously sexual harassment in militaries, as women married to men being promoted up
the military ranks, as former insurgent guerrillas wanting their share of
places in the new state army—may see *more,* not less, militarization as
the solution to their own problems. When these women look at the
gendered politics of militarization, they see male decision makers reluctant to integrate women fully into militarized roles. Patriarchy, according to their analysis, is not the bedfellow of militarization; rather, patriarchy is the barrier to women's and girls' full militarization.

It is not surprising, then, that the Okinawa feminists who mobilized local anger after the U.S. marines' rape of the schoolgirl in 1995
and those Washington-based American feminists who attracted the
most media attention when they charged an admiral with a sexist
mindset appeared to be traveling along parallel political roads. They
consequently never formed an alliance. Each group of women was
taking political risks by being so forthright in critiquing masculinized
behavior. Women in each group defined themselves as feminists. Each
group was taking on the state. But they had quite dissimilar—though
maybe not wholly incompatible—approaches to patriarchy's relationship to militarization. The Okinawan feminists acted on the theory
that dismantling both Japanese and American militarism was the only
guarantor of physical safety and political agency for women. By contrast, those American feminists acting through Congress and lobbying
the Defense Department believed that withdrawing military bases
from Okinawa was not a feminist priority; their aim was to challenge
sexism inside the American military, exposing an admiral's encouragement of prostitution, so that women wanting to make careers as
American military personnel could operate in an atmosphere free of
misogyny.

It might be tempting for women working on behalf of women oppressed by militarization and those working on behalf of women seeking greater opportunities through militarization to imagine that they
have nothing in common with each other or, worse, that they are each

other's political adversaries. But this belief would leave unexamined the full range of gendered militarization. That process treats women as distinct from men; that process virtually always privileges masculinity, even when some women do gain some new opportunities from being included. Militarization is also a process that relies on women in different circumstances not seeing that underlying dynamic. Analyzing is one thing; what a person does with that analysis is another. It would amount to an intellectual loss to step away from understanding militarizing decision makers' complete panoply of gendered maneuvers simply because some of the women thus militarized may shrink from forming political alliances with some of the other women militarized.

Those women who, as feminists, have confronted militarization have found that the effort poses risks—not just the risk of courting ridicule or arrest, but the risk of producing consequences that might reinvigorate patriarchy. Here are just five of the puzzles revealed in the course of the present research:

First: How can feminists lobbying against sexist practices inside militarized institutions (armed forces, defense factories, national security agencies, foreign affairs legislative committees, the UN's peacekeeping forces) reach their objectives

without

assigning to those institutions a superior worth in the political culture?

Second: How can feminists who draw upon maternal consciousness to politically activate women (who usually feel as though they have no place to voice their opinions in public affairs) do so

without

reducing women to mothers and

without

making motherhood the sole legitimate space in which women can take political action?

Third: How can feminists make visible the uses of rape in warfare and mobilize support for women raped by soldiers

without

allowing women who have endured rape to be turned into symbols of "national humiliation" or allowing news of rapes to inflame masculinized revenge?

Fourth: How can feminists peel back a military's protective covering to show the institution's cultural reliance on sexism and homophobia

without

permitting women's entrance into and promotion within that military to be interpreted as steps toward all women's "first-class citizenship"?

Fifth: How can feminists ensure that more women with feminist consciousnesses are appointed to policy posts within the state and international agencies

without

the sacrifice of a gender-smart critical approach to militarization becoming the price of admission?

Again, it is the breadth of militarizing processes and the rewards flowing from them to many women as well as most men that complicate feminists' relationships to militarization.

Today that complexity is intensified by the ongoing internationalization of militarizing processes. International political processes are driven by specific decisions, whether those decisions are in the form of lending foreign military trainers, managing overseas bases, expanding NATO, investing corporations' capital in countries ruled by militarized regimes, negotiating reparations for past wars, performing UN peacekeeping duties, diaspora funding of civil wars, constructing the images of soldiers through a globalized media, international marketing of weaponry, diplomatically negotiating the creation of a permanent war crimes tribunal. In each of these international political processes, those decisions will not just have different implications for women than for men; those decisions will depend on particular, if varied, constructions of what it means to be "feminine." Femininity as a concept and women as actors are not merely relevant to creating a useful domestic political analysis. Femininity as a concept and women as actors need to be made the objects of analytical curiosity when we are trying to make sense of international political processes. A major stumbling block on the road to ongoing militarization—between and within states—could take the form of feminist curiosity.

Endnotes

CHAPTER 1

1. New York's Metropolitan Museum of Art mounted a special exhibition, Swords Into Ploughshares: Military Dress and the Civilian Wardrobe, September—November, 1995. The curators put on display civilian fashion inspired by military uniforms that ranged from those of the American general Dwight Eisenhower and Mussolini's Black Shirts, to those of the Queen's Own Oxfordshire Hussars. See Amy M. Spindler, "From Lethal Cause to Artistic One," *New York Times,* 15 September 1995. For the August 1996 issue of *George,* the up-market commercial New York magazine, fashion designers such as Chanel, Miuccia Prada, and Calvin Klein were asked to propose uniforms. The request was sparked by American public debates about the benefits and drawbacks of requiring public school children to dress in uniforms, but the designers and the magazine publisher (John Kennedy Jr.) also took up the wider concern about militaristic values that uniforms might imply. See Amy M. Spindler, "Designers Put Their Minds to Uniformity," *New York Times,* 14 May 1996.

2. A recent cross-disciplinary study of the militarization of American society from the 1930s into the 1990s is Michael S. Sherry, *In the Shadow of War: The United States since the 1930s* (New Haven: Yale University Press, 1995).

3. Jacklyn Cock, professor of sociology, University of Witswatersrand, correspondence with the author, April 1996. See also Jacklyn Cock, "A Sociological Account of Light Weapons Proliferation in Southern Africa," in *Light Weapons and International Security,* ed. J. Singh (Washington, D.C.: British American Security Council, 1995), 63–86.

4. See, for instance, Stuart A. Wright, ed., *Armageddon in Waco: Critical Perspectives on the Branch Davidian Conflict* (Chicago: University of Chicago Press, 1996).

5. For a critical profile of Idaho Republican Helen Chenoweth, the woman Congressional representative most sympathetic to at least some of the patriotic militias' analyses, see Sidney Blumenthal, "Her Own Private Idaho," *The New Yorker Magazine*, 10 July 1995, 27–33.

6. An eye-opening account of the deliberately cultivated dependence of American leaders of psychology on the U.S. national security doctrine is Ellen Herman, *The Romance of American Psychology: Political Culture in the Age of Experts* (Berkeley: University of California Press, 1995).

7. The question of whether Carmen Miranda was able to maintain control over her own remarkable talent and stardom once she entered the Hollywood studio system of the 1940s is provocatively explored in the 1995 documentary film by Brazilian director Helena Solberg entitled *Carmen Miranda: Bananas Is My Business*.

8. I am grateful to Tim LeDoux of Clark University for alerting me to Washington's 1940s wartime film diplomacy with Latin America. For an investigation of the Hollywood studios' active role in—and substantial benefits from—post–World War II military occupation in Europe, see Reinhold Wagnleitner, "American Cultural Diplomacy, Hollywood, and the Cold War in Central Europe," *Rethinking Marxism* 7, no. 1 (spring 1994): 31–47.

9. See, for example, the complicated story of the famous Berlin cabaret singer Claire Waldoff, a lesbian, whom Nazi officials tried, not always successfully, to mobilize to entertain German troops during World War II: "'Get the Men Out-Out-Out of Parliament!'—Claire Waldoff (1884–1957)," in Claudia Schoppmann, *Days of Masquerade: Life Stories of Lesbians during the Third Reich* (New York: Columbia University Press, 1996), 57–75.

10. Russia's 1995 legislative election was a different sort of khaki election in that it came on the heels of the Russian army's humiliatingly hollow victory against insurgents in the region of Chechnya. In the campaign run-up to the 17 December 1995 national elections for the Duma, considerable notice was given to the number of army generals running for legislative seats. No one party sponsored all the generals-turned-political candidates; they were spread among the governing party and several opposition parties. The Russia Is Our Home Party, the party backing President Boris Yeltsin, reportedly ran 123 military officers, including 23 generals, with the support of their superior, the Defense Minister. See Steven Erlanger, "Russian Military Seeks Wider Power by Putting Officers Up for Parliament," *New York Times*, 24 November 1995. On all sides, military officers not only promised that the presence of career military men in the fledgling democratic legislature would bring Russian citizens both greater stability and national pride, they also claimed that their political influence would win the military a bigger slice of the limited budgetary pie, thus reducing the physical hardships being endured by the conscript soldier sons of voters. See Olivia Ward, *Toronto Star*, 5 November 1995. It was not clear, however, whether Russian voters were willing to be so electorally militarized. One of the most notable of the opposition party military candidates, Afghan war hero and nationalist Aleksandr Ledbed, won his own seat, but his party, the Congress of Russian Communities, failed to win the 5 percent of the

popular vote that would qualify it for the Duma. Despite its militarized candi-date list, The Russia Is Our Home Party came in behind both the Communist party and the ultranationalist Liberal Democratic Party. See Alessandra Stan-ley, "Communists Lead the Ruling Party by 2 to 1 in Russia," *New York Times,* 19 December 1995. In the weeks following the legislative election, there was speculation that General Ledbed would run in 1996 against Yeltsin for the Russian presidency. In this election, he would be sponsored by the Communist party, the largest in the new Duma, ensuring that the status of the military would remain a central issue in Russian electoral politics. See Michale Specter, "Army Hero Enters Russian Race, Posing a Big Threat to Reformers," *New York Times,* 29 December 1995. Ledbed lost, but has remained a prominent figure in Russia's unstable politics.

11. Lisa Brandes, "The Gender Gap and Attitudes toward War" (paper presented for the annual meeting of the Midwest Political Science Association, Chicago, 9–11 April 1992). Lisa Brandes is a professor of political science at Tufts University, Medford, Mass. See also Carol Bacchi, "Women and Peace through the Polls," working paper no. 8, Peace Research Centre, Australian National University, Canberra, Australia, 1986.

12. Alan Travis, "Majority Say Bomb Iraq," *The Guardian,* 10 February 1998. The poll, conducted by the Guardian and the British polling firm ICM, was conducted by telephone across Britain during February 6, 7, and 8, 1998. Among its other findings was that younger Britons were more supportive of the government's bombing threat than were older Britons (65 percent of 18- to 34-year-olds versus 51 percent of Britons over age 65), a reversal of earlier pat-terns of opinion regarding views on war.

13. For a discussion of this phenomenon in the United States during the 1990-91 Gulf War, see Cynthia Enloe, *The Morning After: Sexual Politics at the End of the Cold War* (Berkeley: University of California Press, 1993), 173–76.

14. Alexandra Marks, "Gender Gap Narrows over Kosovo," *The Chris-tian Science Monitor,* 30 April 1999.

15. For descriptions of the debates among British suffragists during World War I, see Sandra Stanley Holton, *Suffrage Days: Stories from the Women's Suffrage Movement* (New York: Routledge, 1996), 211–26; Susan Kingsley Kent, *Making Peace: The Reconstruction of Gender in Interwar Britain* (Princeton: Princeton University Press, 1993), 31–50; Ray Strachey, *The Cause: A Short History of the Women's Movement in Great Britain* (London: Virago, 1978), 337–45. For American suffrage leaders' strategic attitude to-ward their government's World War I involvement, see Sara Hunter Graham, *Woman Suffrage and the New Democracy* (New Haven: Yale University Press), 99–127. For the history of the Women's International League for Peace and Freedom, see Catherine Foster, *Women for All Seasons: The Story of the Women's International League for Peace and Freedom* (Athens: University of Georgia Press, 1989); and Ruth Roach Pierson, ed., *Women and Peace: Theo-retical, Historical, and Practical Perspectives* (London: Croom Helm, 1987). For a comparison of British and American suffragists' debates over whether to

support their respective governments' World War I policies, see Sheila Rowbotham, *A Century of Women: The History of Women in Britain and the
United States* (New York: Vintage, 1997), 64–115.

16. For a recent study of difficulties in creating and maintaining an international feminist organization based on genuine equality in the early twentieth
century, a study that includes the Women's International League for Peace and
Freedom, see Leila Rupp, *Worlds of Women: The Making of an International
Women's Movement* (Princeton: Princeton University Press, 1997).

17. Tony Marcano, "Famed Riveter in War Effort, Rose Monroe Dies at
77," *New York Times,* 2 June 1997. As her obituary explains, Rose Monroe
was actually one of two models for "Rosie." Rosalind P. Walter, from Long Island, New York, served as the inspiration for Kay Kyser's song "Rosie the Riveter." It was after the song had already become a popular hit and after the dis-
tribution of the well-known poster portraying a woman in a bandanna flexing
her muscle and declaring "We Can Do It!" that Rose Monroe was discovered
by the actor Walter Pigeon while she was working as a riveter at the Willow
Run Aircraft Factory. Pigeon chose her to appear in a promotional film for war
bonds. For more on the history and contemporary politics of women in war industries, see "Rosie the Riveter: Women in Defense Industries," in Cynthia Enloe, *Does Khaki Become You? The Militarization of Women's Lives* (London:
Pandora/Harper Collins, 1988), 173–206; and "Turning Artillery into Ambulances," in Enloe, *The Morning After,* 38–70.

18. Jeff Gerth and Tim Weiner, "Arms Makers See Bonanza in Selling
NATO Expansion," *New York Times,* 29 June 1997.

19. Gerth and Weiner, "Arms Makers See Bonanza."

20. Recent studies contributing to this ongoing reconsideration of American and British women in World War II war work are Judy Barrett Litoff and
David Smith, *American Women in a World at War* (Wilmington, Del.: Scholarly Resources Books, 1997); and Dorothy Sheridan, ed., *Wartime Women*
(London: Mandarin, 1990). For a fresh investigation of the ambivalent attitudes of American women working in 1990s weapons factories, see Robin L.
Riley, "Circumstantial Warriors: Militarism, Gender, and the Discourses of Defense" (Ph.D. diss., Department of Conflict Resolution, Syracuse University,
1999).

21. This account is based on Stephanie Gutmann, "Ready to Lift That
Copter (And Don't Call Her 'Doll')," *New York Times,* 3 August 1997. The
newspaper's editors placed this story in the financial section of the paper. Most
stories about toys can be read in the financial sections; toys are a big business.

22. See, for instance, Ximena Bunster, "The Mobilization and Demobilization of Women in Militarized Chile," in *Women in the Military System,* ed.
Eva Isaksson (New York: St. Martin's Press, 1988), 210–24; for information
on the subtle processes of militarization in women's lives in early 1990s Croatia, see Slavenka Drakulic, *The Balkan Express: Fragments from the Other
Side of War* (New York: W. W. Norton, 1993). For a rare record of women
from different ethnic groups in the former Yugoslavia, many of whom were active in the feminist peace group Women in Black, and for conversations about
wartime mothering as well as other issues in women's wartime lives, see

"Compilation of Informations on Crimes of War against Women in ex-Yugoslavia—Actions and Initiatives in their Defence" (a collection produced and distributed by Women Living under Muslim Laws, Montpelier, France, 1994).

23. For a provocative study of American women who see the military as aiding them in mothering their sons, see "Turning to Uncle Sam," in *Mothers of Sons*, ed. Linda Rennie Forcey (New York: Praeger, 1987), 117–35.

24. Liz Fekete and Frances Webber, "The Human Trade," *Race and Class* 39, no. 1 (1997): 67.

25. As of 1996, according to Anita Gradin, European Commissioner on Immigration Affairs, an estimated 500,000 Eastern European and African women were living in EU countries illegally, many having been smuggled in by crime syndicates. Precisely because they have to pay so much money to the smugglers, who in turn point to the formidable border obstacles, the procurers are going to extraordinary lengths (12-hour days, multiple male customers, high quotas, intimidation, torture) to force the procured women to earn back those fees, plus a profit. See Fekete and Webber, "The Human Trade," 71.

26. For an analysis of the steps taken toward the militarization of the American local police forces, Federal Border Patrol, and Immigration and Naturalization Service in their increasingly integrated operations along the U.S. side of the U.S.-Mexican border in the late 1990s, see Christian Parenti, "Crossing Borders," in *These Times*, March 1998, 15–17.

27. Eric L. Wee, "JROTC Advances on High Schools," *Washington Post*, 18 December 1995.

28. Wee, "JROTC Advances."

29. This fact and the information that follows comes from Catherine Lutz and Lesley Bartlett, *Making Soldiers in the Public Schools: An Analysis of the Army JROTC Curriculum* (Philadelphia: American Friends Service Committee, 1995). Data regarding the gender and racial composition of JROTC units is found on pages 6–9. For 1998 figures, see Youth and Militarism Program, American Friends Service Committee, "Is JROTC a Wise Use of Class Time?" (American Friends Service Committee, Philadelphia, Pa., June 1998, pamphlet).

30. I am grateful to Anne Boylan, professor of women's studies at the University of Delaware, for sharing these experiences and analyses with me in a conversation at the Berkshire Conference on the History of Women held at the University of North Carolina, Chapel Hill, on 7 June 1996.

31. For more on the JROTC program and the debates it has provoked in local communities, see Rick Jahnkow, "Countering Pentagon Propaganda: Activists Confront Recruiters, Promote Alternatives to Military for Youth," *Resist*, July/August 1997, 1–4; and Project on Youth and Non-Military Opportunities, "Air Force JROTC Curriculum Evaluation: Some Areas of Concern" (Project on Youth and Non-Military Opportunities, Encinitas, Calif., 1994, typescript). The Project on Youth and Non-Military Opportunities failed to persuade the San Diego school board not to adopt the JROTC program.

32. Harold Jordan, "Making Student Soldiers: JROTC Academies," *On Watch: Newsletter of the National Lawyers Guild Military Task Force* (San Diego, Calif.) 16, nos. 2–3 (November 1995): 5. See also Jonathan S. Lindsey,

"Parents Protest Military's Role in the Classroom," *Christian Science Monitor,*
5 October 1995.

33. An especially helpful account of how the military policy on homosexuality became a major American political issue is Chris Bull, "And the Ban Played On," *The Advocate,* 9 March 1993, 36–43.

34. For a very insightful disentanglement of the American military's often confusing twists and turns in its policy on homosexuality, see Gary Lehring, *Officially Gay: Politics, Policies, and the Public Construction of Sexual Difference* (Philadelphia: Temple University Press, forthcoming). A study commissioned by the Department of Defense to assess the efficacy of the ban, a study that found the government's policy unreasonable, is National Defense Research Institute, "Sexual Orientation and U.S. Military Personnel Policy: Options and Assessment" (Santa Monica, Calif.: Rand Corporation, 1993). Pentagon officials did not like Rand's conclusions and disregarded its recommendations. See also Craig Rimmer, ed., *Gay Rights, Military Wrongs: Political Perspectives on Lesbians and Gays in the Military* (New York: Garland Press, 1996).

35. Letter from Sanford D. Bishop, Congressional representative for the Second District of Georgia, 24 August 1995. African American women's multiplicity of reasons for joining the U.S. army during World War II is wonderfully recalled in Brenda Moore's new history of the Women's Army Corps 6888th, the only all-black women's unit to be deployed overseas during the war. See Brenda Moore, *To Serve My Country, To Serve My Race* (New York: New York University Press, 1995).

36. Insights into the ongoing debates over the dilemma in post-apartheid South Africa are provided by South African feminist sociologist Jacklyn Cock. See Cock, *Women and War in South Africa* (Cleveland, Ohio: Pilgrim Press, 1993); and more recently, Cock, "Forging a New Military out of Old Enemies: Women in the South African Military" (paper presented at the Conference on Women in the Military, Women's Research and Education Institute, Washington, D.C., 2 December 1994). For descriptions of South African gay men's experiences in the pre-Mandela, apartheid-era military, see Mark Gevisser and Edwin Cameron, eds., *Defiant Desire: Gay and Lesbian Lives in South Africa* (New York: Routledge, 1995); and Matthew Krouse, ed., *The Invisible Ghetto: Lesbian and Gay Writing from South Africa* (Johannesburg: The Gay Men's Press, 1993).

37. The organization that has provided legal counseling and defense for women soldiers charged with homosexuality, charges that often stem from a woman's rejection of male soldiers' sexual advances, is Servicemembers Legal Defense Network, Washington, D.C. See also Winni S. Weaver, *Lesbians in the Military Speak Out* (Northboro, Mass.: Madwomen Press, 1993); Mary Ann Humphrey, *My Country, My Right to Serve: Experiences of Gay Men and Women in the Military, World War II to the Present* (New York: HarperCollins, 1990); Randy Shilts, *Conduct Unbecoming: Gays and Lesbians in the U.S. Military* (New York: St. Martin's Press, 1993); Steven Zeeland, *Barrack Buddies and Soldier Lovers: Dialogues with Gay Young Men in the U.S. Mili-*

tary (New York: Haworth Press, 1993); and Steven Zeeland, *Sailors and Sexual Identity* (New York: Haworth Press, 1995).

38. For a description of how the ideas of director Barbra Streisand, featured actor Glenn Close, and author Margarethe Cammermeyer came together to shape the film's production, see Sue Carswell, "An Officer and a Gentlewoman," *Out*, February 1995, 56–60. The book that served as the basis for the film is Cammermeyer, *Serving in Silence* (New York: Penguin, 1994).

39. Quoted in David Johnston and Deborah Sontag, "Reno's Loner Image Hides a More Complex Reality," *New York Times*, 23 November 1997.

40. Johnston and Sontag, "Reno's Loner Image."

41. Linda Matthews, "She Asks, She Tells," *New York Times*, 16 May 1996. During the 1998 Congressional campaign, Cammermeyer ran in the Democratic primary in Washington State, but lost. In 1996, those American college audiences to whom Cammermeyer spoke were divided on the relationship between the state and heterosexism, and the division was in significant measure along gender lines. Incoming first-year college students from across the United States were asked whether they agreed with the statement, "It is important to have laws prohibiting homosexuality." A total of 33.5 percent of the students agreed with the statement; 45 percent of men agreed, as did 24.1 percent of women. These data are reproduced in Sheila Mann, "Gender Differences in College Students' Interest in Political Science and Politics," *Women's Caucus in Political Science Quarterly* 15, no. 2 (January 1998): 4–5.

42. National Organization for Women, "Brief for Amicus Curiae, in the Case before the Supreme Court of the United States, Bernard Roster, Director of Selective Service, v. Robert L. Goldberg et al.," Washington, D.C., 1980.

43. Sherri Paris, "Not That Anybody Asked Me But ..." *Lavender Reader* (Santa Cruz, Calif.), fall 1991, 11. Another cogent critique of the militarizing subtext of the gays-in-the-military debate is found in Neta C. Crawford, "Out of the Closet and into a Straight Metal Jacket? Why I'm Unhappy about 'Gays in the Military,'" originally published in *Sojourner*, June 1993, reprinted in *Frontline Feminism*, ed. Karen Kahn (San Francisco: Aunt Lute Press, 1995), 70–74.

44. Urvashi Vaid, *Virtual Equality: The Mainstreaming of Gay and Lesbian Liberation* (New York: Anchor Books, 1995), 146–77. For a description of the gay political campaign from the vantage point of David Mixner, the man who is credited with persuading Bill Clinton in 1992 to actively court the gay vote and to make the campaign pledge to lift the ban on gays and lesbians in the military, see David Mixner, *Stranger among Friends* (New York: Bantam Books, 1996).

45. Vaid, *Virtual Equality*, 151.

46. For investigations of feminists' responses to the risks of engaging with the state on its own terms, see Anna Yeatman, *Bureacrats, Technocrats, Femocrats: Essays on the Contemporary Australian State* (Sydney: Allen and Unwin, 1990); Suzanne Franzway, Dianne Court, and R. W. Connell, *Staking a Claim: Feminism, Bureaucracy, and the State* (Sydney: Allen and Unwin, 1989); Hester Eisenstein, *Inside Agitators: Australian Femocrats and the State*

(Philadelphia: Temple University Press, 1996); and R. Amy Elman, ed., *Sexual Politics and the European Union* (Providence, R.I.: Berghahn Books, 1996).

47. Joni Seager, *Earth Follies: Coming to Feminist Terms with the Global Environmental Crisis* (New York: Routledge, 1993), 14–69; also Joni Seager, "Patriarchal Vandalism: Militaries and the Environment," in *Dangerous Intersections: Feminist Perspectives on Population, Environment, and Development,* ed. Joel Silliman and Ynestra King (Boston: South End Press, 1999), 163–88.

48. Debra L. Dodson et al., *Voices, Views, and Votes: The Impact of Women on the 103rd Congress* (New Brunswick, N.J.: Center for the American Woman and Politics, Rutgers University, 1995), 9.

49. Servicemembers Legal Defense Network (SLDN), "Conduct Unbecoming: The Fourth Annual Report on 'Don't Ask, Don't Tell, Don't Pursue'" (Washington, D.C.: Servicemembers Legal Defense Network, February 1998, 4–5, typescript). See also Tim Weiner, "Military Discharges of Homosexuals Soar," *New York Times,* 7 April 1998.

50. SLDN, "Conduct Unbecoming." SLDN's 1998 findings were reported in Steven Lee Myers, "Gay Group's Study Finds Military Harassment Rising," *New York Times,* 15 March 1999. For another source of updates on legal challenges to the 1993 modified gay ban policy, see Mary Newcombe and Kathleen Gilberd, "Litigating the Military's Policy on Homosexuality," *On Watch: Newsletter of the National Lawyers Guild Military Task Force* 16, nos. 2–3 (November 1995): 12–13; and Kathleen Gilberd, "Military Policy on Homosexuality," *On Watch: Newsletter of the National Lawyers Guild Military Task Force* 16, nos. 2–3 (November 1995): 13–14.

51. Jennifer Egan, "Uniforms in the Closet," *New York Times Magazine,* 28 June 1998, 26–31, 40, 48, 56.

52. "Navy Approves Retention of Lesbian Officer," *Minerva's Bulletin Board* (Pasadena, Md.), summer 1995, 6. *Minerva's Bulletin Board* and *Minerva* are journals that report on women in the military and are published by the Minerva Center, Pasadena, Maryland.

53. In March 1995, Judge Eugene H. Nickerson of the Federal District Court in Brooklyn, N.Y., concluded in the case of *Able v. United States* that the Clinton policy of "don't ask, don't tell, don't pursue" was a violation of the First and Fifth Amendments and that it catered to the fears and prejudices of heterosexual troops. He called the Defense Department's rationale for the gay ban "nothing less than Orwellian." The federal government filed an appeal, scheduled to be heard in the U.S. Court of Appeals for the Second Circuit. Newcombe and Gilberd, "Litigating the Military's Policy"; and Don Van Natta Jr., "Recusal Halts Court Appeal in a Gay Case," *New York Times,* 20 December 1995. For more on gay men and lesbians in the military, see Gregory M. Herek, Jared B. Jobe, and Ralph M. Carney, eds., *Out in Force: Sexual Orientation and the Military* (Chicago: University of Chicago Press, 1996).

54. "Appeals Court Upholds Military on Homosexuals," *New York Times,* 16 February 1997. See also Janet E. Halley, *Don't: A Reader's Guide to the Military's Anti-Gay Policy* (Durham, N.C.: Duke University Press, 1999).

55. For personal accounts of life as a lesbian in the Israeli military, see Tracy Moore, ed., *Lesbiot: Israeli Lesbians Talk about Sexuality, Feminism, Judaism, and their Lives* (New York: Cassell, 1995). For accounts by gay South African men of their experiences in the apartheid regime's military, see Matthew Krouse, "The Arista Sisters, September 1984: A Personal Account of Army Drag," and Ivan Toms, "Ivan Toms Is a Fairy? The South African Defense Force, the End Conscription Campaign, and Me," both in Gevisser and Cameron, *Defiant Desire,* 209–18 and 258–63. For a discussion of the Australian debate over the homosexual ban, see Enloe, *The Morning After,* 89. Carol Johnson believes that the Australian government of Prime Minister Paul Keating took the initiative to end the ban on gays and lesbians in the military as part of the Labour Party leadership's wider goal of promoting social and political inclusion throughout Australian society for the sake of making Australia more competitive in the post–Cold War international economy. In other words, lifting the ban was neither chiefly a military policy nor a cultural policy, but an economic policy. See Johnson, "Negotiating the Politics of Inclusion: Women and Australian Labor Governments 1983 to 1995," *Feminist Review,* no. 52 (1996): 102–17. In Canada, following the lift of the ban on gay men and lesbians serving in the military, the Canadian parliament went on to pass, with the support of the Liberal government of Prime Minister Jean Chretien, legislation outlawing discrimination against homosexuals. See Clyde H. Farnsworth, "Legislature Acts to Widen Gay Rights in Canada," *New York Times,* 10 May 1996. In taking this positive action, the Canadian government followed in the political footsteps of South Africa's post-apartheid government, which in 1996 passed a new national constitution that included—for the first time in the international history of constitution writing—sexual orientation as a category protected from discrimination.

56. Roger Tredre, "Straight and Gay Unite to Boost Pride by 160,000," *The Observer* (London), 25 June 1995. I am indebted to Debbie Licorish for so energetically monitoring the British press coverage of the gays-in-the-military issue.

57. At the same time that American voters were considering retired general Colin Powell as a presidential candidate, Russian voters were facing a remarkable number of retired generals-turned-civilian politicians. In autumn 1995, ten generals were running for seats in the Russian parliament under the banners of nine different political parties. See "Russia: A Real General Election," *The Economist,* 23 September 1995, 44.

58. These international rankings are derived from the 1997 annual arms sale survey conducted by the Congressional Research Service. Of all the global weapons sales orders in 1996, U.S. companies received 35.5 percent. British companies garnered 15.1 percent of the total, putting them just ahead of Russian companies (most still state-owned), which received 14.6 percent of the total. See Philip Shanon, "U.S. Increases Its Lead in World Market for Weapons," *New York Times,* 16 August 1997.

59. These data and a summary of budgetary and other current cross-pressures facing the Conservative government's minister of defense in 1995 are

detailed in Tim Webb, "A Man under Fire," *New Statesman and Society,* 4 August 1995, 22–23. For a commentary on the new Labour government's likelihood of reducing Britain's reliance on militarism in its foreign policy, see John Lloyd, "Into the Ethical Dimension," *New Statesman,* 25 July 1997, 28–29.

60. Travis, "Majority Say Bomb Iraq."

61. R. W. Apple Jr., "Clinton's Positive Approach: The Alliance is Alive and Kicking," *New York Times,* 26 April 1999.

62. The firsthand accounts of what led a small group of Welsh women in 1981 to walk from Cardiff to Greenham and there to create an all-women's antinuclear peace camp outside the gates of the United States Air Force base (one of dozens scattered across the Cold War British landscape) and accounts of why and how this initially small group burgeoned into a thousands-strong nationwide women's peace campaign that shook the Conservative government are graphically detailed in Alice Cook and Gwyn Kirk, *Greenham Women Everywhere* (Boston: South End Press, 1983); Barbara Harford and Sarah Hopkins, eds., *Greenham Common: Women at the Wire* (London: Women's Press, 1984); Caroline Blackwood, *On the Perimeter* (London: Penguin, 1985); and Lynn Wilson, "Epistomology and Power: Ethnography at Greenham," in *Anthropology for the Nineties,* ed. Johnetta Cole (New York: Free Press, 1988), 42–58. For the most recent analyses of the Greenham Common Women's Peace Camp, see Sasha Roseneil, *Disarming Patriarchy: Feminism and Political Action at Greenham* (Milton Keynes, U.K.: Open University Press, 1995); and Jill Liddington, *The Long Road to Greenham: Feminism and Anti-Militarism in Britain since 1820* (Syracuse, N.Y.: Syracuse University Press, 1991).

63. This perspective is most fully presented in Edmund Hall, *We Can't Even March Straight: Homosexuality in the British Armed Forces* (London: Vintage, 1995). See also Edmund Hall, "Burning Sense of Injustice," *The Guardian,* 19 July 1995.

64. Owen Bowcott, "Judgement Reserved in Challenge by Gays," *The Guardian,* 12 October 1995.

65. "Gays in the Military: Hello, Soldier," *The Economist,* 9 September 1995, 61.

66. Clare Dyer, "Forces' Gay Ban Referred to Europe by High Court," *The Guardian,* 14 March 1996.

67. Coverage of the evolving challenge to the ban on gay men and lesbians in the British military includes Aine McCarthy, "Lesbians and Gays Dismissed from Armed Forces," *Everywoman,* September 1994, 8; "'Perverse' MOD Faces Challenge," *Stonewall Newsletter* 3, no. 2 (April 1995): 1; Mark Storey and George Jones, "Labour to Lift Homosexual Ban in Forces," *Daily Telegraph,* 22 April 1995; Trudie Rabbet, "MOD to Review Gay Policy," *The Guardian,* 9 July 1995; Richard Norton-Taylor, "MOD Rethinks Gays Ban," *The Guardian,* 5 September 1995; "Gays in the Military: Hello, Soldier"; Owen Bowcott, "Sacked Gays Renew Fight against MoD," *The Guardian,* 10 October 1995.

68. Quoted in Hall, *We Can't Even March Straight,* 12.

69. For a discussion of the construction of gay rights as internationally recognized human rights, see Nicole LaViolette and Sandra Whitworth, "No Safe Haven: Sexuality as a Universal Human Right and Gay and Lesbian Activism in International Politics," *Millennium: Journal of International Studies* 23, no. 3 (1994): 563–88.

70. Bradford Booth, "Women and Homosexuals in the Armed Forces: Policies and Practices in 18 European and North American Nations," appendix to David R. Segal, Mady Wechsler Segal, and Bradford Booth, "Gender and Sexual Orientation Diversity in Modern Military Forces: Cross-National Patterns," in *Beyond Zero Tolerance: Discrimination in the Military,* ed. Judith Reppe and Mary Katzenstein (New York: Routledge, 1999), 237–50.

71. The most complete description of the British military's 1995 policy and practice regarding gay men and lesbians—and the current challenges being made against them—is by a British journalist who himself was forced out of the Royal Navy because he was gay. See Hall, *We Can't Even March Straight.*

72. Quoted in Hall, *We Can't Even March Straight,* 45–46.

73. McCarthy, "Lesbians and Gays Dismissed."

74. Rebecca Smithers, "New Campaign to End Armed Forces Gay Ban," *The Guardian,* 10 February 1996. A 1996 documentary film that focuses on the case of Callum Morgan, a woman officer in the Royal Air Force accused of being a lesbian, is *Disgraceful Conduct,* directed by Eve Webber. The film is described by Natalie Alicia in "Action or Play," *Everywoman,* March 1996, 25.

75. Owne Bowcott, Ben Stewart, and Chris Zinn, "Minister Firm against Gays in the Military," *The Guardian,* 5 March 1996.

76. Bowcott, Stewart, and Zinn, "Minister Firm against Gays."

77. Peter Tatchell, *We Don't Want to March Straight: Masculinity, Queers, and the Military* (London: Cassell, 1995).

78. Ibid., 38.

79. Ibid., 46.

80. David Fairhall, "Armed Forces Justified in Banning Gays, Say MPs," *The Guardian,* 8 May 1996.

81. Fairhall, "Armed Forces Justified."

82. Michael White, "MPs Vote to Keep Forces Ban on Gays," *The Guardian,* 10 May 1996.

83. White, "MPs Vote."

84. Eight Labour MPs who were present voted to sustain the Defence Ministry's ban on homosexuals. See White, "MPs Vote."

85. Mary Riddell, "Do As We Say, Not As We Do," *New Statesman and Society,* 17 May 1996, 18–19.

86. "Who's Wearing the Trousers?" *Everywoman,* June 1996, 6.

87. "Forces Ban on Gays to Be Lifted," *Daily Mirror* (London), 7 April 1999. For more discussion of Britain's judicial processes, including their increasing intertwining with European judicial institutions as both are shaping bans on homosexuals in the military, see Paul Skidmore, "Sexuality and the UK Armed Forces: Judicial Review of the Ban on Homosexuality," in *Politics of Sexuality,* ed. Terrell Carver and Veronique Mottier (London: Routledge,

1999). For the Labour government's and gay rights legal experts' respective strategies to win cases concerning discrimination against gay men and lesbians in British workplaces and in the military in the arena of the European Court of Justice in Luxembourg, see Lucy Ward, "Officials Try to Delay Gays Test Case," *The Guardian,* 14 January 1998; and Clare Dyer, "Lesbian Couple Lose Test Case on Perks at Work," *The Guardian,* 18 February 1998.

88. Martin Linton, "Tories Most Liberal-Minded about Gay MPs, Poll Reveals," *The Guardian,* 16 December 1995. This poll, conducted for the Guardian by the ICM polling firm, posed this question: "If a person is a declared homosexual living in a stable relationship with a partner, which of the following jobs should they be allowed to take?" The job categories listed were: in teaching, in the church, in the police service, in the armed forces, and as an MP. A majority of Britons polled approved of a declared homosexual holding jobs in all five categories. The highest support—78 percent—was for as an MP. In all five categories, British women expressed more approval than did men. The newspaper's headline is a bit misleading, since Conservative voters ("Tories") approved of a declared homosexual serving as an MP by 81 percent, while Labour voters approved by 80 percent and Liberal Democrat voters approved by 81 percent. Where Conservative voters did stand out was on the question of the armed forces: 81 percent of Conservative voters approved, versus just 68 percent of Labour voters and 70 percent of Liberal Democrat voters. There were differences along economic class lines too: while only 58 percent of middle-class professionals approved of declared homosexuals serving in the armed forces, 66 percent of respondents in both the lower middle class and skilled working class approved. Regarding all five job categories, respondents from the middle and upper middle classes voiced lower approval than did respondents from the lower middle and skilled working class. In all five job categories, respondents from the manual laboring class and the poorest classes expressed the lowest approval ratings.

89. Roseneil, *Disarming Patriarchy;* Liddington, *The Long Road to Greenham.*

90. For cross-national women's analyses of militarism, see, for example, Miriam Cooke and Roshni Rustomji-Kerns, eds., *Blood into Ink: South Asian and Middle Eastern Women Write War* (Boulder, Colo.: Westview Press, 1994); Miriam Cooke and Angela Woolacott, eds., *Gendering War Talk* (Princeton: Princeton University Press, 1993); Sharon MacDonald, Pat Holden, and Shirley Ardener, eds., *Images of Women in Peace and War* (Madison: University of Wisconsin Press, 1987); Jane S. Jaquette, ed., *The Women's Movement in Latin America,* 2d ed. (Boulder, Colo.: Westview Press, 1994); Jean Bethke Elshtain and Sheila Tobias, eds., *Women, Militarism, and War* (Savage, Md.: Rowman and Littlefield, 1990); Eva Isaksson, ed., *Women and the Military System* (New York: St. Martin's Press, 1988); Ruth Roach Pierson, ed., *Women and Peace* (London: Croom Helm, 1987); Christine Sylvester, "Patriarchy, Peace, and Women Warriors," in Linda Rennie Forcey, ed., *Peace: Meanings, Politics, Strategies* (Westport, Conn.: Greenwood Press, 1989), 97–112; and Lois Ann Lorentzen and Jennifer Turpin, eds., *The Women and War Reader* (New York: New York University Press, 1998).

CHAPTER 2

1. Carol van Driel-Murray, "Gender in Question," in *Theoretical Roman Archeology: Second Conference Proceedings,* ed. Peter Rush (Aldershot, UK: Avebury, 1995), 9.

2. Carol van Driel-Murray in conversation with the author at the Conference on Ethnic Soldiering, University of Leiden, Leiden, Netherlands, 13–14 January 1995.

3. Van Driel-Murray, "Gender in Question," 26–48.

4. Burton Hacker, "Women and Military Institutions in Early Modern Europe: A Reconnaissance," *Signs* 6, no. 4 (summer 1981): 648.

5. Ute Daniel, The War from Within: German Working-Class Women in the First World War (New York: Berg, 1997), 140–146.

6. John Willoughby, "The Sexual Behavior of American GIs during the Early Years of the Occupation of Germany," *Journal of Military History* 62 (January 1998): 155–174.

7. Robert Shaffer, "A Rape in Beijing, December 1946: GIs, Nationalist Protest, and U.S. Foreign Policy" (paper presented at the annual meeting of the American Historical Association, Seattle, Wash., 9 January 1998). I am grateful to Robert Shaffer, a doctoral candidate at Rutgers University, for sharing his revealing research with me.

8. Katharine Moon, *Sex among Allies: Military Prostitution in U.S.-Korea Relations* (New York: Columbia University Press, 1997), 3.

9. Hacker, "Women and Military Institutions," 653.

10. Samuel Hutton, quoted in Roy Palmer, ed., *The Rambling Soldier: Military Life through Soldiers' Songs and Writing* (London: Peguin Books, 1977), 152–53.

11. Carol Hymowitz and Michaele Weisman, *A History of Women in America* (New York: Bantam, 1978), 29.

12. Drawing on British military records, a wonderfully detailed account of the numbers and activities of British women officially integrated into the British army during its operations against the American rebels is contained in Don N. Hagist, "The Women of the British Army during the American Revolution," *Minerva: Quarterly Report on Women and the Military* 13, no. 2 (summer 1995): 29–85.

13. Hagist, "Women of the British Army."

14. This firsthand account appears in Hymowitz and Weissman, *History of Women in America,* 29.

15. John Rees, " 'The Multitude of Women': An Examination of the Numbers of Female Camp Followers with the Continental Army," *Minerva: Quarterly Report on Women and the Military* 14, no. 2 (summer 1996): 2.

16. Ibid.

17. Ibid.

18. Ibid.

19. Quoted in Hacker, "Women and Military Institutions," 654.

20. Kristin Waters (guest lecture at the Seminar on Women and Militarization, Clark University, Worcester, Mass., 20 February 1995). This discussion of

the relationship between Griffiss Air Force Base and Kristin Waters and her family is based on her lecture and on subsequent correspondence and conversations during 1995. Kristin Waters is a philosopher who teaches women's studies at Holy Cross College, Worcester, Mass.

21. *Daily Sentinel,* 15 November 1994.

22. Waters, lecture.

23. Quoted in Hacker, "Women and Military Institutions," 651.

24. For some Japanese women's early reactions to remilitarization, see Tono Haruhi, "Women Do Not Allow War!" *AMPO* (Toyko) 13, no. 4 (1981): 17–20.

25. Lory Manning and Jennifer E. Griffith, *Women in the Military: Where They Stand* (Washington, D.C.: Women's Research and Education Institute, 1998), 26. For annual updates on the profiles of military forces around the world, some of which (not all) include data by gender, see also International Institute of Strategic Studies, *The Military Balance* (London: Oxford University Press).

CHAPTER 3

1. Feminist Majority Foundation, "Draft Commitments" (Feminist Majority Foundation, Washington, D.C., August 1995, photocopy). I am grateful to Christine Onyango of the Feminist Majority for her insights on this pre-Beijing conference process.

2. Christine Onyengo, in conversation with the author, 6 October 1995.

3. Janice G. Raymond, "Prostitution as Violence against Women: NGO Stonewalling in Beijing and Elsewhere," *Women's Studies International Forum* 21, no. 1 (1996): 1–9. For a collection that starts from the proposition that women in prostitution should be seen just as women choosing a particular form of work, see Kamala Kempadoo and Jo Doezema, eds., *Global Sex Workers* (New York: Routledge, 1998).

4. Mary Gibson, *Prostitution and the State in Italy, 1860–1915* (New Brunswick: Rutgers University Press, 1986), 174–76.

5. Neici Zeller, "To Live the Modern Life" (paper presented at the Berksire Conference on Women's History, Chapel Hill, N.C., 9 June 1996). This paper analyzed the impact on women of U.S. Marine Corps' 1916 to 1924 occupation of the Dominican Republic. Neici Zeller is with the History Department of the University of Illinois, Chicago.

6. See, for instance, Jill Harsin, *Policing Prostitution in Nineteenth-Century Paris* (Princeton: Princeton University Press, 1985); "Sex Workers and Sex Work," special issue of *Social Text,* no. 37 (winter, 1993); Wathinee Boonchalaksi and Philip Guest, *Prostitution in Thailand,* (Nakhonpathom, Thailand: Institute for Population and Social Research, Mahidol University, 1994); Laurie Bernstein, *Sonia's Daughters: Prostitutes and their Regulation in Imperial Russia,* (Berkeley: University of California Press, 1995); Asia Rights Watch, *Rape for Profit: Traffiking of Nepali Women to India's Brothels* (New York: Human Rights Watch, 1995); Gail Hershatter, *Dangerous Pleasures: Prostitution and Modernity in Twentieth Century Shanghai* (Berkeley: University of California

Press, 1997). The first global mapping of the international prostitution trade—that is, tracking where male sex tourists come from and where they go to, where those women drawn into prostitution come from and where they are sent to—appears in Joni Seager, "The Global Sex Trade," *The State of Women in the World Atlas* (New York: Penguin Books, 1997), map 18, 54–55.

7. In her classic account, Kathleen Barry has been especially persuasive in arguing that prostitution is an industry that involves male power used to create and keep women as prostitutes. See Kathleen Barry, *Female Sexual Slavery* (New York: Avon, 1979). Barry's recent sequel to her original book is Kathleen Barry, *The Prostitution of Sexuality: The Global Exploitation of Women* (New York: New York University Press, 1995).

8. Quoted in Janet Murray, ed., *Strong Minded Women* (New York and London: Pantheon 1982), 397.

9. Ibid.

10. Laura Hapke, "Conventions of Denial in Prostitution: Late Nineteenth Century American Anti-Vice Narrative," Michigan Occasional Papers in Women's Studies (University of Michigan, Ann Arbor, 1982).

11. Mary Elizabeth Massey, *Women in the Civil War* (Lincoln: University of Nebraska Press, 1994), 262–64.

12. Francis X. Clines, "Archeology Find: Capital's Best Little Brothel," *New York Times,* 18 April 1999. The two archeologists who made the find are Donna Seifert and Elizabeth Barthold O'Brien.

13. Myna Trustram, "Marriage and the Victorian Army at Home: The Regulation of Soldiers' Relationships with Women and the Treatment of Soldiers' Wives" (Ph.D. thesis, Department of Social Administration, University of Bristol, July 1981), 357–58.

14. Myna Trustram, "Distasteful and Derogatory? Examining Soldiers for Venereal Disease," in *Sexual Dynamics of History,* ed. Feminist History Group (London: Pluto Press, 1983).

15. Ibid.

16. Quoted in Murray, *Strong Minded Women,* 436.

17. Judith Walkowitz, *Prostitution and Victorian Society* (London: Cambridge Unversity Press 1980), 108. Walkowitz also analyzes the political alliances within the repeal movement, alliances that expanded as the acts themselves expanded to police women, not just for military security but also in the name of social order. See also Nancy Boyd, *Three Victorian Women Who Changed Their World: Josephine Butler, Octavia Hill, and Florence Nightingale* (London and New York: Oxford University Press 1982).

18. Susan Kingsley Kent, *Sex and Suffrage in Britain, 1860–1914* (Princeton: Princeton University Press, 1990). See especially pp. 60–79.

19. Ibid., 60–70.

20. Sir Alexander Arbuthnot, member of the British Council in India in 1888, quoted in Philippa Levine, "Rereading the 1890s: Venereal Disease as Constitutional Crisis in Britain and British India," *The Journal of Asian Studies* 55, no. 3 (August 1996): 588.

21. Philippa Levine, "'A Brothel is not a Brothel': Racial Meaning, Configurations of Prostitution, and Imperial Power in British India," (unpub-

lished paper, 1995), 3. Philippa Levine is Professor of History at the University of Southern California. For more on the politics of the British Contagious Diseases Acts in colonial India, see Radha Kumar, *The History of Doing: An Illustrated Account of Movements for Women's Rights and Feminism in India, 1800–1990* (London: Verso, 1995), 34–37; Antoinette M. Burton, "The White Women's Burden: British Feminists and 'The Indian Women,' 1865–1915," in *Western Women and Imperialism: Complicity and Resistence,* ed. Nupur Chaudhuri and Margaret Strobel (Bloomington: Indiana University Press, 1992), 141–45.

22. The issues of *Dawn* make intriguing reading. They are available in the Fawcett Library in London. I have discussed Butler's overseas antiprostitution campaign at greater length in *Bananas, Beaches, and Bases: Making Feminist Sense of International Politics* (Berkeley: University of California Press, 1990). There recently has been an outpouring of provocative scholarship investigating the complicated relationships between those British women who saw themselves as advocates of imperial reform and the Indian women that they believed they were supporting. See, for instance, Kumari Jayawardena, *The White Woman's Other Burden: Western Women and South Asia During British Rule* (New York: Routledge, 1995); Barbara N. Ramusack and Antoinette Burton, eds., "Feminism, Imperialism, and Race: A Dialogue between India and Britain," special issue of *Women's History Review* 3, no. 4 (1994); "Feminist Politics—Colonial/Postcolonial Worlds," special issue of *Feminist Review,* no. 49 (1995); Anne McClintock, *Imperial Leather: Race, Gender, and Sexuality in the Colonial Contest* (New York: Routledge, 1995).

23. Margot Badran, *Feminists, Islam, and Nation* (Princeton: Princeton University Press, 1995), 192–200.

24. Susan Kingsley Kent, *Making Peace: The Reconstruction of Gender in Interwar Britain* (Princeton: Princeton University Press, 1993), 28–29. I was initially helped in understanding the World War I CD Acts politics by conversations with historian Jennifer Gould, London, May 1982.

25. Philippa Levine, "'Walking the Streets in a Way No Decent Woman Should': Women Police in World War I," *Journal of Modern History* 66 (March 1994): 42.

26. Ibid., 44.

27. Philippa Levine, "Battle Colors: Race, Sex, and Colonial Soldiery in World War I," *Journal of Women's History* 9, no. 4 (winter 1998): 103–4. See also Levine, *The Subject Body: Prostitution, Venereal Disease, and the Sexual Politics of Race, 1860–1918* (forthcoming). For a further description of the U.S. Army's attempts to control male soldiers' sexual behavior in World War I, see Nancy K. Bristow, *Making Men Moral: Social Engineering during the Great War* (New York: New York University Press, 1996).

28. From the monument in Avarua, Rarotonga, Cook Islands, July 1995.

29. Levine, "Battle Colors," 4.

30. Ibid., 13.

31. Ibid.

32. Claudia Schoppmann, *Days of Masquerade: Life Stories of Lesbians during the Third Reich* (New York: Columbia University Press, 1996), 21.

33. John Ellis, *The Sharp End of War: The Fighting Man in World War II* (London: Corgi Books, 1982), 303.

34. Ibid., 303–4.

35. Ibid., 304.

36. Ibid., 379.

37. Ibid., 308.

38. For a discussion of the French militaries' policy—especially French officers' role as procurers that was revealed in a Corsican trial—see Barry, *Female Sexual Slavery*, 67–70, 70–71.

39. The best description to date of the World War II organization of military prostitution in Hawaii is Beth Bailey and David Farber, *The First Strange Place: The Alchemy of Race and Sex in World War II Hawaii* (New York: Free Press, 1992), 95–132. I have elaborated in more detail on the Hawaii prostitution wartime politics in *The Morning After: Sexual Politics at the End of the Cold War* (Berkeley: University of California Press, 1993), 145–47.

40. A new book by two women's studies professors at the University of Hawaii details the militarization of present-day Hawaiian culture: Kathy E. Ferguson and Phyllis Turnbull, *Oh, Say, Can You See?: The Semiotics of the Military in Hawaii* (Minneapolis: University of Minnesota Press, 1999).

41. This section is based on Karen Anderson, *Wartime Women: Sex Roles, Family Relations, and the Status of Women during World War II* (Westport, Conn.: Greenwood Press, 1981), 104–8.

42. Ibid., 108.

43. Australian feminist historians are freshly examining World Wars I and II prostitution politics to reassess the impacts of those wars on Australian women. See Joy Damousi and Marilyn Lake, eds., *Gender and War: Australians in the Twentieth Century* (New York: Cambridge University Press, 1995); Julie Tisdale, "Venereal Disease and the Policing of the Amateur in Melbourne during World War I," *Lilith: A Feminist History Journal*, no. 9 (autumn 1996): 33–50; Marilyn Lake, "Female Desires: The Meaning of World War II," in *Feminism and History*, ed. Joan Wallach Scott (New York: Oxford University Press, 1996), 429–52.

44. Susan Brownmiller, *Against Our Will* (New York: Bantam, 1976), 94–95, describes the French military's system of mobile field brothels in Vietnam.

45. Barry, *Female Sexual Slavery*, 71.

46. U.S. veteran quoted in Mark Baker, *Nam* (New York: Quill Books, 1982), 53.

47. Quoted by Barry, *Female Sexual Slavery*, 72.

48. This information was provided by a social scientist who acted as a consultant on race relations to the U.S. military during the Vietnam war, conversation with the author, June 1982. He wished to remain anonymous. For confirmation, see Jonathan Shay, *Achilles in Vietnam: Combat Trauma and the Undoing of Character* (New York: Touchstone Books, 1994), 160.

49. James W. Trullinger, *Village at War* (Stanford: Stanford University Press, 1994), 134–35.

50. James E. Westheider, *Fighting on Two Fronts: African-Americans and the Vietnam War* (New York: New York University Press, 1997), 83–84.

51. During his investigation into racial conflict within the U.S. military during the Vietnam War, James E. Westheider found that between 1968 and 1972, hostilities escalated between American black and white male soldiers on and around U.S. bases in Vietnam, Germany, Labrador, Thailand, and the United States. The most common sites of hostilities were not on the front lines near combat, but in the rear in mess halls, enlisted men's clubs, and civilian bars and brothels. Ibid., 86. See also Baker, *Nam,* 206.

52. Westheider, *Fighting on Two Fronts,* 87. For another account of the experiences of black male soldiers in the Vietnam War, see Stanley Goff and Robert Sanders with Clark Smith, *Brothers: Black Soldiers in Nam* (San Francisco: Presidio Press, 1982).

53. Kathleen Barry, *The Prostitution of Sexuality* (New York: New York University Press, 1995), 122–64.

54. One place to start is an Australian doctoral thesis: Gavin Hart, "The Impact of Prostitution on Australian Troops on Active Service in a War Environment—With Particular Reference to Sociological Factors Involved in the Incidence and Control of Venereal Disease" (M.D. thesis, University of Adelaide, Adelaide, Australia, January 1974). I am grateful to Philippa Levine for telling me of this thesis.

55. Ibid., 135–36.

56. Stanley Karnow, "Saigon," *Atlantic Monthly,* November 1981, 15.

57. Le Thi Quy, "Prostitution in Vietnam" (Center for Women's Studies, Social Science Research Center, Hanoi, 1995, photocopy), 2. For analyses by contemporary Vietnamese women's studies researchers, see Kathleen Barry, ed., *Vietnam's Women in Transition* (New York: St. Martin's Press, 1996).

58. For a Vietnamese analysis of the economic hardships pushing more women into prostitution in the mid-1990s, see Barry, *Vietnam's Women in Transition.*

59. In 1995, there was vague discussion of reopening Cam Ran Bay, site of one of the largest U.S. military bases in Vietnam in the1960s and 1970s, to American naval ships once again. Twenty years after its closure, the U.S. base is remembered by some local Vietnamese residents, today buffeted by the Hanoi government's market reforms, as the supplier of jobs, not as the site of militarized, commercialized sex. See Tim Larimer, "At a Vietnam Port, the U.S. Navy Is Sadly Missed," *New York Times,* 8 August 1995.

60. I have explored the gendered politics of tourism at greater length in *Bananas, Beaches, and Bases: Making Feminist Sense of International Politics* (Berkeley: University of California Press, 1990), 19–41.

61. Ryan Bishop and Lillian S. Robinson, *Night Market: Sexual Cultures and the Thai Economic Miracle* (New York: Routledge, 1998), 159.

62. Khin Thitsa, *Providence and Prostitution: Image and Reality for Women in Buddhist Thailand* (London: Change International Reports, 1980), 15.

63. Gregory F. DeLaurier, "Thailand 1970," *Peace Review* 8, no. 2 (June 1996): 231. This article appears in a special issue of *Peace Review* entitled "War and Rememberance," guest edited by Michael Webber and Rodney Watkins.

64. Ibid., 232.

65. Ibid., 233. Gregory DeLaurier currently teaches politics at Ithaca College. Upon return from Thailand, he became one of the founding members of the Ithaca Chapter of the Veterans for Peace.

66. Khin Thitsa, *Providence and Prostitution.*

67. John Pilger, "Thailand: Frogmarched into Slavery," *New Statesman* 20 (August 1982): 10–12. See also Tim Bond, *The Price of a Child* (London: Anti-Slavery Society, 1980).

68. Thanh-Dam Truong, *Sex, Money, and Morality: Prostitution and Tourism in South-East Asia* (London: Zed Press, 1990), 80. See also Asia Watch and Women's Rights Watch, *A Modern Form of Slavery: Trafficking of Burmese Women and Girls into Brothels in Thailand* (New York: Human Rights Watch, 1993); Lenore Manderson and Margaret Jolly, eds., *Sites of Desire, Economics of Pleasure: Sexualities in Asia and the Pacific* (Chicago: Chicago University Press, 1997); Rita Nakashima Brock and Susan Brooks Thistlewaite, *Casting Stones: Prostitution and Liberation in Asia and the United States* (San Francisco: Fortress Press, 1996). For analyses of prostitution in Thailand in the mid-1990s, see Boonchalaksi and Guest, *Prostitution in Thailand,* and Bishop and Robinson, *Night Market.*

69. K. Torugsa et al., "The Temporal Trend of HIV Seroprevalence among Young Men Entering the Royal Thai Army, 1989–91," (Washington, D.C., Walter Reed Army Institute of Research, 1992, typescript). I am indebted to Kari Hartwig of the AIDS Control and Prevention Project, Bangkok, for her correspondence with me about the roles of the Thai military in AIDS prevention. For a description of the British army's prostitution and AIDS prevention policies in Belize, see Stephanie Kane, "Prostitution and the Military in Belize: Planning AIDS Intervention in Belize," *Social Science and Medicine* 36, no. 7 (1993): 965–79.

70. For insightful case studies of Asian women who have achieved new access to affluence in the 1980s and 1990s, see Maila Stivens and Krishna Sen, eds., *Sex and Power in Affluent Asia* (New York: Routledge, 1999). This collection comes out of the "New Rich of Asia" research project of the Asia Research Center, Murdoch University, Australia.

71. Kamol Hengkietisak, "Sex Exploitation: A Green Harvest of a Different Kind," *Friends of Women Newsletter* 5, no. 1 (June 1994): 16–19. Friends of Women is a Thai feminist organization whose members press the government to enforce laws against the procurement and abuse of women in the sex trade: Friends of Women, 1379/30 Soi Praditchai, Pahonyothin Rd., Bangkok 10400, Thailand. I am also indebted to Alison Cohn for sharing with me her research on girls sold into prostitution by impoverished families among the hill tribe minorities of northern Thailand: Alison Cohn, "Hill Tribe Prostitution: An Overview" (Clark University, Worcester, Mass., 1990, typescript). According to AIDS prevention professionals, education campaigns in Thailand have begun to show positive results: fewer Thai men were visiting brothels in late 1995 than in the early 1990s; more Thai women working in brothels were demanding that their male clients wear condoms; from 1990 to 1995, actual condom use by male brothel customers rose from 30 percent to 60 percent in brothels surveyed; the number of Thais newly infected with HIV in 1990 was

approximately 215,000, but by the year 2000, that figure was expected to drop to 90,000. Nonetheless, by the turn of the century, AIDS was expected by health experts to become Thailand's leading cause of death. These data and projections were collected by: Philip Shenon, "AIDS Epidemic, Late to Arrive, Now Explodes in Populous Asia," *New York Times,* 21 January 1996.

72. I am grateful to Parissara Liewkeat, Thai feminist and Women's Studies doctoral candidate, for sharing with me her analysis of the current laws shaping prostitution in Thailand in our conversation at Clark University, Worcester, Mass., September 1997.

73. The description that follows relies on reporting by Steven Erlanger in "Thai Bar Girls Greet Sailors Like Heroes," *New York Times,* 25 March 1991.

74. Ibid.

75. Ibid.

76. Paul Hutchcroft, "US bases, US bosses: Filipino workers at Clark and Subic," *AMPO* (Toyko) 14, no. 2 (1982): 37.

77. Ibid.

78. For a comparison of British and American militaries' effects on prostitution and their common reliance on racism, see David J. Pivar, "Military Prostitution and Colonial Peoples: India and the Philippines, 1885–1917," *Journal of Sex Research* 17, no. 3 (August 1981): 256–69.

79. Leopoldo M. Moselina, "Olongapo's R & R Industry: A Sociological Analysis of Institutionalized Prostitution," *Makatao: An Interdisciplinary Journal for Students and Practitioners of the Social Sciences* (Asian Social Institute, Manila) 1, no. 11 (January–June 1981): 10.

80. Ibid., 16.

81. Quoted in ibid., 16.

82. Ibid.

83. Sandra Sturdevant and Brenda Stoltzfus, *Let the Good Times Roll: Prostitution and the U.S. Military in Asia* (New York: The New Press, 1992), 45–165.

84. Buklod Center, "Hospitality—What Price? The U.S. Navy at Subic Bay ... and the Women's Response" (Buclod Center, 1 Davis Street, New Banican, Olongapo City, Philippines, 1990, pamphlet).

85. Moselina, "Olongapo's R & R Industry," 16–17.

86. Ibid., 17.

87. Anne-Marie Hilsdon, *Madonnas and Martyrs: Militarism and Violence in the Philippines* (Sydney: Allen and Unwin, 1995), 100–101.

88. Nelia Sancho, Maria Angelica Layador, Lorna Barile, eds., *Issues and Problems of Filipino Migrants, Military Prostitution, and Sex Tourism in the Philippines* (Manila: Asian Women Human Rights Council, 1993), 131.

89. See Hilsdon, *Madonnas and Martyrs.*

90. For more on the various strands of the Filipino women's movement, see Delia Aguilar, "Toward a Reinscription of Nationalist Feminism," *Review of Women's Studies* 4, no. 2 (1994–95): 1–14; Delia Aguilar, *The Feminist Challenge: Initial Working Principles toward Reconceptualizing the Feminist Movement in the Philippines* (Manila Asia Social Institute, 1989).

91. Barry, *Prostitution of Sexuality,* 148. For more on the gendered politics of the U.S. military bases conversion process, see Farah Godrej, "The Prostitution Industry Surrounding U.S. Military Bases in the Philippines" (honors thesis, Department of Government, Clark University, Worcester, Mass., 1994). For an American Defense Department official's view of the early negotiations leading to the base closures, see Georgia C. Sadler (Captain, U.S. Navy), "Philippine Bases: Going, Going, Gone" (Proceedings, U.S. Naval Institute, November 1988), 89–96. For alternative proposals for the base conversions, see Peace Education Division, *Swords into Plowshares: Economic Conversion and the U.S. Bases in the Philippines* (Philadelphia: American Friends Service Committee, 1990).

92. Louise Carolin, "Military Maneuvers," *Everywoman* (London), May 1996, 8. Along with the Buklod Center, other organizations have begun to provide alternative jobs training for women in Olongapo, for instance, Approtech Asia Magallanes Intramuros, Manila 1002, Philippines. For Filipino feminists' formal proposal to the government of a national economic blueprint that would both shrink the prostitution industry and provide alternative bases of economic security to Filipinas who in the 1990s are driven to look to prostitution as a career, see The National Commission on the Role of Filipino Women, *Philippine Plan for Gender-Responsive Development, 1995–2025* (Manila: The Government of the Philippines, 1995.

93. Sturdevant and Stoltzfus, *Let the Good Times Roll,* 48–111. An unusually detailed account of the elaborate international business system that has developed to trade Filipinas' bodies for profit is Chris de Stoop, *They Are So Sweet, Sir: The Cruel World of Traffickers in Filipinas and Other Women* (Manila: Limitless Asia, 1994). This book was originally published in French in Belgium in 1992 and was translated from the French to English by Francois Hubert-Baterna and Louise Hubert-Baterna.

94. I am grateful to Angela Yang, a Filipina feminist, for tutoring me on the internal politics of Filipina migration abroad as mail-order brides and as entertainers. The results of her research are "The Mail-Order Bride Industry" (Department of Government, Clark University, Worcester, Mass., 1996, typescript); and "Filipinas Migrating as Entertainers to Japan" (honors thesis, International Development Program, Clark University, Worcester, Mass., 1998).

95. These figures are cited in Yang, "The Mail-Order Bride Industry," drawing on data from The National Commission on the Role of Filipina Women, *Filipina Women Migrants* (Manila: The National Commission of the Role of Filipina Women, 1996), 20.

96. Wendy Kauffman, *Morning Edition,* National Public Radio, 11 June 1996.

97. I am grateful to both Jan Pettmen, Director of Women's Studies at the Australian National University, and Sheila Jeffries, of the University of Melbourne, for their informative conversations with me about current Filipina Australian organizing and analyses. Jan Pettman notes that advertisements in Australian newspapers for mail-order brides began by offering Filipina

women, then began offering Thai and Malaysian women and by the early 1990s were offering Russian women. See Jan Pettman, *Worlding Women: A Feminist International Politics* (Sydney: Allen and Unwin, 1996), 185–207. See also Kathryn Robinson, "Of Mail Order Brides and 'Boys Own' Tales: Representations of Asian-Australian Marriages," in "The World Upside Down: Feminisms in the Antipodes," special issue of *Feminist Review,* no. 52 (spring 1996): 53–68.

98. See Jan Pettman, "Women on the Move: Globalization, Gender, and the Changing International Division of Labor" (paper presented at the Australian National University, 29 August 1996).

99. The Australian branch of the Women's International League for Peace and Freedom (WILPF) in 1996 began a campaign to compel the Australian government to require a woman-respecting code of conduct for any U.S. troops invited by the Australian government to use Australian territory as a training ground. For WILPF, this new campaign is seen as part and parcel of their work that has included supporting Asian women survivors of the Japanese imperial government's World War II sexual slavery system. I am grateful to Yumi Lee, WILPF's Australian National Coordinator, for this information obtained during our conversation on 28 June 1996.

100. Yang, *Filipinas Migrating as Entertainers to Japan;* Yayori Matsui, "The Plight of Asian Migrant Women Working in Japan's Sex Industry," in *Japanese Women: New Feminist Perspectives on the Past, Present, and Future,* ed. Kumiko Fujimura-Fanselow and Atsuko Kameda (New York: The Feminist Press, 1995), 309–22. Other Japanese feminists have been monitoring Japan's media portrayal of the Filipina migrant woman, where she has been represented typically as a hostess in the country's sex industry. See Ann Kaneko, "In Search of Ruby Moreno," *AMPO Japan-Asia Quarterly Review* 25, no. 4 (1994), and 26, no. 1 (1995): 66–70. Thai feminists also have been alarmed at the rising numbers of Thai women who have been recruited to migrate to Japan only to find, once there, that they are to work in the sex trade. See Etain McDonnell and Karuna Buakumsri, "Prostitutes in Japan: A Shriek of Silence," *Friends of Women Newsletter* (Bangkok) 4, no. 2 (December 1993), 13–17.

101. Matsui Yayori, "Asian Migrant Women in Japan," in *Broken Silence: Voices of Japanese Feminism,* ed. Susan Buckley (Berkeley: University of California Press, 1997), 150. See also Sturdevant and Stoltzfus, *Let the Good Times Roll,* 254–99. For an exposé by a Belgian journalist of the operations of those business entrepreneurs who run the organizations trafficking in Filipino women overseas, see de Stoop, *They Are So Sweet, Sir.* See also Sietske Altink, *Stolen Lives: Trading Women into Sex and Slavery* (Binghamton, N.Y.: The Haworth Press, 1996).

102. Saundra Sturdevant, "Notes from the Field: The U.S. Military and Sexual Violence against Women," *Bulletin of Concerned Asian Scholars* 27, no. 4 (1995): 93. For an analysis of the mayor of Manila's attempts to crack down on prostitution and in the process blaming women in prostitution for the city's international reputation for degeneracy, see Neferti Xina Tadiar,

"Manila's New Metropolitan Form," in *Discrepant Histories: Translocal Essays on Filipino Cultures,* ed. Vicente L. Rafael (Philadelphia: Temple University Press, 1995), 285–307.

103. Edward A. Gargan, "Traffic in Children Is Brisk (Legacy of the Navy?)," *New York Times,* 11 December 1997. On the same day, but pages away in the financial section of the paper, appeared Gargan's article on the economic success of the Subic Bay industrial park: Edward A. Gargan, "Last Laugh for the Philippines," *New York Times,* 11 December 1997.

104. Linda Greenhouse, "Facet of Immigration Law Is Argued," *New York Times,* 5 November 1997.

105. Stephen R. Shalom, "Bases by Another Name: U.S. Military Access in the Philippines," *Bulletin of Concerned Asian Scholars* 29, no. 4 (1997), 78.

106. Ibid., 81.

107. Coalition Against Trafficking in Women (CATW), Electronic Newsletter, no. 1 (20 April 1998), www.uri.edu/artsci.wms/hughes/catw. In the U.S., the American Friends Service Committee (AFSC) has been active in raising public awareness of the implications of the Defense Department's seeking new military access to Philippine towns. I am grateful to Joe Gerson of the AFSC and Daniel Boone Schirmer of the Boston Friends of the Filipino People for their sharing with me their information on the evolving basing negotiations. The Gabriela activists' linkage between signing the SOFA and sponsoring a Centennial celebration beauty contest is made in *KaWOMENan: A Publication of Gabriela Network* (New York) (spring 1998): 2, 4, 7.

108. Bang-Soon Yoon, "Military Sexual Slavery: Political Agenda for Feminist Scholarship and Activism" (paper prepared for the Non-Governmental Organization Forum on Women, Hairou, China, 1995). This forum was held in conjunction with the Fourth UN Conference on Women, Beijing, China. Bang-Soon Yoon, a specialist on the Korean military sex slave issue, is a political scientist and director of women's studies at Central Washington University, Ellensburg, Washington.

109. This description of a Japanese military "comfort women" operation in World War II China is from Kim Il Myon, *Tenno no Guntai to Chosenjin Ianfu* [The Emperor's Forces and Korean Comfort Women] (Tokyo, 1976), quoted by George Hicks, *The Comfort Women: Sex Slaves of the Japanese Imperial Forces* (New York: W.W. Norton, 1995), 47. For a historical account of the Japanese imperial government's earlier overseas prostitution policy, that is, the 1905–1930 period following its victory in the Russo-Japanese War, see Mikiso Hane, *Peasants, Rebels, and Outcasts: The Underside of Modern Japan* (New York: Pantheon Books, 1982), 218–25.

110. A detailed account of the step-by-step evolution of Japanese military commanders' prostitution policies implemented in China and Korea between 1932 and 1945 (and the rationales underlying each step) is provided in Yuki Tanaka, *The Origin of the "Comfort Women" System* (New York: Routledge, forthcoming). See also Chin Sung Chung, "Korean Women Drafted for Military Sexual Slavery by Japan," in *True Stories of the Korean Comfort Women,* ed. Keith Howard (New York: Cassell, 1998), 14. This collection of firsthand

accounts by nineteen surviving Korean women who were forced to serve as prostitutes was initiated by the Korean Council for the Women Drafted for Military Sexual Slavery by Japan.

111. The following report of Amanita Ballahadiu's story of her experiences as a World War II Japaneese military sex slave—the term she and younger Filipina feminists prefer—is derived from notes I took during her talk at Wellesley College, Wellesley, Mass., 1 November 1993. Amanita Ballahadiu spoke in Tagalog, one of the Philippines' principal languages. Her words were translated by Nelia Sancho, a well-known Filipina activist. This talk was part of a U.S. tour of "comfort women" organized by the Filipina women's organization Gabriela.

112. The organization formed to support the Filipina former "comfort women" is the Task Force on Filipina Victims of Military Sexual Slavery by Japan, P.O. Box 190, 1099 Manila, Philippines. See also Maria Rosa Henson, *Comfort Woman: A Filipina's Story of Prostitution and Slavery under the Japanese Military* (Lanham, Md.: Rowman and Littlefield, 1999).

113. Kim Tokchin, "I Have Much to Say to the Korean Government," in Howard, *True Stories,* 42–43.

114. Ibid., 44–45.

115. Nicholas D. Kristof, "Fearing G.I. Occupiers, Japan Urged Women into Brothels," *New York Times,* 27 October 1995. For further analysis of American officials' motivations for suppressing accounts of the Japanese "comfort women" system and for initially accepting a post-surrender proposition system designed by Japanese officials for American male occupying soldiers, see Yuki Tanaka, "U.S. Military Indifference towards 'Comfort Women,'" *Bulletin of Concerned Asian Scholars,* forthcoming.

116. Kristof, "Fearing G.I. Occupiers."

117. Ibid.

118. Ibid. For a fictional account of Japanese citizens' responses to the ending of the war and to the calls from their government for women to service the arriving American occupiers, see Hisako Matsubara, *Cranes at Dusk* (London: Futura Publications, 1985).

119. Chunghee Sarah Soh, "The Korean 'Comfort Women': Movement for Redress," *Asian Survey* 36, no. 12 (1997): 1226–40.

120. Insook Kwon, "Feminism and Nationalism" (master's thesis, Womens Studies Program, Rutgers University, New Brunswick, N.J., 1997). Insook Kwon currently is finishing a dissertation on South Korean women's militarized consciousness in the women's studies doctoral program at Clark University, Worcester, Mass. See also Elaine H. Kim and Chungmoo Choi, eds., *Dangerous Women: Gender and Korean Nationalism* (New York: Routledge, 1997); Chungmoo Choi, guest editor, "The Comfort Women: Colonialism, War, and Sex," special issue of *Positions: East Asia Cultures Critique* 5, no. 1 (spring 1997).

121. Yamazaki Hiromi, "Military Sexual Slavery and the Women's Movement," *AMPO Japan-Asia Quarterly Review,* vol. 25, no. 4, (1994), and vol. 26, no. 1 (1995): 53. This entire issue of AMPO is devoted to articles by Japanese feminists. In another article in the same issue, a Korean Japanese feminist

(that is, a member of Japan's own resident Korean minority, called the *zainichi*) cautions her fellow Korean Japanese women to look carefully at the World War II sexual slavery issue as it is being played out within their ethnic community in the 1990s. She criticizes those Korean Japanese men who portray the "comfort women" policy as merely derived from racism rather than from a combination of racism and sexism. She urges that the World War II revelations be used to raise the issues of sexism within the Korean culture. Kim Pu Ja, "Seeing Sexual Slavery from a Zainichi Perspective," Ibid., 86–87. This article and others from this special issue of AMPO have been published in AMPO, *Voices from the Japanese Women's Movement* (Armonk, N.Y: M.E. Sharpe, 1996). A documentary film on the history of the "comfort women" and the silencing of that history is *Senso Daughters,* directed by Noriko Sekiguchi, distributed by First Run Icarus Films, 1989. In 1995, another documentary film about the women's experiences of wartime sexual slavery was released in South Korea and Japan: *Murmuring,* directed by Byun Young Joo. Byun told an interviewer that she "wanted to go beyond the Japanese-Korean relationship with this documentary. In a wider perspective, wherever there is warfare—in Bosnia, for example—women (are among) the first victims" (Norma Reveler, "Murmurs of Despair," *The Daily Yomiuri,* 12 October 1995). I am grateful to Grace Cho for bringing this article to my attention. A book examining the "comfort women" policy, among other Japanese imperial government World War II wartime practices, is Yuki Tanaka, *Hidden Horrors: Japanese War Crimes in World War II* (Colorado Springs, Colo.: Westview Press, 1996).

122. For a Japanese feminist analysis of the current sexual politics in Japan, see Kuniko Funabashi, "Pornographic Culture and Sexual Violence," in *Japanese Women: New Feminist Perspectives on the Past, Present, and Future,* ed. Kumiko Fujimura-Fanselow and Atsuka Kameda (New York: The Feminist Press, 1995), 260–61. See also Masanori Yamaguchi, "Men on the Threshold of Change," in Fujimura-Faneslow and Kameda, *Japanese Women,* 247–54.

123. Rebecca Jennison, "Feminist Visions: Contemporary Women Artists Remember the War" (paper presented at the Berkshire Conference on the History of Women, University of North Carolina, Chapel Hill, N.C., 7 June 1996). Rebecca Johnson is at Kyoto Seiko University, Kyoto, Japan. For more on the works of Shimada Yoshiko, see Hagiwara Hiroko, "Comfort Women and Patriotic Mothers: Recent Works by Shimada Yoshiko," *Visions International,* March 1996, 6–8.

124. See, for example, Noriyo Hayakawa, "Feminism and Nationalism in Japan, 1868–1945," *Journal of Women's History* 7, no. 4 (1996): 108–19.

125. Mayumi Maruyama, "Lobbying Weak at Forum," *Asahi Evening News* (Tokyo), 19 September 1996. By May 1996, the government-sponsored Asian Women's Fund had raised "only a fraction of the money that is necessary," and its most prominent promoter, Tomiichi Murayama, wife of the former Socialist prime minister, had resigned in protest over the Liberal Democratic Party government's lukewarm response to demands that the government make full apologies for the wartime enslavement of Asian women. See Nicholas D. Kristof, "Japan Fund for War's 'Comfort Women' Is in Crisis," *New York Times,* 13 May 1996.

126. "World War II Sex Slaves Receive Apology," *Boston Globe,* 23 June 1996.

127. Ibid.

128. Takemi Chieko, "Killing Us Twice: The Asian Women's Fund," *AMPO Japan-Asia Quarterly Review* 27, no. 3 (1998): 14–16.

129. "Japan Court Backs 3 Brothel Victims," *New York Times,* 28 April 1998. A week earlier the newly elected president of South Korea, Kim Dae Jung, announced that his administration would stop seeking direct compensation from the Japanese government for South Korean "comfort women" and would distribute monetary compensations to those survivors from its own budget See Stephanie Strom, "Seoul Won't Seek Japan Funds for War's Brothel's Women," *New York Times,* 22 April 1998. For more on the Japanese politics of World War II apologies, see Ryuji Mukae, "Japan's Diet Resolution on World War II," *Asian Survey* 36, no. 10 (October 1996).

130. The details that follow are from a presentation made by Kim Yeon Ja at Wellesley College, Wellesley, Mass., 8 February 1995, as part of an event organized by Katharine Moon, a professor of political science at Wellesley College. Kim Yeon Ja is active in The Women's Human Rights Committeee National Campaign for Eradication of Crime by U.S. Troops in Korea, Room 708, Christian Blvd., 136–46, Yunchi-Dong, Chongro-ku, Seoul, South Korea 110–470.

131. Katharine Moon, *Sex among Allies: Military Prostitution in U.S.-Korea Relations* (New York: Columbia University Press, 1997), 22–24. See also Sturdevant and Stoltzfus, *Let the Good Times Roll,* 166–239.

132. Moon, *Sex among Allies,* 25. See also Katharine Moon, "Military Prostitution and the Hypermasculinization of Militarized Women," in *Inside/Outside: Women and the U.S. Military,* ed. Francine D'Amico and Laurie Weinstein (New York: New York University Press, 1998).

133. A similar case has been made the basis of a fictional plot. Written by Martin Limon, who served in the U.S. Army for ten years in South Korea, this novel provides some insight into how American military personnel wove the bars and prostitution industry around their bases into their own lives. See Martin Limon, *Jade Lady Burning* (New York: Soho Press, 1992). For another autobiographically inspired novel about American military prostitution in Korea, see Heinz Insu Fenkl, *Memories of My Ghost Brother* (New York: Penguin Books, 1997).

134. This understanding is derived from my conversations, under the promise of anonymity, with three U.S. mid-career military officers during a Defense Department–sponsored conference, Annapolis, Maryland, 16 September 1993.

135. Katharine Moon, *Sex among Allies: Military Prostitution in U.S.-Korea Relations* (New York: Columbia University Press, 1997). Moon's research is based on U.S. government minutes of meetings of the U.S.-Korea Status of Forces Joint Committee in 1971 through 1976 as well as on oral histories of women working in the bars around the U.S. bases. Kim Yeon Ja is one of those women.

136. Westheider, *Fighting on Two Fronts,* 144.

137. Moon, *Sex among Allies,* 331.

138. For a nuanced investigation of the complex relationships between early Korean feminism and nationalism and imperialism (Western and Japanese), see Insook Kwon, "'The Korean New Women's Movement' in 1920s Korea: Rethinking the Relationship between Imperialism and Women,"*Gender and History* 10, no. 3 (November 1998): 381–405. For more on feminists' interpretations of Korean women's experiences of capitalism, see Seung-Kyung Kim, *Class Struggle or Family Struggle? The Lives of Women Factory Workers in South Korea* (New York: Cambridge University Press, 1997); and Jeong-Lim Nam, "Women's Role in Export Dependence and State Control of Labor Unions in South Korea," *Women's Studies International Forum* 17, no. 1 (1994): 57–67.

139. Soung-ai Choi, "Whose Honor, Whose Humiliation: Women, Men, and the Economic Crisis," *Asian Women Workers Newsletter* 17, no. 2 (April 1998): 15–16.

140. For more on Korean feminists' debates about nationalism—and nationalists—see Kyung-Ai Kim, "Nationalism: An Advocate of, or a Barrier to, Feminism in South Korea," *Women's Studies International Forum* 19, nos. 1–2 (1996): 65–74. This special issue is devoted to gender, ethnicity, and nationalism and is edited by Barbara Einhorn. See also Yung-Hee Kim, "Under the Mandate of Nationalism: Development of Feminist Enterprises in Modern Korea, 1860–1910," *Journal of Women's History* 7, no. 4 (winter 1995): 120–36.

141. See, for instance, *The Women Outside,* directed by J.T. Takagi and Hye Jung Park (New York: Third World Newsreel, 1995) and *Camp Arirang,* directed by Diana S. Lee and Grace Yoon-Kyung Lee (New York: Third World Newsreel, 1995).

142. This quotation and those that follow are from J.T. Takagi and Hye Jung Park's film on women now working and who have recently worked as prostitutes around U.S. bases in South Korea. Some of these women have married American male soldiers and moved to the United States. Their experiences as new immigrants are also documented. See J.T. Takagi and Hye Jung Park, *The Women Outside.*

143. Uma Narayan, "'Mail-Order' Brides: Immigrant Women, Domestic Violence, and Immigration Law," *Hypatia* 10, no. 1 (winter 1995): 106–7.

144. Doreen Carvajal, "Oldest Profession's Newest Home," *New York Times,* 28 May 1995.

145. Ibid.

146. Ibid.

147. Sandra Whitworth, "Gender, Race, and the Politics of Peacekeeping," in *A Future for Peacekeeping?* ed. Eddie Moxon-Browne (London: Macmillan, forthcoming). The Cambodian Women's Association (P.O. Box 2334, Phnom Penh, Cambodia) has published their own study of prostitution in Cambodia: *Selling Noodles, The Traffic in Women and Children in Cambodia* (Phnom Penh, Cambodia: Cambodian Women's Association, 1996).

148. "Letters: An Open Letter to Yasushi Akashi (head of the UN operation in Cambodia in 1994)," *Phnom Penh Post,* 4 October 1994. I am grateful

to Liz Bernstein, one of the letter's signers, for sending me a copy of this letter. In 1995, a survey by the French humanitarian aid group Medicins Sans Frontiere revealed that, out of 200 prostitutes or sex workers tested in the northwest province of Cambodia, 92 percent were HIV positive. See Kari Hartwig, "Women's Health in an Age of Globalization" (keynote address of the conference on Women's Health in an Age of Globalization sponsored by Payap University and McCormick Faculty of Nursing, Chiang Mai, Thailand, 6 February 1995), 10. See also Gayle Kirshenbaum and Marina Gilbert, "Who's Watching the Peacekeepers?" *Ms. Magazine,* May/June 1994, 10–15.

149. Penny Edwards, "Imaging the Other in Cambodian Nationalist Discourse before and during the UNTAC Period," in *Propaganda, Politics, and Violence in Cambodia,* ed. Steve Heder and Judy Ledgerwood (Armonk, N.Y.: M. E. Sharpe, 1996), 62–63. See also Judy Ledgerwood, "Politics and Gender Negotiating Conceptions of the Ideal Woman in Present Day Cambodia," *Asia Pacific Viewpoint* 37, no. 2 (August 1996): 139–52.

150. "Virgin Territory," *The Economist,* 2 March 1996, 37. One of the organizations working to end the trafficking in women in Asia has published the following proceedings: The Coalition against Trafficking in Women in Asia, "Women Empowering Women" (proceedings of the Human Rights Conference on the Trafficking of Asian Women, Ateneo di Manila University, Quezon City, Philippines, April 1993). Cambodian human rights advocates welcomed the new Cambodian government's passage in January 1996 of a new law making illegal the trafficking of people, but have criticized Cambodian policy makers and courts for failing to prosecute those involved in prostitute procurement. See Debra Boyce, "Rescued Prostitutes Present Theater of Their Lives," *Bangkok Post,* 28 August 1996.

151. United Nations Division for the Advancement of Women and the Department for Policy Coordination and Sustainable Development, "The Role of Women in United Nations Peace-keeping," *Women 2000,* (December 1995): 8. This journal is published by the UN Division for the Advancement of Women, New York.

152. Ibid.

153. Gayle Kirshenbaum, "In UN Peacekeeping, Women Are an Untapped Resource," *Ms. Magazine,* January/February 1997, 20–21. See also Judith Hicks Stiehm, "United Nations Peacekeeping: Men's and Women's Work," in *Gender Politics in Global Governance,* ed. Mary K. Meyer and Elisabeth Prugl (Lanham, Md.: Rowman and Littlefield, 1999), 41–57.

154. Barbara Crosscttc, "When Peacekeepers Turn into Troublemakers," *New York Times,* 7 January 1996.

155. "U.N. Focuses on Peacekeepers Involved in Child Prostitution," *New York Times,* 9 December 1996.

156. I am grateful to several UN officials who asked to remain anonymous for sharing their thoughts on peacekeeping with me in conversations from May 1997 through May 1998.

157. Lillian A. Pfluke, "Direct Ground Combat in Bosnia: Clear as Mud," *Minerva's Bulletin Board,* spring 1996, 10.

158. Ian Fisher, "French Zone, British Zone, Alchohol-Free Zone," *New York Times,* 7 January 1996.

159. This report from the Hungarian towns of Kaposvar and Taszar is based on Stephen Kinzer, "Bosnia-Bound G.I.'s Energize Merchants of Hungary Town," *New York Times,* 4 December 1995.

160. Ibid. In May 1996 several Hungarian women working for the food concessionaires (the chief contractor is Brown and Root) that had the Defense Department contracts in Taszar, Hungary, lodged complaints of sexual harassment. According to one report, "The complaints have cast a cloud on what both sides have sought to depict as exemplary relations since the 3,500 American soldiers stationed here began arriving in the region in December." "Hungarians Say Americans Harass Them," *Boston Globe,* 5 May 1996.

161. Jane Perlez, "G.I. Charm Overcomes Anxieties in Hungary," *New York Times,* 5 December 1996.

162. The account presented here is based on my conversations between October 1995 and August 1996 with several Defense Department officials who were active participants in this policy-making process. Because the process remains delicate, I agreed not to give their names.

163. Fred Pang, Assistant Secretary of Defense, U.S. Department of Defense, Washington, D.C., "Memorandum for Assistant Secretary of the Army (Manpower and Reserve Affairs), Assistant Secretary of the Navy (Manpower and Reserve Affairs), Assistant Secretary of the Air Force (Manpower, Reserve Affairs, Installations, and Environment), Subject: Anti–Child Prostitution Effort," 30 July 1996. The quotations that follow come from this same memorandum.

164. "DOD Represented at World Congress," *Military Family* (a U.S. Department of Defense periodical), fall 1996, 2.

165. Telephone conversation with the author, 5 September 1996. In 1998, Carolyn Becraft was promoted to the civilian post of Assistant Secretary of the Navy. She made a point of taking with her to the new post responsibility for implementing the Defense Department's anti-child prostitution policy.

166. Pang, "Memorandum ... Anti–Child Prostitution Effort."

167. Ibid.

CHAPTER 4

1. The writer who deserves credit for drawing feminists' attention early on to rape in war and to the feminist politics of addressing rape in war is Susan Brownmiller in her book *Against Our Will: Men, Women, and Rape* (New York: Penguin Books, 1976).

2. Atina Grossman, "A Question of Silence: The Rape of German Women by Occupation Soldiers," *October Magazine,* no. 72 (spring 1995): 55. Atina Grossman, a historian at Columbia University, did not set out initially to investigate wartime rapes in Germany; rather, her interest was in the politics of abortion. But she came across German health documents that revealed that German authorities in –1945 and 1946 had suspended the Nazi-era antiabor-

tion law under pressure from German women who came to doctors saying that they had been made pregnant as a consequence of being raped by occupying soldiers, mostly soldiers of the Soviet Red Army. Upon careful further research, Grossman has discovered (1) that the situations in which the rapes occurred were diverse and occasionally, in the women's own minds, came confusingly close to prostitution or even consensual sex (though in these cases it was largely in order to gain some protection for themselves and/or their daughters); (2) that many raped German women did not feel burdened by a sense of individual guilt—a feeling often experienced by women who have been raped—because they saw themselves as part of a larger collective, not as lone victims, and because they were able to draw on their own wartime, Nazi-fostered stereotypes of Russians as "brutes"; (3) that East German communist authorities who, after the war, tried to raise the issue of the widespread rapes were silenced, along with the women who had experienced those assaults, in the name of the new Cold War political realities in what was becoming a Soviet-dominated East Germany (pp. 43–63).

3. See, for instance, Ritu Menon and Kamla Bhasin, *Borders and Boundaries: Women in India's Partitition* (New Brunswick, N.J.: Rutgers University Press, 1998).

4. For a report on Haitian women health activists' gradual exposure of rape by soldiers to sustain the former military regime, see Sharon Lerner, "Haitian Women Demand Justice," *Ms. Magazine,* July/August 1998, 10–11. For the central role played by Indonesian feminist human rights groups in revealing soldiers' use of rape to intimidate Chinese Indonesians during the May 1998 protests that led to the fall of President Suharto, see Seth Mydans, "In Jakarta, Reports of Numerous Rapes of Chinese in Riots," *New York Times,* 10 June 1998.

5. In the wake of the anti-Suharto rioting in Indonesia in May 1998, women's centers and human rights groups documented rapes of scores of women whom the male rioters picked out for assault because they were presumed to be Chinese Indonesian women. Immediately after the riots, news accounts focused on the anti-Chinese character of the looting and arson that accompanied the rioting and explained (not necessarily excused) the protestors' actions by noting that the ethnic Javanese-dominated Suharto regime's "crony-ist" politics favored Indonesian ethnic Chinese large company owners (though burning down small shops owned by ethnic Chinese appeared to have less to do with a critique of governmental elite corruption and more to do with long-standing Indonesian racism). Only a month later could women's center activists accumulate sufficient information to substantiate the rapes of ethnic Chinese women, from the ages of ten to fifty-five, that occurred alongside the looting and arson. According to Ita F. Nadia of the Sita Kayam women's aid center in Jakarta, not only were rapes systematically committed by men in groups, but they were perpetrated by men in the Indonesian army wearing civilian clothes. Lending credence to this analysis was documentation of previous rapes of local women by male Indonesian soldiers during their counterinsurgency operations on the contested island of East Timor and even in villages where the government had been seeking to appropriate land. See Seth Mydans,

"In Jakarta, Reports of Numerous Rapes of Chinese in Riots," *New York Times,* 10 June 1998; and Human Rights Watch, *Indonesia: The Damaging Debate on Rapes of Ethnic Chinese Women* (New York: Human Rights Watch, 1998).

6. In the U.S. military system, the Department of Veterans Affairs usually sees those American military women who have been raped by American military men. The women often are treated for post-traumatic stress syndrome (PTSS). They commonly do not seek post-rape services until they are veterans, that is, until they have left the service. This delay means that the uniformed armed services themselves—and their senior officials—can continue behaving as though their male soldiers' rapes of their woman soldiers is a nonproblem. I am grateful to Carolyn Prevatte, Executive Director of the Defense Advisory Committee on Women in the Services (DACOWITS), for this information, obtained in a conversation on 5 September 1996. For rapes by U.S. male soldiers of U.S. women soldiers during the 1990–91 Gulf War, see Cynthia Enloe, *The Morning After: Sexual Politics at the End of the Cold War* (Berkeley: University of California Press, 1992), 190–92.

Canadian women who have been raped by fellow male soldiers while serving in the Canadian armed forces have long been silent, but in 1998 they began speaking to journalists. They described a common set of experiences: being sexually assaulted when a new young recruit by a fellow soldier, often just above them in rank; being disbelieved or treated dismissively when they reported the assault to a senior officer; being harassed when transferred to another unit by men there who had heard distorted versions of the women's earlier complaints; finally, resigning from the military, often suffering from mental and physical stress. See Jane O'Hara, "Rape in the Military," *Maclean's,* 25 May 1998, 15–21; and Jane O'Hara, "Abuse of Power," *Maclean's,* 13 July 1998, 16–20.

7. For a ground-breaking historical exploration of the sexualized relationships, many of which took the form of homosexual rape between invading men of Europe and indigenous men of the Americas—both of whom often were socialized into militarized attitudes—see Richard Trexler, *Sex and Conquest: Gendered Violence, Political Order, and the European Conquest of the Americas* (Ithaca, New York: University Press, 1995).

8. See, for instance, Women's Rights Watch, "Widespread Rape of Somali Women Refugees" (New York: Human Rights Watch, October 1993); and United Nations High Commissioner for Refugees, "Sexual Violence against Refugees" (Geneva: UNHCR, 1995). See also Maryanna Schmuki, "Shedding Their Refugee Skins: Constructions of Women Refugees and International Aid Regimes" (master's thesis, International Development Program, Clark University, Worcester, Mass., 1997). For more on women as refugees, see Doreen Indra, ed., *Engendering Forced Migration* (New York: Berghahn Books, 1999).

9. The most recent case of British soldiers stationed overseas being convicted of rape while off duty occurred in Cyprus, where for almost two decades British soldiers have been stationed as members of a UN peacekeeping operation. In 1994, three British soldiers serving with a peacekeeping

Green Jackets regiment stationed in Cyprus were arrested on charges of kid-
napping, raping, and then murdering a twenty-three-year-old Danish woman.
There had been little public discussion among Britons about the army's
Cyprus mission. Only two years later did violent conflict between the island's
Greeks and Turks prompt renewed diplomatic attention to the society divided not only by ethnic distrust, but by foreign regime's aspirations and
Cold War fears. Thus in 1994, it took a rape and murder to stir British commentators to pay attention to their troops in the Mediterranean. A decade
earlier soldiers were describing to one journalist confusions and frustrations
that may have provided some of the fuel for the later rape. But to have been
taken as warning signals of future militarized sexual assault, even these hints
would have to have been listened to with feminist ears:

> "I'm not all that struck on being here in this observation post on the line between
> the Greeks and the Turks ... Where we're billeted back in the old factory there's
> no telly ... I don't like the island much, it seems a bit of a dump to me." (Len, a
> private)

> "What precisely we're doing here I don't know. We're supposed to be part of the
> United Nations force and I did think that might mean a few joint exercises. But so
> far there's been nothing like that: it's all very boring." (Stanley, a Lance corporal)

> "We're not really needed in the military sense: there's no adrenalin flowing."
> (Tony, a corporal)

> "We get a series of visitors out here of course, from generals down. For them it's
> just a holiday, combining what they call 'An inspection' which takes about an
> hour, then a nice little ten-day holiday on a free trip." (Michael, a captain)

> "I'd say we have less than normal trouble with the soldiers ... When you walk
> out in the towns or wherever you go you have to wear uniform: that's British uni-
> form but with the light blue beret ... One or two brothels but not many of our
> lads go into them, they haven't the money to throw around compared to some of
> the other UN troops, and girls tend to favour those." (Don, a sergeant)

In the aftermath of the rape and murder, the British soldiers' male superiors
tried both to explain and to distance themselves from the misogyny of rank-
and-file men. Spokesmen for the army explained that raping was the outburst
of young military men "cooped up" with too little to do. After the men's convictions two years later, Brigadier Arthur Denaro, deputy commander of the
British forces in Cyprus, declared, "This was not a trial of the Green Jackets,
nor of the forces on Cyprus, nor of the army as a whole." This account is
based on Tony Parker, Soldier, Soldier (London: Coronet Books, 1985),
190–94; and Christopher Price, "Cyprus Rape and Killing Case," New Stateman and Society, 5 April 1996, 8.

10. Kakazu Katsuko and the Okinawa Women's History Group, "Map of
Japanese Military Brothels in Okinawa," Okinawa: Peace, Human Rights,
Women, Environment, no. 4 (February 1997): 4.

11. Nicholas Kristof, "Okinawa Ponders Lessons of a Larger Invasion than
D-Day," New York Times, 24 June 1995.

12. Saundra Sturdevant, "Okinawa Then and Now," in Saundra Sturdevant and Brenda Stoltzfus, Let the Good Times Roll: Prostitution and the U.S.
Military in Asia (New York: The New Press, 1992), 246.

13. Andrew Pollack, "Okinawans Send Message to Tokyo and U.S. to Cut Bases," *New York Times* 9 September 1996.

14. Quoted by Kristof, "Okinawa Ponders Lessons."

15. Nishi Tomoko, "The Bases Seen by High School Students," *AMPO: Japan-Asia Quarterly Review* 27, no. 1 (1996): 32–37. I am grateful to Ogawa Yoko of the Clark International Development Program for alerting me to the public expressions by Okinawan high school students in the aftermath of the September 1995 rape.

16. Andrew Pollack, "Marines Seek Peace with Okinawa in Rape Case," *New York Times,* 8 October 1995; and Rick Mercier, "Lessons from Okinawa," *AMPO Japan-Asia Quarterly Review* 27, no. 1 (1996): 28.

17. Takazato Suzuyo, "The Past and Future of Unai, Sisters of Okinawa," in *Voices from the Japanese Women's Movement,* ed. AMPO (Armonk, N.Y.: M. E. Sharpe, 1996), 139.

18. Ibid., 133–43. See also Mercier, "Lessons from Okinawa," 30.

19. Quotations from an October 1995 survey of high school students taken by Okinanwan teacher Shinjo Toshiaki, himself a supporter of Okinawa's greater autonomy from Japan and from the U.S. military. See Tomoko, "Bases Seen by High School Students," 34.

20. I am grateful to Daniel Boone Schirmer for keeping me informed on Asian anti-bases campaigns. He is a long-time Cambridge, Massachusetts, peace activist who has invested great energy into making American citizens aware of the impacts of their military's bases on the lives of Filipinos and Japanese.

21. In conversation with Takazato Suzuyo and Carolyn Francis, activists in the Okinawa feminist antimilitarism campaign, Cambridge, Mass., 24 February 1998.

22. These portraits of Marines Rodrico Harp, 21, and Kendrick Ledet, 20, both of Griffin, Georgia, and Seaman Marcus Dion Gill, 22, of Woodville, Texas, are drawn from: Ronald Smothers, "Accused Marines' Kin Incredulous," *New York Times,* 6 November 1995.

23. The three men's female relatives sought out independent lawyers, not trusting either the Japanese defense attorneys or the U.S. military's Okinawa command to provide effective defense counsel. Smothers, "Accused Marines' Kin Incredulous." See also Ronald Smothers, "Protests by Relatives," *New York Times,* 8 November 1995.

24. For a meticulous investigation of the ways in which institutional racism operated in the U.S. military's justice system during the Vietnam War era, see James E. Westheider, *Fighting on Two Fronts: African Americans and the Vietnam War* (New York: New York University Press, 1996). In 1921, African American feminist and suffragist Mary Church Terrell criticized her white feminist colleagues in the recently formed Women's League for Peace and Freedom (WILPF) for their apparently too-willing agreement to accept rumor-based charges that American black male soldiers stationed in Germany after the end of World War I were assaulting German women. Responding to Terrell's objection, fellow WILPF member Jane Addams agreed and urged Terrell not to resign from WILPF. See Rosalyn Terborg-Penn, "Discontented Black Feminist: Prelude and Postscript to the Passage of the Nineteenth Amendment," in *"We Specialize in the Wholly Impossible": A Reader in Black Women's History,* ed.

Darlene Clark Hine, Wilma King, and Linda Reed (Brooklyn, N.Y.: Carlson Publishers, 1995), 487–503.

25. This series of articles initiated by reporter Russell Carollo and later continued by Jeff Nesmith appeared in the *Dayton Daily News,* Dayton, Ohio, on 1, 2, 3, 4, 7, 8 October 1996. I am grateful to Japanese journalist Norio Okada for bringing these articles to my attention.

26. Detective Sammy Peavy, Escambia County Sheriff's Department, Florida, quoted in Russell Carollo, "Escaping Justice: Sex Offenders Find Leniency in System," *Dayton Daily News,* 1 October 1995. I am indebted to Madeline Morris of the Duke University Law School for sharing her recent research on the U.S. military's record regarding defining and prosecuting rapes committed by military personnel. See, for instance, Madeline Morris, "By Force of Arms: Rape, War, and Military Culture," *Duke Law Journal.* 45, no. 4 (1996): 652–782; Madeline Morris, "In War and Peace: Incidence and Implications of Rape by Military Personnel," in *Beyond Zero Tolerance: Discrimination in the Military,* ed. Mary Katzenstein and Judith Reppy, (Lanham, Md.: Rowman and Littlefield, 1999).

27. Quoted by Smothers, "Protests by Relatives."

28. This narrative was pieced together by a *New York Times* reporter in Okinawa from the three accused men's confessions, their defense lawyers' descriptions, and the charges of the prosecutors. See Andrew Pollack, "One Guilty Plea in Okinawa Rape; Two Others Admit Role," *New York Times,* 8 November 1995.

29. For instance, Marine Private Rodrico Harp admitted that he had participated in the kidnapping, but denied that he had raped the girl, claiming the U.S. Navy investigators had compelled him to confess to the rape as well. "Japan Rape Confession Was Forced, Marine Says," *New York Times,* 5 December 1995.

30. Saundra Sturdevant and Brenda Stolzfus, "Kin: The Bar System," in Sturdevant and Stolzfus, *Let the Good Times Roll,* 256.

31. Karen DeWitt, "In Japan, Blacks as Ousiders," *New York Times,* 6 December 1995. For instance, Karen Hill Anton, an African American reporter for the *Japan Times,* told DeWitt, "Some Blacks come here prepared to face, and repel, racism ... But if they can let down their armor, they will recognize that they are first and foremost part of that larger group called gaijin (foreigners)."

32. Quoted by Art Pine, "US Admiral Retires under Pressure: Retracts Okinawa Rape Remark," *Boston Globe,* 18 November 1995.

33. Ibid.

34. The Pentagon's own exposure of the Department of the Navy's cover-up of its initial investigation of the goings-on at the Tailhook Association September 1991 convention is included in Department of Defense, Office of Inspector General, "Tailhook 91, Part 1: Review of the Navy Investigation" (Washington, D.C.: Department of Defense, September 1992). For a detailed account of the Tailhook affair, see Jean Zimmerman, *Tailspin: Women at War in the Wake of Tailhook* (New York: Doubleday, 1995).

35. My conversation with a civilian official in the Department of Defense who is close to personnel policy issues, 16 May 1996.

36. Sturdevant and Stoltzfus, *Let the Good Times Roll,* 240–99.

37. Suzuyo and Francis, conversation, Cambridge, Mass., 24 February 1998.

38. Okinawa Christian Peace Center, "Okinawa—Peace, Human Rights, Women, Environment: 1996–1997 Report" (Ginowan-shi, Okinawa, 1997), 25–27. This point also was reconfirmed by Japanese antiviolence feminist scholar and activist Kazuka Watanabe in her comments as chair of the panel "Women, the Pacific War, and Representation in Japan" at the Berkshire Conference on the History of Women, University of North Carolina, Chapel Hill, 7 June 1996.

39. Takazato Suzuyo, in conversation with the author, Cambridge, Mass., 24 February 1998.

40. Mercier, "Lessons from Okinawa," 30.

41. These activities are spelled out in a publicly distributed letter from Keiko Itokazu and Suzuyo Takazato, cochairpersons, Okinawan Women Act against Military Violence, Naha City, Okinawa, 11 December 1995.

42. "Japan: Three Jailed for Rape," *Far Eastern Economic Review,* 21 March 1996, 13; Andrew Pollack, "3 U.S. Servicemen Convicted of Rape of Okinawa Girl," *New York Times,* 7 March 1996.

43. Charles A. Radin, "Rape in Japan: The Crime That Has No Name," *Boston Globe,* 8 March 1996. For more discussions of the analyses of violence made by Japanese feminists, see Sandra Buckley, *Broken Silence: Voices of Japanese Feminism* (Berkeley: University of California Press, 1996). For a detailed account of the ways in which most rape cases fail to reach the courts in Britain and, if they do, fail to bring convictions, see Sue Lees, *Carnal Knowledge: Rape on Trial* (London: Penguin, 1996).

44. Nicholas D. Kristof, "U.S. Will Return Base in Okinawa," *New York Times,* 13 April 1996.

45. A month later a twenty-year-old American sailor from Minnesota was arrested on the charge of cutting the throat and stealing the handbag of a twenty-year-old Japanese woman as she walked in a park early one morning near a U.S. base in Sasebo, a town on the Japanese island of Kyushu. Prompted by the continuing debate among Japanese about the American military presence, U.S. naval authorities responded by imposing a midnight-to-5:30 A.M. curfew on sailors stationed on Kyushu. See "U.S. Sailors Placed on Curfew in Japan," *Boston Globe,* 28 July 1996.

46. The first referendum was held in September 1996. In December 1997, another referendum was held, this one in the Okinawan city of Nago, site of a proposed new offshore heliport for the U.S. forces. Women's groups were among those that held rallies to persuade citizens to vote no. The central government campaigned vigorously to win over local voters, but 53 percent of Nago voters cast ballots in opposition to the heliport. In the wake of the referendum, the prime minister held meetings with Okinawa's governor and Nago's mayor, with the result being a decision to go ahead with the building of the heliport: Massamichi Sebastian Inoue, John Purves, and Mark Selden, "Okinawa Citizens, U.S. Bases, and the Dugong," *Bulletin of Concerned Asian Scholars* 29, no. 4 (1997): 82–86.

47. Okinawa Christian Peace Center, "1996–1997 Report," 4–12.

48. For a detailed description of the analyses and strategies of Okinawan feminists in the two years following the September 1995 rape, see Sandra Shin-Young Park, "For a World without Bases: The Okinawan Feminist Movement against U.S. Japan Alliance Politics and Militarization" (unpublished senior thesis, The Committee on Degrees in the Social Sciences, Radcliffe College, Harvard University, Cambridge, Mass., March 1997).

49. Suzuyo and Francis, conversation. Both have noted that Admiral Macke seemed out of touch with the financial realities of his men: in 1995, the cost of ladies' drinks and bar fines in the entertainment establishments around the American bases in Okinawa was probably more than most enlisted men could afford on their salaries; the result was that some of the flashiest entertainment businesses had closed and many Filipina workers were compelled to move into shadier establishments in narrow side streets.

50. Suzuyo and Francis, conversation. Suzuyo told of being asked by some of the Nago women to lead them at the head of the walk, but she declined, saying that they should lead the walk themselves, that they didn't need a prominent woman elected official to provide them with legitimacy.

51. Ibid.

52. For a brief yet provocative discussion by an Iraqi reformer of the use of systematic, bureaucratized rape by the regime of Saddam Hussein against women suspected of being the regime's opponents, see Kanan Makiya, *Cruelty and Silence: War, Tyranny, Uprising, and the Arab World* (London: Jonathan Cape, 1993), 295-300. For a detailed account of the occasional use of rape and the more frequent threats of rape and other forms of sexual harassment by Israeli security personnel against detained Israeli Jewish peace activists and especially against Palestinian women during the years of the Intafada, see Teresa Thornhill, "Making Women Talk: The Interrogation of Palestinian Women Detainees" (Lawyers for Palestinian Human Rights, London, 1992), 28-34. Indian feminists have made "police rape" a major issue, conceptualizing assaults by police and other male security personnel as evidence not only of a patriarchal state system, but also of a sexualized form of counterinsurgency undertaken by security forces when they are enaged in suppressing alleged domestic insurgents. See, for example, Radha Kumar, *The History of Doing: An Illustrated Account of Movements for Women's Rights and Feminism in India, 1800-1990* (London: Verso, 1995), 127-42. The first Amnesty International documentation of police rape in India is Amnesty International, "Rape and Sexual Abuse: Torture and Ill Treatment of Women in Detention" (Amnesty International, New York, January 1992). Amnesty International's most recent report on the governmental abuse, including rape, of women held in police or military custody is Amnesty International, "Human Rights Are Women's Rights" (Amnesty International, London, 1995), 85-116. For Mayan Guatemalan women's own accounts of the governmental army's use of rape to "discipline" women in highland Indian villages—often persuading young Mayan men who had been conscripted into the army and into militarized civil patrols that it was their right and duty to sexually assualt female members of their own communities—see Maria Stern-Pettersson, "Reading in/Security in Mayan Women's Narratives" (Ph.D. diss., Department of Devel-

opment and Peace Studies, University of Gotesborg, Gotesborg, Sweden, 1998). On rape as a tool of state control during Haiti's era of militarized rule, see Women's Rights Watch, "Rape in Haiti: A Weapon of Terror" (Human Rights Watch, New York, July 1994).

53. Sarah Benton, "Women Disarmed: The Militarization of Politics in Ireland 1913–23," *Feminist Review,* no. 50 (summer 1995): 164. This special issue of *Feminist Review* is devoted to Irish feminism and is guest edited by Mary Hickman and Ailbhe Smyth.

54. Ibid., 162–65. Anita Nesai, a Sri Lankan feminist (and former Peace Fellow at Radcliffe College's Bunting Institute) long active in cross-ethnic efforts to end her country's fourteen-year-old civil war, believes that the Sri Lankan military has during 1995–96 introduced a policy that has notably reduced the incidence of rape by government male soldiers against Tamil women. According to Nesai, this very reduction suggests that rapes in earlier years of the conflict were officially tolerated, perhaps even encouraged, as part of a larger war-waging strategy against the Tamil community. In conversation with the author, Cambridge, Mass., 25 June 1996.

55. For an analysis of how class, gender, political ideology, and sexuality were simultaeously negotiated—and how that often ambivalent negotiation was portrayed by Filipino women writers—during the months preceding Marcos' fall, see Jacqueline Siapno, "Alternative Filipina Heroines: Contested Tropes in Leftist Feminisms," in *Bewitching Women, Pious Men: Gender and Body Politics in Southeast Asia,* ed. Aihwa Ong and Michael G. Peletz (Berkeley: University of California Press, 1995), 216–43.

56. For a detailed and critical analysis of low intensity conflict doctrine, see Michael Klare and P. Kornbluh, eds., *Low Intensity Warfare: Counterinsurgency, Proinsurgency, and Anti-terrorism in the Eighties* (New York: Pantheon, 1988).

57. A valuable feminist social science analysis of low intensity conflict's use in the Philippines is Anne-Marie Hilsdon, *Madonnas and Martyrs: Militarism and Violence in the Philippines* (Sydney: Allen and Unwin, 1995).

58. "Women Victims of Militarization," *Gabriela Women's Update* 3, no. 7 (August-September 1987): 6. See also Gabriela, "The Women's Movement and the Militarization Issue," Proceedings, Fourth Annual Conference, Manila, March 1987.

59. Hilsdon, *Madonnas and Martyrs,* 112.

60. Ibid., 118.

61. For an exploration of theraputic recovery practices developed especially for women who have undergone trauma due to militarized torture and exile, see Inger Agger, *The Blue Room* (Atlantic Highlands, N.J.: Zed Books, 1992).

62. Hilsdon, *Madonnas and Martyrs,* 21.

63. Alfred McCoy, historian at the University of Wisconsin, is in the midst of an ambitious multigenerational study of the institutional culture of the Philippines military, from its creation by the U.S. colonial administration, to its role in the post-Marcos era. See Alfred McCoy, "'Same Banana': Hazing and Honor at the Philippine Military Academy," *Journal of Asian Studies* 54, no. 3

(August 1995): 689–726; Alfred McCoy, "The RAM Boys" (paper presented at the International Studies Association, Toronto, 22–26 March 1997).

64. Hilsdon, *Madonnas and Martyrs,* 19.

65. U.S. Department of State, *Country Reports on Human Rights Practices for 1993* (Washington, D.C.: U.S. Government Printing Office, 1994), 718–21.

66. Raquel Edralin-Tiglao and Rowena Martha S. Beltran, "The Women's Crisis Centre, Manila: Empowering Survivors of Violence," *Arrows for Change* 1, no. 3 (December 1995): 4. *Arrows for Change* is the publication of the Asian-Pacific Resource and Research Centre for Women in Kuala Lumpur, Malaysia.

67. Nancy Caro Hollander, "The Gendering of Human Rights: Women and the Latin American Terrorist State," *Feminist Review* 22, no. 1 (spring 1996): 68. For a detailed ethnographic study of Guatemalan Indian women who witnessed and survived rape as well as the killing of family members during the counterinsurgency war of the 1970s and 1980s, see Linda Green, *Fear as a Way of Life* (New York: Columbia University Press, 1999).

68. Several women novelists have attempted to create credible portraits of those men who have become torturers. Ninotchka Rosca, a Filipina feminist, active in the U.S. branch of the Filipino women's organization Gabriela, has created a character who is a military officer-become-torturer/rapist during the latter years of the Marcos regime. See her novel, *State of War* (New York: Simon and Schuster, 1988). Jordanian British novelist Fadia Faqir has created a multidimensional fictional character, a Jewish Israeli security interrogator who also uses torture as a matter of official routine. See her novel *Nisanit* (New York: Penguin Books, 1987). A recent Israeli documentary film that explores the presumptions and afterthoughts of both Israeli male soldiers who were complicit in beatings of Palestinians during the 1980s Intafada and those who refused to participate is Eduyot Associates, *Testimonies,* 1993.

69. Ximena Bunster-Burotto, "Surviving without Fear: Woman and Torture in Latin America," in *Women and Change in Latin America,* ed. June Nash and Helen Safa (South Hadley, Mass.: Bergin and Garvey Publishers, 1986), 297–326. This research draws as well on interviews conducted with women torture survivors from then-military-ruled Argentina and Uruguay; similar gender patterns were found in all three governments' use of sexualized torture. I am indebted to Ximena Bunster for years of eye-opening conversations about the analyses, priorities, and strategies devised by Chile's remarkable feminist movement, in which she has been both a recorder and a participant. Upon the restoration of civilian democratic rule, Ximena Bunster resumed her post as Professor of Anthropology at the University of Chile in Santiago. For more on the internal culture of the Chilean military in the 1950s–1980s, see Pamela Constable and Arturo Valenzuela, *Chile under Pinochet: A Nation of Enemies* (New York: Norton, 1991), 40–63.

70. Bunster-Burotto, "Surviving without Fear," 308.

71. For more on the formation of the Chilean women's movement during the Pinochet era and in the years during which democracy was restored, see Patricia M. Chuchryk, "From Dictatorship to Democracy: The Women's Movement in Chile," in *The Women's Movement in Latin America,* 2d ed., ed. Jane S. Jaquette (Boulder, Colo.: Westview Press, 1994), 65–108; DAWN, *Al-*

ternatives: The Food, Energy, and Debt Crisis in Relation to Women (Rio de Janeiro: Editora Rosa dos Tempos, 1991). Latin American women novelists have written accounts revealing the subtle interactions of class, gender, familial status, personality, and ideology amid the pressures of military rule and its immediate aftermath. See, for instance, Argentinian writers Alicia Portnoy, *The Little School* (Pittsburgh, Pa.: Cleis Press, 1986) and Luisa Valenzuela, *Bedside Manners* (New York: Serpent's Tail, 1994).

72. Bunster-Burotto, "Surviving without Fear," 307. Ximena Bunster also has written an account of women's activism inside the Chilean anti-torture movement that was organized during the 1970s and 1980s: "Non-Violent Alternatives in Chile's Quest for Democracy" (report for the Program on Nonviolent Sanctions in Conflict and Defense Center for International Affairs, Harvard University, Cambridge, Mass., 1989).

73. Bunster-Burotto, "Surviving without Fear," 308–9. The article includes specific details of several forms of sexual abuse used by the military torturers. These details are included by Ximena Bunster not to "excite" the reader, but to provide a sense of how physicality was integral to the torturers' misogyny and to provide the reader with some understanding of what recovery would have to entail if the interviewees survived.

74. A scientific journal, *Torture,* was launched in 1991 to report on studies of both the effects of torture and the medical and psychological treatment of torture victims. There are now centers for victims of torture in Poland, Guatemala, Denmark, Iran, and the United States. One of the first, the Rehabilitation and Research Center for Torture Victims, was created in 1982 in Copenhagen, Denmark, in recognition of the numbers of refugees from Latin American military dictatorships who had gone into exile in Denmark. An American counterpart, the Center for Victims of Torture in Minneapolis, estimates that between 200,000 and 400,000 survivors of torture are living now in the United States. Daniel Goleman, "A Promising Medical Specialty Emerges to Help Torture Victims," *New York Times,* 9 July 1996.

75. Bunster-Burotto, "Surviving without Fear," 312.

76. Ximena Bunster, "Watch for the Little Nazi Man That All of Us Have Inside: The Mobilization and the Demobilization of Women in Militarized Chile," *Women's Studies International Forum* 11, no. 5 (1988): 228–35. For a detailed study of how both the Pinochet regime and American foreign policy makers tried to manipulate conservative Chilean women, see Margaret Power, *Gendered Allegiances: The Construction of a Rightist, Cross-Class Women's Movement in Chile, 1964–1973* (State College: Pennsylvania State University Press, forthcoming).

77. In neighboring Argentina, social scientists had found that domestic violence had actually increased during the years of military rule. Hollander, "The Gendering of Human Rights," 64.

78. This understanding of the early 1990s Chilean women's movement's legislative priorities is based on conversations with a number of Chilean women activists and legislators during a visit to Santiago in April 1994.

79. Catherine Bonnet, Doctors without Frontiers, New York, quoted by Melinda Lorenson, "No Woman Was Spared," *Ms. Magazine,* May/June 1996, 25.

80. Claire Duchen, "Summary of a Report from Rwanda, and a Call for Action, written by Dr. Catherine Bonnet on Behalf of Medecins sans Frontieres," *Women's Studies International Forum* 18, nos. 5–6 (September–December, 1995): ix.

81. Human Rights Watch Africa, *Genocide in Rwanda April–May 1994* (New York: Human Rights Watch, May 1994). I have written at greater length about how older Hutu male elite men organized young Hutu men into militias in Cynthia Enloe, "When Feminists Think about Rwanda," *Cultural Survival Quarterly* 19, no. 1 (spring 1995): 25–29. This special issue of *Cultural Survival* is devoted to "Women and War" and is edited by Carolyn Nordstrom.

82. Women's Rights Watch, *Shattered Lives: Sexual Violence during the Rwandan Genocide and its Aftermath* (New York: Human Rights Watch, 1996), 18–19. The most thoroughly documented report on the 1994 violence in Rwanda is Alison Des Forges, *"Leave None to Tell the Story": Genocide in Rwanda* (New York: Human Rights Watch, 1999).

83. "Rape and Forced Pregnancy in War and Conflict Situations," Reproductive Freedom and Human Rights, 30 April 1996, 1–11. This publication is from the Center for Reproductive Law and Policy, 120 Wall Street, New York, New York. During the 1971 civil war in Pakistan, out of which Bangladesh was created, an estimated 400,000 Bengali women were raped by male soldiers serving in the Pakistani army; of these, an estimated 250,000 women became pregnant, some pregancies thought by observers to have been the result deliberately sought by these soldiers and possibly their commanders as well (p. 9).

84. Duchen, "Report from Rwanda."

85. Shana Swiss and Joan E. Giller, "Rape as a Crime of War: A Medical Perspective," *Journal of the American Medical Association* 270 (4 August 1993): 614. Shana Swiss is director of the Women's Program of the Boston-based Physicians for Human Rights; she worked in Liberia during 1994 and 1995 to create a program to serve the health needs of women from diverse ethnicities and to address health needs that stemmed from that country's civil war, among which were sexual violence and domestic battering. Joan Giller participated in rape crisis intervention while with the Medical Foundation of Kampala, Uganda.

86. Conversation with the author, Cambridge, Mass., January 1996. For more on the postwar efforts of Rwanda women to organize, see "Hutu, Tutsi Women Rebuilding," *Ms. Magazine,* March/April 1998, 11; Laura Flanders, "Rwanda's Living Casualties," *Ms. Magazine,* March/April 1998, 27–29.

87. Joni Seager, *The State of Women in the World: An International Atlas* (New York: Penguin Books, 1997). For a recent report on what appears to be an emerging pattern of rapes during 1995–96 in Mexico's southern state of Chiapas that were committed by men intent upon silencing, suppressing, and demoralizing women who supported the mainly Indian rebels of the Zapatista National Liberation Army, see Rachel Kamel, "Sexual Violence in Chiapas: Too Close for Comfort?" (Philadelphia: American Friends Service Committee, 1996). Kamel's report is based chiefly on evidence collected by the independent Women's Center in San Cristobal de las Casas, the state capital of Chiapas. By early 1996, the Women's Center had documented 50 rape cases involving

members of the government's security forces or ununiformed men who appeared to act in support of those forces' campaign against the Zapatistas. For a detailed account of military rapes in Burma, see Betsy Apple, *School for Rape: The Burmese Military and Sexual Violence* (Bangkok: Earthrights International, 1998).

88. Preliminary, but rigorously collected, evidence of the Milosevic regime's systematic use of rape by men in its several armed forces operating against the ethnic Albanian majority of the province of Kosovo was gathered by human rights monitors of the Organization for Security and Cooperation in Europe (OSCE). The OSCE's early findings are reported in Jane Perelz, "Serbs Seal Off 700,000 Refugees Who Face Starvation, U.S. Says," *New York Times,* 10 April 1999; Carlotta Gall, "Refugees Crossing Kosovo Border Tell of Rapes and Killings," *New York Times,* 20 April 1999; and Carlotta Gall, "European Group Cites Evidence of War Crimes," *New York Times,* 24 April 1999.

89. This multipronged cause is the conclusion of several feminist analysts who have examined recent wars in which rape was widespread. See Elaine Scarry, *The Body in Pain: The Making and Unmaking of the World* (New York: Oxford University Press, 1985); Carolyn Nordstrom, "Women and War: Observations from the Field," *Minerva: Quarterly Report on Women and the Military* 9, no. 1 (1991): 1–15; Hilary McCollum, Liz Kelly, and Jill Radford, "Wars against Women," *Trouble and Strife,* no. 28 (spring 1994): 12–19; and Ruth Seifert, "The Second Front: The Sexual Violence in Wars," *Women's Studies International Forum* 19, nos. 1/2 (1996): 35–43.

90. Alexandra Stiglmayer, "The War in the Former Yugoslavia," in *Mass Rape: The War against Women in Bosnia-Herzegovina,* ed. Alexandra Stiglmayer (Lincoln: University of Nebraska Press, 1994), 25.

91. Ibid.

92. Quoted in: Marlise Simons, "For First Time, Court Defines Rape as War Crime," *New York Times,* 28 June 1996. Two years later, the Hague Tribunal heard its first accused enter a plea of guilty to rape as a war crime. If the plea had been accepted by the judges, it would have marked the first time in the history of international law that an international court had convicted a person of rape as a separate crime against humanity. Dragoljub Kunarac, 37, was a Bosnian Serb commander of a paramilitary unit. The two rapes of Bosnian Muslim women that he himself perpetrated and those in addition that he supervised occurred in the eastern Bosnian town of Foca in 1992. See Marlise Simons, "An Ex-Bosnian Serb Commander Admits Rape of Muslims in War," *New York Times,* 10 March 1998. Several days after his guilty plea, its legality was thrown into doubt, however. Tribunal justices, meticulous throughout the war crimes proceedings in their attention to defendants' rights, announced that they were not satisfied that Kunarac fully understood the charges. In response to the judges' further questioning, he seemed rather vague about the events, but instead told the court," I came here voluntarily to tell the truth … How great my guilt is, is up to you to decide." "Guilty Plea by a Serb Rejected at War Tribunal," *New York Times,* 14 March 1998.

93. For a ground-breaking feminist investigation of an international organization, the International Labor Organization, see Sandra Whitworth, *Femi-*

nism and International Relations: Towards a Political Economy of Gender in Interstate and Non-Governmental Institutions (New York: St. Martin's Press, 1994). See also Margaret E. Galey, "Promoting Nondiscrimination against Women: The UN Commission on the Status of Women," *International Studies Quarterly,* no. 23 (June 1979): 290–305; Elisabeth Prugl, "Gender in International Organization and Global Governance: Critical Review of the Literature," *International Studies Association Research Note* 21, no. 1 (winter 1996): 15–24.

94. Simons, "Court Defines Rape as War Crime."

95. A thoughtful analysis of the changes necessary to make it possible for Bosnian women to appear as witnesses in the Hague is by feminist international legal theorist Julie Mertus. See "Only a War Crimes Tribunal: Triumph of the 'International Community,' Pain of the Survivors," in *The War Crimes Tribunal,* ed. N. Courtjul (1999). See also Julie Mertus et al., eds., *The Suitcase: Refugees' Voices from Bosnia and Croatia* (Berkeley: University of California Press, 1996). For more on what it means for a woman to come forward as a witness at the Hague, see Sarah Maguire, "Dispatches from the Front Line," *Trouble and Strife,* no. 36 (winter 1997/98): 2–5.

96. James C. McKinley Jr., "UN Tribunal Convicts Rwandan of '94 Genocide," *New York Times,* 3 September 1998.

97. Naomi Klein, "Is War Crimes Prosecution in the Right Hands?" *Ms. Magazine,* July/August 1996, 22–23.

98. Barbara Crossette, "U.N. Prosecutor Urges New Criminal Court," *New York Times,* 7 December 1997; Barbara Crossette, "U.S. Budges at U.N. Talks on a Permanent War-Crimes Court," *New York Times,* 18 March 1998; Eric Schmitt, "Pentagon Battles Plans for International War Crimes Tribunal," *New York Times,* 14 April 1998.

99. Charlotte Graves Patton, "UN NGO Report Focuses on Status of Women," *International Studies Newsletter* 25, no. 2 (1998): 5; Bharati Sadasivam, "Global Voices," *Sibyl* (London), no. 1 (March/April 1998): 29.

100. "Last Call for Integrating Women's Human Rights into the International Criminal Court," *Forum News* 11, no. 1 (April 1998): 14. The *Forum News* is published by the Asia Pacific Forum on Women, Law, and Development, YMCA Building, 11 Sermsuk Road, Soi Mengrairasmi, Chiangmai, Thailand. The Women's Caucus for Gender Justice in the International Criminal Court can be contacted via the Law School, City University of New York, New York. For an account of the last-minute behind-the-scenes bargaining over the treaty's provisions on rape, see Alessandra Stanley, "Semantics Stalls Pact Labeling Rape a War Crime," *New York Times,* 9 July 1998.

101. Alessandra Stanley, "U.S. Dissents, But Accord Is Reached on War-Crime Court," *New York Times,* 18 July 1998.

102. In May 1998, the first guilty plea was entered in the Rwanda War Crimes Tribunal in Arusha, Tanzania. Jean Kambanda, former prime minister of Rwanda in a regime of the Hutu-dominated political party, the Mouvement Democratique Populaire, which came to power in April 1994, pleaded guilty in front of tribunal justice Lamity Kama of Senegal to four charges of genocide and two charges of crimes against humanity. He confessed that he took delib-

erate steps to incite and to plan massacres of Tutsis and of those Hutus seen to be supportive of Tutsis. See James C. McKinley Jr., "Ex-Premier Admits He Led Massacres in Rwanda in 1994," *New York Times,* 2 May 1998. Among the other Rwandan prisoners awaiting trials or verdicts in Arusha are men whose charges include inciting or supervising mass rapes of Tutsi women and Hutu women married to Tutsi men.

103. Principal sections of the indictments issued by the International Criminal Court were reprinted in "The Charges," *New York Times,* 28 May 1999. For a Canadian analysis of Arbour's performance as chief prosecutor and her likely future career in Canada, see Barry Came, "The Trials of Louise Arbour," *Maclean's,* 24 May 1999, 34–37.

104. Jutta Joachim, "How Women's Issues Get on the UN's Agenda: International Women's Organizations and Violence against Women" (paper presented at the International Studies Association Annual Conference, San Diego, Calif., 20 April 1996); Rebecca Cook, ed., *Human Rights of Women* (Philadelphia: University of Pennsylvania Press, 1994); Joanna Kerr, ed., *Ours by Right: Women's Rights as Human Rights* (Atlantic Highlands, N.J.: Zed Press, 1993); Amnesty International, *Human Rights Are Women's Rights* (London: Amnesty International, 1995); Human Rights Watch Women's Rights Project, *The Human Rights Watch Global Report on Women's Human Rights* (New York: Human Rights Watch, 1995); Georgina Ashworth, *Changing the Discourse: A Guide to Women and Human Rights* (London: Change–International Reports: Women and Society, 1990).

105. Simons, "Court Defines Rape." For further feminist analysis of the modes and conclusions of investigations of numbers of women raped—often multiply—between 1992 and 1996 in the war in the former Yugoslavia, see Stiglmayer, *Mass Rape;* Beverly Allen, *Rape Warfare: The Hidden Genocide in Bosnia-Herzegovina and Croatia* (Minneapolis: University of Minnesota Press, 1996).

106. Klein, "War Crimes Prosecution," 22.

107. Allen, *Rape Warfare,* 73–74. Allen is quoting directly from the "Mazowiecki Report," whose formal citation is United Nations General Assembly Security Council, "The Situation of Human Rights in the Territory of the Former Yugoslavia," Document A/48/92, S/25341, 26 February 1993.

108. Alexandra Stiglmayer, "The Rapes in Bosnia-Herzegovina," in Stiglmayer, *Mass Rape,* 147–61.

109. United Nations General Assembly, "Final Report of the Commission of Experts Established Pursuant to Security Council Resolution 780 (1992)," General Document S/1994/674, 27 May 1972, quoted directly by Allen, *Rape Warfare,* 43.

110. Bosnian official census figures as cited by Tom Gjelten, *Sarajevo Daily* (New York: HarperCollins, 1995), 9–10.

111. This argument about Titoist nation-building strategy's reliance on militarism is made by Bette Denich in her chapter "Of Arms, Men, and Ethnic War in (Former) Yugoslavia," in *Feminism, Nationalism, and Militarism,* ed. Constance R. Sutton (Arlington, Va.: Association for Feminist Anthropology of the American Anthropological Association, 1995), 64–65.

112. Stasa Zajovic, "About 'Cleansing,'" in *Women for Peace,* ed. Stasa Zajovic (Belgrade: Women in Black, 1994), 65.

113. Lepa Mladjenovic and Vera Litricin, "Belgrade Feminists 1992: Separation, Guilt, and Identity Crises," *Feminist Review,* no. 45 (autumn 1993): 113–19. This special issue is entitled "Thinking through Ethnicities."

114. For the pre-1991 beginnings of Serbian feminist groups, see Donna M. Hughes, Lepa Mladjenovic, and Zoica Mrsevic, "Feminist Resistance in Serbia," *European Journal of Women's Studies* 2 (1995): 509–32.

115. Quoted in the Women in Black's occasional newletter, Belgrade, June 1996, 3. The information here on Serbian women's antimilitarism groups is derived from: Maja Korac, "Understanding Ethnic-National Identity and Its Meaning: Questions from Women's Experience," *Women's Studies International Forum* 19, nos. 1–2 (1996): 133–43; Zajovic, *Women for Peace;* "Compilation of Information on Crimes of War against Women in Ex-Yugoslavia—Actions and Initiatives in their Defense," Update No. 3 (Women Living under Muslim Laws, Grabels, France, 1994). Women Living under Muslim Laws has developed a close working relationship with the Belgrade chapter of Women in Black out of the belief that feminists opposing misogynist militarism have a common stake in overcoming constructed barriers of religion, ethnicity, and state status. The address of Women Living under Muslim Laws is boite postale 23, 34790 Grabels, Montpelier, France.

116. See, for instance, Zajovic, *Women for Peace.*

117. Ibid.

118. "The Reactions of Passers-by to the Protests of the Women in Black," in Zajovic, *Women for Peace,* 12–13.

119. See, for instance, Dubravka Ugresic's critique of the Tudjman government's effort to manipulate Croat folklore for the sake of nationalist mobilization: Dubravska Ugresic, "Balkan Blues," *Storm,* no. 6 (1994). This special issue of *Storm* entitled "Out of Yugoslavia" features writers of the former Yugoslavia and is edited by British historian Joanna Labon. This special issue of *Storm* has been published in book form: Joanna Labon, ed., *Balkan Blues:Writing out of Yugoslavia* (Evanston, Ill.: Northwestern University Press, 1994). Ugresic's piece appears as "Balkan Blues," 3–36.

120. A documentary film that explores both the systematic rapes carried on by Serbian militamen in the Omarska camp and the efforts of two Bosnian women to make their own sense of that experience and to develop nonnationalist organizations to provide services and to collect testimonies for the Hague tribunal is *Calling the Ghosts—A Story of Rape, War, and Women,* directed by Mandy Jacobson and Karmen Jelincic, Bowery Productions, New York, 1996. The filmmakers themselves are candidly aware of the choices they had to make during the three years of filming and editing in order to ensure that their film would not be used to promote militarized nationalism. Correspondence and conversation with Mandy Jacobson and Karmen Jelincic, August 1996.

121. See, for instance, Maja Povrzanovic, "Crossing the Borders: Croatian War Ethnographies," in *Narodna Umjetnost: Croatian Journal of Ethnology and Folklore Research* 32, no. 1 (1995): 91–106. See also Lada Cale Feldman,

Ines Prica, and Reana Senjkovic, eds., *Fear, Death, and Resistance: An Ethnography of War—Croatia 1991–1992* (Zagreb, Croatia: Institute of Ethnology and Folklore Research, 1993).

122. The Conference on the "(En)gendering of Violence: Terror, Domination, Recovery," held at the University of Zagreb, Zagreb, Croatia, 27–28 October 1995, was organized by Maria Olujic, of the Institute for Applied Social Research, University of Zagreb. I was one of the invited participants. The conference was cosponsored by the Center for Slavic and East European Studies of the University of California, Berkeley. For Maria Olujic's research findings, see Maria Olujic, "Sexual Coercion and Torture in the Former Yugoslavia," *Cultural Survival Quarterly* 19, no. 1 (spring 1995): 43–45. Croatia also has an autonomous feminist movement, whose relations with the Tudjman government are cool. In 1995, women active in the movement launched a freestanding Women's Studies program, independent of the University of Zagreb. Among the courses they designed and offered were "Imagining the Feminine," "Women's Identity," "Feminism, Women, and the Public World," "Feminism and Linguistics," "Video Art by Women," and "A Feminist Approach to Violence against Women." I am grateful to Biljana Kasic of the Zagreb Women's Studies Program for sharing information of this project with me.

123. Women in Black newsletter, Belgrade, June 1996. The conference being announced was held in Novi Sad, 1–4 August 1996.

124. Korac, "Understanding Ethnic-National Identity," 138.

125. Wenona Giles and Maja Korac, of the Centre for Feminist Studies, York University, Ontario, Canada, have launched an international research project on the experiences and conditions of women who have been made refugees by war. Their project—The Women in Conflict Zones Network, or WICZNET—includes women in the former Yugoslavia. Among the project's concerns are the pressures on women to deny their own subjective understandings of their experiences and, instead, to allow others—family members and, especially, nationalists from their ethnic communities—to define their experiences' meaning for them. Conversations and correspondence with Maja Korac and Wenona Giles, 1995 through 1998. For an analysis of how different groups of women in the former Yugoslavia have related to the political changes in the 1990s, see Maja Korac, "The Power of Gender in the Transition from State Socialism to Ethnic Nationalism, Militarization, and War: The Case of Post-Yugoslav States" (Ph.D. diss., Graduate Programme in Sociology, York University, Ontario, Canada, 1998).

126. The June 1996 preliminary program for the August 1996 international meeting organized by the Belgrade Women in Black listed the implications of the peace accords as the topic for the first workshop; lesbianism and political responsibility was listed as the topic of the second session.

127. This point was made by a group of women inside U.S.-based human rights organizations in a letter they addressed to then-U.S. United Nations Ambassador Madeleine Albright, dated 14 December 1995, after the signing of the Dayton Peace Accords and on the eve of the NATO peacekeeping operation in Bosnia. The letter was distributed by one of the signers, Ann Eisenberg,

Assistant Director, Jacob Blaustein Institute for the Advancement of Human Rights, New York, New York. I am grateful to Ann Eisenberg for sharing this letter with me.

128. Chris Hedges, "100,000 Serbs Take to Streets against Milosevic," *New York Times,* 26 November 1996; Chris Hedges, "In Serbian Leader's Home, Corruption is Corrosive," *New York Times,* 29 November 1996; Vladimir Arsenijevic, "Belgrade's Philosophers of Freedom," *New York Times,* 30 December 1996.

129. Belgrade Women's Lobby, "Women, Let's Whistle!" translated and reprinted in *Women Living under Muslim Laws* (Grabels, Montpellier, France) (spring 1997): 28.

130. Stasa Zajovic, Zorica Trifunovic, and Lino Veljak, "Report about the Protest in Serbia," *Women Living under Muslim Laws* (Grabels, Montpellier, France) (spring 1997): 24–27. Steve Crawshaw, "The Reign of Bitter Apathy," *New Statesman,* 7 November 1997, 26–27.

131. Jane Perlez, "Many Serbs Would Just Rather Not Fight to Keep Kosovo," *New York Times,* 12 March 1998.

132. Stasa Zajovic, "Report on the Current Situation at Kosovo, Serbia, and Montenegro," *Compilation of Information—Women Living under Muslim Laws* (winter 1998): 1–5; Women in Black, "Prevent War in Kosovo," *Compilation of Information—Women Living under Muslim Laws* (winter 1998): 18; Chris Hedges, "Kosovo: Yet Another Act in the Balkan Tragedy," *New York Times,* 30 April 1998. For an analysis of the politics of Kosovo, see Julie Mertus, *Kosovo: How Myths and Truths Started a War* (Berkeley: University of California Press, 1999).

133. Autonomous Women's Groups in Belgrade, Women in Black against War, Autonomous Women's Center against Sexual Violence, Feminist Publishers 94, Center for Women's Studies, Belgrade Women's Lobby, "War in Kosovo—The Logics of Patriarchy," in *Compilation of Information—Women Living under Muslim Laws* (spring-summer-fall 1998): 7–8.

134. Sonia E. Alvarez, "The (Trans)formation of Feminism(s) and Gender Politics in Democratizing Brazil," in Jaquette, *Women's Movement in Latin America,* 13–64; Maria del Carmen Feijoo with Marcela Maria Alejandra Nari, "Women and Democracy in Argentina," in Jaquette, *Women's Movement in Latin America,* 109–31; Jo Fisher, *Out of the Shadows: Women, Resistance, and Politics in South America* (London: Latin America Bureau, 1993); Regina Rodriguez, Ximena Bunster, and Cynthia Enloe, eds., *La Mujer Ausente: Derechos Humanos en el Mundo,* 2d ed. (Santiago: Isis International, 1997).

CHAPTER 5

1. I have gained an appreciation for Jane Austen's worldly awareness and artistic choices from conversations with two specialists in British women novelists: Serena Hilsinger of Clark University, and Ruth Perry of M.I.T.: conversations with the author, 1995–96.

2. Jane Austen's *Pride and Prejudice* was published in 1813. It is through the eyes of her heroine, Elizabeth Bennet, that Austen reveals the dubiousness of the appeal of the army officers, such objects of fascination to Elizabeth's sisters when they arrive on leave into their small village. Jane Austen, *Pride and Prejudice* (New York: Penguin Books, 1985).

3. Jane Austen, *Persuasion* (New York: Bantam Books, 1984), 86.

4. Ibid., 61.

5. General Sir John Adye in a confidential report to the British Secretary for War, 1881, quoted in Myna Trustram, "Marriage and the Victorian Army at Home: the Regulation of Soldiers' Relationships with Women and the Treatment of Soldiers' Wives" (Ph.D. diss., Department of Social Administration, University of Bristol, July 1981), 63. The book to which this dissertation led is Myna Trustram, *Women of the Regiment: Marriage and the Victorian Army* (Cambridge: Cambridge University Press, 1984).

6. For a fresh look at the long historical twists and turns in Western societies' rationales for, and rules to control, heterosexualized marriage, see E. J. Graff, *What Is Marriage For?* (Boston: Beacon Press, 1999).

7. Augustus Stafford, quoted by Trustram, "Marriage and the Victorian Army at Home," 332.

8. This condition was exposed as an especially significant factor obstructing military wives' identification with the women's movement in the mid-1970s. See Lynne R. Dobrofsky and Constance T. Batterson, "The Military Wife and Feminism," *Signs* 2, no. 3 (spring 1977): 675–84. Researching an earlier version for this chapter on military wives prompted me thereafter to start investigating the complicated lives of diplomatic wives in order to see what light those complications would shed on the processes of foreign policy making. Findings from that investigation are published in "Diplomatic Wives," Chapter 5 of Cynthia Enloe, *Bananas, Beaches, and Bases: Making Feminist Sense of International Politics* (Berkeley: University of California Press, 1990), 93–123.

9. Deborah Harrison and Lucie Laliberte, *No Life Like It: Military Wives in Canada* (Toronto: James Lorimer and Company, 1994), 52–53.

10. Minnyetta Marie Boone, "P.M.S.: Patriarchal Militarized Society" (unpublished paper, Clark University, Worcester, Mass., 1995). This paper was based on Minnyetta Marie Boone's interview with her own mother, whose husband was in the U.S. Army during the mid-1970s and 1980s.

11. Eric Schmitt, "Marriage and Fighting Go Together," *New York Times*, 19 December 1993.

12. Trustram, "Marriage and the Victorian Army at Home."

13. Eighteenth-century British recruiting patter quoted in Roy Palmer, ed., *The Rambling Soldier* (Harmondsworth: Penguin, 1977), 9. See also Trustram, *Women of the Regiment*.

14. Trustram, "Marriage and the Victorian Army at Home," 41.

15. Ibid., 53.

16. Ibid., 356.

17. Conversation with Shauna Whitworth, research director of the Military Family Resource Center in Springfield, Virginia, March 1982. At that time the

center was a nongovernmental but Defense Department–funded agency specializing in issues concerning U.S. military wives and children. In the mid-1980s, the center was incorporated into the Defense Department. Thus its newsletter, *Military Family,* should no longer be read as an even quasi-independent publication.

18. Kathleen Furukawa and Shauna Whitworth, "American Military Families: Basic Demographics" (Springfield, Va.: Military Family Support Center YMCA, 1984), 20. This is the same center that has since been absorbed—along with its publications and archives—into the U.S. Defense Department.

19. Ibid., 19.

20. Military Family Demographics, "Profile of the Military Family" (Arlington, Va.: Personnel Support, Families, and Education Office of Family Policy, Military Family Resource Center, December 1995), 19.

21. Ibid., 16.

22. Doreen M. Lehr, "Madwoman in the Military's Attic: Mental Health and Defense Department Policy in the Lives of U.S. Air Force Wives" (Ph.D. diss., Union Institute, Cincinnati, Ohio, 1993), 89. See also Laurie Weinstein and Christie White, eds., *Wives and Warriors* (Westport, Conn.: Greenwood Publishers, 1996). Two doctoral dissertations that investigate Defense Department policies toward military wives and families as well as the wives' reactions to those policies are Donna Alvah, " 'Unofficial Ambassadors': American Military Families Overseas Cold War Foreign Relations 1945–1962" (Ph.D. diss., Department of History, University of California, Santa Barbara, 2000); and Daniela Brancaforte, "Identities in Camouflage: An Ethnography of U.S. Army Wives" (Ph.D. diss., Department of Anthropology, Princeton University, 1999).

23. Lehr, "Madwoman in the Military's Attic," 89.

24. See, for example, Ann Crossly and Carol Keller, *The Army Wife Handbook* (Sarasota, Fla.: ABI Publishers, 1994).

25. A new study of French women whose husbands were captured by the Germans during World War II has found that the wives of prisoners of war who struggled to sustain their household during the difficult war years did not, to the author's surprise, end the war with a greater appreciation of their own autonomy and skills equal to any man's. Rather, according to historian Sarah Fishman, most of these women seemed quite happy to restore their husbands to the patriarchal head of household role when they returned in 1944 and 1945. See Sarah Fishman, *We Will Wait: Wives of French Prisoners of War, 1940–1945* (New Haven: Yale University Press, 1991), 167.

26. Particularly striking is the militarized devotion of wives of the now-aging American pilots who dropped, and those trained to drop, two atomic bombs on Japan in 1945. These women have not only provided for forty years individual moral support to their own husbands at a time when the latter's actions have come under less favorable scrutiny, they also take active part in the Ladies Auxiliary, a side car to the Veterans of the U.S. Army Air Force 509th Composite Group, the organization formed by their husbands. This story is sensitively spelled out in Kristen M. Kazokas, "The Lasting Effects: The Military Influence Has Played in the Life of Mary Godfrey" (Worcester, Mass.: Clark University, unpublished typescript, 1995).

27. We know remarkably little about the experiences and thoughts of women married to senior military officers in countries in which the military has extraordinary access to business opportunities. One of the few researchers to raise this question is Chilean anthropologist Ximena Bunster in her "Mobilization and Demobilization of Women in Militarized Chile," in *Women and the Military System,* ed. Eva Isaksson (New York: St. Martins Press, 1988), 210–24. Also, a tantalizing mere hint is contained in a study of the changing class system of Taiwan. Under the 1949–1987 political system, a member of the military officer corps was considered a member of the middle class; since the success of the democratizing process in the 1980s and 1990s, marrying a man pursuing a military career is no longer deemed the surest way for a woman to improve her class status via marriage. See J.J. Chu, "Taiwan: A Fragmented 'Middle Class' in the Making," in *The New Rich in Asia,* ed. Richard Robison and David S.G. Goodman (New York: Routledge, 1996), 207–24.

28. Robert Lowry, *The Armed Force of Indonesia* (Sydney: Allen and Unwin, 1996), 128.

29. Mark Landler, "Unrest Deepens in Indonesia, But Suharto Offers Defiance," *New York Times,* 10 May 1998.

30. John McBeth, "The Line of Fire: Army's Choice Is between Suharto and Saving the Country," *Far Eastern Economic Review,* 21 May 1998, 20–22.

31. *Morning Edition,* National Public Radio, 25 May 1998.

32. I am grateful to Maria S. Stevens, an Indonesian feminist researcher, for first alerting me to the efforts of Suharto to co-opt senior civil service and military male officials by organizing their wives.

33. An analysis of the early years of the SSAFA is contained in Trustram, "Marriage and the Victorian Army at Home," 326–38.

34. Conversation with Hilary Land and Miriam David, Department of Social Administration, University of Bristol, May 1982. When I visited the National Institute of Social Work in London in May 1982—in the midst of the Falklands War, when the press and television were filled with stories about military wives and children—the staff told me that the Institute had virtually no connection with the military or with the few social workers inside the Ministry of Defence. One staff member, however, did wonder aloud whether the Falklands War would result in new official interest in expanding military social work.

35. John Draper, "Clients in Uniform," *Community Care,* 29 March 1979, 27.

36. Ibid., 27–28.

37. Mary Wilson, "Housing Hope Offered to Redundant Soldiers," *The Independent on Sunday* (London), 28 Februrary 1993.

38. Military Family Demographics, "Profile of the Military Family," 30.

39. Alana Blatt, untitled profile of a woman who grew up in the 1980s and early 1990s as the daughter of a U.S. Army officer (Clark University, Worcester, Mass., typescript, 1995).

40. The newsletter *Military Family* is published monthly by the Military Family Resource Center, U.S. Defense Department, Washington, D.C.

41. *New York Times,* 31 July 1982.

42. Ellen Herman, *The Romance of American Psychology: Political Culture in the Age of Experts* (Berkeley: University of California, 1995). A very interesting description of the limits imposed on a social or medical professional working inside the military is Arlene Kaplan Daniels's analysis of the conflicting roles of the U.S. military psychiatrist, a professional who works mostly with soldiers, not their families. Arlene Kaplan Daniels, "The Social Construction of Military Psychiatric Diagnoses," in Hans Peter Dreitzel, ed., *Recent Sociology,* no.2 (1970): 182–205; Polly Toynbee, " 'Yes,' Says the Psychiatrist, 'We Indoctrinate Them in the Forces. Otherwise They Wouldn't Fight,' " *The Guardian,* November 1982. This interview describes British military psychiatrists' roles in the Falklands War.

43. Eric Schmitt, "Stress Follows Troops Home from Gulf," *New York Times,* 16 July 1991.

44. Ibid. See also Julian Ford et al., "Psychological Debriefing after Operation Desert Storm: Marital and Family Assessment and Intervention," *Journal of Social Issues* 49 (winter 1993), 47–58.

45. I tried to think about the gendered politics of the yellow ribbon while the Gulf War was still fresh. These preliminary thoughts are contained in Cynthia Enloe, "The Gendered Gulf: A Diary," *The Morning After: Sexual Politics at the End of the Cold War* (Berkeley: University of California Press, 1993), 161–200.

46. Nina Browne, "Women and the War Show: T.V.'s Gendered Construction of the Homefront," in *Feminism, Nationalism, and Militarism,* ed. Constance R. Sutton (Arlington, Va.: Association of Feminist Anthropology of the American Anthropological Association, 1995), 59.

47. Eric Schmitt, "Victorious in War, Not Yet in Peace," *New York Times,* 29 May 1995.

48. Chris Black, "U.S. Soldiers Battle to Preserve Family Life," *Boston Globe,* 10 January 1995.

49. Ibid.

50. Ibid.

51. My conversations with Carolyn Becraft from1985 to 1995.

52. "Housing and Housing Allowances," *Military Family* (August 1995): 12. The article also noted that 74 percent of unmarried U.S. military personnel lived in government-provided housing.

53. "Task Force Finds Most Military Housing Poor," *The State* (Columbia, S.C.), 20 October 1995.

54. Mady Wechsler Segal and Jesse J. Harris, *What We Know about Army Families* (Alexandria, Va.: U.S. Army Research Institute for the Behavioral and Social Sciences, 1993), 17.

55. Ibid.

56. Ibid., 17–19.

57. Eric Schmitt, "Military Puts Bosnia on the Web," *New York Times,* 17 December 1995.

58. Alan Cowell, "Army Children Express Their Doubts," *New York Times,* 2 December 1995.

59. Ibid.

60. Stephen Kinzer, "The G.I. Families in Germany Soldier On," *New York Times*, 26 December 1995.

61. Ian Fisher, "Calls Home from Bosnia Can Shell a G.I.'s Wallet," *New York Times*, 19 August 1996.

62. Ian Fisher, "Encircled by Peril, G.I.'s Stay Nonchalant," *New York Times*, 13 January 1996.

63. Ian Fisher, "To U.S. Troops in Bosnia, Home Looks Closer," *New York Times*, 11 August 1996.

64. Ibid.

65. For more on U.S. and Canadian military policy makers' efforts to resolve the contradictions in military marriages and military wives' own responses to those efforts, see three chapters in *Wives and Warriors: Women and the Military in the U.S. and Canada*, ed. Laurie Weinstein and Christie White (Westport, Conn.: Greenwood Press, 1997): Laurie Weinstein and Helen Mederer, "Blue Navy Blues: Submarine Officers and the Two-Person Career," 7–18; Barbara Marriott, "The Social Networks of Naval Officers' Wives," 19–34; and Deborah Harrison and Lucie Laliberte, "Gender, the Military, and Military Family Support," 35–54.

66. Mike O'Connor, "A Downsized Army Leans on Reserves for Duty in Bosnia," *New York Times*, 25 May 1998.

67. Philip Shenon, "Top Guns Quitting for Life at Cruising Altitude," *New York Times*, 22 October 1997.

68. Ibid.

69. Ibid.

70. See for instance, Edna Jo Hunter et al., *Military Wife Adjustment: An Independent Dependent* (San Diego, Calif.: Office of Naval Research, 1981); and Edna Jo Hunter and Melissa Pope, *Family Roles in Transition* (San Diego, Calif.: Office of Naval Reseach, 1981).

71. "Momentum Increased in Spouse Employment Programs," *Military Family* (winter 1996): 8.

72. Stephen Kinzer, "Bitter Goodbye: Russians Leave Germany," *New York Times*, 4 March 1994; Stephen Kinzer, "Russian Troops Bid 'Wiedersehen' to Germany," *New York Times*, 1 September 1994.

73. Jane O'Hara, "Fighting Mad," *Maclean's*, 13 April 1998, 14–19.

74. Jane O'Hara, "Rape in the Military," *Maclean's*, 25 May 1998, 15–24.

75. These figures come from a 1992 joint study conducted by the U.S. Departments of Defense and Agriculture, reported in Eric Schmitt, "As Military Pay Slips Behind, Poverty Invades the Ranks," *New York Times*, 12 June 1994.

76. Schmitt, "Poverty Invades the Ranks."

77. Ibid.

78. Eric Schmitt, "School Lunch Bill Leaves Out Military Children," *New York Times*, 9 March 1995.

79. Another plank in the U.S. Republican platform has been opposition to federal support for abortion. During 1995 and 1996, the chair of the Republican-controlled House armed services committee supported legislation that

would make it illegal for overseas military hospitals to provide abortion services to women members of the military and military wives. Abortions already
had been banned in U.S.-located military hospitals. Generally, the Senate was
more supportive of continuing abortion services at overseas hospitals; many
senators had been persuaded by Senators Patty Murray and Edward Kennedy
that it was unfair to compel women stationed abroad to seek abortion procedures in what the two described as often unsafe local facilities. Most of the il-
lustrations used in the congressional debates were of women in the military;
the needs and experiences of military wives were rarely mentioned. See "Senate
Votes for a Repeal of Ban on Some Abortions: Allow Them in Military Hospitals Abroad," *New York Times,* 20 June 1996. See also Jerry Gray, "Emotions
High, House Takes on Abortion: Bill to Bar Procedure at Military Hospitals
Overseas Is Approved," *New York Times,* 16 June 1995.

80. Ellwyn R. Stoddard, "Married Female Officers in a Combat Branch:
Occupation-Family Stress and Future Career Choices," *Minerva: Quarterly
Report on Women and the Military* 12, no. 2 (summer 1994): 1–14.

81. Franklin Pinch, "Military Manpower and Social Change," *Armed
Forces and Society* 8, no. 4 (summer 1982): 584. Some military officials define
many of these "soldier-to-soldier" marriages as marriages of convenience, performed only to acquire certain married soldiers' benefits, such as getting out of
the barracks; once off-base, the two soldiers don't even live with each other.
See *Youth Policy* 3, no. 10 (October 1981): 67–69.

82. Military Family Demographics, "Profile of the Military Family," 18.

83. For my own early efforts to explore the racial and ethnic designing of
militaries, see Cynthia Enloe, *Ethnic Soldiers: State Security in Divided Societies* (London: Penguin Books, 1980).

84. Ibid., 49. A revealing investigation of Britain's gendered and racialized
policy making regarding the wives of its prized Gurkha soldiers is Seira
Tamang, "Nepali Women as Military Wives" (unpublished honors thesis, Department of Government, Clark University, Worcester, Mass., 1992).

85. Military Family Demographics, "Profile of the Military Family," 31.

86. Ibid., 34.

87. See, for example, Mary Leefe Laurence, *Daughter of the Regiment:
Memoirs of a Childhood in the Frontier Army, 1878–1898* (Lincoln: Univer-
sity of Nebraska Press, 1996); Mary Wertsch, *Military Brats: The Legacy of
Childhood inside the Fortress* (New York: Crown Books, 1991); William Jay
Smith, *Army Brat* (New York: Penguin Books, 1982); and James Carroll, *An
American Requiem: God, My Father, and the War That Came between Us*
(New York: Houghton Mifflin, 1996).

88. Charlayne Hunter-Gault, *In My Place* (New York: Vintage Books,
1992), 94.

89. Claire Cummings, "'Georgie'—A Feminist Interviewer Looks at Class
and Race in an Analysis of Women and Militarization," (Clark University,
Worcester, Mass., unpublished typescript, 1995). See also Sidney Werkman
and Peter Jensen, "Resolved: Military Family Life Is Hazardous to the Mental
Health of Children," *Journal of the American Academy of Child Adolescent
Psychiatry* 31, no. 5 (September 1992): 980–95.

90. Heide Fehrenbach (of Colgate University), "Mixed Blood 'Discourses of Race,' Sex and German Democratization" (paper presented at the Berkshire Conference on Women's History, University of North Carolina, Chapel Hill, 8 June 1996). A study of the racial politics of U.S. troops in wartime Britain is Graham Smith, *When Jim Crow Met John Bull: Black American Soldiers in World War II Britain* (New York: St. Martin's Press, 1988).

91. Maria Hoehn (of the University of Pennsylvania), "Amazonen, Veronikas, and Negerliebchen" (paper presented at the Berkshire Conference on Women's History, University of North Carolina, Chapel Hill, 8 June 1996). The observation about the perceived modernity of black soldiers was made at this same conference session by historian Rebecca Boehling, derived from her own research into the sexual politics of late-1940s Germany. See also Robert G. Moeller, *Protecting Motherhood: Women and the Family in the Politics of Postwar West Germany* (Berkeley: University of California Press, 1993).

92. John Willoughby, "The Sexual Behavior of American GIs during the Early Years of the Occupation of Germany," *The Journal of Military History,* no. 62 (January 1998): 155–74.

93. A rarely discussed book by Gertrude Stein, based on her and Alice B. Toklas's own conversations with American male soldiers in postwar France, captures some of these men's hopes, worries, and fantasies about dating local women and about the sorts of marriages awaiting them back home. See Gertrude Stein, *Brewsie and Willie* (New York: Random House, 1946). I am indebted to Julie Abraham of Emory University for bringing this surprising book to my attention.

94. Uma Narayan, "'Male-Order' Brides: Immigrant Women, Domestic Violence, and Immigration Law," *Hypatia* 10, no. 1 (winter 1995): 106.

95. Bok-Lim C. Kim, Amy Izuno Okamura, Naomi Ozawa, and Virginia Forrest, "Women in the Shadows: A Handbook for Service Providers Working with Asian Wives of U.S. Military Personnel" (National Committee Concerned with Asian Wives of U.S. Servicemen, La Jolla, Calif., 1982), 15.

96. The coalition first made its headquarters in La Jolla, California. See also Narayan, "'Male-Order' Brides." See also a documentary film following the experiences of several Korean women who immigrate to the United States as wives of American soldiers: *The Women Outside* (New York: Third World Newsreel, 1996).

97. Quoted in Bok-Lim C. Kim et al., "Women in the Shadows," 53.

98. Doreen M. Lehr, "The Madwoman in the Military's Attic," 89.

99. Eric Schmitt, "Military Struggling to Stem an Increase in Family Violence," *New York Times,* 23 May 1994.

100. Ibid.

101. Ibid.

102. William Duke, quoted in Ibid.

103. This information is based on a report by National Public Radio's Defense Department specialist, Martha Radditz, on *Morning Edition,* National Public Radio, 23 October 1997.

104. "Family Policy Directorate Addresses Needs of Military Families," *Military Family* (spring 1996): 3.

105. Harrison and Laliberte, *No Life Like It,* 187. Deborah Harrison has become the director of the Muriel McQueen Ferguson Centre for Family Violence Research at the University of New Brunswick in Fredericton, Canada. Precisely because one of Canada's largest military bases is located in New Brunswick, the Centre has made the study of military family domestic violence one of its principal projects. In 1996, a coalition of African women's advocates sent out an international "Alert for Action" provoked by a similar militarized context for judging the worthiness of a military wife's charges of violence. The two organizations, the Women and Law Project of Senegal and the Legal Information Centre of the African Network for Integrated Development, claimed that the charges brought by the wife of a Senegalese senior officer were being dismissed by Senegalese authorities chiefly because the government wanted to avoid any public humiliation of a military officer; that is, the well-being of the military was to be the standard against which any woman's charge would be measured. "Alert for Action," Women Living under Muslim Laws, Grabels, France, 25 July 1996. WLUML regularly serves as an international distributor of requests for civil action by women's groups.

106. "Widows Complain of Treatment," *Sydney Morning Herald,* 19 October 1993.

107. Joni Seager, "The Vote," *The State of Women in the World: An International Atlas* (New York: Penguin Books, 1997). The very first Canadian women to win the vote, earlier in 1917, were women serving in the Canadian military as nurses. For more on the Italian fascists' sometimes quite intriguingly ambiguous policies directed at women, see Victoria DeGrazia, *How Fascism Ruled Women: Italy, 1922–1945* (Berkeley: University of California, 1992).

108. *New York Times,* 13 August 1982.

109. "Falklands Fund: Inequality Even in Death," *The Economist,* 7 August 1982. Myna Trustram discusses the variations in Britain philanthropic outpouring that accompanied different wars in "Marriage and the British Victorian Army at Home," 311.

110. I am grateful to Boston science journalist Madeleine Drexler for this information. Among the newsletters published by women is *The Veteran's Voice,* ed. Gina Whitcomb, published by the Desert Storm Justice Foundation, Oklahoma City, Okla.

111. EXPOSE newsletter, February 1982.

112. Ibid.

113. Member of EXPOSE in conversation with the author, 15 March 1982. In July 1982, the U.S. House of Representatives passed the Uniformed Services Former Spouses' Protection Act, which returned to the state courts the question of divorce and military benefits. Congressional Representative Patricia Schroeder, a key supporter of the bill, had been in close communication with the women from EXPOSE. See *New York Times,* 29 July 1982.

114. Member of EXPOSE, conversation with the author, 15 March 1982.

115. Carolyn Becraft, then-director of the Women and the Military Project of the Women's Equity Action League, testimony before the House of Repre-

sentatives Armed Services Subcommittee on Military Personnel and Compensation, Washington, D.C., 1 October 1987; *New York Times,* 20 March 1988.

116. I am grateful to Lucie Laliberte, herself a military wife and one of OS-SOMM's founders, for details about the organization's beginning and its subsequent actions. See also Harrison and Laliberte, *No Life Like It,* 233–40.

117. Lynne Gouliquer, "The Needs and Issues of Military Wives: A Case Study of a Grassroots Struggle and the State," (honors thesis, Department of Sociology, St. Thomas University, Fredericton, New Brunswick, 1995).

118. Theda Skocpol, "America's First Social Security System: The Expansion of Benefits for Civil War Veterans," in her book *Social Policy in the United States* (Princeton: Princeton University Press, 1995), 72–135. See also Theda Skocpol, *Protecting Soldiers and Mothers: The Political Origins of Social Policy in the United States* (Cambridge: Harvard University Press, 1993).

119. A good discussion of the historical evolution of this dilemma in Britain is Elizabeth Wilson, *Women and the Welfare State* (New York and London: Tavistock, 1977). See also Anna Coote and Beatrix Campbell, *Sweet Freedom* (London: Picador, 1982); and Zoe Fairbairns's novel, *Benefits* (London: Virago, 1979). A valuable cross-national exploration of the benefits and traps offered to women by state welfare programs is Linda Gordon, ed., *Women, the State, and Welfare* (Madison: University of Wisconsin Press, 1990).

120. Tony Parker, *Soldier, Soldier* (London: Coronet, 1987), 240.

121. Doreen Lehr, "Do Real Women Wear Uniforms? Invisibility and the Consequences for the U.S. Military Wife" (paper presented at the International Studies Association annual meeting, Chicago, February 1995), 3. See also Doreen Lehr, "Military Wives: Breaking the Silence," in *Gender Camouflage: Women and the U.S. Military,* ed. Francine D'Amico and Laurie Weinstein (New York: New York University Press, 1999).

CHAPTER 6

1. For a new cross-national history of nursing, a history that starts from the idea that nursing is political, see Anne Marie Rafferty, Jane Robinson, and Ruth Elkan, eds., *Nursing History and the Politics of Welfare* (London: Routledge, 1996).

2. A detailed and often surprising study of British nursing leaders' efforts to maximize nurses' militarization during World War II—and the postwar ramifications of their efforts—is Pam Starns, "Military Influence on British Civilian Nursing" (Ph.D diss., Department of History, University of Bristol, Bristol, U.K., 1997). See also Pam Starns, "Fighting Militarism? British Nursing during the Second World War," in *War, Medicine, and Modernity, 1860–1945,* ed. Roger Cooter et al. (London: Sutton Publishing Co., 1999).

3. Burton Hacker, "Women and Military Institutions in Early Modern Europe: A Reconnaissance," *Signs* 6, no. 4 (summer 1981): 657.

4. Ibid., 662.

5. For a historical analysis of the gendered class dynamics shaping nineteenth-century British nursing, see Anne Summers, *Angels and Citizens:*

British Women as Military Nurses 1854–1914 (New York: Routledge & Kegan Paul, 1988).

6. For an interpretation of the diary that Florence Nightingale kept while she traveled abroad, see Michael D. Calabria, *Florence Nightingale in Egypt and Greece: Her Diary and 'Visions'* (Albany: State University of New York Press, 1995).

7. Lytton Strachey, *Florence Nightingale* (New York: Penguin Books, 1997), 11. Strachey first published his profile of Nightingale in 1918 as part of his collection titled *Emminent Victorians,* a book that remains in print.

8. Eva Gamarnikow, "Sexual Division of Labour: The Case of Nursing," in *Feminism and Materialism,* ed. Annette Kuhn and Ann Maria Wolpe (London and Boston: Routledge & Kegan Paul, 1978). See also Celia Davis, ed., *Rewriting Nursing History* (London: Croom Helm, 1980).

9. Excerpts from Mary Seacole, *The Wonderful Adventures of Mrs. Seacole in Many Lands* (1857), reprinted in Margaret Busby, ed., *Daughters of Africa* (New York: Pantheon, 1992), 55.

10. Ibid., 57. For the complete Seacole autobiography, see Ziggie Alexander and Audrey Dewjee, eds., *The Wonderful Adventures of Mary Seacole* (Bristol, U.K.: Falling Wall Press, 1984).

11. Strachey, *Florence Nightingale,* 16–17.

12. A selection of Florence Nightingale's dispatches from the Crimea are included in Eva Figes, ed., *Women's Letters in Wartime, 1460–1945* (London: Pandora Press, 1995).

13. Strachey, *Florence Nightingale,* 35.

14. Ibid.

15. Ibid.

16. Contemporary account by one of the nurses recruited to work with Nightingale in the Crimea, quoted in "Capabilities and Disabilities of Women," *Westminister Review,* January 1909, 31–32.

17. I am grateful to Tim LeDeux of Clark University for his insights derived from his honors thesis research into the debates surrounding the launching of the International Red Cross.

18. This account is drawn from Richard Stites's history of Russian feminism in the nineteenth and early twentieth centuries. See Stites, *The Women's Liberation Movement in Russia* (Princeton: Princeton University Press 1978).

19. Quoted by Stites, *Women's Liberation Movement in Russia,* 30.

20. Lawrence James, *Crimea 1854–56* (London: Hayes Kennedy, 1981), 126.

21. The development of the French military use of women is described by French military sociologist Michael Martin in *Armed Forces and Society* 8, no. 2 (winter 1982).

22. Myna Trustram, *Women of the Regiment: Marriage and the Victorian Army* (Cambridge: Cambridge University Press, 1984).

23. For a feminist analysis of this evolution of British military nursing through the Boer War and World War I, see Summers, *Angels and Citizens.*

24. Louisa May Alcott, "Obtaining Supplies," the first of the short stories collected in Alcott's *Hospital Sketches* (New York: Sagamore Press, 1957;

originally published in 1863), 22. See also Madeleine B. Stern, ed., *The Feminist Alcott: Stories of a Woman's Power* (Boston: Northeastern University Press, 1996).

25. Gerda Lerner, *The Female Experience: An American Documentary* (Indianapolis, Ind.: Bobbs-Merrill, 1977), 180.

26. Elizabeth D. Leonard, *Yankee Women: Gender Battles in the Civil War* (New York: W. W. Norton, 1994), 14. See also Catherine Clinton and Nina Silber, eds., *Divided Houses: Gender and the Civil War* (New York: Oxford University Press, 1992); and John Brumgardt, ed., *Civil War Nurse: The Diary and Letters of Hannah Ropes* (Knoxville, Tenn.: University of Tennessee Press, 1982).

27. Leonard, *Yankee Women*, 15. Clara Barton, as famous for her Civil War nursing as Dorothea Dix was, chose to work without official government sanction so as to maintain more independence. Barton is credited with founding the American Red Cross. She first attracted public notice when she went to the battlefield at Antietam to nurse wounded soldiers while the fighting still raged. See Stephen B. Oates, *A Woman of Valor: Clara Barton and the Civil War* (New York: The Free Press, 1995). The National Museum of Civil War Medicine is planning to create in Frederick, Maryland, a museum commemorating the Battle of Antietam. Clara Barton's role is to be depicted in the new museum.

28. "Old Records Reveal Clara Barton's Role as Sleuth," *New York Times*, 2 December 1997. See also Oates, *A Woman of Valor.*

29. Leonard, *Yankee Women*, 43.

30. Mary Elizabeth Massey, *Women in the Civil War* (Lincoln: University of Nebraska Press, 1995), 45–46. See also Elizabeth D. Leonard, *All the Daring of the Soldier: Women of the Civil War Armies* (New York: W. W. Norton, 1999).

31. For more on the gender politics that shaped each side's war waging and postwar reconstruction, see LeeAnn Whites, *The Civil War as a Crisis in Gender: Augusta, Georgia, 1860–1890* (Athens: University of Georgia Press, 1995); Drew Gilpin Faust, *Mothers of Invention: Women of the Slaveholding South in the American Civil War* (Chapel Hill: University of North Carolina Press, 1996); Marilyn Mayer Culpepper, *Trials and Tribulations: The Women of the American Civil War* (Ann Arbor: University of Michigan Press, 1994); and Jane E. Schultz, "Race, Gender, and Bureaucracy: Civil War Army Nurses and the Pension Bureau," *Journal of Women's History* 6, no. 2 (summer 1994): 44–69.

32. Noralee Frankel, "The Southern Side of 'Glory': Mississippi African-American Women during the Civil War," in *"We Specialize in the Wholly Impossible": A Reader in Black Women's History,* ed. Darlene Clark Hine, Wilma King, and Linda Reed (New York: Carlson Publishing, 1995), 335–41.

33. For an insightful analysis of public reaction to African American men's soldiering in Cuba, see Amy Kaplan, "Black and Blue on San Juan Hill," in *Cultures of United States Imperialism,* ed. Amy Kaplan and Donald E. Pease (Durham, N.C.: Duke University Press, 1993), 219–37.

34. Linda Rochelle Lane, "The Military," in *Black Women in America: An Historical Encyclopedia*, vol. 2, ed. Darlene Clark Hine, Elsa Barkley Brown, and Rosalyn Terborg-Penn (Bloomington: Indiana University Press, 1993), 793.

35. Connie L. Reeves, "The Military Woman's Vanguard: Nurses," in *It's Our Military Too! Women and the U.S. Military*, ed. Judith Hicks Stiehm (Philadelphia: Temple University Press, 1996), 89.

36. Quoted in a paper presented by Margaret Scobey and Philip Kalish to the Inter-University Seminar on Armed Forces and Society, a meeting ground of academic social scientists and military personnel specialists in the United States and other NATO countries, Chicago, Illinois, October 1980.

37. For instance, see Joan I. Roberts and Thetis M. Group, eds., *Feminism and Nursing: An Historical Perspective of Power, Status, and Political Activism* (Westport, Conn.: Greenwood Publishing Group, 1996).

38. Darlene Clark Hine, "Nursing, World War I," in Hine, Brown, and Terborg-Penn, *Black Women in America*, 891.

39. Ibid., 892.

40. Reeves, "The Military Woman's Vanguard: Nurses," 98.

41. Summers, *Angels and Citizens*, 181.

42. Ibid.

43. Katie Holmes, "Day Mothers and Night Sisters: World War I Nurses and Sexuality," in *Gender and War: Australians at War in the Twentieth Century*, ed. Joy Damousi and Marilyn Lake (Cambridge: Cambridge University Press, 1995), 45–46.

44. Joni Seager, *The State of Women in the World: An International Atlas* (New York: Penguin Books, 1997), 124.

45. Regina Schulte, "The Sick Warrior's Sister: Nursing during the First World War," trans. Pamela Selwyn, in *Gender Relations in German History*, ed. Lynn Abrams and Elizabeth Harvey (Durham, N.C.: Duke University Press, 1997), 126–27.

46. Quoted by Schulte, "The Sick Warrior's Sister," 127.

47. Ibid.

48. British novelist Pat Barker's award-winning trilogy provides an unusual look into the psychological toll that this sort of war took on British soldiers and into the emergence of a medical professional response to what came to be known as shell shock: Pat Barker, *Regeneration* (New York: Penguin Books, 1991); *The Eye in the Door* (New York: Dutton, 1994); and *The Ghost Road* (New York: Dutton, 1995).

49. Quoted by Sharon Ouditt, *Fighting Forces, Writing Women: Identity and Ideology in the First World War* (New York: Routledge, 1994), 21. For more on Vera Brittain, see Deborah Gorham, *Vera Brittain: A Feminist Life* (Cambridge, Mass.: Blackwell, 1996). Vera Brittain's own account is in Vera Brittain, *Testament of Youth* (originally published in 1933; reissued in Britain by Virago, 1978, and in the United States by Westview Books, 1980).

50. A. J. P. Taylor, *English History, 1914–1945* (New York: Oxford University Press, 1965), 61. See also Jay Winter and Blaine Bagget, *The Great War and the Shaping of the 20th Century* (New York: Penguin Books, 1996), 178–95. Winter and Bagget conclude that "for the British the first day of the

Somme was eight times more expensive in human life than was Waterloo ... More than chivalry was lost on the battlefields of the Somme. The first
day of July was a cultural shock from which Britain, a society nurtured on economic mastery and naval strength, has never fully recovered" (p. 195).

51. Radclyffe Hall, "Miss Ogilvy Finds Herself," in *The Other Persuasion,*
ed. Seymour Kleinberg (New York: Vintage Books, 1977), 46. Hall's short
story was first published in Britain in 1926.

52. Ibid., 47.

53. Judy Yung, *Unbound Feet: A Social History of Chinese Women in San
Francisco* (Berkeley: University of California Press, 1995), 254.

54. Ibid., 253.

55. For American women nurses' own rememberances of their World War
II experiences, see Diane Burke Fessler, *No Time for Fear: Voices of American
Military Nurses in World War II* (Ann Arbor: University of Michigan Press,
1996).

56. Quoted by Darlene Clark Hine in her paper "Mabel Seaton Stater: The
Integration of Black Nurses into the Armed Forces, World War II" (presented
at the Berkshire Conference of Women Historians, Vassar College, June 1981),
9. See also Darlene Clark Hine, *Black Women in White: Racial Conflict and
Cooperation in the Nursing Profession* (Bloomington: Indiana University
Press, 1989).

57. For a political profile of Mabel K. Staupers, see Darlene Clark Hine,
"Mabel K. Staupers and the Integration of Black Nurses into the Armed Forces
during World War II," in *Hine Sight: Black Women and the Reconstruction of
American History* (Bloomington: Indiana University Press, 1994), 183–202.
For the original correspondence of the NACGN to government officials that
called for desegregation of military nursing, see *National Association of Colored Graduate Nurses Records, 1908–1951* (Wilmington, Del.: Scholarly Resources Publishers, 1995).

58. Darlene Clark Hine, "Nursing," in Hine, Brown, and Terborg-Penn,
Black Women in America, 890. For more on the evolution of African American nursing politics, see Stephanie J. Shaw, *What a Woman Ought to Be and
to Do: Black Professional Women Workers during the Jim Crow Era* (Chicago:
University of Chicago Press, 1996).

59. I have traced this ethnicized and racialist process as it has affected male
soldiers in Britain, the United States, the Soviet Union, South Africa, Iraq, Israel, Canada, and elsewhere in my *Ethnic Soldiers* (London: Penguin Books,
1980) and in *Police, Military, and Ethnicity* (New Brunswick: Transaction
Books, 1980).

60. Reina J. Pennington, "Offensive Women: Women in Combat in the Red
Army" (paper presented at the Berkshire Conference on Women and History,
Chapel Hill, N.C., June 1996), 7–8. This paper is due to be published in *The
Soldier's Experience of War, 1939–1945,* ed. Paul Addison and Angus Calder
(London: Pimlico Press, forthcoming). Pennington is completing a dissertation
on women in the Soviet Military in World War II for the Department of His-
tory, University of South Carolina, Columbia, S.C.

61. Pennington, "Offensive Women," 8.

62. Ibid., 7. Pennington draws this quotation from a collection of interviews with Soviet women veterans that was assembled and published in Moscow in the late 1980s during the period of perestroika, when more open public discussion of questionable historical interpretations became possible. That collection is Svetlana Alexiyevich, *War's Unwomanly Face* (Moscow: Progress Publishers, 1988).

63. Reeves, "The Military Woman's Vanguard: Nurses," 105–6.

64. Ibid., 104.

65. Patricia L. Walsh, *Forever Sad the Heart* (New York: Avon Books, 1982).

66. Ministry of Defence, London, 1981.

67. LaVonne Camp, "Letters: 50 Years of Remembering," *New York Times Book Review,* 4 June 1995, 7.

68. Ibid.

69. The data that follow are from a 1982 National Opinion Research Center General Social Survey entitled "Public Acceptance of Roles for Women in the Military" and are included in A. Wade Smith, "Public Attitudes," in *Who Defends America? Race, Sex, and Class in the Armed Forces,* ed. Edwin Dorn (Washington, D.C.: Joint Center for Political Studies Press, 1989), 129.

70. Rapid changes in military medical technology since the Second World War have made less tenable the myth that nurses work far from combat. In 1942, the U.S. Army created its first Mobile Army Surgical Hospital Unit. Out of this experiment came the famous MASH units, popularly known through reruns of the American television comedy series *MASH,* which is set in a medical unit in the South Korea war during the 1950s. The last MASH unit was decommissioned in Korea in June 1997. They would be replaced with the newest form of battlefield medical care. A formal decommissioning military ceremony was held, and actors from the television series were invited to attend. The line between a theater of war and an electronic screen had become blurred. *All Things Considered,* National Public Radio, 11 June 1997.

71. Karen G. Turner with Phan Thanh Hao, *Even the Women Must Fight: Memories of War from North Vietnam* (New York: John Wiley and Sons, 1998). I read this important book while it was still in manuscript form. The figures cited here, derived from Vietnamese historians' research, are contained early in Chapter 1.

72. The following description of Le Thi Than is derived from the English translation of a journalistic account that appeared in the Hanoi literary monthly *Van Nghe* in January 1997. The piece is by Minh Chuyen and entitled in English, "Go to the Pagoda, Meeting with …" The translation, in typescript, was done by Phan Thanh Hao.

73. Turner, *Even the Women Must Fight.* For more on women in many countries who have been combatants in guerrilla insurgent armies, see my *Does Khaki Become You? The Militarization of Women's Lives* (London: Pandora Press/HarperCollins, 1988).

74. Karen Turner, in conversation with the author, 5 June 1997. Turner is a professor of history at Holy Cross College, Worcester, Mass.

75. The book that first compelled American officials and the general public—and many military nurses—to confront the postwar traumas experienced by American military nurses as a result of their service in Vietnam is Lynda Van Devanter, *Home Before Morning: Story of an Army Nurse in Vietnam* (New York: Beaufort Books, 1983).

76. John O'Brien, "New VA Clinic Will Serve Women Veterans," *The Post-Standard* (Syracuse, N.Y.), 4 November 1995.

77. Ibid.

78. Ibid. For more on women's contracting PTSD because of experiences in the military—some of those experiences coming from sexist intimidation from their male colleagues—and for more on women veterans' efforts to make the VA take PTSD among women seriously, see Donna M. Dean, *Warriors without Weapons: The Victimization of Military Women* (Pasadena, Md.: Minerva Center, 1997).

79. For more on *China Beach*, see Sasha Torres, "War and Remembrance: Television Narrative, National Memory and 'China Beach'," *Camera Obscura*, nos. 33 and 34 (1996): 140–58.

80. The Vietnam Women's Memorial was promoted not only by American women who served as nurses but by women who served in other military posts in Vietnam as well. The Washington Mall women's monument, dedicated in 1993, was designed by scultor Glenna Goodacre. The monument project was supported by, funded by, and continues to be overseen by the Vietnam Women's Memorial Project, Inc. The Memorial is open to the public and can be viewed in Washington, D.C., near the more famous Vietnam Memorial Wall. The Vietnam Women's Memorial Project has its offices at #302, 2001 5th Street, Washington, D.C., 20009.

81. Lily Lee Adams told her story to author Kathryn Marshall. It provides one chapter for Marshall's book, *In the Combat Zone* (New York: Penguin Books, 1988), 206–30.

82. Adams quoted in Marshall, *In the Combat Zone*, 214–19.

83. Ibid., 221–22.

84. Karen Johnson, vice president of the National Organization for Women, described her Vietnam War experience and its long-term effects on her career, first in the U.S. Air Force and more recently as a civilian activist, at a conference at Cornell University, Ithaca, New York, 26–28 January 1996, and later in a Los Angeles public radio interview in 1996 in which we both participated. I am grateful to Professors Mary Katzenstein and Judith Reppy of Cornell University for organizing this valuable conference and its successors to explore the interaction of race and gender in the contemporary U.S. military. More information on their project can be obtained by contacting Katzenstein and Reppy at the Peace Studies Program, Cornell University, Ithaca, New York. For another dimension of Johnson's military experience, see Karen Johnson, "Autobiography: An Officer and a Feminist," in *Gender Camouflage: Women and the U.S. Military*, ed. Francine D'Amico and Laurie Weinstein (New York: New York University Press, 1999).

85. Johnson, presentation.

86. U.S. Department of Defense, "Occupational Profile of Active Duty Women in the Defense Department, Fiscal Year 1995" (Washington, D.C.: Defense Manpower Data Center, 30 September 1995).

87. Ibid. According to the same Defense Department data, 14.8 percent of all women military officers in mid-1995 were in administrative posts while 9.8 percent were in engineering and maintenance posts. Among all the women in enlisted ranks (that is, non-officers), 15.6 percent were in health care—military nurses are all ranked as officers—while 32.9 percent were in support and administrative roles.

88. Brenda L. Moore, "A Changing Military: Implications for the Future Role of Women" (paper presented at the conference entitled "Women in Uniform: Strategies for Success in Military, Police, and Fire Fighting Services," sponsored by the Women's Research and Education Institute, Washington, D.C., 10–11 December 1996), 7.

89. It is analytically risky to imagine patriarchy as fixed, unmalleable. Patriarchal systems, that is, have survived for so many generations not because they are rigid but because they are adaptable. For instance, new feminist research on women activists in Egypt reveals that while nursing was being so insistently feminized in patriarchal 1920s Europe, in Egypt, where Britain continued to station its imperial troops, nursing was a profession controlled by men, men who claimed that only male nurses could work closely with male physicians, only male nurses could work in intimate proximity to male patients. The only women nurses in Egypt in the 1910s and 1920s—decades of widespread Egyptian feminist militancy—were British women. In the imperial order of race and gender, these British women nurses could gain professional access where Egyptian women could not. This social order did not make international sisterhood among feminists easy. See Margot Badran, *Feminists, Islam, and Nation* (Princeton: Princeton University Press, 1995), 181.

CHAPTER 7

1. This chapter is the beneficiary of the editorial skills of Lois Brynes.

2. Judith Miller, "Selling the Government Like Soap; It Seems to Work," *New York Times*, 14 September 1997.

3. Stephen Kurkjan and Matthew Brelis, "Cohen Orders Safety Probe for Military," *Boston Globe*, 7 August 1997.

4. Miller, "Selling the Government Like Soap."

5. For a study of the British government's policies intended to manage the Nepali women married to their Gurkha soldiers, perhaps the sole feminist analysis of the Gurkhas, see Seira Tamang, "Nepali Women as Military Wives," (honors thesis, Department of Government, Clark University, Worcester, Mass., 1992). See also Lionel Caplan, *Warrior Gentlemen: "Gurkhas" in the Western Imagination* (Providence, R.I.: Berghahn Books, 1995). My own efforts to understand scores of governments' efforts to manipulate ethnic identities to fill their ranks is *Ethnic Soldiers* (London: Penguin Books, 1980). For more on the responses of ethnic communities to state military personnel policies, see Alison Berstein, *American Indians and World War II* (Norman:

Oklahoma University Press, 1991); Alison Berstein, "Military Service," in *Native America in the Twentieth Century,* ed. Mary B. Davis (New York: Garland Publishers, 1994), 341–43; James E. Westheider, *Fighting on Two Fronts: African Americans and the Vietnam War* (New York: New York University Press, 1997); and N. F. Dreisziger, ed., *Ethnic Armies: Polyethnic Armed Forces* (Waterloo, Ontario: Wilfred Laurier University Press, 1990). Recent studies of these community debates that are informed with more attention to gender include Brenda Moore, *To Serve My Country, To Serve My Race: The Story of the Only African American WACs Stationed Overseas during World War II* (New York: New York University Press, 1996); Claire M. Tylee, "Womanist Propaganda, African American Great War Experience, and Cultural Strategies of the Harlem Renaissance," *Women's Studies International Forum* 20, no. 1 (1997): 153–63. For an eye-opening account of the British military's confusion over when and how to use black West Indian women as volunteers during World War II, a political confusion that was generated in part by British diplomats' eagerness not to offend the segregationist sensibilities of their white American allies, see Ben Bousquet and Colin Douglas, *West Indian Women at War: British Racism in World War II* (London: Lawrence and Wishart, 1991). For more on the ways in which racism combined with sexism to shape World War II negotiations between the American and British allied forces, see Graham Smith, *When Jim Crow Met John Bull: Black American Soldiers in World War II Britain* (New York: St. Martin's Press, 1988).

6. J. T. Warner and B. J. Asch, "The Economics of Military Manpower," in *Handbook of Defense Economics,* vol. 1, ed. K. Hartley and T. Sandler (New York: Elsevier, 1995), 440–58.

7. David Filipov, "Thousands Flee Russia's Brutal Military," *Boston Globe,* 14 June 1998.

8. The proceedings of this conference are contained in J. Eric Fredland, Curtis L. Gilroy, Roger D. Little, and W. S. Sellman, eds., *Professionals on the Front Line: Two Decades of the All-Volunteer Force* (Washington, D.C.: Brassey's, 1996).

9. The "propensity to enlist" findings are detailed in Edwin Dorn, "Sustaining the All-Volunteer Force," in Fredland et al., *Professionals on the Front Line,* 6; and in Mark Eitelberg, "The All-Volunteer Force after Twenty Years," Fredland et al., *Professionals on the Front Line,* 66–67. Edwin Dorn, a longtime nongovernmental advocate of African Americans receiving fair treatment in the military had, by 1993, been appointed by President Bill Clinton to the senior Pentagon civilian post of Under Secretary of Defense for Personnel and Readiness. It was in this role that Edwin Dorn hosted the 1993 conference and wrote this chapter. Just prior to being selected by President Clinton, Dorn had been a research fellow at the Brookings Institution. In the 1980s, as an independent policy analyst with the Joint Center for Political Studies, a respected Washington-based black political institute, Dorn had edited *Who Defends America? Race, Sex, and Class in the Armed Forces* (Washington, D.C.: Joint Center for Political Studies, 1989). My own contribution to that volume is "Lessons from Other Times, Other Places" (pp. 133–57). In 1997, Edwin Dorn resigned from the Defense Department to take up his new post as direc-

tor of the Lyndon Johnson School of Public Policy at the University of Texas, the first African American to direct the school.

The assessments here of the tenor of the conference derive from my own observations of this gathering, held at the U.S. Naval Academy on 15–17 September 1993. I presented a paper there, though neither as a Defense Department official nor as a Defense Department contractor, in which I raised the issue of military prostitution's implicit message to potential and recent recruits. The paper appears as "Women, Men, and Soldiering after the Cold War," in Fredland et al., *Professionals on the Front Line*, 256–65.

10. Dorn, "Sustaining the All-Volunteer Force," 6.

11. Steven Lee Myers, "Enlistments Falling, Navy Lowers Education Standard," *New York Times*, 16 January 1999; Diana Jean Schemo, "Kosovo War Doesn't Do Much for U.S. Recruiting," *New York Times*, 16 May 1999.

12. Mike Causey, "The Federal Diary: Women Surviving the Cuts," *Washington Post*, 23 May 1997. According to this same report, during the period from 1993 to 1996, the Agency for International Development cut 31.9 percent of its jobs and the State Department eliminated more than 10 percent of its jobs.

13. William Reno, a political scientist at Florida International University, is among the scholars who have most closely monitored the post–Cold War emergence of mercenary companies. See William Reno, "Privatizing War in Sierra Leone," *Current History* 96, no. 610 (May 1997): 227–30. See also William Reno, *Warlord Politics and African States* (Boulder, Colo.: Lynne Rienne Publishers, 1998).

14. "Company Will Make War No More for Africans," *New York Times*, 11 December 1998.

15. The Young Marines was created by the Marine Corps in 1958 but has expanded in recent years; in 1998, it involved nearly 8,000 boys and girls nationwide. The programs of drills and campouts occur after school and on weekends. The children wear camouflage fatigues and drill with fake guns. About half the children in the program have family members (mothers, fathers, brothers, sisters) who are in the military. The children's parents pay a $40 entrance fee and a $10 annual fee. The Young Marines are taught by members of the Marine Corps. See Dana Hull, "The Littlest Leatherheads," *Washington Post*, 22 March 1998.

16. Guy Goodwin-Gill and Ilene Cohn, *Child Soldiers* (New York: Oxford University Press, 1996), 163. See also Human Rights Watch, *The Scars of Death: Children Abducted by the Lord's Resistance Army in Uganda* (New York: Human Rights Watch, 1997); and Kriju Peters and Paul Richards, "'Why We Fight': Voices of Youth Combatants in Sierra Leone," *Africa* 68, no. 2 (1998): 183–210.

17. Ibid., 207.

18. Ibid.

19. Malathi de Alwis, "Paternal States and Baby Brigades: Violence in the Name of the Nation" (paper written for the Conference on Children and Nationalism, Centre for Child Research, Trondheim, Norway, May 1994).

Malathi de Alwis is an anthropologist at the University of Chicago. On Tamil rebels' uses of women warrior myths, see Sitralega Maunaguru, "Gendering Tamil Nationalism: The Construction of 'Woman' in Projects of Protest and Control," in *Unmaking the Nation: The Politics of Identity and History in Modern Sri Lanka,* ed. Predeep Jeganthan and Qadri Ismail (Colombo, Sri Lanka: Social Scientists' Association, 1995), 161–62; Pamela Price, "Revolution and Rank in Tamil Nationalism," *The Journal of Asian Studies* 55, no. 2 (May 1996): 359–83. Prominent American feminist author Barbara Ehrenreich has explored the cross-cultural attraction of the war-inspiring mother and woman warrior myths in her *Blood Rites: Origins and History of the Passions of War* (New York: Henry Holt, 1997).

20. Ziauddin Sardar, "Two Asian Thugs Square Up, " *New Stateman* (London), 5 June 1998, 11.

21. For a historical account of conscription, military and nonmilitary, see Gregory J. Kasza, *The Conscription Society: Administered Mass Organizations* (New Haven: Yale University Press, 1995).

22. Nira Yuval-Davis, *Gender and Nation* (London: Sage Publications, 1997). See also a special issue of *Feminist Review* devoted to citizenship: Helen Crowly, Gail Lewis, Prina Werbner, and Nira Yuval-Davis, guest editors, "Citizenship: Pushing the Boundaries," *Feminist Review,* no. 57 (autumn 1997). See also Suad Joseph, "Gender and Citizenship in Middle Eastern States," in a special issue of *Middle East Report* entitled "Gender and Citizenship in the Middle East," no. 1198 (January–March 1996): 4–11.

23. In the United States, the most recent phase in this long-developing feminist debate began in 1980 when the National Organization for Women submitted a friend-of-the-court brief in the Supreme Court case challenging the new military selective service law. See National Organization for Women, "Brief for Amicus Curiae, in the Case before the Supreme Court of the United States, Bernard Roster, Director of Selective Service v. Robert L. Goldberg et al., Washington, D.C., October Term, 1980." As passed by Congress, the selective service law required only young men, upon turning eighteen years of age, to register for potential military service. Since the military draft had been ended by Congress in 1973, mandatory military service was not likely, though it was legally possible. NOW's leadership at the time was convinced that excluding women from this registration and thus from potential military service deprived them of a sine qua non of American citizenship, that is, the duty to militarily defend their country. The Supreme Court decided against NOW and the other challengers. In the late 1990s, military registration remains a males-only requirement system. It is males, therefore, who can be forced to forfeit their federal college financial aid if they fail to register on their eighteenth birthdays—thereby militarizing educational assistance. At the time of the U.S. legal dispute, an international response to the NOW analysis appeared. See Wendy Chapkis, ed., *Loaded Questions: Women in the Military* (Amsterdam: Transnational Institute, 1981).

24. Ayse Girl Karayzgan, "National Security, Identity, and National Service in Turkey" (paper presented at the annual meeting of the International Studies

Association, Toronto, 22–26 March 1997). The author is pursuing this research as part of her doctoral dissertation in political science at Duke University, Durham, N.C.

25. North Atlantic Treaty Organization, *Women in NATO* (Brussels: International Military Staff, NATO Headquarters, 1994), 36.

26. Linda Kerber, *Women of the Republic: Intellect and Ideology in Revolutionary America* (Chapel Hill, N.C.: University of North Carolina, 1980).

27. Dubravka Ugrei, quoted by Vesna Nikolic-Ristanovic in "War, Nationalism, and Mothers," in a special issue of *Peace Review* on "Women and War," *Peace Review* 8, no. 3 (September 1996): 359.

28. Steven Erlanger, "Serb Conscripts Drift into Hiding," *New York Times,* 5 April 1999; Carlotta Gall, "Wives Protest and General Sends Troops Back Home," *New York Times,* 21 May 1999; and Carlotta Gall, "Protests Are Resumed by Families of Yugoslav Reservists Ordered Back to Duty in Kosovo," *New York Times,* 25 May 1999.

29. Joni Seager, *The State of Women in the World Atlas* (New York: Penguin Books, 1997), 124.

30. Claudia Koonz, *Mothers in the Fatherland: Women, the Family, and Nazi Politics* (New York: St. Martin's Press, 1986); Victoria De Grazia, *How Fascism Ruled Women: Italy, 1922–1945* (Berkeley: University of California Press, 1992); Atina Grossman, *Reforming Sex: The German Movement for Birth Control and Abortion Reform* (New York: Oxford University Press, 1995). For a historical analysis of an American mothers' movement that flirted with fascist ideas in its campaign to keep the U.S. out of World War II, see Glen Jeansonne, *Women of the Far Right: The Mothers Movement and World War II* (Chicago: University of Chicago Press, 1997).

31. For an analysis of Croatian women's partial success in compelling the Tudjman regime to withdraw its nationalist, maternalist, pro-natalist grand plan at the start of its militarizing campaign in 1992, see Vesna Kesic, "From Respect to Rape," *War Report,* September 1995, 36–38. For more on motherhood as the basis for women's antimilitarism activism, see Malathi de Alwis, "Motherhood as a Space of Protest: Women's Political Participation in Contemporary Sri Lanka," in *Appropriating Gender: Women's Activism and the Politicization of Religion in South Asia,* ed. Amrita Basu and Patricia Jeffrey (New York: Routledge, 1998), 185–202.

32. Jok Madut Jok, "Militarism, Gender, and Reproductive Risk: The Case of Abortion in Southern Sudan" (paper presented at the conference on "Militarism and Gender," Women's Studies Program, University of Wisconsin, Madison, 13 October 1997.

33. The first woman to be appointed to Vietnam's Politburo—in July 1996—was Nguyen Thi Xuan My, a member of the party's Control Commission. She was the only woman among seventeen men on the Politburo. Six of the Politburo's members came from the military and security services, an increase of two over the previous membership. See Seth Mydans, "Hanoi Names Military Officers to Politburo," *New York Times,* 2 July 1996.

34. Karen Turner, communication with the author, July 1997. For her more extensive analysis of the Hanoi Women's Museum, see Karen Turner with

Phan Thanh Hao, *Even the Women Must Fight: Memories of War from North Vietnam* (New York: John Wiley and Sons, 1998), 25–28. My own thoughts about the messages of a second Vietnamese postwar women's museum, The South Vietnam Women's Museum, created by volunteers in Ho Chi Minh City (formerly Saigon), is "Women after Wars: Puzzles and Warnings," in *Vietnam's Women in Transition,* ed. Kathleen Barry (New York: St. Martin's Press, 1996), 299–316.

35. See Miriam Cooke, *Women and the War Story* (Berkeley: University of California Press, 1996) and Miriam Cooke and Roshini Rustomji-Kerns, eds., *Blood into Ink: South Asian and Middle Eastern Women Write War* (Boulder, Colo.: Westview Press, 1994). For German women's autobiographical war stories that are self-consciously alternative, see Lilo Klug, ed., *Surviving the Fire: Mother Courage and World War II* (Seattle: Open Hand Publishing, 1989); and Claudia Schoppmann, *Days of Masquerade: Life Stories of Lesbians during the Third Reich,* trans. Allison Brown (New York: Columbia University Press, 1996). For a British equivalent of feminist peacetime retelling of mothering stories for the sake of transforming a public's political consciousness, see Melissa Benn, *Madonna and Child: Towards a New Politics of Motherhood* (London: Jonathan Cape, 1998).

36. Nancy Scheper-Hughes, "Maternal Thinking and the Politics of War," special issue on "Women and War," *Peace Review* 8, no. 3 (September 1996): 354. Scheper-Hughes's now-classic ethnographic study of residents of a poor Brazilian shantytown is *Death without Weeping: The Violence of Everyday Life in Brazil* (Berkeley: University of California Press, 1992). In her *Peace Review* article, Scheper-Hughes calls for a refinement of the ideas proposed in one of the most widely discussed analyses of "maternal thinking," that is, Sara Ruddick, *Maternal Thinking: Toward a Politics of Peace* (Boston: Beacon Press, 1989).

37. Lesley Gill, "Creating Citizens, Making Men: The Military and Masculinity in Bolivia," *Cultural Anthropology* 12, no. 4 (1997): 1–27. In the poor neighborhoods of 1980s Cairo, according to Diane Singerman's detailed research, mothers of daughters saw a young man still in the military as a poor marital prospect; these Egyptian women did not believe that such a man had enough financial savings to provide rent for a city apartment after the marriage. Marriageability was assessed by these mothers less in terms of a young man's warrior traits than in terms of his economic resources. See Diane Singerman, *Avenues of Participation: Family, Politics, and Networks in Urban Quarters of Cairo* (Princeton: Princeton University Press, 1995), 86.

38. Margaret Randall is one of the external feminist observers whose analytical attention did not waver. As a sequal to her account of women who became active in the 1970s Sandinista movement (*Sandino's Daughters* [Vancouver: New Star Books, 1981]), Randall wrote *Sandino's Daughters Revisited: Feminism in Nicaragua* (New Brunswick, N.J.: Rutgers University Press, 1994).

39. Helen Collinson, *Women and Revolution in Nicaragua* (Atlantic Highlands, N.J.: Zed Books, 1990), 154–61.

40. Roger N. Lancaster, *Life Is Hard: Machismo, Danger, and the Intimacy of Power in Nicaragua* (Berkeley: University of California Press, 1992), 197.

41. Ibid.

42. I am grateful to Karen Kampwirth, a political scientist at Knox College, Galesburg, Illinois, for sharing with me her insights into the success of Violeta Chamorro and the regenderings of Nicaraguan political life that occurred during the 1990s. See Karen Kampirth, "The Mother of the Nicaraguans: Dona Violeta and the UNO's Gender Agenda," *Latin American Perspectives*, no. 23 (March 1995): 67–86; Karen Kampwirth, "Legislating Personal Politics in Sandinista Nicaragua," *Women's Studies International Forum* 21, no. 1 (1998): 53–64; and Karen Kampwirth, *Feminism and Guerrilla Politics in Latin America* (forthcoming).

43. Linda Green, "Preconditions for Internal Violence: The Delicate Balance between Subsistence, Social Relations, and Suffering" (paper presented at the American Anthropology Association annual meeting, San Francisco, 1–24 November 1996), 2. Linda Green, an anthropologist at the University of Arizona, is the also the author of *Fear as a Way of Life: Mayan Widows in Rural Guatemala* (New York: Columbia University Press, 1998). See also Maria Stern-Pettersson, "Reading in/Security in Mayan Women's Narratives" (Ph.D. diss., Department of Development and Peace Studies, University of Gotesborg, Gotesborg, Sweden, 1998). Women in Colombia who have been organizing against both U.S.-supported governmental militarism and druglord militarism have told observers that one of their chief frustrations is watching their sons, who lack any economic alternatives and who are under extreme pressure to take sides in Colombia's drawn-out internal war, join paramilitaries. One mother of a son asked: "What can I say to them? What are our options? Our boys are being turned into salaried killers." Quoted by Robin Lloyd, "Caught in the Crossfire: Women Take a Stand in the Fight between Corruption and Justice," *Colombia Bulletin: A Human Rights Quarterly* 3, no. 1 (May 1998), 32.

44. A particularly provocative and subtle cinematic treatment of the rocky road to understanding between two Northern Irish women who defined their contrasting wartime identities largely in terms of their mothering of sons is *Some Mother's Son,* a 1996 film (produced by Castle Rock Productions) directed by Terry George, a Northern Irishman, and starring Helen Mirren, the celebrated English actress. In interviews, George and Mirren described their arguments with each other over the film's interpretation, arguments that give the cinematic result a valuable tension. See Dinitia Smith, "A Prison Left Behind Becomes a Career," *New York Times,* 1 January 1997. A thorough analysis of Northern Irish republican Catholic women activists' efforts not to be reduced to merely nationalist mothers and, instead, to create political spaces in which their own voices could be heard is Begona Aretxaga, *Shattering Silence: Women, Nationalism, and Political Subjectivity in Northern Ireland* (Princeton: Princeton University Press, 1997).

45. Maria Sriningih Stevens, "Nurturing the Dream: The Militarization of an American Mother" (unpublished paper, Clark University, Worcester, Mass., April 1997).

46. Linda Rennie Forcey, "Turning to Uncle Sam," Chapter 6 of Forcey's *Mothers of Sons* (New York: Praeger, 1987), 117–35.

47. Quoted in Hull, "The Littlest Leatherheads."

48. For an analysis of the U.S. government's campaign to pressure American mothers into accepting the Selective Service Act of 1917 as an act of patriotic motherhood, see Susan Zeiger, "'She Didn't Raise Her Boy to Be a Slacker': Motherhood, Conscription, and the Culture of the First World War," *Feminist Studies,* no. 1 (spring 1996): 7–39.

49. For discussions of Palestinian women's strategizing as mothers, see Julie Peteet, "Icons and Militants: Mothering in the Danger Zones," *Signs* 23, no. 1 (autumn 1997): 103–30. Peteet notes (page 107) that while under the Ottoman Empire, Palestinian mothers not only did not urge their sons to accept military conscription in the Ottoman forces, they also did not consider service in the imperial military to be a sign of Palestinian maculinity. For more on recent Palestinian politics of motherhood, see Suha Sabbagh, ed., *Palestinian Women of Gaza and the West Bank* (Bloomington: Indiana University Press, 1998). On the Israeli state's construction of the Israeli Jewish woman as mother, see Nitza Berkovitch, "Motherhood as a National Mission: The Construction of Womanhood in the Legal Discourse in Israel," special issue "Cultures of Womanhood in Israel," *Women's Studies International Forum* 20, no. 5/6 (1997): 605–20.

50. Dafna Izraeli, "Gendering Military Service in the Israeli Defense Forces" (typescript), *Israel Social Science Research* 12, no. 1 (1997), 5. Dafna Izraeli is a professor of sociology at Bar-Ilan University, Israel.

51. Rela Mazali, an Israeli feminist, peace activist, and journalist, has written widely on Jewish Israeli mothers, and parents generally, as they sustain the militarization of Israeli culture. Those Mazali articles on which I am relying here include "The Taboo of the Military," *Challenge,* no. 36 (March–April 1996): 18–19; "Parenting Troops: The Summons to Acquiescence" (typescript, 1994); "Raising Boys to Maintain Armies," *British Medical Journal* 311, 9 September 1995, 694; and "Serving the Service: Soldiers Forming Their Parents," originally published in Hebrew in the Israeli feminist journal *Nogah,* September 1997, used here in its English form (typescript, 1997). I also have benefited from many conversations via e-mail with Rela Mazali between 1996 and 1999. For other insights into Israeli feminist analyses of militarization, see Simona Sharoni, *Gender and the Israeli-Palestinian Conflict: The Politics of Women's Resistance* (Syracuse: Syracuse University Press, 1995); Tamar Mayer, ed., *Women and the Israeli Occupation* (New York: Routledge, 1994).

52. Rela Mazali, e-mail correspondence with the author, 5 December 1997.

53. The following analysis draws on the work of Hanna Herzog, Department of Sociology, Tel Aviv University: "Enlisting Mom: Military-Family Relations as Gendering Social Mechanism: The Case of Israel" (typescript, February 1997).

54. See, for instance, Andjelka Milic, "Nationalism and Sexism: Eastern Europe in Transition," in *Europe's New Nationalism,* ed. R. Coplan and J. Feffer (London: Oxford University Press, 1996), 169–83.

55. The photo accompanies Alessandra Stanley, "Mothers Act to Save Their Sons from War," *New York Times,* 11 February 1995. The photo is credited to Agence France-Presse.

56. Among the journalistic accounts of the Mothers of Soldiers Committee are Stanley, "Mothers Act to Save Their Sons"; Fred Kaplan, "Russian Mothers' Fight," *Boston Globe,* 24 January 1995; David Hoffman, "Hell No, Their Boys Won't Go," *Washington Post,* 23–29 October 1995; Ruth Daniloff, "Hope Springs Maternal," *Boston Globe,* 12 May 1996; and Alessandra Stanley, "Russia War Dead Lie in Filth, Awaiting Claim by Their Kin," *New York Times,* 25 August 1996.

57. I discuss this late 1980s political movement in more detail in *The Morning After: Sexual Politics at the End of the Cold War* (Berkeley: University of California Press, 1993), 10–13. For fascinating profiles of women who began to critique the Soviet state's sexism in its latter phase and then were among the first to launch new women's organizations, including the Mothers of Soldiers, in the early years of the new Russian state, see Linda Raccioppi and Katherine O'Sullivan See, *Women's Activism in Contemporary Russia* (Philadelphia: Temple University Press, 1997).

58. David Filipov, "Thousands Flee Russia's Brutal Military," *Boston Globe,* 14 June 1998.

59. Ibid.

60. Valeria Zawilski, "Saving Mothers' Sons" (paper presented at the Conference on Women in Conflict Zones, Eaton Hall, King City, Ontario, 13 May 1997). Valeria Zawilski is a professor of sociology at Trent University, Petersborough, Ontario, Canada.

61. Ibid.

62. Ann Garrels, *Morning Editon,* National Public Radio, 17 November 1997.

63. Quoted in Filipov, "Thousands Flee Russia's Brutal Military." During 1998, members of the Committee of Soldiers' Mothers began to work with the Russian military to persuade young men who had deserted from the army to turn themselves in. The army couldn't guarantee full amnesty but pledged consideration of cause, especially since, as the women activists had shown, so many young men deserted as a result of maltreatment in the army. For their part, the women activists explained that they were willing to engage in this joint effort with that part of the Russian state that had been the object of their sharp criticism because they saw this effort—called "Operation Deserter"—as one way to slow down the rapid rise of young Russian men entering into criminal activity. See Joan Ross Frankson, "Russian Mothers to the Rescue," *Ms. Magazine,* July/August 1998, 12.

64. Anne Eliot Griesse and Richard Stites, "Russia: Revolution and War," in *Female Soldiers—Combatants or Noncombatants?* ed. Nancy Loring Goldman (Westport, Conn.: Greenwood Press, 1981), 79.

65. International Institute for Strategic Studies, *The Military Balance, 1995–1996* (London: Oxford University Press, 1996), 113.

66. See, for instance, Beth Junor, Greenham Commons Women's Peace Camp: A History of Non-Violent Resistence, 1984–1995 (London: Working Press, 1995); Sasha Roseneil, Disarming Patriarchy: Feminism and Political Action at Greenham (Philadelphia: Open University Press, 1995); Marguerite Guzman Bouvard, Revolutionizing Motherhood: The Mothers of the Plaza De

Mayo (Wilmington, Del.: Scholarly Resources Books, 1994); and Rita Arditti, Searching for Life: Grandmothers of the Plaza De Mayo and the Disappeared Children of Argentina (Berkeley: University of California Press, 1999). For a sophisticated study of an earlier American Cold War movement drawing on ideas about motherhood, see Amy Swerdlow, Women Strike for Peace: Traditional Motherhood and Radical Politics in the 1960s (Chicago: University of Chicago Press, 1993).

67. A 1991 survey of "office ladies" in a large Japanese insurance company—young women who used their discretionary incomes to shop, ski, travel overseas—revealed that what they were "most dissatisfied" with in their workplace was the company uniform—not their service to male executives, not their lack of professional career opportunities. See Yuko Ogasawara, Office Ladies and Salaried Men (Berkeley: University of California Press, 1998), 25.

68. Elaine Sciolino, "The British Carried Umbrellas to Waterloo. Don't Laugh," New York Times, 3 August 1997. Sciolino reports that an article in a May 1997 issue of Army Times on the umbrella problem provoked more letter writing by readers than any other subject in recent years.

69. Sciolino, "The British Carried Umbrellas." Several weeks later the New York Times ran an essay on the issue by conservative commentator Stephanie Gutmann. She opined that the Army Chief of Staff had made the proper decision in that carrying an umbrella would add momentum to what she believed were the current trends toward demasculinizing the American military. See Stephanie Gutmann, "The Great Umbrella Debate," New York Times, 9 October 1997.

70. Sciolino, "The British Carried Umbrellas."

71. A Nazi women's organizational directive of 1934, quoted by Schoppmann, Days of Masquerade, 18.

72. Irene V. Guenther, "Nazi 'Chic': German Politics and Women's Fashion," Fashion Theory 1 (1997): 29–58.

73. Nancy Goldman, "The Utilization of Women in Combat: The Armed Forces of Great Britain, World War I, and World War II" (Interuniversity Seminar on Armed Forces and Society, University of Chicago, unpublished manuscript, 1978).

74. Vita Sackville-West, The Woman's Land Army (London: Michael Joseph Ltd., 1944), 90–91.

75. Antonia Lant, Blackout: Reinventing Women for Wartime British Cinema (Princeton: Princeton University Press, 1991), 103–4.

76. Ruth Roach Pierson, "They're Women After All": The Second World War and Canadian Womanhood (Toronto: McClelland and Stewart, 1986), 140.

77. Ibid.

78. Leisa D. Meyer, Creating G.I. Jane: Sexuality and Power in the Women's Army Corps during World War II (New York: Columbia University Press, 1996). For the history of the women who served as air force transport pilots—the WASPS—but who were denied full integration into the military and thus also denied death benefits and pensions, see Molly Merryman, Clipped Wings: The Rise and Fall of the Women Airforce Service Pilots of World War II (New York: New York University Press, 1997).

79. Ibid., 38–40.

80. For discussions of African American WACs' experience as and responses to lesbians, see Meyer, *Creating G.I. Jane,* 170–71; and Moore, *To Serve My Country, To Serve My Race,* 137–38.

81. Meyer, *Creating G.I. Jane,* 153–54.

82. Ibid., 66.

83. Mary Meigs, "A Lesbian WAVE," in *Beyond the Home Front: Women's Autobiographical Writing of the Two World Wars,* ed. Yvonne M. Klein (New York: New York University Press, 1996), 158–59.

84. For a collection of case studies suggesting the range of social trends and political activism even in the apparently hegemonically domesticated 1950s, see Joanne Meyerowitz, ed., *Not June Cleaver: Women and Gender in Postwar America, 1945–1960* (Philadelphia: Temple University Press, 1994). These historians are joining a conversation about postwar U.S.-gendered culture and economy pioneered by Elaine Tyler May's important study, *Homeward Bound: American Families in the Cold War Era* (New York: Basic Books, 1988).

85. Donna M. Dean, *Warriors without Weapons: The Victimization of Military Women* (Pasadena, Md.: Minerva Center, 1998), viii. Dean also appears in a provocative film about American women veterans across several generations who compare their armed forces experiences and call on each other to speak out about topics that had been buried for decades. See Julia Perez, director, *Invisible Forces: Women in the Military,* a 1985 film distributed by the William Joiner Center for the Study of War and Its Social Consequences, University of Massachusetts, Boston.

86. Ibid.

87. Advertisment, U.S. Department of Defense, Washington, D.C., 1981.

88. For a study of the process by which the U.S. Air Force Academy became a coeducational institution, see Judith Hicks Stiehm, *Bring Me Men and Women: Mandated Change at the U.S. Air Force Academy* (Berkeley: University of California Press, 1981). Recent feminist studies of the academies' adjustments—or lack of adjustments—to the entrance of women include, on the army's academy at West Point: Billie Mitchell, "The Creation of Army Officers and the Gender Lie: Betty Grable or Frankenstein?" in *It's Our Military Too: Women and the U.S. Military,* ed. Judith Hicks Stiehm (Philadelphia: Temple University Press, 1996), 35–59; on the navy's academy at Annapolis: Carol Burke, "Pernicious Cohesion," in Stiehm, *It's Our Military Too,* 205–19; and Carol Burke, "Military Folklore," in *Beyond Ground Zero: Discrimination in the Military,* ed. Judith Reppy and Mary Katzenstein (New York: Routledge, 1999).

89. Elizabeth Lutes Hillman, "Uniform Identities: Women, Gender, and Images at the United States Service Academies" (master's thesis, Department of History, University of Pennsylvania, Philadelphia, 1994). See also Elizabeth L. Hillman, "Dressed to Kill? The Paradox of Women in Military Uniforms," in Katzenstein and Reppy, *Beyond Ground Zero.* I am grateful to Beth Hillman for her conversations and conference presentations and for sharing the insights she garnered from her firsthand experience as an officer on the faculty of the Air Force Academy. In 1997, Beth Hillman left the military to pursue a history degree at Yale law school.

90. Hillman, "Uniform Identities," 31.

91. Martha Raddatz, "Women in the Military, Part 3," *Morning Edition,* National Public Radio, 14 May 1997 (typed transcript).

92. Among the spate of recent interesting feminist analyses of the gendered state—and the genderings of particular states—are the following: Ailbhe Smyth, "Paying Our Disrespects to the Bloody States We're In: Women, Violence, Culture, and the State," a special double issue on "Irish Women," *Journal of Women's History* 6, no. 4, and 7, no. 1 (winter/spring 1995); Ailbhe Smyth, "States of Change: Reflections on Ireland in Several Uncertain Parts," in a special issue on "The Irish Issue: The British Question," *Feminist Review,* no. 50 (summer 1995): 24–43; "The New Politics of Sex and the State," a special issue of *Feminist Review,* no. 48 (autumn 1994); M. Jacqui Alexander, "Erotic Autonomy as a Politics of Decolonization: An Anatomy of Feminist and State Practice in the Bahamas Tourist Economy," in *Feminist Genealogies, Colonial Legacies, Democratic Futures,* ed. M. Jacqui Alexander and Chandra Mohanty (New York: Routledge, 1997), 63–100; Jan Jindy Pettman, *Worlding Women: A Feminist International Politics* (Sydney: Allen and Unwin, 1996); Marysia Zalewski and Jane Parpart, eds., *The "Man" Question in International Relations* (Boulder, Colo.: Westview, 1998); Ann Tickner, "You Just Don't Understand: Troubled Engagements between Feminists and IR Theorists," *International Studies Quarterly* 41 (1997): 611–32; Ann Tickner, *Gender in International Relations* (New York: Columbia University Press, 1992); Jongwoo Han and Lily H.M. Ling, "Authoritarianism in the Hypermasculinized State: Hybridity, Patriarchy, and Capitalism in Korea," *International Studies Quarterly* 42 (1998): 53–78; Deniz Kandiyoti, ed., *Women, Islam, and the State* (Philadelphia: Temple University Press, 1996); Diane Singerman, *Avenues of Participation;* Shirin M. Rai and Geraldine Lievesley, eds., *Women and the State: International Perspectives* (London: Taylor and Francis, 1996); Dorothy McBride Stetson and Amy G. Mazur, *Comparative State Feminism* (Thousand Oaks, Calif.: Sage Publications, 1995); Nira Yuval-Davis and Floya Anthias, eds., *Woman-Nation-State* (London: Macmillan, 1989); Anne Showstack Sassoon, ed., *Women and the State* (London: Unwin and Hyman, 1987); V. Spike Peterson, *Gendered States* (Boulder, Colo.: Lynne Rienner Publishers, 1992); Anne Phillips, *Engendering Democracy* (University Park: Pennsylvania State University Press, 1991); and Carole Patemen, *The Sexual Contract* (Stanford, Calif.: Stanford University Press, 1988).

93. I am grateful to Professors Mary Katzenstein and Judith Reppy, both of Cornell University, for having organized this interesting meeting at the Defense Department, Washington, D.C., 4 April 1997. It was one part of a larger multiyear project on gender and military culture, funded by the Ford Foundation. The resultant book is Katzenstein and Reppy, *Beyond Ground Zero.*

94. On the 1991 Tailhook Association convention and its political aftermath, see Department of the Navy: Office of the Inspector General, *Tailhook I, Part 1: Review of the Navy's Investigations* (Washington, D.C.: Department of Defense, September 1992); and Office of the Inspector General, *The Tailhook Report* (New York: St. Martin's Press, 1993). The latter is the full and unedited Part 2 of the inspector general's report and covers in eye-opening detail what happened in the Hilton during the September 1991 Tailhook convention. For

feminist analyses of the many strands in the Tailhook scandal, see Jean Zimmerman: *Women at War in the Wake of Tailhook* (New York: Doubleday, 1995); Francine D'Amico, "Deinstitutionalizing the Military's 'Women's Problem,'" in *Wives and Warriors,* ed. Laurie Weinstein and Christine White (Westport, Conn.: Bergin and Garvey, 1997), 79–98; Renee Goldsmith Kasinsky, "Tailhook and the Construction of Sexual Harassment in the Media: 'Rowdy Navy Boys' and Women Who Made a Difference," *Violence Against Women* 4, no. 1 (February 1998): 81–99; "Lt. Hultgren and the 'Hot Dogs'—A Bad Year for Navy Flyers," *Minerva's Bulletin Board* (summer 1995): 1; and Susan Barnes, "WANDAS Forum: Sibling Rivalry in the Navy—Tom Cruise Meets His Little Sister," *Minerva's Bulletin Board* (winter 1995): 10–12. In addition, for analyses of Tailhook's later aftershocks, see Peter J. Boyer, "Admiral Boorda's War," *The New Yorker,* September 1996, 33–49; and Philip Shenon, "Five Years Later, Navy Is Still Reeling from Tarnish of Tailhook Incident," *New York Times,* 20 May 1996.

95. Journalist Elaine Sciolino almost single-handedly broke the Kelly Flinn story that prompted a national debate over the military's policies not only toward women as pilots but toward marriage and adultery and toward the classic sexual double standard. See Elaine Sciolino, "From a Love Affair to a Court Martial," *New York Times,* 11 May 1997. Eventually Kelly Flinn was spared a court martial but was compelled to resign from the air force. Her own post-resignation account is Kelly Flinn, *Proud To Be* (New York: Random House, 1997).

Accounts of widespread sexual harassment at the army's Aberdeen, Md., base include Sara Rimer, "At Maryland Post, Talk Is of Shame," *New York Times,* 14 November 1996; Eric Schmitt, "Female Legislators Push Generals for Answers," *New York Times,* 19 November 1996; Eric Schmitt, "Teaching Army's Teachers Gets Tougher," *New York Times,* 24 November 1996; Elaine Sciolino, "Sergeant Convicted of 18 Counts of Raping Female Subordinates," *New York Times,* 30 April 1997; Eric Schmitt, "Army Turns Off Phone Line for Sexual Misconduct Reports," *New York Times,* 14 June 1997. For background on the Defense Department policies and military institutional cultural inclinations that set the stage for the Aberdeen assaults, see Linda Bird Franke, *Ground Zero: The Gender Wars in the Military* (New York: Simon and Schuster, 1997). The fact that at Aberdeen the several sergeants charged were all African American men and all the women complainants were white enlisted women provoked considerable discussion over whether the army had pursued its sexual harassment investigations in a racist manner, even though the secretary of the army, the official who ordered the investigations, was at that time an African American civilian male, Togo West. See, for instance, Peter T. Kilborn, "Five Women Say Sex Charges in Army Case were Coerced," *New York Times,* 12 March 1997.

96. The policy debate between Congress, the White House, and the Defense Department—as well as between conservative and feminist groups outside government who acted as the principal lobbyists in the struggle—was carried on in part through a series of commissioned reports, each by a committee of experts on military personnel issues composed of people with varied views and military associations and purporting to have reached their conclusions re-

garding the realities of women in the military ("men in the military" was not labeled the issue) based on unbiased evidence. See Defense Advisory Committee on Women in the Military, "Memorandum to the Secretary of Defense, regarding Military Installation Visits" (Department of Defense, Washington, D.C., January 1998); Secretary of the Army, "Senior Review Panel Report on Sexual Harassment," vols. 1 and 2 (Department of Defense, Washington, D.C., July 1997); Inspector General of the Army, "Special Inspection of Initial Entry Training Equal Opportunity/Sexual Harassment Policies and Procedures" (Department of the Army, Department of Defense, Washington, D.C., 22 July 1997). A further study commissioned by the secretary of defense on the conditions experienced by women in the late 1990s U.S. military is Margaret C. Harrell and Laura L. Miller, *New Opportunities for Military Women: Effects upon Readiness, Cohesion, and Morale* (Santa Monica, Calif.: Rand Corporation, 1997). See also Mary Fainsod Katzenstein and Judith Reppy, eds., *Beyond Zero Tolerance: Discrimination in Military Culture* (Lanham, Md.: Rowman and Littlefield, 1999).

97. See Mary Fainsod Katzenstein, *Faithful and Fearless: Moving Feminist Protest inside the Church and the Military* (Princeton: Princeton University Press, 1998).

98. Margot Badran, *Feminists, Islam, and Nationalism: Gender and the Making of Modern Egypt* (Princeton: Princeton University Press, 1995), 187–88.

99. For more by and about Australian feminists who have attempted to pursue feminist goals by taking official posts inside the Australian government, see Sophie Watson, ed., *Playing the State: Australian Feminist Interventions* (London: Verso, 1990); Anna Yeatman, *Bureaucrats, Technocrats, Femocrats* (Sydney: Allen and Unwin, 1990); Suzanne Franzway, Dianne Court, and R. W. Connell, *Staking a Claim: Feminisms, Bureaucracy, and the State* (Sydney: Allen and Unwin, 1989); and Hester Eistenstein, *Inside Agitators: Australian Femocrats and the State* (Philadelphia: Temple University Press, 1996).

100. The United Nations commissioned a series of country case studies to assess women's policy-making influence inside governments: Center for Social Development and Humanitarian Affairs, "Participation of Women in Decision-Making for Peace: Case Study on Sweden" (New York: United Nations Publications, 1989); Center for Social Development and Humanitarian Affairs, "Women in Decision-Making: Case Study on Greece" (New York: United Nations Publications, 1991); Center for Social Development and Humanitarian Affairs, "Women in Decision-Making: Case Study on Costa Rica" (New York: United Nations Publications, 1991). See also the worldwide map of proportion of seats in government cabinets held by women in Seager, *The State of Women in the World Atlas*, 90–91.

101. Cornell political scientist Mary Katzenstein has monitored and compared the theorizing and strategizing of two groups of American feminists working within two patriarchal institutions. See Katzenstein, *Faithful and Fearless*.

102. Defense Manpower Data Center, "U.S. Active Duty Servicewomen by Branch of Service, Status, Race, and Hispanic Origin as of April 30, 1997" (U.S. Department of Defense, Washington, D.C., 30 April 1997).

103. "Selected Statistics on Women in the U.S. Armed Forces and Civilian Firefighting and Police Operations" (Washington, D.C.: Women's Research and Education Institute, December 1998).

104. Defense Manpower Data Center, "U.S. Active Duty Servicewomen." The categories employed here are of the Defense Department's own making.

105. Lory Manning, "News from the International Front," *Minerva's Bulletin Board* (summer 1998): 7.

106. For more on women in the German military, see Ruth Seifert, "Gender and Military: Budeswehr Officers on the Issue of Integration of Women into the Army," (Hamburg, Fuhrungsakamie der Bundeswehr, typescript, 1995); Ruth Seifert and Christine Eiffert, eds., *Gender and the Military* (Hamburg: German Sociological Association, 1998).

107. Roger Cohen, "Over There, Different Rules on Sex," *New York Times,* 7 June 1997. This article notes that neither the French nor the British have the American-style rules that prohibit personal relationships between male and female soldiers of different ranks.

108. I am grateful to Austrian feminist Katrin Kriz for informing me of this change in Austrian military policy.

109. Jane O'Hara, "Rape in the Military," *Maclean's,* 25 May 1998, 14–24; Jane O'Hara, "Rape in the Military: Speaking Out," *Maclean's,* 1 June 1998, 14–20; John Geddes and Stephanie Nolen, "Answering the Call," *Maclean's,* 8 June 1998, 28–31.

110. For a detailed feminist analysis of the Canadian airborne unit's behavior in Somalia and the political dynamics of the civilian public investigation that ensued, see Sandra Whitworth, *Bullies in Blue Berets: Gender, Race, and the Politics of Peacekeeping* (Boulder, Colo.: Lynne Rienner Publishers, forthcoming).

111. "Canada's Army Seeks Women for Combat," *New York Times,* 18 June 1998.

112. Amelia Gentleman, "Campaign by Army to Woo Women and Blacks," *The Guardian,* 4 April 1998. See also David Fairhill, "Equality Promised to Black Soldiers," *The Guardian,* 14 October 1997; Ian Burrell, "Army's Black and Asian Recruitment Drive Turns to Kitchner for a Role Model," *The Independent,* 14 October 1997. I am indebted to British feminist Debbie Licorish for these press articles.

113. Figures on women in the British military are from Lory Manning and Jennifer Griffith, *Women in the Military: Where They Stand* (Washington, D.C.: Women's Research and Education Institute, 1997), 26. Data on black and Asian Britons in the British military are from Alan Travis and David Bowen, "A Beacon Burning Darkly," *The Guardian,* 2 October 1997. Both sets of data are derived from the Ministry of Defence's own sources.

114. Quoted in Gentleman, "Campaign by Army to Woo."

115. Jacklyn Cock, *Women and War in South Africa* (Cleveland, Ohio: Pilgrim Press, 1993).

116. Among the accounts of what has happened to women combatants in insurgent forces after their respective wars are Karen Kampwirth, *Feminism and Guerrilla Politics in Latin America* (forthcoming); Randall, *Sandino's*

Daughters; Randall, *Sandino's Daughters Revisited;* Lois M. Smith and Alfred Padula, *Sex and Revolution: Women in Socialist Cuba* (New York: Oxford University Press, 1996); "Eritrea: The Kitchen Calls," *The Economist,* 25 June 1994, 46; Turner, *Even the Women Must Fight;* Marina Lazreg, *The Eloquence of Silence: Algerian Women in Question* (New York: Routledge, 1994); Sita Ranchod-Nilsson, "From the Margins of the State to the Center of the Cultural Crisis: Women and the Reconfiguration of the One-Party State in Zimbabwe," in *The African State at Critical Juncture,* ed. Leonard Villon and Philip Huxtable (Boulder, Colo.: Lynne Rienner Publishers, 1997); Irene Staunton, *Mothers of the Revolution: The War Experiences of Thirty Zimbabwean Women* (Bloomington: Indiana University Press, 1991); and Christine Sylvester, *Producing "Women" and "Progress" in Zimbabwe's First Decade* (forthcoming). I also gave consideration to the causes and consequences of women's roles as combatants in armed insurgencies in my *Does Khaki Become You? The Militarization of Women's Lives* (London: Pandora Press/HarperCollins, 1988).

117. Jacklyn Cock, "Banal Militarism" (paper presented at a conference of Militarism and Internationalizing Women's Studies, University of Wisconsin, Madison, 4 October 1997); for more on the post-apartheid South African military's gendered evloution, see Jacklyn Cock, "Forging a New Army Out of Old Enemies: Women in the South African Military," a special issue on "Rethinking Women's Peace Studies," *Women's Studies Quarterly* 23, nos. 3 and 4 (fall/winter 1995): 97–111.

118. Edwin Dorn, Under Secretary of Defense, "Memorandum: Guidelines for Investigating Threats against Service Members Based on Alleged Homosexuality" (Department of Defense, Washington, D.C., 24 March 1997).

CONCLUSION

1. Virginia Woolf, *Three Guineas* (New York: Harcourt Brace, 1938).

2. For Woolf's thoughts about the writing of *Three Guineas* and about its critical reception, see Anne Oliver Bell, ed., *The Diary of Virgina Woolf: Volume 5, 1936–1941* (New York: Harcourt Brace, 1984), 52–193.

3. I am grateful to the members of the Women in Conflict Zones Network and staff people from UNICEF for sharing with me in conversations their observations on trends in humanitarian aid operations. The coordinators of WICZNET are Wenona Giles and Maja Korac, both of York University, Ontario, Canada.

4. I am grateful to Insook Kwon of South Korea and Ximena Bunster of Chile for having shared with me their own experiences of participating in prodemocracy movements that, at decisive moments, witnessed such militarizing decisions. See also Seungsook Moon, "Civil Society, Gender, and Women's Movements in South Korea" (typescript, Women's Studies Program, Vassar College, Poughkeepsie, N.Y., 1998). For a description of a deliberately nonmasculinized form of protest against the Indonesian militarized regime led by President Suharto, see Richard Lloyd Parry, "After the Crash: The Demonstrator," *Granta,* no. 62 (summer 1998): 132–33.

5. For investigations of women's efforts in Northern Ireland to create cross-communal organizations, see Cynthia Cockburn, *The Space between Us* (London: Zed Press, 1998). I am also grateful to Ailbhe Smyth of University College, Dublin, for sharing with me information from her own work with such Irish cross-border and cross-communal women's groups.

6. I am indebted to Marysia Zalewski of the University of Wales, Aberyswyth, and to Christine Sylvester of the Australian National University for making me more aware of the theoretical implications of this feminist debate.

SELECTED BIBLIOGRAPHY

Abrams, Lynn, and Elizabeth Harvey, eds. *Gender Relations in German History*. Durham, NC: Duke University Press, 1997.

Adams, Abigail. "The 'Military Academy': Metaphors of Family Life for Pedagogy and Public Life." In *Wives and Warriors: Women and the Military in the United States and Canada*, edited by Laurie Weinstein and Christie C. White, 63–77. Westport, CT: Bergin and Garvey, 1996.

Aguilar, Delia. "Toward a Reinscription of National Feminism." *Review of Women's Studies* 4, no. 2 (1994–95): 1–14.

Alcott, Luisa May. *Hospital Sketches*. New York: Sagamore Press, 1957.

Alexander, M. Jacqui, and Chandra Mohanty, eds. *Feminist Genealogies, Colonial Legacies, Democratic Futures*. New York: Routledge, 1997.

Alexander, Ziggie, and Audrey Dewjee, eds. *The Wonderful Adventures of Mary Seacole*. Bristol, UK: Falling Wall Press, 1984.

Allen, Beverly. *Rape Warfare: The Hidden Genocide in Bosnia-Herzegovina and Croatia*. Minneapolis: University of Minnesota Press, 1996.

Alvarez, Sonia E. "The (Trans)formation of Feminism(s) and Gender Politics in Democratizing Brazil." In *The Women's Movement in Latin America*, 2d ed., edited by Jane Jaquette, 13–64. Boulder, CO: Westview Press, 1994.

Amnesty International. *Human Rights Are Women's Rights*. London: Amnesty International, 1995.

Amnesty International. *Rape and Sexual Abuse: Torture and Ill Treatment of Women in Detention*. New York: Amnesty International, January 1992.

AMPO-Japan Asia Quarterly Review. *Voices from the Japanese Women's Movement*. Armonk, NY: M. E. Sharpe, 1996.

Anderson, Karen. *Wartime Women: Sex Roles, Family Relations, and the Status of Women during World War II*. Westport, CT: Greenwood Press, 1981.

Apple, Betsy. *School for Rape: The Burmese Military and Sexual Violence.* Bangkok: Earthrights International, P.O. Box 12, Lard Phrao Junction, Lard Phrao, Bangkok 10901, Thailand, 1998.

Arditti, Rita. *Searching for Life: The Grandmothers of the Plaza de Mayo and the Disappeared Children of Argentina.* Berkeley: University of California Press, 1999.

Aretxaga, Begona. *Shattering Silence: Women, Nationalism, and Subjectivity in Northern Ireland.* Princeton: Princeton University Press, 1997.

Ashworth, Georgina. *Changing the Discourse: A Guide to Women and Human Rights.* London: Change–International Reports: Women and Society, 1990.

Asia Rights Watch. *Rape for Profit: Trafficking of Nepali Women to India's Brothels.* New York: Human Rights Watch, 1995.

Austen, Jane. *Persuasion.* New York: Bantam Books, 1984.

Austen, Jane. *Pride and Prejudice.* New York: Penguin Books, 1985.

Bacchi, Carol. "Women and Peace through the Polls." Working Paper No. 8, Peace Research Centre, Australian National University, Canberra, 1986.

Badran, Margot. *Feminists, Islam, and Nation.* Princeton: Princeton University Press, 1995.

Bailey, Beth, and David Farber. *The First Strange Place: The Alchemy of Race and Sex in World War II Hawaii.* New York: Free Press, 1992.

Barker, Pat. *Regeneration.* New York: Penguin, 1991.

Barnes, Susan. "WANDAS Forum: Sibling Rivalry in the Navy—Tom Cruise Meets His Little Sister." *Minerva's Bulletin Board* (winter 1995): 10–12.

Barry, Kathleen. *The Prostitution of Sexuality: The Global Exploitation of Women.* New York: New York University Press, 1995.

Barry, Kathleen, ed. *Vietnam's Women in Transition.* New York: St. Martin's Press, 1996.

Benn, Melissa. *Madonna and Child: Towards a New Politics of Motherhood.* London: Jonathan Cape, 1998.

Berkovitch, Nitza. "Motherhood as a National Mission: The Construction of Womanhood in the Legal Discourse in Israel." In a special issue titled "Cultures of Womanhood in Israel." *Women's Studies International Studies Forum* 20, nos. 5/6 (1997): 605–20.

Bernstein, Alison. *American Indians and World War II.* Norman: Oklahoma University Press, 1991.

Bishop, Ryan, and Lillian Robinson. *Night Market: Sexual Cultures and the Thai Economic Miracle.* New York: Routledge, 1998.

Blackwood, Caroline. *On the Perimeter.* London: Peguin, 1985.

Boonchalaksi, Wathinee, and Philip Guest. *Prostitution in Thailand.* Nakhonpathom, Thailand: Institute for Population and Social Research, Mahidol University, 1994.

Bousquet, Ben, and Colin Douglas. *West Indian Women at War: British Racism in World War II.* London: Lawrence and Wishart, 1991.

Bouvard, Marguerite Guzman. *Revolutionizing Motherhood: The Mothers of the Plaza de Mayo.* Wilmington, DE: Scholarly Resources Books, 1994.

Bristow, Nancy K. *Making Men Moral: Social Engineering during the Great War.* New York: New York University Press, 1996.

Brittain, Vera. *Testament of Youth.* London: Virago, 1978.

Brownmiller, Susan. *Against Our Will.* New York: Bantam, 1976.

Buckley, Susan, ed. *Broken Silence: Voices of Japanese Feminism.* Berkeley: University of California Press, 1997.

Bull, Chris. "And the Band Played On." *The Advocate,* 9 March 1993, 36–43.

Bunster, Ximena. "'Watch for the Little Nazi Man That All of Us Have Inside': The Mobilization and Demobilization of Women in Militarized Chile." *Women's Studies International Forum* 11, no. 5 (1988): 228–35.

Bunster, Ximena. "Non-Violent Alternatives in Chile's Quest for Democracy." Report for the Program on Nonviolent Sanctions in Conflict and Defense, Center for International Affairs, Harvard Unversity, Cambridge, MA, 1989. Unpublished typescript.

Bunster-Burotto, Ximena. "Surviving without Fear: Women and Torture in Latin America." In *Women and Change in Latin America,* edited by June Nash and Helen Safa, 297–326. South Hadley, MA: Bergin and Garvey Publishers, 1986.

Burke, Carol. "Pernicious Cohesion." In *It's Our Military Too!* edited by Judith Hicks Stiehm, 205–19. Philadelphia: Temple University Press, 1996.

Cammermeyer, Margarethe. *Serving in Silence.* New York: Penguin, 1994.

Carver, Terrell, and Veronique Mottier, eds. *Politics of Sexuality.* London: Routledge, 1999.

Center for Reproductive Law and Policy. "Rape and Forced Pregnancy in War and Conflict Situations." *Reproductive Freedom and Human Rights,* 30 April 1996, 1–11.

Chapkis, Wendy, ed. *Loaded Questions: Women in the Military.* Amsterdam: Transnational Institute, 1981.

Choi, Chungmoo, ed. "The Comfort Women: Colonialism, War, and Sex." In a special issue of *Positions: East Asia Cultures Critique* 5, no. 1 (spring 1997).

Choi, Soung-ai. "Whose Honor, Whose Humiliation: Women, Men, and the Economic Crisis." *Asian Women Workers Newsletter* (Hong Kong) 17, no. 2 (April 1998): 15–16.

Chuchryk, Patricia M. "From Dictatorship to Democracy: The Women's Movement in Chile." In *The Women's Movement in Latin America,* 2d ed., edited by Jane Jaquette, 65–108. Boulder, CO: Westview Press, 1994.

Clark, Darlene, Wilma King, and Linda Reed, eds. *"We Specialize in the Wholly Impossible": A Reader in Black Women's History.* Brooklyn, NY: Carlson Publishers, 1995.

Clinton, Catherine, and Nina Silber, eds. *Divided Houses: Gender and the Civil War.* New York: Oxford University Press, 1992.

Cock, Jacklyn. "Forging a New Army Out of Old Enemies: Women in the South African Military." In a special issue titled "Rethinking Women's Peace Studies." *Women's Studies Quarterly* 23, nos. 3 and 4 (fall/winter 1995): 97–111.

Cock, Jacklyn. "A Sociological Account of Light Weapons Proliferation in Southern Africa." In *Light Weapons in International Security,* edited by J. Singh, 34–51. Washington, DC: British American Security Council, 1995.

Cock, Jacklyn. *Women and War in South Africa.* Cleveland, OH: Pilgrim Press, 1993.

Cockburn, Cynthia. *The Space between Us.* New York: St. Martin's Press, 1998.

Cohn, Carol. "Gays in the Military: Texts and Subtexts." In *The "Man Question" in International Relations,* edited by Marysia Zalewski and Jane Parpart, 129–49. Boulder, CO: Westview Press, 1998.

Cook, Alice, and Gwyn Kirk. *Greenham Women Everywhere.* Boston: South End Press, 1983.

Cook, Rebecca, ed. *Human Rights of Women.* Philadelphia: University of Pennsylvania Press, 1994.

Cooke, Miriam. *Women and the War Story.* Berkeley: University of California Press, 1996.

Cooke, Miriam, and Roshini Rustomji-Kerns, eds. *Blood into Ink: South Asian and Middle Eastern Women Write War.* Boulder, CO: Westview Press, 1994.

Cooke, Miriam, and Angela Woollacott, eds. *Gendering War Talk.* Princeton: Princeton University Press, 1993.

Copelon, Rhonda. "Surfacing Gender: Reconceptualizing Crimes against Women in Time of War." In *The Women and War Reader,* edited by Lois Ann Lorentzen and Jennifer Turpin, 63–79. New York: New York University Press, 1998.

Coronel, Sheila, and Ninotchka Rosca. "For the Boys: Filipinas Expose Years of Sexual Slavery by the U.S. and Japan." *Ms. Magazine,* November/December 1993, 10–17.

Crawford, Neta C. "Out of the Closet and into a Straight Metal Jacket? Why I'm Unhappy about 'Gays in the Military.'" In *Frontline Feminism,* edited by Karen Kahn, 70–74. San Francisco: Aunt Lute Press, 1995.

Crossette, Barbara. "When Peacekeepers Turn into Troublemakers." *New York Times,* 7 January 1996.

D'Amico, Francine, and Laurie Weinstein, eds. *Gender Camouflage: Women and the U.S. Military.* New York: New York University Press, 1999.

Damousi, Joy, and Marilyn Lake, eds. *Gender and War: Australians in the Twentieth Century.* New York: Cambridge University Press, 1995.

Daniel, Ute. *The War from Within: German Working Class Women in the First World War.* New York: Berg, 1997.

De Alwis, Malathi. "Moral Mothers and Stalwart Sons." In *The Women and War Reader,* edited by Lois Ann Lorentzen and Jennifer Turpin, 254–71. New York: New York University Press, 1998.

De Alwis, Malathi. "Motherhood as a Space of Protest: Women's Political Participation in Contemporary Sri Lanka." In *Appropriating Gender: Women's Activism and the Politicization of Religion in South Asia,* edited by Amrita Basu and Patricia Jeffrey, 185–202. New York: Routledge, 1998.

Dean, Donna M. *Warriors without Weapons: The Victimization of Military Women.* Pasadena, MD: Minerva Center, 1997.

Defense Manpower Data Center. "U.S. Active Duty Servicewomen by Branch of Service, Status, Race, and Hispanic Origin as of April 30, 1997." Washington, DC: U.S. Department of Defense, 30 April 1997.

DeGrazia, Victoria. *How Fascism Ruled Women: Italy, 1922–1945.* Berkeley: University of California Press, 1992.

Des Forges, Alison. *"Leave None to Tell the Story": Genocide in Rwanda.* New York: Human Rights Watch, 1999.

Dobrofsky, Lynne R., and Constance T. Batterson. "The Military Wife and Feminism." *Signs* 2, no. 3 (spring 1977): 675–84.

Dombrowski, Nicole A., ed. *Woman and War in the Twentieth Century.* Levittown, NY: Garland Publishers, 1998.

Dorn, Edwin, ed. *Who Defends America? Race, Sex and Class in the Armed Forces.* Washington, DC: Brassey, 1989.

Dorn, Edwin, Under Secretary of Defense. "Memorandum: Guidelines for Investigating Threats against Service Members Based on Alleged Homosexuality." Washington, DC: U.S. Department of Defense, 24 March 1997.

Drakulic, Slavenka. *The Balkan Express: Fragments from the Other Side of the War.* New York: W.W. Norton, 1993.

Dreisziger, N.F., ed. *Ethnic Armies: Polyethnic Armed Forces.* Waterloo, Ontario: Wilfred Laurier University Press, 1990.

Ehrenreich, Barbara. *Blood Rites: Origins and History of the Passions of War.* New York: Henry Holt and Co., 1997.

Einhorn, Barbara, ed. "Gender, Ethnicity, and Nationalism." In a special issue of *Women's Studies International Forum* 19, nos. 1–2 (1996).

Eisenstein, Hester. *Inside Agitators: Australian Femocrats and the State.* Philadelphia: Temple University Press, 1996.

Elshtain, Jean Bethke, and Sheila Tobias, eds. *Women, Militarism, and War.* Savage, MD: Rowman and Littlefield, 1990.

Enloe, Cynthia. "All the Men Are in the Militias, All the Women Are Victims: The Politics of Masculinity and Femininity in Nationalist Wars." In *The Women and War Reader,* edited by Lois Ann Lorentzen and Jennifer Turpin, 50–62. New York: New York University Press, 1998.

Enloe, Cynthia. *Bananas, Beaches, and Bases: Making Feminist Sense of International Politics.* Berkeley: University of California Press, 1990.

Enloe, Cynthia. *Does Khaki Become You? The Militarization of Women's Lives.* London: Pandora Press/HarperCollins, 1988.

Enloe, Cynthia. *Ethnic Soldiers: State Security in Divided Societies.* London: Penguin Books, 1980.

Enloe, Cynthia. *The Morning After: Sexual Politics at the End of the Cold War.* Berkeley: University of California Press, 1993.

Enloe, Cynthia. "When Feminists Think about Rwanda." *Cultural Survival Quarterly* 19, no. 1 (spring 1995): 25–29.

Ericksen, E. Gordon. *African Company Town: The Social History of a Wartime Planning Experiment.* Dubuque, IA: Wm. C. Brown, 1964.

Faquir, Fadia. *Nisanit.* New York: Penguin Books, 1987.

Faust, Drew Gilpin. *Mothers of Invention: Women of the Slaveholding South in the American Civil War.* Chapel Hill: University of North Carolina Press, 1996.

Fehrenbach, Heide. "Mixed Blood: Discourses of Race, Sex, and German Democratization." Unpublished paper presented at the Berkshire Conference on Women's History, Chapel Hill, University of North Carolina, June 1996.

Feinman, Ilene. "Citizenship Rites: Feminist Soldiers and Feminist Antimilitarists." Unpublished book manuscript, Santa Cruz, CA, 1998.

Feldman, Lada Cale, Ines Prica, and Reana Senjkovic, eds. *Fear, Death, and Resistance: An Ethnology of War—Croatia 1991–1992.* Zagreb: Institute of Ethnology and Folklore Research, 1993.

Ferguson, Kathy E., and Phyllis Turnbull. *Oh, Say, Can You See? The Semiotics of the Military in Hawaii.* Minneapolis: University of Minnesota Press, 1998.

Figes, Eva, ed. *Women's Letters in Wartime, 1460–1945.* London: Pandora Press, 1995.

Fisher, Jo. *Out of the Shadows: Women, Resistance, and Politics in South America.* London: Latin America Bureau, 1993.

Flanders, Kaura. "Rwanda's Living Casualties." *Ms. Magazine,* March/April 1998, 27–29.

Flinn, Kelly. *Proud To Be.* New York: Random House, 1997.

Forcey, Linda Rennie. *Mothers of Sons.* New York: Praeger, 1987.

Forcey, Linda Rennie, ed. *Peace: Meanings, Politics, Strategies.* Westport, CT: Greenwood Press, 1989.

Foster, Catherine. *Women for All Seasons: The Story of the Women's International League for Peace and Freedom.* Athens: University of Georgia Press, 1989.

Frankson, Joan Ross. "Russian Mothers to the Rescue." *Ms. Magazine,* July/August 1998, 12.

Franzway, Suzanne, Dianne Court, and R. W. Connell. *Staking a Claim: Feminism, Bureaucracy, and the State.* Sydney: Allen and Unwin, 1989.

Fredland, J. Eric, Curtis L. Gilroy, Roger D. Little, and W. S. Sellman, eds. *Professionals on the Front Line: Two Decades of the All-Volunteer Force.* Washington, DC: Brassey's, 1996.

Fujimura-Fanselow, Kumiko, and Atsuko Kameda, eds. *Japanese Women: New Feminist Perspectives on the Past, Present, and Future.* New York: The Feminist Press, 1995.

Gevisser, Mark, and Edwin Cameron, eds. *Defiant Desire: Gay and Lesbian Lives in South Africa.* New York: Routledge, 1995.

Gill, Lesley. "Creating Citizens, Making Men: The Military and Masculinity in Bolivia." *Cultural Anthropology* 12, no. 4 (1997): 1–27.

Goldman, Nancy Loring. *Female Soldiers—Combatants or Noncombatants?* Westport, CT: Greenwood Press, 1981.

Goodwin-Gill, Guy, and Ilene Cohn. *Child Soldiers.* New York: Oxford University Press, 1996.

Gorham, Deborah. *Vera Brittain: A Feminist Life.* Cambridge, MA: Blackwell, 1996.

Gouliquer, Lynne. "The Needs and Issues of Military Wives: A Case Study of a Grassroots Struggle and the State." Unpublished honors thesis, Department of Sociology, St. Thomas University, Fredericton, New Brunswick, 1995.

Graff, E. J. *What Is Marriage For?* Boston: Beacon Press, 1999.

Grayzel, Susan R. *Women's Identities at War.* Chapel Hill: University of North Carolina Press, 1999.

Green, Linda. *Fear As a Way of Life: Mayan Widows in Rurual Guatemala.* New York: Columbia University Press, 1999.

Grossman, Atina. "A Question of Silence: The Rape of German Women by Occupation Soldiers." *October Magazine,* no. 72 (spring 1995): 43–63.

Guenther, Irene V. "Nazi 'Chic': German Politics and Women's Fashion." *Fashion Theory* 1 (1997): 29–58.

Gusterson, Hugh. *Nuclear Rites: A Weapons Laboratory at the End of the Cold War.* Berkeley: University of California Press, 1996.

Gutmann, Stephanie. "The Great Umbrella Debate." *New York Times,* 9 October 1997.

Hacker, Burton. "Women and Military Institutions in Early Modern Europe: A Reconnaissance." *Signs* 6, no. 4 (summer 1981): 641–55.

Hagist, Don N. "The Women of the British Army during the American Revolution." *Minerva: Quarterly Report on Women and the Military* 13, no. 2 (summer 1995): 29–85.

Hall, Edmund. *We Can't Even March Straight: Homosexuality in the British Armed Forces.* London: Vintage, 1995.

Hall, Radclyffe. "Miss Ogilvy Finds Herself." In *The Other Persuasion,* edited by Seymour Kleinberg. New York: Vintage Books, 1977.

Han, Jungwoo, and Lily H. M. Ling. "Authoritarianism in the Hypermasculinized State: Hybridity, Patriarchy, and Capitalism in Korea." *International Studies Quarterly* 42 (1998): 53–78.

Harford, Barbara, and Sarah Hopkins, eds. *Greenham Common: Women at the Wire.* London: Women's Press, 1984.

Harrell, Margaret C., and Laura Miller. *New Opportunities for Military Women.* Santa Monica, CA: Rand Corporation, 1997.

Harrison, Deborah, and Lucie Laliberte. *No Life Like It: Military Wives in Canada.* Toronto: James Lorimer and Co., 1994.

Haruhi, Tono. "Women Do Not Allow War!" *AMPO* 13, no. 4 (1981): 17–20.

Hayakawa, Noriyo. "Feminism and Nationalism in Japan, 1868–1945." *Journal of Women's History* 7, no. 4 (1996): 108–19.

Herder, Steve, and Judy Ledgerwood, eds. *Propaganda, Politics, and Violence in Cambodia.* Armonk, NY: M. E. Sharpe, 1996.

Herek, Gregory M., Jared B. Jobe, and Ralph M. Carney, eds. *Out in Force: Sexual Orientation and the Military.* Chicago: University of Chicago Press, 1996.

Herman, Ellen. *The Romance of American Psychology: Political Culture in the Age of Experts.* Berkeley: University of California Press, 1995.

Herzog, Hanna. "Enlisting Mom: Military-Family Relations as a Gendering Social Mechanism—The Case of Israel." Department of Sociology, Tel Aviv University, February 1997. Typescript.

Hickman, Mary, and Ailbhe Smyth, eds. "The Irish Issue: The British Question." Special issue of *Feminist Review,* no. 50 (summer 1995).

Hicks, George. *The Comfort Women: Sex Slaves of the Japanese Imperial Forces.* New York: W. W. Norton, 1995.

Hillman, Elizabeth Lutes. "Uniformed Identities: Women, Gender, and Images at the United States Service Academies." Unpublished master's thesis, Department of History, University of Pennsylvania, Philadelphia, 1994.

Hilsdon, Anne-Marie. *Madonnas and Martyrs: Militarism and Violence in the Philippines.* Sydney: Allen and Unwin, 1997.

Hine, Darlene Clark. *Hine Sight: Black Women and the Reconstruction of American History.* Bloomington: Indiana Press, 1994.

Hine, Darlene Clark, Elsa Barkley Brown, and Rosalyn Terborg-Penn, eds. *Black Women in America: An Historical Encyclopedia,* vols. I and II. New York: Carlson Publishing, 1995.

Hoehn, Maria. "Amazons, Veronikas, and Negerliebchen." Unpublished paper presented at the Berkshire Conference on Women's History, Chapel Hill, University of North Carolina, June 1996.

Hoganson, Kristin L. *Fighting for American Manhood: How Gender Politics Provoked the Spanish-American and Philippine-American Wars.* New Haven, CT: Yale University Press, 1998.

Howard, Keith, ed. *True Stories of the Korean Comfort Women.* New York: Cassell, 1997.

Human Rights Watch. *The Scars of Death: Children Abducted by the Lord's Resistance Army in Uganda.* New York: Human Rights Watch, 1997.

Human Rights Watch. *Indonesia—The Damaging Debate on Rapes of Ethnic Chinese Women.* New York: Human Rights Watch, 1998.

Human Rights Watch/Asia and Women's Rights Watch. *A Modern Form of Slavery: Trafficking of Burmese Women and Girls into Brothels in Thailand.* New York: Human Rights Watch, 1993.

Humphrey, Mary Ann. *My Country, My Right to Serve: Experiences of Gay Men and Women in the Military, World War II to the Present.* New York: HarperCollins, 1990.

Hunter-Gault, Charlayne. *In My Place.* New York: Vintage Books, 1992.

Hymowitz, Carol, and Michaele Weisman. *A History of Women in America.* New York: Bantam, 1978.

Indra, Doreen, ed. *Engendering Forced Migration.* New York: Berghahn Books, 1998.

International Institute of Strategic Studies. *The Military Balance.* London: Oxford University Press, 1998.

Isaksson, Eva, ed. *Women and the Military System.* New York: St. Martin's Press, 1988.

Izraeli, Dafna. "Gendering Military Service in the Israeli Defense Forces." *Israeli Social Science Research* 12, no. 1 (1997): 13–27.

Jahnkow, Rick. "Countering Pentagon Propaganda: Activists Confront Recruiters, Promote Alternatives to Military for Youth." *Resist Newsletter,* July/August 1997, 1–4.

Jaquette, Jane S., ed. *The Women's Movement in Latin America,* 2d ed. Boulder, CO: Westview Press, 1994.

Jeansonne, Glen. *Women of the Far Right: The Mothers Movement and World War II.* Chicago: University of Chicago Press, 1997.

Johnson, Carol. "Negotiating the Politics of Inclusion: Women and the Australian Labor Governments 1983 to 1995." *Feminist Review,* no. 52 (1996): 102–17.

Johnson, Karen. "Autobiography: An Officer and a Feminist." In *Gender Camouflage: Women and the U.S. Military,* edited by Francine D'Amico and Laurie Weinstein, 123–41. New York: New York University Press, 1999.

Jok, Madut Jok. "Militarism, Gender, and Reproductive Risk: The Case of Abortion in Southern Sudan." Unpublished paper presented at the Conference on Militarism and Gender, Women's Studies Program, University of Wisconsin, Madison, 13 October 1997.

Jordan, Harold. "Making Student Soldiers: JROTC Academies." *On Watch: Newsletter of the National Lawyers Guild Military Task Force* (San Diego, CA) 16, nos. 2–3 (November 1995): 5.

Joseph, Suad. "Gender and Citizenship in Middle East States." In a special issue titled "Gender and Citizenship in the Middle East." *Middle East Report,* no. 198 (January-March 1996): 4–11.

Junor, Beth. *Greenham Commons Women's Peace Camp: A History of Non-Violent Resistance, 1984–1995.* London: Working Press, 1995.

Kahn, Karen, ed. *Frontline Feminism.* San Francisco: Aunt Lute Press, 1995.

Kakazu, Katsuko, and the Okinawa Women's History Group. "Map of Japanese Military Brothels in Okinawa." *Okinawa: Peace, Human Rights, Women, Environment,* no. 4 (February 1997): 4.

Kampwirth, Karen. "Legislating Personal Politics in Sandinista Nicaragua, 1979–1992." *Women's Studies International Forum* 21, no. 1 (1998): 53–64.

Kandyoti, Deniz, ed. *Women, Islam, and the State.* Philadelphia: Temple University Press, 1996.

Kane, Stephanie. "Prostitution and the Military in Belize: Planning AIDS Intervention in Belize." *Social Science and Medicine* 36, no. 7 (1993): 965–79.

Kaplan, Amy, and Donald Pease. *Cultures of United States Imperialism.* Durham, NC: Duke University Press, 1993.

Katzenstein, Mary Fainsod. *Faithful and Fearless: Moving Feminist Protest inside the Church and Military.* Princeton: Princeton University Press, 1998.

Katzenstein, Mary Fainsod, and Judith Reppy, eds. *Beyond Zero Tolerance: Discrimination in Military Culture.* Lanham, MD: Rowman and Littlefield, 1999.

Kent, Susan Kingsley. *Making Peace: The Reconstruction of Gender in Interwar Britain.* Princeton: Princeton University Press, 1993.

Kent, Susan Kingsley. *Sex and Suffrage in Britain, 1860–1914*. Princeton: Princeton University Press, 1990.

Kerber, Linda. *The Constitutional Right to Be Ladies*. New York: Farrar Strauss, 1998.

Kim, Elaine H., and Chungmoo Choi, eds. *Dangerous Women: Gender and Korean Nationalism*. New York: Routledge, 1997.

Kim, Seung-Kyung. *Class Struggle or Family Struggle? The Lives of Women Factory Workers in South Korea*. New York: Cambridge University Press, 1997.

Kirshenbaum, Gayle. "In UN Peacekeeping, Women Are an Untapped Resource." *Ms. Magazine,* January/February 1997, 20–21.

Kirshenbaum, Gayle, and Marina Gilbert. "Who's Watching the Peacekeepers?" *Ms. Magazine,* May/June 1994, 10–15.

Klein, Naomi. "Is War Crimes Prosecution in the Right Hands?" *Ms. Magazine,* July/August 1996, 22–23.

Koonz, Claudia. *Mothers in the Fatherland: Women, the Family, and Nazi Politics*. New York: St. Martins Press, 1986.

Korac, Maja. "Understanding Ethnic-National Identity and Its Meaning: Questions from Women's Experience." *Women's Studies International Forum* 19, nos. 1/2 (1996): 133–43.

Korac, Maja. *Linking Arms: Women and War in Post-Yugoslavia States*. Uppsala, Sweden: Life and Peace Institute, 1998.

Korac, Maja. "The Power of Gender in the Transition from State Socialism to Ethnic Nationalism, Militarization, and War: The Case of Post-Yugoslav States." Unpublished Ph.D. dissertation, Graduate Programme in Sociology, York University, North York, Ontario, Canada, 1998.

Kristof, Nicholas D. "Fearing G.I. Occupiers, Japan Urged Women into Brothels." *New York Times,* 27 October 1995.

Kumar, Radha. *The History of Doing: An Illustrated Account of Movements for Women's Rights and Feminism in India, 1800–1990*. London: Verso, 1995.

Kwon, Insook. "'The New Women's Movement' in 1920s Korea: Rethinking the Relationship between Imperialism and Women." *Gender and History* 10, no. 3 (November 1998): 381–405.

Labon, Joanna, ed. *Balkan Blues: Writing Out of Yugoslavia*. Evanston, IL: Northwestern University Press, 1994.

Lancaster, Roger. *Life Is Hard: Machismo, Danger, and the Intimacy of Power in Nicaragua*. Berkeley: University of California Press, 1992.

Lant, Antonia. *Blackout: Reinventing Women for Wartime British Cinema*. Princeton: Princeton University Press, 1991.

LaViolette, Nicole, and Sandra Whitworth. "No Safe Haven: Sexuality as a Universal Human Right and Gay and Lesbian Activism in International Politics." *Millennium: Journal of International Studies* 23, no. 3 (1994): 563–88.

Lehr, Doreen M. "Madwoman in the Military's Attic: Mental Health and Defense Department Policy in the Lives of U.S. Air Force Wives." Ph.D. dissertation, Union Institute, Cincinnati, OH, 1993.

Lehring, Gary. *Officially Gay: Politics, Policies, and the Public Construction of Sexual Difference.* Philadelphia: Temple University Press, 1999.

Leonard, Elizabeth D. *Yankee Women: Gender Battles in the Civil War.* New York: W. W. Norton, 1994.

Leonard, Elizabeth D. *All the Daring of a Soldier: Women of the civil War Armies.* New York: W. W. Norton, 1999.

"Letters: An Open Letter to Yasushi Akashi." *Phnom Penh Post,* 4 October 1994.

Levine, Philippa. "'Walking the Streets in a Way No Decent Woman Should': Women Police in World War One." *Journal of Modern History,* no. 66 (1994): 34–78.

Levine, Philippa. "Battle Colors: Race, Sex, and Colonial Soldiery in World War II." *Journal of Women's History* 9, no. 4 (1998): 104–30.

Liddington, Jill. *The Long Road to Greenham: Feminism and Anti-Militarism in Britain since 1820.* Syracuse, NY: Syracuse University Press, 1991.

Lorentzen, Lois Ann, and Jennifer Turpin, eds. *The Women and War Reader.* New York: New York University Press, 1998.

Lowry, Robert. *The Armed Forces of Indonesia.* Sydney: Allen and Unwin, 1996.

Lutz, Catherine, and Lesley Bartlett. *Making Soldiers in the Public Schools: An Analysis of the Army ROTC Curriculum.* Philadelphia: American Friends Service Committee, June 1995.

MacDonald, Sharon, Pat Holden, and Shirley Ardner, eds. *Images of Women in Peace and War.* Madison: University of Wisconsin Press, 1987.

Mackie, Vera. *Creating Socialist Women in Japan: Gender, Labour, and Activism, 1900–1937.* Cambridge: Cambridge University Press, 1997.

Makiya, Kanan. *Cruelty and Silence: War, Tyranny, Uprising, and the Arab World.* London: Jonathan Cape, 1993.

Manning, Lory, and Jennifer E. Griffith. *Women in the Military: Where They Stand.* Washington, DC: Women's Research and Education Institute, 1998.

Marshall, Kathryn. *In the Combat Zone.* New York: Penguin Books, 1988.

Massey, Mary Elizabeth. *Women in the Civil War.* Lincoln: University of Nebraska Press, 1995.

Maunaguru, Sitralega. "Gendering Tamil Nationalism." In *Unmaking the Nation: The Politics and History of Sri Lanka,* edited by Pradeep Jeganthan and Qadri Ismail, 158–69. Colombo: Sri Lanka Social Scientists' Association, 1995.

May, Elaine Tyler. *Homeward Bound: American Families in the Cold War.* New York: Basic Books, 1988.

Mayer, Tamar, ed. *Women and the Israeli Occupation.* New York: Routledge, 1994.

Mazali, Rela. "Raising Boys to Maintain Armies." *British Medical Jounal* 311 (September 1995): 694.

Mazali, Rela. "The Taboo of the Military." *Challenge,* no. 36 (March-April 1996): 18–19.

Mazurana, Dyan E., and Susan R. McKay. *Women and Peacebuilding.* Montreal: International Centre for Human Rights and Democratic Development, 1999.

McCoy, Alfred. " 'Same Banana': Hazing and Honor at the Philippine Military Academy." *Journal of Asian Studies* 54, no. 3 (August 1995): 689–726.

McDonnell, Etain, and Karuna Buakumsri. "Prostitutes in Japan: A Shriek of Silence." *Friends of Women Newsletter* (Bangkok) 4, no. 2 (December 1993): 13–17.

Meigs, Mary. "A Lesbian Wave." In *Beyond the Home Front: Women's Autobiographical Writing of the Two World Wars,* edited by Yvonne M. Klein, 155–61. New York: New York University Press, 1996.

Melman, Billie, ed. *Borderlines: Genders and Identities in War and Peace, 1870–1930.* New York: Routledge, 1998.

Merryman, Molly. *Clipped Wings: The Rise and Fall of the Women Airforce Service Pilots of World War II.* New York: New York University Press, 1997.

Mertus, Julie. *Kosovo: How Myths and Truths Started a War.* Berkeley: University of California Press, 1999.

Mertus, Julie, et al., eds. *The Suitcase: Refugees' Voices from Bosnia and Croatia.* Berkeley: University of California Press, 1996.

Meyer, Leisa D. *Creating G.I. Jane: Sexuality and Power in the Women's Army Corps during World War II.* New York: Columbia University Press, 1996.

Meyer, Mary K., and Elisabeth Prugl, eds. *Gender Politics in Global Governance.* Lanham, MD: Rowman and Littlefield, 1999.

Meyerowitz, Joanne, ed. *Not June Cleaver: Women and Gender in Postwar America, 1945–1960.* Philadelphia: Temple University Press, 1994.

Milic, Andjelka. "Nationalism and Sexism: Eastern Europe in Transition." In *Europe's New Nationalism,* edited by R. Coplan and J. Feffer, 169–83. London: Oxford University Press, 1996.

Military Family Resource Center. *Military Family Demographics: Profile of the Military Family.* Arlington, VA: Personnel Support, Families and Education Office of Family Policy, Military Family Resource Center, U.S. Department of Defense, December 1995.

Mladjenovic, Lepa, and Vera Litricin. "Belgrade Feminists 1992: Separation, Guilt, and Identity Crises." *Feminist Review,* no. 45 (autumn 1993): 113–19.

Moon, Katharine. *Sex among Allies: Military Prostitution in U.S.-Korea Relations.* New York: Columbia University Press, 1997.

Moon, Seungsook. "Gender, Militarization, and Universal Male Conscription in South Korea." In *The Women and War Reader,* edited by Lois Ann Lorentzen and Jennifer Turpin, 90–100. New York: New York University Press, 1998.

Moore, Brenda L. "A Changing Military: Implications for the Role of Women." Unpublished paper presented at the Conference on Women in Uniform, sponsored by the Women's Research and Education Institute, Washington, DC, December 1996.

Moore, Brenda L. *To Serve My Country, To Serve My Race.* New York: New York University Press, 1995.

Moore, Tracy, ed. *Lesbiot: Israeli Lesbians Talk about Sexuality, Feminism, Judaism, and their Lives.* New York: Cassell, 1995.

Morris, Madeline. "By Force of Arms: Rape, War, and Military Culture." *Duke Law Journal* 45, no. 4 (1996): 652–782.

Mydans, Seth. "In Jakarta, Reports of Numerous Rapes of Chinese in Riots." *New York Times,* 10 June 1998.

Narayan, Uma. "'Mail-Order' Brides: Immigrant Women, Domestic Violence, and Immigration Law." *Hypatia* 10, no. 1 (winter 1995): 105–10.

The National Commission on the Role of Filipino Women. *Philippine Plan for Gender-Responsive Development, 1995–2025.* Manila: Government of the Philippines, 1995.

National Defense Research Institute. *Sexual Orientation and U.S. Military Personnel Policy: Options and Assessment.* Santa Monica, CA: Rand Corporation, 1993.

National Organization for Women. "Brief for Amicus Curiae, in the Case Before the Supreme Court on the United States, Bernard Roster, Director of Selective Service, v. Robert L. Goldberg et al." Washington, DC: National Organization for Women, 1980.

Nordstrom, Carolyn, ed. "Women and War." A special issue of *Cultural Survival Quarterly* 19, no. 1 (spring 1995).

North Atlantic Treaty Organization. *Women in NATO.* Brussels: International Military Staff, NATO Headquarters, 1994.

O'Hara, Jane. "Rape in the Military." *Maclean's,* 25 May 1998, 15–21.

O'Hara, Jane. "Abuse of Power: Critics Say the Military Justice System has Failed." *Maclean's,* 13 July 1998, 16–20.

O'Hara, Jane. "Of Rape and Justice: Has Anything Really Changed in the Canadian Military?" *Maclean's,* December 1998, 16–21.

Office of the Inspector General. *The Tailhook Report.* New York: St. Martin's Press, 1993.

Olujic, Maria. "Sexual Coercion and Torture in the Former Yugoslavia." *Cultural Survival Quarterly* 19, no. 1 (spring 1995): 43–45.

Ong, Aihwa, and Michael G. Peletz, eds. *Bewitching Women, Pious Men: Gender and Body Politics in Southeast Asia.* Berkeley: University of California Press, 1995.

Ouditt, Sharon. *Fighting Forces, Writing History: Identity and Ideology in the First World War.* New York: Routledge, 1994.

Park, Sandra Shin-Young. "For a World without Bases: The Okinawa Feminist Movement against U.S. Japan Alliance Politics and Militarization." Unpublished senior thesis, The Committee on Degrees in the Social Sciences, Radcliffe College, Harvard University, Cambridge, MA, March 1997.

Parker, Tony. *Soldier, Soldier.* London: Coronet Books, 1985.

Pennington, Reina J. "Offensive Women: Women in Combat in the Red Army." Unpublished paper presented at the Berkshire Conference on Women's History, Chapel Hill, University of North Carolina, June 1996.

Perlez, Jane. "G.I. Charm Overcomes Anxieties in Hungary." *New York Times,* 5 December 1996.

Peterson, V. Spike, and Anne Sisson Runyan. *Global Gender Issues,* 2d ed. Boulder, CO: Westview Press, 1999.

Pettman, Jan. *Worlding Women: A Feminist International Politics.* Sydney, Australia: Allen and Unwin, 1996.

Pierson, Ruth Roach. *"They're Women After All": The Second World War and Canadian Womanhood.* Toronto: McClelland and Stewart, 1986.

Pierson, Ruth Roach, ed. *Women and Peace: Theoretical, Historical, and Practical Perspectives.* London: Croom Helm, 1987.

Pitter, Laura, and Alexandra Stiglmayer. "Will the World Remember? Can the Women Forget." *Ms. Magazine,* March/April 1993, 19–22.

Povrzanovic, Maja. "Crossing the Borders: Croatian War Ethnographies." *Narodna Umjetnost: Craotian Journal of Ethnology and Folklore Research* 32, no. 1 (1995): 91–106.

Prugl, Elisabeth. "Gender in International Organization and Global Governance." *International Studies Association Research Notes* 21, no. 1 (winter 1996): 15–24.

Raccioppi, Linda, and Katherine O'Sullivan See. *Women's Activism in Contemporary Russia.* Philadelphia: Temple University Press, 1997.

Ramusack, Barbara N., and Antoinette Burton. "Feminism, Imperialism, and Race: A Dialogue between India and Britain." A special issue of *Women's History Review* 3, no. 4 (1994).

Ranchod-Nilsson, Sita. "From the Margins of the State to the Center of the Cultural Crisis: Women and the Reconfiguration of the One-Party State in Zimbabwe." In *The African State at Critical Juncture,* edited by Leonard Villon and Philip Huxtable, 132–53. Boulder, CO: Lynne Rienner Publishers, 1997.

Randall, Margaret. *Sandino's Daughters.* Vancouver: New Star Books, 1981.

Randall, Margaret. *Sandino's Daughters Revisited: Feminism in Nicaragua.* New Brunswick, NJ: Rutgers University Press, 1994.

Randall, Vicky, and Georgina Waylen, eds. *Gender, Politics, and the State.* New York: Routledge, 1998.

Reno, William. *Warlord Politics and African States.* Boulder, CO: Lynne Rienner Publishers, 1998.

Rimmer, Craig, ed. *Gay Rights, Military Wrongs: Political Perspectives on Lesbians and Gays in the Military.* New York: Garland Press, 1996.

Rodriquez, Regina, Ximena Bunster, and Cynthia Enloe, eds. *La Mujer Ausente: Derechos Humanos en el Mundo,* 2d ed. Santiago: Isis International, 1997.

Roseneil, Sasha. *Disarming Patriarchy: Feminism and Political Action at Greeham.* Milton Keynes, UK: Open University Press, 1995.

Rowbotham, Sheila. *A Century of Women: The History of Women in Britain and the United States.* New York: Vintage, 1997.

Ruddick, Sara. "'Women of Peace': A Feminist Construction," in *The Women and War Reader,* edited by Lois Ann Lorentzen and Jennifer Turpin, 213–26. New York: New York University Press, 1998.

Rupp, Leila. *Worlds of Women: The Making of an International Women's Movement.* Princeton: Princeton University Press, 1997.

Sackville-West, Vita. *The Woman's Land Army.* London: Michael Joseph, 1944.

Sadler, Georgia C. "Philippine Bases: Going, Going, Gone." *Proceedings,* U.S. Naval Institute, November 1988, 89–96.

Sales, Rosemary, and Jeanne Gregory. "Refugee Women in London: The Experiences of Somali Women." *Refuge: Canada's Periodical on Refugees* 17, no. 1 (February 1998): 16–20.

Scary, Elaine. *The Body in Pain: The Making and Unmaking of the World.* New York: Oxford University Press, 1985.

Scheper-Hughes, Nancy. "Maternal Thinking and the Politics of War." In *The Women and War Reader,* edited by Lois Ann Lorentzen and Jennifer Turpin, 227–33. New York: New York University Press, 1998.

Schmitt, Eric. "Stress Follows Troops Home From Gulf. "*New York Times,* 16 July 1991.

Schmitt, Eric. "As Military Pay Slips Behind, Poverty Invades the Ranks." *New York Times,* 12 June 1994.

Schmitt, Eric. "Pentagon Battles Plans for International War Crimes Tribunal." *New York Times,* 14 April 1998.

Schmuki, Maryanna. "Human Rights: Setting the Stage for Protecting Refugee Women." *Refuge: Canada's Periodical on Refugees* 17, no. 1 (February 1998): 4–9.

Schoppmann, Claudia. *Days of Masquerade: Life Stories of Lesbians during the Third Reich.* New York: Columbia University Press, 1996.

Schultz, Jane E. "Race, Gender, and Bureaucracy: Civil War Nurses and the Pension Bureau." *Journal of Women's History* 6, no. 2 (summer 1994): 44–69.

Sciolino, Elaine. "The British Carried Umbrellas to Waterloo. Don't Laugh." *New York Times,* 3 August 1997.

Sciolino, Elaine. "From a Love Affair to a Court Martial." *New York Times,* 11 May 1997.

Seager, Joni. *Earth Follies: Coming to Feminist Terms with the Global Environmental Crisis.* New York: Routledge, 1993.

Seager, Joni. *The State of Women in the World Atlas.* New York: Penguin Books, 1997.

Secretary of the Army. "Senior Review Panel Report on Sexual Harassment." Vols. 1 and 2. Washington, DC: U.S. Department of Defense, July 1997.

Segal, Mady Wechsler, and Jesse J. Harris. *What We Know about Army Families.* Alexandria, VA: U.S. Army Research Institute for the Behavioral and Social Sciences, 1993.

Seifert, Ruth. "The Second Front: Sexual Violence in Wars." *Women's Studies International Forum* 19, nos. 1/2 (1996): 35–43.

Seifert, Ruth, and Christine Eiffert, eds. *Gender and the Military.* Hamburg: German Sociological Association, 1998.

Servicemembers Legal Defense Fund. "Conduct Unbecoming: The Fourth Annual Report on 'Don't Ask, Don't Tell, Don't Pursue.'" Washington, DC: Servicemembers Legal Defense Fund, February 1998.

Sharoni, Simona. *Gender and the Israeli-Palestinian Conflict: The Politics of Women's Resistance.* Syracuse: Syracuse University Press, 1995.

Shay, Jonathan. *Achilles Heel in Vietnam: Combat Trauma and the Undoing of Character.* New York: Touchstone Books, 1994.

Sheridan, Dorothy, ed. *Wartime Women.* London: Mandarin, 1990.

Shilts, Randy. *Conduct Unbecoming: Gays and Lesbians in the U.S. Military.* New York: St. Martin's Press, 1993.

Singerman, Diane. *Avenues of Participation: Family, Politics, and Networks in Urban Quarters of Cairo.* Princeton: Princeton University Press, 1995.

Sinha, Mrinalini, Donna J. Guy, and Angela Woollacott, eds. "Feminisms and Internationalism." A special issue of *Gender and History* 10, no. 3 (November 1998).

Skocpol, Theda. *Protecting Soldiers and Mothers: The Political Origins of Social Policy in the United States.* Cambridge: Harvard University Press, 1993.

Smith, Graham. *When Jim Crow Met John Bull: Black American Soldiers in World War II Britain.* New York: St. Martin's Press, 1988.

Smith, Lois M., and Alfred Padula. *Sex and Revolution: Women in Socialist Cuba.* New York: Oxford University Press, 1996.

Smyth, Ailbhe. "Paying Our Disrespects to the Bloody States We're In: Women, Violence, Culture, and the State." In a special double issue entitled "Irish Women." *Journal of Women's History* 6, no. 4, and 7, no. 1 (winter/spring 1995): 68–83.

Soh, Chunghee Sarah. "The Korean 'Comfort Women': Movement for Redress." *Asian Survey* 36, no. 12 (1997): 1226–40.

Stanley, Alessandra. "Russian Woman Sails Solo in a Sea of Cadets." *New York Times,* 27 March 1998.

Starns, Pam. "Fighting Militarism? British Nursing during the Second World War." In *War, Medicine, and Modernity, 1860–1945,* edited by Roger Cooter et al. London: Sutton Publishing, 1999.

Stein, Gertrude. *Brewsie and Willie.* New York: Random House, 1946.

Stiehm, Judith Hicks. *Bring Me Men and Women: Mandated Change at the U.S. Air Force Academy.* Berkeley: University of California Press, 1981.

Stiehm, Judith Hicks, ed. *It's Our Military Too! Women and the U.S. Military.* Philadelphia: Temple University Press, 1996.

Stiglmayer, Alexandra, ed. *Mass Rape: The War Against Women in Bosnia-Herzegovina.* Lincoln: University of Nebraska Press, 1994.

Stoddard, Ellwyn R. "Married Female Officers in a Combat Branch: Occupation-Family Stress and Future Career Choices." *Minerva: Quarterly Report on Women and the Military* 12, no. 2 (summer 1994): 1–14.

Strachey, Lytton. *Florence Nightingale.* New York: Penguin Books, 1997.

Sturdevant, Saundra, and Brenda Stoltzfus. *Let the Good Times Roll: Prostitution and the U.S. Military in Asia.* New York: The New Press, 1992.

Summerfield, Penny. *Reconstructing Women's Wartime Lives.* New York: Manchester University Press, 1998.

Summers, Anne. *Angels and Citizens: British Women as Military Nurses 1854–1914.* New York: Routledge and Kegan Paul, 1988.

Sutton, Constance, ed. *Feminism, Nationalism, and Militarism.* Arlington, VA: Association for Feminist Anthropology of the American Anthropological Association, 1995.

Swerdlow, Amy. *Women Strike for Peace: Traditional Motherhood and Radical Politics in the 1960s.* Chicago: Chicago University Press, 1993.

Swiss, Shana, and Joan E. Giller. "Rape as a Crime of War: A Medical Perspective." *The Journal of the American Medical Association* 270 (4 August 1993): 614.

Sylvester, Christine. "Patriarchy, Peace, and Women Warriors." In *Peace: Meanings, Politics, Strategies,* edited by Linda Rennie Forcey, 97–112. Westport, CT: Greenwood Press, 1989.

Tamang, Seira. "Nepali Women as Military Wives." Unpublished honors thesis, Department of Government, Clark University, Worcester, MA, 1992.

Tanaka, Yuki. "U.S. Military Indifference towards 'Comfort Women.'" *Bulletin of Concerned Asian Scholars,* forthcoming.

Tatchell, Peter. *We Don't Want to March Straight: Masculinity, Queers and the Military.* London: Cassell, 1995.

Thitsa, Khin. *Providence and Prostitution: Image and Reality for Women in Buddhist Thailand.* London: Change: International Reports, 1980.

Thornhill, Teresa. *Making Women Talk: The Interrogation of Palestinian Women Detainees.* London: Lawyers for Palestinian Human Rights, 1992.

Tickner, J. Ann. "You Just Don't Understand: Troubled Engagements between Feminists and IR Theorists." *International Studies Quarterly* 41 (1997): 611–32.

Tisdale, Julie. "Venereal Disease and the Policing of the Amateur in Melbourne during World War I." *Lilith: A Feminist History Journal,* no. 9 (autumn 1996): 33–50.

Trustram, Myna. *Women of the Regiment: Marriage and the Victorian Army.* Cambridge: Cambridge Unversity Press, 1984.

Turner, Karen, with Phan Thanh Hao. *Even the Women Must Fight: Memories of War from North Vietnam.* New York: John Wiley and Sons, 1998.

Turshen, Meredith, and Clotilde Twagiramariya, eds. *What Women Do in Wartime: Gender and Conflict in Africa.* New York: Zed Books, 1998.

U.S. Department of Defense, Office of Inspector General. *Tailhook 91, Part 1: Review of the Navy Investigation.* Washington, DC: Department of Defense, September 1992.

U.S. Department of State. *Country Reports on Human Rights Practices for 1993.* Washington, DC: U.S. Government Printing Office, 1994.

Vaid, Urvashi. *Virtual Equality: The Mainstreaming of Gay and Lesbian Liberation.* New York: Anchor Books, 1995.

Van Devanter, Lynda. *Home Before Morning: Story of an Army Nurse in Vietnam.* New York: Beaufort Books, 1983.

Van Driel-Murray, Carol. "Gender in Question." In *Theoretical Roman Archeology: Second Conference Proceedings,* edited by Peter Rush, 9–48. Aldershot, UK: Avebury, 1995.

Walkowitz, Judith. *Prostitution and Victorian Society.* London: Cambridge University Press, 1980.

Weaver, Winnie S. *Lesbians in the Military Speak Out.* Northboro, MA: Madwomen Press, 1993.

Weber, Cynthia. "Something's Missing: Male Hysteria and the U.S. Invasion of Panama." In *The "Man Question" in International Relations,* edited by Marysia Zalewski and Jane Parpart, 150–68. Boulder, CO: Westview Press, 1998.

Wee, Eric L. "JROTC Advances on High Schools." *Washington Post,* 18 December 1995.

Weinstein, Laurie, and Christie C. White, eds. *Wives and Warriors: Women and the Military in the United States and Canada.* Westport, CT: Bergin and Garvey, 1996.

Weitz, Margaret Collins. *Sisters in the Resistance: How Women Fought to Free France 1940–1945.* New York: John Wiley and Sons, 1995.

Wertsch, Mary. *Military Brats: The Legacy of Childhood inside the Fortress.* New York: Crown Books, 1991.

Westheider, James E. *Fighting on Two Fronts: African-Americans and the Vietnam War.* New York: New York University Press, 1997.

Whites, LeeAnn. *The Civil War as a Crisis in Gender: Augusta, Georgia, 1860–1890.* Athens, GA: University of Georgia Press, 1995.

Whitworth, Sandra. *Bullies in Blue Berets: Gender, Race, and the Politics of Peacekeeping.* Boulder, CO: Lynne Rienner Publishers, 1999.

Whitworth, Sandra. *Feminism and International Relations: Towards a Political Economy of Gender in Interstate and Non-Governmental Institutions.* New York: St. Martin's Press, 1994.

Whitworth, Sandra. "Gender, Race, and the Politics of Peacekeeping." In *A Future for Peacekeeping?* edited by Eddie Moxon-Browne. London: Macmillan, 1999.

Willoughby, John. "The Sexual Behavior of American GIs during the Early Years of the Occupation of Germany." *Journal of Military History* 62 (January 1998): 155–74.

Wilson, Lynn. "Epistomology and Power: Ethnography at Greenham." In *Anthropology for the Nineties,* edited by Johnetta Cole, 42–58. New York: Free Press, 1988.

Winter, Jay, and Blaine Bagget. *The Great War and the Shaping of the 20th Century.* New York: Penguin Books, 1996.

Women in Black, eds. *Compilation of Information on Crimes of War against Women in ex-Yugoslavia—Actions and Initiatives in their Defence.* Montpelier, France: Women Living Under Muslim Laws, 1994.

Women's Research and Education Institute. "Selected Statistics on Women in the U.S. Armed Forces and Civilian Firefighting and Police Occupations." Unpublished report, Women's Research and Education Institute, Washington, DC, December 1998.

Women's Rights Project. *The Human Rights Watch Global Report on Women's Human Rights*. New York: Human Rights Watch, 1995.

Women's Rights Watch. *Widespread Rape of Somali Women Refugees*. New York: Human Rights Watch, 1993.

Women's Rights Watch. *Rape in Haiti: A Weapon of Terror*. New York: Human Rights Watch, July 1994.

Women's Rights Watch. *Shattered Lives: Sexual Violence during the Rwanda Genocide and its Aftermath*. New York: Human Rights Watch, 1996.

Yeatman, Anna. *Bureaucrats, Technocrats, Femocrats: Essays on the Contemporary Australian State*. Sydney: Allen and Unwin, 1990.

Yung, Judy. *Unbound Feet: A Social History of Chinese Women in San Francisco*. Berkeley: University of California Press, 1995.

Yuval-Davis, Nira. *Gender and Nation*. London: Sage Publications, 1997.

Zajovic, Stasa, ed. *Women for Peace*. Belgrade: Women in Black, 1994.

Zajovic, Stasa. "Report on the Current Situation at Kosovo, Serbia, and Montenegro." In *Compilation of Information* (edited by Women Living under Muslim Laws, Montpelier, France) (winter 1998): 1–5.

Zajovic, Stasa, Zorica Trifunovic, and Lino Veljak. "Report about the Protest in Serbia." *Women Living Under Muslim Laws* (spring 1997): 24–27.

Zalewski, Marysia, and Jane Parpart, eds. *The "Man Question" in International Relations*. Boulder, CO: Westview Press, 1998.

Zawilski, Valeria. "Saving Mothers' Sons." Unpublished paper presented at the Conference on Women in Conflict Zones, Eaton Hall, King City, Ontario, 13 May 1997.

Zeeland, Steven. *Barrack Buddies and Soldier Lovers: Dialogues with Gay Young Men in the U.S. Military*. New York: Haworth Press, 1993.

Zeiger, Susan. "'She Didn't Raise Her Boy to Be a Slacker': Motherhood, Conscription, and the Culture of the First World War." *Feminist Studies* 23, no. 1 (autumn 1993): 103–30.

Zimmerman, Jean. *Tailspin: Women at War in the Wake of Tailhook*. New York: Doubleday, 1995.

Index

violence, 49, 148–49, 150. *See also* domestic violence; rape; torture
Violent Crime Control and Law Enforcement Act (U.S.), 105
Virgin Mary, and Chilean feminine respectability, 129
volunteering, involuntary
  and Becraft, Carolyn, 173
  and Britain's SSAFA, 166–67
  and ex-wives, 194
  and ideal militarized wife, 164
  and military husbands, 183
  U.S. Defense Department directive, 161, 173
  and working wives, 179
  See also nurses
voters. *See* elections
voting rights. *See* suffrage; suffragists

Wales, 27, 60. *See also* Britain
Walkowitz, Judith, 57
Walsh, Patricia L., 220–21
war, 2–3, 6–7, 43, 147. *See also specific wars*
war crimes. *See* international war crimes tribunals; rape; torture
Warsaw Pact, 180
Washington, George, 43
Waters, Kristin, 43–44
WAVES (U.S. Navy women's corps), 267–68, 269
We Can't Even March Straight (Hall), 29
We Don't Want to March Straight (Tatchell), 29
welfare. *See* social welfare
Well of Loneliness, The (Hall), 214
widows, 41, 42, 192–93
Wilkinson, John, 27
Wilson, Woodrow, 211
Wirth, Timothy, 49
witch-hunts, 16–17, 28, 281
wives, xii, xiii, 153–58, 295–96
  and Britain's SSAFA, 166–67
  and camp followers, 38, 40–41, 42, 43, 44
  Dinka, 248
  divorce and separation, 170–78
  and domestic violence, 189–91
  exclusion of, 156–57
  and family/social services, 166–70
  militant, 191–97
  militarized ideal, 161, 162–66
  nurses as, 219–20
  as political problem, 158–62
  and prostitutes, 51, 63, 97–98
  race and ethnicity, 183–88
  and reenlistment, 174

working, 178–82
See also marriage
Woman's Autonomous Association, 91
women, 297–300
  camp followers, 37–45, 199, 209, 241
  civilian, 241–42
  civil servants, 279
  comfort women, 79–89, 297
  diversity of, 297
  and gender gaps, 6–7
  girlfriends, xii, 170
  mannish, 263
  and masculinity, 34
  and militarism, 36
  and military policy, 37
  and military's status, 45, 47
  rights of, 49 (*see also* human rights)
  soldiers
    fashion, 261–72
    feminist perspectives on, 273–87
    husbands of, 182–83
    and military policy, 244, 245
    in peacekeeping operations, 101–2
    and prostitutes, 51
    recruitment of, 47–48, 237–38, 240
    Russia, 259–60
    Soviet Union, 217–18
    Turkey, 246
    Vietnam, 249
  suffragists, 7–9, 15, 57–58, 59, 60
  widows, 41, 42, 192–93
  See also feminism/feminists; lesbians; motherhood; mothers; nurses; prostitutes/prostitution; rape; wives
Women and Mothers for Peace (Israel), 256
Women in Black (Serbia), 143, 144, 145, 147, 148
Women Outside, The (documentary), 97
Women Police Service, 60
Women's Caucus for Gender Justice in the International Criminal Court, 138
Women's Crisis Centre (Philippines), 128
Women's Development Association, 99
Women's Equity Action League, 173, 194
Women's International League for Peace and Freedom (WILPF), 8
women's movement
  Britain, 25–26, 58
  United States, second wave, 48, 133, 188, 189, 224
  See also feminism/feminists
Women's Museum (Vietnam), 249
Women's National Secretariat (Chile), 131

Compositor: Impressions Book and Journal Services, Inc.
Text: 10/13 Sabon
Display: Sabon, Meta Plus Book, and Meta Plus Bold